Political Foundations of Judicial Supremacy

PRINCETON STUDIES IN AMERICAN POLITICS
Historical, International, and Comparative Perspectives

Ira Katznelson, Martin Shefter, and Theda Skocpol, series editors

A list of titles in this series appears at the back of the book

Political Foundations of Judicial Supremacy

THE PRESIDENCY, THE SUPREME COURT, AND CONSTITUTIONAL LEADERSHIP IN U.S. HISTORY

Keith E. Whittington

PRINCETON UNIVERSITY PRESS

PRINCETON AND OXFORD

Copyright © 2007 by Princeton University Press
Published by Princeton University Press, 41 William Street, Princeton, New Jersey 08540
In the United Kingdom: Princeton University Press, 3 Market Place,
Woodstock, Oxfordshire OX20 1SY

Library of Congress Cataloging-in-Publication Data

Whittington, Keith E.
Political foundations of judicial supremacy : the presidency, the Supreme
Court, and constitutional leadership in U.S. history / Keith E. Whittington.
p.   cm. — (Princeton studies in American politics)
Includes index.
ISBN-13: 978-0-691-09640-7 (hardcover : alk. paper)
ISBN-10: 0-691-09640-6 (hardcover : alk. paper)
1. United States. Supreme Court. 2. Judicial review—United States.
3. Political questions and judicial power. I. Title.
KF8748.W48 2007
347.73'12—dc22
2006022598

British Library Cataloging-in-Publication Data is available

This book has been composed in Sabon

Printed on acid-free paper. ∞

pup.princeton.edu

Printed in the United States of America

1   3   5   7   9   10   8   6   4   2

For Taylor and Jimmy

Whoever hath an absolute authority to interpret any written or spoken laws, it is he who is truly the lawgiver, to all intents and purposes, and not that person who first wrote or spoke them.

—*Bishop Benjamin Hoadly, "Sermon Preached Before King George I"*

It is emphatically the province and duty of the judicial department to say what the law is.

—*Chief Justice John Marshall,* Marbury v. Madison

Contents

Preface

THIS IS A BOOK ABOUT the authority of the judiciary, and particularly the Supreme Court, to determine the meaning of the Constitution. It seeks to understand why the judiciary has that authority and looks for the answer in the incentives facing the individuals occupying the various institutions of government. Judicial supremacy largely consists of the ability of the Supreme Court to erase the distinction between its own opinions interpreting the Constitution and the actual Constitution itself. The Court claims the authority not only to look into the meaning of the Constitution as a guide to the justices' own actions, but also and more importantly to say what the Constitution means, for themselves and for everyone else. Political leaders, and most importantly presidents, have generally been willing to lend their support to those sorts of claims by the Court.

The book is secondarily about departmentalism, the Jeffersonian idea that each branch of government has an equal authority and responsibility to interpret the Constitution when performing its own duties. Conceptually and historically, departmentalism has been the primary alternative to judicial supremacy. For the departmentalist, the Court's interpretations of the Constitution might be persuasive or adequate, but the Court has no special institutional authority to say what the Constitution means. The judiciary is one institution among many that is trying to get the Constitution right, but the other branches of government have no responsibility to take the Court's reading of the Constitution as being the same as the Constitution itself. Departmentalism has enjoyed moments of prominence in American constitutional thought and practice, but most political leaders have eschewed this kind of independent responsibility for reading the Constitution. Presidents and political leaders have generally preferred that the Court take the responsibility for securing constitutional fidelity.

In examining the development of the judicial authority to interpret the Constitution over the course of American history—the political foundations of judicial supremacy—the book focuses particularly on the relationship between the president and the Supreme Court and touches on a variety of broader concerns, such as the politics of the exercise of judicial review and the bases for judicial independence. It is not a history of judicial review or constitutional law per se. Likewise, it does not attempt to provide a comprehensive treatment of the relationship between the president and the Supreme Court. As a consequence, some notable episodes of judicial-presidential interaction—such as the Supreme Court's review of President Harry Truman's steel mill seizure during the Korean War—are left unaddressed when they do not shed additional light on the problem of the judicial authority to interpret the Constitution (an authority that Truman never questioned). The central concern of the book is with why politicians have been so eager to anoint the judges as the "ultimate interpreters" of the Constitution, a mantle that judges have been only too happy to accept.

This book has been in gestation for longer than I once expected. One consequence is that I have benefited from the support and conversation of many colleagues and institutions during the time that I have been thinking about issues relating to this book, and it is unlikely that I can adequately acknowledge them all. Bits and pieces of work relating to this book have been presented at a number of workshops, conferences, and colloquia over the last few years, and I appreciate greatly those opportunities to work out these ideas and the many participants who prodded me to work on them some more. I am particularly thankful for those gluttons for punishment who have listened to and read pieces and versions of this project through much of its development and who have been particularly generous with their time and attention, and whose own scholarship has often deepened my own thinking on these issues. They include Jack Balkin, Willie Forbath, Barry Friedman, Paul Frymer, Howard Gillman, Mark Graber, Ken Kersch, Larry Kramer, Sandy Levinson, Andrew Polsky, Scot Powe, Corey Robin, Reva Siegel, Stephen Skowronek, Mark Tushnet, and my colleagues at Princeton University. I also appreciate the support of the American Council of Learned Societies, the John M. Olin Foundation, the University of Texas Law School, the James Madison Program in American Ideals and Institutions, and Princeton University during the time I was working on this project. Some materials in this book are drawn from work previously published in *Polity* (vol. 33, no. 3, Spring 2001, pp. 365–95), the *American Political Science Review* (vol. 99, no. 4, November 2005, pp. 583–96), and *Constitutional Politics* (Princeton University Press, 2001) and are used here by permission.

I particularly appreciate the patience of my family as I worked on this project, especially since I often tested that patience. I will always associate this book with events that interceded during the time that I was "working" on it. Just when I thought I was about to begin this project, my daughter was born. Just when I thought I was about to work on this project in earnest, her grandfather was killed in the destruction of the World Trade Center. They did not share enough time together, and this book is dedicated to them.

ONE

The Politics of Constitutional Meaning

THE CONSTITUTION IS OFTEN thought to transcend our current disagreements and to have settled our fundamental political arguments. Its text embodies our most fundamental commitments, those things about which we no longer disagree, such as the content of our "self-evident" truths and "unalienable rights." The Founding constituted order out of chaos, setting an authoritative higher law over the discord of politics. We may understand the meaning of that law differently than did those who framed it, but the Constitution remains a source of determinate answers to even our hardest political questions.

We may come to disagree about the proper interpretation of even such a Constitution, however. In such cases, the judiciary is thought to become an essential guardian of the constitutional order. By issuing an authoritative interpretation of the Constitution, the judiciary, and especially the Supreme Court, secures order and reestablishes agreement. Without such an authoritative interpreter, the constitutional order would threaten to dissolve back into political discord. Daniel Webster, one of our nation's most incisive constitutional thinkers, captured this sense of constitutional order well. When faced with the argument that the individual states that formed the Union could determine the terms of the Union and the meaning of the Constitution, Webster recoiled. Could it be possible to leave the meaning of the Constitution not in the hands of "one tribunal" but in the hands of multiple "popular bodies, each at liberty to decide for itself, and none bound to respect the decisions of others; and each at liberty, then to give a new construction on every new election of its own members?" Could such a thing be "fit to be called a government? No sir. It should not be denominated a constitution. It should be called, rather, a collection of topics, for everlasting controversy; heads of debate for a disputatious people. It would not be a government. It would not be adequate to any practical good, nor fit for any country to live under."[1] Constitutions require a single, authoritative interpreter, subject to neither popular pressure nor electoral instability. Constitutional government, Webster and others have argued, requires judicial supremacy.

---

[1] *Debates in Congress*, 21st Cong., 1st sess. (1830), 6:78.

Webster's views were controversial in the early nineteenth century, but they are widely accepted now. At least in the United States, judicial supremacy is often regarded as essential to constitutionalism. The legal roots of the current consensus are often traced to Chief Justice John Marshall. In his 1803 opinion in the case of *William Marbury v. James Madison*, Marshall, having characterized the Constitution as the "fundamental and paramount law of the nation," importantly declared, "It is emphatically the province and duty of the judicial department to say what the law is."[2] This was a strong claim to judicial authority over the interpretation of constitutional meaning. The judiciary "must of necessity expound and interpret that rule." It was the "very essence of the judicial duty" to determine the meaning of the Constitution and to lay aside those statutes that contradicted that fundamental law.[3] "The Constitution is either a superior paramount law" subject to judicial interpretation and application, or it is "absurd."[4]

Marshall did temper this strong claim, however. In the context of the time, it was clear that other political institutions had been actively engaged in interpreting the Constitution and that those interpretations were broadly accepted as authoritative. The Constitution, Marshall recognized, was not in the hands of the judges alone. He concluded his opinion more modestly, arguing that surely "the framers of the constitution contemplated that instrument as a rule for the government of *courts*, as well as of the legislature." How could a judge uphold his own duties to the Constitution if its text "is closed upon him, and cannot be inspected by him?"[5] The courts did not so much have authority over the Constitution and over other political actors as they had the obligation not to "close their eyes on the Constitution, and see only the law."[6]

By the mid–twentieth century, the justices of the Supreme Court had abandoned such tempering statements. In 1958, Chief Justice Earl Warren, speaking for a unanimous court, offered his own interpretation of John Marshall's famous sentence declaring the judicial duty to "say what the law is." In response to state government officials who questioned the judicial authority to define constitutional meaning, the chief justice noted that "it is only necessary to recall some basic constitutional propositions which are settled doctrine."[7] The Warren Court instructed, "This decision

---

[2] Marbury v. Madison, 5 U.S. (1 Cranch) 137, 177 (1803).

[3] Ibid., 178.

[4] Ibid., 177.

[5] Ibid., 180.

[6] Ibid., 178.

[7] Cooper v. Aaron, 358 U.S. 1, 17 (1958). The opinion was in fact drafted by Justice William Brennan. Bernard Schwartz, *Super Chief* (New York: New York University Press, 1983), 295–96. But compare this fit of post–New Deal modesty: "There is no reason to doubt

declared the basic principle that the federal judiciary is supreme in the exposition of the law of the Constitution, and that principle has ever since been respected by this Court and the Country as a permanent and indispensable feature of our constitutional system. It follows that the interpretation of the Fourteenth Amendment enunciated by this Court in the *Brown* case is the supreme law of the land." It concluded, "Every state legislator and executive and judicial officer is solemnly committed by oath pursuant to Art. VI, cl. 3, 'to support *this* Constitution. "[8] Four years later, the Court was obliged to again explain to the state governments that the Supreme Court is the "ultimate interpreter of the Constitution."[9] Within a decade the Court had repeated those words first to the Congress and then to the president, and insisted that the power to interpret the meaning of the Constitution "can no more be shared with the Executive Branch than the Chief Executive, for example, can share with the Judiciary the veto power."[10]

Constitutional maintenance, in this view, requires an independent judiciary with the authority to articulate the meaning of the Constitution and have all other political actors defer to those judicial interpretations. Without judicial supremacy, government officials would be free to ignore constitutional requirements with impunity. The Court has recently employed another favored quote from *Marbury* to that effect, arguing in *Boerne* that "if Congress could define its own powers by altering the Fourteenth Amendment's meaning, no longer would the Constitution be 'superior paramount law, unchangeable by ordinary means.' It would be 'on a level with ordinary legislative acts, and, like other acts, . . . alterable when the legislature shall please to alter it.' " The Court concluded, "Under this approach, it is difficult to conceive of a principle that would limit congressional power."[11] Implicit in this argument was the equation between the "Fourteenth Amendment's meaning" and the Court's own recent interpretation of that text. The Court later clarified what was at stake in the case, offering that "our national experience teaches that the Constitution

---

that this Court may fall into error as may other branches of the Government. Nothing in the history of attitude of this Court should give rise to legislative embarrassment if in the performance of its duty a legislative body feels impelled to enact laws which may require the Court to reexamine its previous judgments or doctrine. . . . It can reconsider a matter only when it is again properly brought before it in a case or controversy; . . . the new case must have sufficient statutory support." Helvering v. Griffiths, 318 U.S. 371, 400–401 (1942).

[8] Cooper, 18 (emphasis added).

[9] Baker v. Carr, 369 U.S. 186, 211 (1962).

[10] U.S. v. Nixon, 418 U.S. 683, 704 (1974). See also Powell v. McCormack, 395 U.S. 486, 521 (1969).

[11] City of Boerne v. Flores, 521 U.S. 507, 529 (1997), quoting from Marbury v. Madison, 5 U.S. (1 Cranch) 137, 177 (1803). See also Kimel v. Florida Board of Regents, 528 U.S. 62, 81 (2000); Board of Trustees v. Garrett, 121 U.S. 955 (2001).

is preserved best when each part of the government respects both the Constitution and the proper actions and determinations of the other branches," in particular current judicial precedent.[12] It is for the Supreme Court to "speak before all others for [the nation's] constitutional ideals."[13] The Constitution cannot be maintained as a coherent law unless the Court serves as its "ultimate interpreter," whose understandings of the constitutional text supersede any others and which other government officials are required to adopt.

Those who advocate judicial supremacy, including the Court itself, tend to treat it as a matter of normative directive and accomplished fact. The Court has claimed that judicial supremacy follows logically from the constitutional design and that since Marshall's declaration of judicial independence "that principle has ever since been respected by this Court and the Country."[14] But of course this was wishful thinking on the part of the justices. Their very assertion of the principle of judicial supremacy in *Cooper* came in response to southern politicians denying that the Court had the authority to bind the states to its own controversial constitutional interpretations. American history is littered with debates over judicial authority and constitutional meaning. Although powerful federal officials have usually acceded to the Court's claims, judicial authority has often been contested by important segments of the populace, from abolitionists to labor unions to segregationists to pro-life advocates.

If judicial supremacy cannot simply be assumed to exist, then it must be politically constructed. This book is concerned with the process by which judicial supremacy has been constructed over the course of American history. Rather than treating the judicial authority to determine constitutional meaning as a matter of legal doctrine, this book treats it as a political problem to be overcome. It asks why other powerful political actors might recognize such an authority and defer to the judiciary's particular interpretations of the Constitution. It considers some of the political incentives facing elected politicians and how they often lead politicians to value judicial independence and seek to bolster, or at least refrain from undermining, judicial authority over constitutional meaning. An examination of the political considerations of elected officials sheds light on how constitutions are constructed and maintained in politically fractious environments. For constitutions and institutions like judicial review to exist in historical reality and be more than imagined moral abstractions, there must be political reasons for powerful political actors to support them over time. Fortunately, for judicial review, there are such reasons.

[12] Ibid., 535–36.
[13] Planned Parenthood v. Casey, 505 U.S. 833, 868 (1992).
[14] Cooper v. Aaron, 358 U.S. 1, 18 (1958).

The struggle for judicial authority has occurred within our constitutional framework, not in opposition to it. The judiciary is not the sole guardian of our constitutional inheritance, and interpretive authority under the Constitution has varied over time. At some points in American history, the Court has been able to make strong claims on its own behalf, as it did in *Cooper*, and others have been willing to recognize that authority. At other points, however, elected officials have strongly asserted their own authority to interpret constitutional meaning and sharply challenged the judiciary's monopoly on constitutional wisdom. For those who view judicial supremacy as an "indispensable feature of our constitutional system," such challenges can only be regarded as deeply threatening to cherished constitutional values. An examination of the reasons for the periodic waning of judicial authority, however, provides a more nuanced view of constitutionalism. Within the American context, judicial authority has often waned precisely when constitutionalism is being taken most seriously in the larger political community.

This book is particularly concerned with how the separation of powers and the structure of American political parties have affected the institutional struggle for constitutional leadership over the course of American history. Presidents—in their capacity as heads of the government, as national political leaders, and as national party leaders—have been particularly important in determining the relative authority of the Supreme Court to say what the Constitution means. Presidents may challenge the supremacy of the Court as a constitutional interpreter, or presidents may defer to the supremacy of the Court on constitutional matters and encourage other political actors to defer also. The political incentives that lead presidents to choose either to challenge or to defer to the Court's constitutional leadership have shaped both the substance of our constitutional understandings and practices and the place of the judiciary within the constitutional order. Through much of American history, presidents have found it in their interest to defer to the Court and encourage it to take an active role in defining the Constitution and resolving constitutional controversies. Even before the Supreme Court claimed that it was the ultimate interpreter of the Constitution, political leaders had already asserted the same thing. The strategic calculations of political leaders lay the political foundation for judicial supremacy.

The Theory of Judicial Supremacy

This book is primarily concerned with judicial supremacy, not judicial review per se. These two concepts should be distinguished. Although judicial supremacy entails judicial review, judicial review need not entail judicial supremacy. The authority of the Supreme Court to exercise the power of judicial review is potentially controversial in its own right. Certainly the argument that John Marshall offered on behalf of the Court's power of judicial review in *Marbury* is problematic.[15] The basic concept of judicial review is readily recognizable, however, even divorced from any particular justificatory theory. The doctrine of judicial review refers to the authority of a court, in the context of deciding a particular case, to refuse to give force to an act of another governmental institution on the grounds that such an act is contrary to the requirements of the Constitution. Judges, in this reading, are the agents of the people, not merely of the legislature. As such, they have an independent responsibility to adhere to the mandates of the Constitution, even when they contradict the instructions of the legislature. The power of judicial review as exercised by American courts can be further distinguished from the power of abstract constitutional review as exercised by some European courts.[16] The power of judicial review only authorizes courts to refuse to apply a law in a particular case in a manner that contradicts the terms of the Constitution. Judicial constitutional decisions arise only in the context of specific controversies, and the broader applicability of those decisions is a function of precedent and common-law reasoning. By contrast, the power of abstract constitutional review allows a constitutional court to directly evaluate the text of a law prior to its application, or even its formal adoption, for its consistency with constitutional requirements and to exercise a veto to block the promulgation of the law or to issue instructions to the legislature as to how to avoid the constitutional difficulty. The possibility of abstract review clarifies the distinctly "judicial" nature of American-style constitutional review, which arises only in the context of normal judicial proceedings and develops through common-law mechanisms. Abstract constitutional review is similar to the American presidential veto and is essentially "legislative" in character.

The concept of judicial supremacy does not focus on the specific act of review itself. Judicial supremacy refers to the "obligation of coordinate officials not only to obey that [judicial] ruling but to follow its reasoning in future deliberations."[17] A model of judicial supremacy posits that the

[15] For critiques of Marshall's argument in *Marbury*, see Edward S. Corwin, "*Marbury v. Madison* and the Doctrine of Judicial Review," *Michigan Law Review* 12 (1914): 538; Alexander M. Bickel, *The Least Dangerous Branch* (Indianapolis: Bobbs-Merrill, 1962), 1–14; William W. Van Alstyne, "A Critical Guide to *Marbury v. Madison*," *Duke Law Journal* 1969 (1969): 1.

[16] E.g., Alec Stone, *The Birth of Judicial Politics in France* (New York: Oxford University Press, 1992).

[17] Walter F. Murphy, "Who Shall Interpret? The Quest for the Ultimate Constitutional Interpreter," *Review of Politics* 48 (1986): 407.

Court does not merely resolve particular disputes involving the litigants directly before them or elsewhere in the judicial system. It also authoritatively interprets constitutional meaning. For the judicial supremacist, the Court defines effective constitutional meaning such that other government officials are bound to adhere not only to the Court's disposition of a specific case but also to the Court's constitutional reasoning. Judicial supremacy requires deference by other government officials to the constitutional dictates of the Court, even when other government officials think that the Court is substantively wrong about the meaning of the Constitution and in circumstances that are not subject to judicial review. Judicial supremacy asserts that the Constitution is what the judges say it is, not because the Constitution has no objective meaning or that courts could not be wrong but because there is no alternative interpretive authority beyond the Court. As Justice Robert Jackson once ironically noted to somewhat different effect, "We are not final because we are infallible, but we are infallible only because we are final."[18]

It is this authority to say what the Constitution means—not merely to refuse to enforce laws that conflict with the Constitution—that has historically been subject to the greatest challenge and which raises the most interesting questions about the theory and practice of constitutionalism. Admittedly, doubts about judicial supremacy may also lead to doubts about judicial review, and it is usually the specific exercise of judicial review that raises political challenges to judicial supremacy. Nonetheless, there is political and logical space for rejecting judicial supremacy while accepting judicial review. Contrary to the Court's assertion, it is even possible for the judiciary to accept congressional interpretations of constitutional meaning without abandoning the (admittedly reduced) power of judicial review. Not every act of legislation implies an act of deliberate constitutional interpretation by Congress. Indeed, it is not uncommon for Congress to include a disclaimer in its legislation that nothing in the statute should be construed to violate the terms of the Constitution. Even Congress recognizes that it can make mistakes, and judicial review is a convenient mechanism for correcting those errors. What is more constitutionally important are the instances when the Court tells Congress that the legislature's constitutional judgments are wrong. The judiciary's authority to set its opinions about the correct meaning of the Constitution above those of Congress, the president, or the electorate is at the root of judicial supremacy. As Jeremy Waldron has usefully pointed out, it is this elite rejection of popular judgments on deeply contested matters of fundamental political principle that is the most troubling aspect of the institution of judicial review for democratic and liberal the-

---

[18] Brown v. Allen, 344 U.S. 443, 540 (1953).

ory.[19] Moreover, given the particular significance of the U.S. Constitution to American national and political identity, judicial supremacy implies much more than the exercise of a veto power by a particularly privileged government institution or the laying aside of statutory details as legally void. In the context of judicial supremacy, the opinions of the Court have the capacity to mark some political contestants and their positions as distinctly un-American and beyond the pale of legitimate American political discourse.

There are a number of justifications for judicial supremacy, and these justifications tend to overlap with the more political justifications for judicial review.[20] For some, judicial supremacy is essential to preserving the rule of law and preventing constitutional anarchy. Thinking particularly of the competing constitutional assertions of the state governments, this was Daniel Webster's concern when he asked his congressional colleagues, "[C]ould anything be more preposterous than to make a government for the whole Union, and yet leave its powers subject, not to one interpretation, but to thirteen, or twenty-four, interpretations? Instead of one tribunal, established by and responsible to all, with power to decide for all, shall constitutional questions be left to four and twenty popular bodies, each at liberty to decide for itself, and none bound to respect the decisions of the others?" He doubted whether the government would be capable "of long existing" under such circumstances.[21] For others, the value of judicial supremacy is not in its capacity to provide authoritative legal settlements, but in its capacity to provide substantively desirable legal outcomes. The judiciary alone serves as a "forum of principle" within the American constitutional system, capable of focusing on "questions of justice" free from the din of "the battleground of power politics."[22] For still others, judicial supremacy is regarded as "a permanent and indispensable feature of our constitutional system" because the Court alone functions as a countermajoritarian institution securing the liberties

[19] Jeremy Waldron, *Law and Disagreement* (New York: Oxford University Press, 1999).

[20] Traditional, "legal" justifications for judicial review, such as those offered in the *Marbury* opinion itself, have fewer implications for judicial supremacy since they emphasize the Constitution's relevance to the judicial resolution of particular cases rather than the importance of the judiciary to maintaining the Constitution. See also Edward A. Hartnett, "A Matter of Judgment, Not a Matter of Opinion," *New York University Law Review* 74 (1999): 123.

[21] *Debates in Congress*, 21st Cong., 1st sess. (1830), 6:78. The fear of constitutional anarchy without judicial supremacy has been carefully argued more recently and more generally; see Larry Alexander and Frederick Schauer, "On Extrajudicial Constitutional Interpretation," *Harvard Law Review* 110 (1997): 1371.

[22] Ronald Dworkin, *A Matter of Principle* (Cambridge: Harvard University Press, 1985), 71.

of individuals and political minorities.[23] Unfettered by political interests or popular prejudices, the judiciary can penetrate to the true meaning of the Constitution and the subtle requirements of its principled commitments. Some questions—questions of justice and rights—are too important to be left in the hands of legislative majorities or "the people themselves."[24] Judicial supremacy insures that they are not.[25]

The *Marbury* myth asserts that judicial supremacy has been with us from the beginning, an unproblematic deduction from the nature of constitutionalism itself. The Supreme Court has been a prime purveyor of this view, but the Court is not alone. Advocates of judicial supremacy frequently recur to *Marbury* in order to avoid questions about the foundations of judicial supremacy. Ronald Dworkin, for example, raised the "mysterious matter" of "whose answer should be taken to be authoritative" in regard to constitutional meaning only to dismiss it as of no practical importance. After all, this interpretive "authority is already distributed by history, and details of institutional responsibility are matters of interpretation, not of invention from nothing." He offers that "the most straightforward interpretation of American constitutional practice shows that our judges have final interpretive authority," the evidence for which is simply *Marbury*.[26]

Judicial supremacy itself rests on political foundations. The judiciary may assert its own supremacy over constitutional interpretation, but such claims ultimately must be supported by other political actors making independent decisions about how the constitutional system should operate. The Court's self-referential reliance on a few sentences from John Marshall's opinion in *Marbury* may be used to establish the doctrine of judicial supremacy, but it is the purest bootstrapping to imagine that it establishes judicial supremacy as a political practice. As the *Cooper* Court at least recognized, the assertion of judicial supremacy is only meaningful if other powerful political actors acquiesce to that declaration. There is a robust tradition of authoritative constitutional interpretation outside the courts, however, which undermines the narrative of unchallenged judicial supremacy. The judiciary has provided only one source of commentary on the meaning of the Constitution, and that commentary has not always been the most important one in translating constitutional text into real-

---

[23] Cooper v. Aaron, 358 U.S. 1, 18 (1958).

[24] Alexander Hamilton, James Madison, and John Jay, *The Federalist Papers*, ed. Clinton Rossiter (New York: American Library, 1961), No. 78, 469.

[25] For a more elaborate and critical examination of these arguments, see Keith E. Whittington, "Extrajudicial Constitutional Interpretation: Three Objections and Responses," *North Carolina Law Review* 80 (2002): 773.

[26] Ronald Dworkin, *Freedom's Law* (Cambridge: Harvard University Press, 1996), 34, 35.

ity.[27] A coherent theory of judicial supremacy must somehow explain how this long tradition of political constitutional discourse is consistent with the model of the Court as the ultimate constitutional interpreter.

The Puzzles of Judicial Supremacy

A number of important empirical and normative questions remain to be answered about the theory of judicial supremacy. Treating judicial supremacy simply as a legal doctrine, justified by the authority of precedent, does little to advance our understanding of judicial supremacy and how it might fit within the constitutional order. Once we move beyond the mere assertion that the Constitution somehow "requires" judicial supremacy and that the judiciary always determines constitutional meaning, we are left with difficult problems of explaining the relative success of judicial supremacy over competing possibilities and the consequences for our constitutional system of both judicial supremacy and challenges to it. Ultimately, these empirical and normative concerns are related. In particular, I think that we will be able to gain a more complete appreciation of the normative issues associated with judicial supremacy if we examine its political and historical roots.

The most basic empirical question to be asked concerns the political foundations of judicial supremacy. Judicial supremacy did not emerge as a fully formed and politically dominant constitutional theory at the time of the Founding or in the early years of the nation's history, as legal theories emphasizing the *Marbury* precedent might suggest. It is the modern Court, not the early Court, that has been most aggressive in asserting the reality of judicial supremacy. Even the more limited institution of judicial review developed gradually. The political foundations for the secure exercise of the Court's power to review legislation for its constitutionality were laid over the course of decades by the Marshall Court and were still weak when the Taney Court issued its *Dred Scott* decision. Mark Graber in particular has insightfully laid bare the Court's long political struggle to establish the power of judicial review, and any exploration of the political foundations of judicial supremacy must be equally sensitive to the logic

---

[27] See, e.g., Louis Fisher, *Constitutional Dialogues* (Princeton: Princeton University Press, 1988); Bruce Ackerman, *We the People*, 2 vols. (Cambridge: Harvard University Press, 1991, 1998), vol. 1; David P. Currie, *The Constitution in Congress*, 3 vols. (Chicago: University of Chicago Press, 1997, 2001, 2005); Keith E. Whittington, *Constitutional Construction* (Cambridge: Harvard University Press, 1999); Larry D. Kramer, *The People Themselves* (New York: Oxford University Press, 2004).

of judicial politics.[28] Given the evident power of elected government officials to intimidate, co-opt, ignore, or dismantle the judiciary, we need to understand why they have generally chosen not to use that power and instead to defer to judicial authority.

Just as the rise of judicial supremacy requires a political explanation, so do challenges to judicial supremacy. In the legal mode, challenges to judicial supremacy, such as departmentalism, are often treated simply as flawed constitutional theories. Occasional departmentalist episodes in American history are products of intellectual mistakes. Of course, these particular intellectual mistakes do not look entirely innocent, so the legal analysis has been readily linked to political analyses emphasizing challenges to judicial supremacy as self-interested behavior by those who had lost in court.[29] The history of the *Cooper* case itself provides an exemplar of such politically opportunistic challenges to judicial supremacy in the form of Governor Orval Faubus. It was Faubus who called out the National Guard in 1957 to prevent the desegregation of the Little Rock schools, which in turn led to the litigation in *Cooper* and the Court's ultimate effort to "answer the premise of the actions of the Governor and Legislature that they are not bound by our holding in the *Brown* case."[30] Although Faubus initially denied that he was "defying the orders of the United States Supreme Court" in calling out the Guard to maintain "order," he later declared that "the Supreme Court decision is not the law of the land."[31] For Faubus, the challenge to the judicial authority to

[28] Mark A. Graber, "The Non-Majoritarian Difficulty: Legislative Deference to the Judiciary," *Studies in American Political Development* 7 (1993): 35; Graber, "The Passive-Aggressive Virtues: *Cohens v. Virginia* and the Problematic Establishment of Judicial Power," *Constitutional Commentary* 12 (1995): 67; Graber, "Federalist or Friends of Adams: The Marshall Court and Party Politics," *Studies in American Political Development* 12 (1998): 229; Graber, "Establishing Judicial Review? *Schooner Peggy* and the Early Marshall Court," *Political Research Quarterly* 51 (1998): 7; Graber, "Naked Land Transfers and American Constitutional Development," *Vanderbilt Law Review* 53 (2000): 71; Graber, "Establishing Judicial Review: *Marbury* and the Judiciary Act of 1789," *Tulsa Law Review* 38 (2003): 609. See also Michael McCann, "How the Supreme Court Matters in American Politics: New Institutionalist Perspectives," in *The Supreme Court in American Politics*, ed. Howard Gillman and Cornell Clayton (Lawrence: University Press of Kansas, 1999); Kramer, *The People Themselves*.

[29] In concluding his response to Edwin Meese's 1986 Tulane speech criticizing judicial supremacy, Paul Brest wrote, "Would he have made the same speech if a majority of the Supreme Court supported the Administration's views on issues such as abortion and school prayer? The transparent political motives underlying Mr. Meese's radical proposal demonstrates why at least the Attorney General ought not to be entrusted with the power to contradict judicial decisions." Paul Brest, "Meese, the Lawman, Calls for Anarchy," *New York Times*, 2 November 1986, sec. 4, p. 23.

[30] Cooper v. Aaron, 358 U.S. 1, 17 (1958).

[31] Quoted in Daniel A. Farber, "The Supreme Court and the Rule of Law: *Cooper v. Aaron* Revisited," *University of Illinois Law Review* 1982 (1982): 393, 397.

determine constitutional meaning simply gave a veneer of legitimacy to the state's resistance to federal policies that were unpopular with the governor's constituents.

Also in 1957, the political scientist Robert Dahl provided a more systematic explanation for conflicts between the Court and the elected branches at the national level. Extrapolating from the example of the New Deal, Dahl posited that the Court would obstruct congressional majorities only when the membership of the Court lagged a rapid change in the dominant electoral coalition.[32] In normal circumstances, the justices who had been appointed by the president and confirmed by the Senate would operate in partnership with the elected branches of government. In the rare circumstances of electoral instability, however, new congressional majorities might find their policies being rejected by holdover justices who had been appointed by the recently dethroned party. By implication, political attacks on the Court were an effort to overcome judicial obstruction of important federal policies. Unfortunately, the use of the judicial veto has not been closely correlated with such electoral transitions, and political attacks on judicial supremacy do not correspond with periods of unusual judicial activism.[33] The failure of the obstructionist Court hypothesis has left scholars without an adequate explanation for such periods of resistance to judicial authority. With the exception of Roosevelt's Court-packing plan, elected officials appear to have attacked the Court without justification, perhaps out of a hysterical overreaction to earlier grievances. Court-curbing measures appear to be an emotional release, not a rational strategy to advance policy objectives—a psychological phenomenon, not a political one.[34] The reconstruction of a political explanation for such challenges to the courts is an important starting point for understanding fluctuations in judicial authority.

Normative and legal theories of judicial supremacy also face the difficulty of integrating their absolutist formal claims on behalf of judicial authority with the empirical reality of constitutional politics. The pervasiveness of constitutional politics intrudes into arguments on behalf of judicial supremacy in various ways. Even strong advocates of judicial supremacy recognize some realm of nonjudicial constitutional interpretation, from the preliminary interpretive efforts of the legislature in passing statutes to the independent efforts of the House of Representatives in

[32] Robert A. Dahl, "Decision-Making in a Democracy: The Supreme Court as a National Policy-Maker," *Journal of Public Law* 6 (1957): 279.

[33] This thesis is considered in more detail in chapter 2.

[34] E.g., David Adamany, "The Supreme Court's Role in Critical Elections," in *Realignment in American Politics*, ed. Bruce Campbell and Richard Trilling (Austin: University of Texas Press, 1980), 244–46.

identifying an impeachable offense. At the very least, the nonexclusivity of judicial constitutional interpretation creates complications for theories of judicial supremacy.[35] At the same time, however, those who wish to call attention to the pervasiveness of constitutional politics must also explain the surfeit of constitutional law. In some fashion, judicial authority to interpret constitutional meaning must be related to the ongoing practice of constitutional politics. The Constitution inside the courts must be reconciled with the Constitution outside the courts.

The most basic normative question to be asked is whether judicial supremacy is essential to constitutionalism. Many scholars and judges have assumed that it is. The Rehnquist Court was clear in identifying the judicial authority as the ultimate interpreter of the Constitution with the capacity of a constitution to constrain political actors, who could otherwise alter or ignore the terms of the Constitution at will as it suited their immediate needs.[36] Likewise, the Warren Court asserted that judicial supremacy was an "indispensable feature of our constitutional system."[37] Challenges to judicial supremacy thus appear to be attacks on constitutionalism itself. Without judicial supremacy, "the civilizing hand of a uniform interpretation of the Constitution crumbles" and the "balance wheel in the American system" would be lost.[38] Many scholars have therefore been distressed to find that judicial supremacy has not been more widely accepted and more politically effective. The rejection of judicial supremacy is tantamount to the rejection of judicial independence. Gerald Rosenberg, for example, has argued that the judiciary is least likely to resist political initiatives precisely "when it is the most necessary" to do so, when the Court's interpretations are being challenged.[39] The prior assumptions of the judicial supremacy model of constitutionalism render political pressure on the judiciary deeply problematic and the supposed foundations of constitutional values quite insecure. But we cannot know when "judicial independence" is "most necessary" unless we more carefully consider the constitutional significance of what goes on outside the courtroom.

[35] See also Scott E. Gant, "Judicial Supremacy and Nonjudicial Interpretation of the Constitution," *Hastings Constitutional Law Quarterly* 24 (1997): 359.

[36] City of Boerne v. Flores, 521 U.S. 507, 529 (1997).

[37] Cooper v. Aaron, 358 U.S. 1, 18 (1958).

[38] Laurence Tribe, quoted in Stuart Taylor Jr., "Liberties Union Denounces Meese," *New York Times*, 24 October 1986, A 17; Anthony Lewis, "Law or Power?" *New York Times*, 27 October 1986, A 23.

[39] Gerald N. Rosenberg, "Judicial Independence and the Reality of Political Power," *Review of Politics* 54 (1992): 394.

The Logic of Constitutional Authority

The starting point for much of our thinking about the judiciary and constitutional interpretation is the assumption of a rigid distribution of interpretive authority. We tend to assume that some institution must simply have the authority to determine constitutional meaning, and that other institutions must have the corresponding obligation to defer to that authority. Most often, interpretive authority is assumed to be vested in the judiciary, producing judicial supremacy. A variety of normative, legal, and doctrinal rationales supports the existence of judicial supremacy and the Court's right and responsibility to issue authoritative interpretations of disputed constitutional commitments. Less often, but more provocatively, some have asserted that interpretive authority is most appropriately invested in some other institution, usually Congress or the president, which is then to be regarded as supreme over the other branches of government. A final option is to distribute interpretive authority across multiple institutions, each "supreme within its sphere," to borrow a phrase from John Marshall,[40] but none supreme over all parts of the Constitution. This theory of "fixed departmentalism" "accepts that there is such a thing as authoritative interpretation in a given matter, but rejects the notion of a single supreme interpreter regarding all matters. Instead, allocation of interpretive authority varies by topic or constitutional provision."[41] The Court's political questions doctrine, for example, recognizes that some constitutional questions may be authoritatively resolved outside the judiciary, such as the meaning of the "high crimes and misdemeanors" impeachment standard or the substantive requirements of the republican guarantee clause.[42] These interpretive questions have been allocated to the political branches to answer. The various potential constitutional interpreters have "different areas of competence." Allocating interpretive authority among those different branches according to their particular area of competence would both "decreas[e] the scope of judicial authority" and reduce if not eliminate conflicts between the judiciary and the other branches of government over interpretive authority.[43] Although these ap-

---

[40] McCulloch v. Maryland, 17 U.S. (4 Wheat.) 316, 405 (1819).

[41] Gant, "Judicial Supremacy," 384. Gant very usefully distinguishes this theory of fixed departmentalism from "fluid departmentalism," in which "allocations are made but are not unalterable" or "no allocation can be made at all . . . all departments have an equal claim as interpretive agents in all matters," though he seems to find fixed departmentalism to be the more common theory. Ibid.

[42] On the political questions doctrine, see Baker v. Carr, 369 U.S. 186 (1962); Luther v. Borden, 48 U.S. (7 How.) 1 (1849); Coleman v. Miller, 307 U.S. 433 (1939); Goldwater v. Carter, 444 U.S. 996 (1979).

[43] Murphy, "Who Shall Interpret?" 417.

proaches disagree sharply on where interpretive authority should be located, they all agree that ultimate interpretive authority can be located somewhere. There is a correct and stable answer to the question "Who shall interpret?" that can be deduced from the structure, purpose, or specific provisions of the Constitution.

In this book, I want to develop a different logic, a political rather than a legal logic. Over the course of American history, there has been no single, stable allocation of interpretive authority. Rather, various political actors have struggled for the authority to interpret the Constitution. They have sought to displace other potential constitutional interpreters and to assert their own primary authority to determine the content of contested constitutional principles. That struggle for interpretive authority has varied in its intensity over time. Often, political actors have been content to defer to the interpretive authority of others. Quite often, they have chosen to defer to the judiciary and have been willing to support claims of judicial supremacy. At times, however, the struggle has been intense and involved leading political figures. At times, others who have been able to make a compelling case that they understand the Constitution better than the courts have displaced the judiciary as the authoritative interpreter of the Constitution. They have not been content to refrain from entering the judiciary's peculiar area of competence, but have instead argued forthrightly that in a democracy the Constitution is too important to be left in the hands of the judges alone.

Challenges to judicial supremacy can come from several directions, from Congress or the president, from state officials or private citizens. For a variety of reasons, however, those challenges are likely to be most fully and significantly developed by the president. Individual legislators, state officials, or citizens may all question judicial supremacy to relatively little effect. Given the inherently controversial nature of the Court's activities, there is likely to always be an undercurrent of resistance to judicial supremacy. The interesting question is when that undercurrent becomes the mainstream and the authority of the judiciary to determine constitutional meaning becomes a politically salient problem attracting the attention and sympathies of powerful political actors. Given the status and power of the presidency, executive challenges to judicial supremacy are likely to represent the most important ones.

Legislative challenges to judicial supremacy are also likely to be inherently limited in their aspirations. At the extreme, a congressional challenge to the Court's authority would imply legislative supremacy in interpreting the Constitution. Legislative supremacy, however, would tend to subvert the power of judicial review itself. Unsurprisingly, given this result, commentators tend to find "few systematic assertions of legislative supremacy since the nation's founding."[44] Unable to develop explicit theories of legislative supremacy, congressional challenges to judicial authority are more likely to take the form of criticisms of particular judicial decisions. Unable to say that Congress is a more authoritative interpreter of the Constitution than the Court, legislators are instead likely to content themselves with saying that the Court has made a mistake in some particular constitutional decision. Congress is more likely to try to enter into a dialogue with the Court over a particular constitutional interpretation than to challenge the Court's authority as the ultimate interpreter. This limited aspiration tends to be reinforced by the sequence of legislative and judicial actions, in which the Court at least formally can always have the last word. Congress finds it difficult to express a challenge to judicial authority without "enacting a lawsuit" and inviting a reassertion of judicial supremacy, as in the *Boerne* case.[45] Congress can readily deny the exclusivity of judicial constitutional interpretation, but it cannot easily challenge the claim that the Court is the ultimate constitutional interpreter.[46]

As a challenge to judicial supremacy departmentalism supports coordinate interpretation of the Constitution by the legislative branch as readily as by the executive branch, but it is no accident that presidents have historically been the primary exponents of departmentalism. Presidents are better positioned to challenge judicial authority than is the legislature. Holding the "power of the sword," presidents have the opportunity to act more directly on judicial decisions and after the Court has spoken. More generally, presidents have a variety of high-profile opportunities to challenge judicial supremacy without subjecting themselves to judicial review and response, from the informal power of the bully pulpit to the formal veto and pardoning powers. More ambitiously, the presidency is a hierarchical rather than a collective institution. The "unity" of the executive means that the president need only consult his own conscience before challenging the Court, whereas the fractious deliberations of Congress weaken and muddy any legislative challenge to the judiciary. The "energy," "decision, activity," and "dispatch" that Alexander Hamilton admired in the executive has public as well as administrative conse-

---

[44] Gant, "Judicial Supremacy," 374.

[45] The Religious Freedom Restoration Act has been criticized as a strategic and normative mistake precisely because it approached the Court as an antagonist rather than as a collaborator. Neal Devins, "How Not to Challenge the Court," *William and Mary Law Review* 39 (1998): 645.

[46] As the Court emphasized in *Powell*, the political questions doctrine carving out areas of the Constitution for congressional interpretive responsibility remains, after all, judicial doctrine. The Court always controls the carving, in effect delegating some interpretive disputes to the legislature to resolve but retaining the authority to rescind that delegation, as it in fact had done in the legislative reapportionment cases. Powell v. McCormack, 395 U.S. 486, 521 (1969); Baker v. Carr, 369 U.S. 186, 209–36 (1962).

quences.[47] The president has a visibility that enhances his authority and gives weight to his pronouncements. The president has emerged as the "interpreter-in-chief," who can "make politics" by redefining the political landscape.[48] Individual legislators speak, but the legislative body can only act.[49] Only the president and the judiciary can and regularly do combine their actions with statements about their larger meaning and justification. Through his public statements the president is capable of expressing a constitutional vision that can stand opposed to that offered in the opinions of the Court.

Presidents are political leaders, and it is the logic of leadership in the American political system that has particular consequences for judicial authority. Almost by accident, presidents alter their political environment. They cannot help but lead. Their electoral campaigns shape the legislative agenda. Their public pronouncements echo across the political landscape. Their actions disrupt existing policy and political networks. If presidents are natural leaders, the demands of leadership also structure and constrain their behavior. Individual presidents must determine what it means to lead well in their particular historical and political context.

Presidential authority is rarely considered in the analysis of the presidency, but is rather subsumed in the related notions of power and influence. From that perspective, the powers of the presidency are fairly fixed by constitutional text, precedent, and tradition. The creation or recognition of a new power by one president necessarily empowers his successors, as with the growth of the policy veto, or the war powers, or the removal power. Presidential interpretation of the Constitution is generally understood in the same way. If one president can successfully challenge judicial supremacy, then all his successors must have the same power. Departmentalism, or more specifically presidential review, would become a part of the office of the presidency as if it had been written into Article II of the Constitution, just like the veto or pardoning power (and just like the power of judicial review for the Court).[50] Some presidents may be more or less skilled or effective in the use of their inherited powers, but their political arsenal is the same.

[47] Hamilton, Madison, and Jay, *The Federalist Papers*, No. 70, 424.

[48] Mary E. Stuckey, *The President as Interpreter-in-Chief* (Chatham, NJ: Chatham House, 1991); Stephen Skowronek, *The Politics Presidents Make* (Cambridge: Harvard University Press, 1993).

[49] See also, Waldron, *Law and Disagreement*, 119–46; Kenneth A. Shepsle, "Congress is a 'They,' Not an 'It': Legislative Intent as an Oxymoron," *International Review of Law and Economics* 12 (1992): 239.

[50] E.g., Frank H. Easterbrook, "Presidential Review," *Case Western Reserve Law Review* 40 (1990): 905; Michael S. Paulsen, "The Most Dangerous Branch: The Executive Power to Say What the Law Is," *Georgetown Law Journal* 83 (1994): 217.

As an effort to understand constitutional authority, this approach is wrong. Constitutional authority is fluid, not fixed. Presidents cannot all make the same leadership claims on their fellow political actors. As Stephen Skowronek has emphasized, "[A] president's authority hinges on the warrants that can be drawn from the moment at hand to justify action and secure the legitimacy of the changes affected."[51] The president is both empowered and constrained by the set of partisan commitments and informal political resources that he brings with him to the office and builds during his term. Thus, although all presidents have quite a bit of power to effect political change, not all presidents can do so successfully, and the political response to those changes is neither uniform across presidencies nor strictly a function of the political skill of individual presidents. The authority for a president to act is structured by the expectations of other political actors, which help define "what is appropriate for a given president to do."[52] All presidents are disruptive of the status quo and change their political environments. Not all presidents, however, have the authority to explain and legitimate those changes. All presidents can and do talk about the Constitution. Not all presidents can speak with authority.

This book will examine fluctuations in judicial interpretive authority primarily in the context of the presidential leadership task. The problems of presidential leadership provide a useful, though not exclusive, perspective on the struggle for constitutional authority within the American system over time, the incentives facing political actors to support or undermine judicial authority, and the opportunities available to the judiciary to assert and develop their own claims to authority. Political actors defer to the authority claims of the courts because the judiciary can be useful to their own political and constitutional goals, or at least because challenging the Court may be too politically costly. Judicial authority must be won and defended, and at the expense of other potential constitutional interpreters.

Political Goals and Constraints

A president has two overriding imperatives. He wishes to advance his agenda and to maintain his political coalition. Presidential agendas vary over time. Some presidents have broad and ambitious agendas. Others have narrow and modest agendas. Presidents would prefer to be able to define their own political agenda and not merely advance a preset list of initiatives drawn from a party platform or the congressional calendar.

---

[51] Skowronek, *The Politics Presidents Make*, 18.
[52] Ibid.

That is, presidents want to lead. Few are content with the role of a mere clerk, though such a role was more common in the nineteenth century, and all hope to occupy the office in their own right and to leave their individual stamp on the nation.

The presidential office is unique in American politics, and it invites its occupant to make expansive claims to the authority to lead the nation. Moreover, part of the presidential agenda is likely to involve constitutional meaning. The Constitution is foundational in American politics, not only in the sense that it establishes the boundaries of legal action but also in the sense that it authorizes, invites, and structures political activity. An implicit or explicit constitutional discourse comes naturally to presidents, not because they are the special caretakers of our constitutional tradition but because their visions of political leadership lead them to push the boundaries of that tradition. The president "tells us stories about ourselves, and in so doing he tells us what sort of people we are, how we are constituted as a community. We take from him not only our policies but our national self-identity."[53] Because presidential ambitions are foundational, the Constitution becomes a basic resource and constraint.

In addition to defining and promoting an agenda, presidents are obliged to maintain their political coalition. This is in part an instrumental good: maintaining coalitional stability facilitates implementation of the presidential agenda. It is also a distinct presidential imperative. To a greater or lesser degree, presidents are representatives of a preexisting political coalition. That coalition places independent demands on the president, which the president will likely seek to meet both out of a sense of political obligation, in payment for earlier assistance rendered, and in expectation of future legacies. Whether for independent or instrumental reasons, however, presidents must expend resources nurturing political coalitions. The president will be required to pursue an agenda that is secondary to his own but favored by coalition members, and he will be expected to help build and to avoid damaging coalitional strength, though such coalitional obligations are not historically constant. Nineteenth-century presidents, for example, were more beholden to their parties than were twentieth-century presidents.

A president cannot afford to simply be a policy entrepreneur or a "policy wonk." He is also by necessity a coalition leader. The president and vice president are the only nationally elected political officers. As a political candidate, the president is highly visible and must appeal to an unusually diverse constituency. The electoral success of a presidential candidate depends on his ability both to take control of the existing party establishment and to consolidate new support around his campaign and presi-

[53] Stuckey, *Interpreter-in-Chief*, 1.

dency. The legislative success of a president likewise depends on his ability to mobilize partisan supporters within Congress and to build new legislative coalitions around particular policy proposals.

In pursuing these twin goals of advancing a substantive agenda and promoting a stable coalition, presidents are faced with a variety of constraints that limit their ability to realize these goals. Such constraints will help determine the presidential strategy in pursuing his objectives. They impose limits on what is possible and force presidents to make choices. They may also be sufficiently internalized so as to shape the types of goals that the president formulates in the first place. That is, we should be equally concerned with the formation of presidential goals and with the choice of strategies that the president might adopt to advance those goals.

Presidents are constrained in part by limited resources. The presidential supply of certain resources, such as time, is finite, which imposes opportunity costs and prevents presidents from pursuing every issue that they might favor. Presidents must pick their battles, and they must prioritize their agenda. Every issue that the president might pursue would require some expenditure of time and energy in order to shape alternatives, formulate strategies, mobilize supporters, and the like. Although some issues might, in the abstract, be resolvable by a given president, they may be crowded off the presidential agenda by more pressing concerns that are more politically salient, more intensely preferred, or more practically consequential. The need for prioritization is felt in the arena of constitutional disputes as much as it is in routine policy disputes. Debates over abortion, euthanasia, and religious liberty may readily rise to the top of the political agenda and demand attention from political leaders, whereas the requirements of a criminal defendant's right to counsel or police interrogation techniques may never receive full political consideration.

Presidents also have limited powers that necessitate their reliance on other political actors. In order to advance his agenda, the president must usually win support for his policies from other political actors, in Congress and elsewhere, with their own, independent political and policy concerns. Although the powers of the presidency are limited, they are not necessarily fixed. Presidents often struggle over the contours of their office as well as over government policy. In seeking to advance their primary goals, presidents are likely to push the boundaries of their inherited office and encourage others to recognize their expanded powers.

The president is also constrained by the strength of his coalition. A presidential agenda may be hard to pursue if legislative support is weak or lacking, as when the opposition party controls one or both houses of Congress. Similarly, the presidential coalition may itself be diffuse or fragmented, limiting the president's ability to focus support for a particular agenda. Somewhat differently, the presidential coalition may be relatively brittle, even if it momentarily retains control of crucial government institutions. Legislative majorities may splinter or face electoral losses if forced to act on an ambitious positive agenda. The relative vulnerability or strength of the presidential coalition will alter calculations of whether and how to pursue individual agenda items, while also shifting the priority between the president's own positive agenda and his coalitional maintenance responsibilities.

Presidents may also be constrained by the broader ideological and institutional context within which they must operate. The president cannot be idiosyncratic in defining his agenda. The credibility of the president's agenda depends in part on its fit within the larger ideological and institutional environment within which it is offered. An individual president is structured by a preexisting regime. The Eisenhower administration, for example, was partly prefigured by its arriving in the context of the modern presidency and the post–New Deal era. Despite Eisenhower's own preferences for congressional leadership and smaller government, he did not have the option of emulating Calvin Coolidge, even if he had the desire to do so. Similarly, in the shadow of Ronald Reagan, Bill Clinton's political legacy will be shaped more by deficit reduction and welfare reform than by such activist proposals as health care reform that he might have otherwise favored.

The presidential challenge is both to pursue his goals within these constraints and to attempt to loosen the constraints themselves. The judiciary may be either one of these felt constraints or a means for managing or even overcoming the various tensions inherent in the presidential task. We tend to think of the judiciary as a constraint on the president and political actors generally, imposing constitutional limits on them and impinging on their natural tendency to ignore constitutional obligations. As a consequence, there is a tendency to assume that judicial authority is always under threat from political leaders. At best that threat is inactive, as when the legislature favors policies that the Court finds to be within the legislature's constitutional discretion to enact. In such instances the judiciary is tolerated, but only because it is irrelevant. At worst the threat to judicial authority becomes active, most notably if the Court were to strike down laws that enjoy widespread popular support. It is in such circumstances that the "countermajoritarian difficulty" is faced most squarely and judicial authority may be expected to wane.

A better appreciation of the goals and constraints facing political leaders, however, should force us to modify that view. The judicial authority to interpret the Constitution may be an opportunity as well as a hindrance to political actors seeking to advance substantive agendas and maintain vulnerable coalitions. An autonomous judiciary with the power to resolve divisive constitutional issues may well be a solution to a variety of problems that political leaders face. Moreover, the political constraints facing presidents may in turn strengthen the Court, helping to insulate it from political attacks. Interpretive authority cannot be wrested from the judiciary without being placed elsewhere. Dissatisfaction with the Court must be linked with some plausible alternative to judicial supremacy before judicial authority can be seriously challenged. For most of American history there has been no such plausible alternative.

The Political Context of Constitutional Authority

These considerations can be framed in the context of three basic situations in which political leaders might find themselves. Each of these situations reflects a different set of incentives facing political leaders and thus a distinct set of likely strategic choices. In particular, these strategic environments reflect the presidential relationship to the constitutional and political regime. Bruce Ackerman, for example, defines a constitutional regime as "the matrix of institutional relationships and fundamental values that are usually taken as the constitutional baseline in normal political life."[54] Similarly, Stephen Skowronek refers to partisan regimes as "the commitments of ideology and interest embodied in preexisting institutional arrangements."[55] These webs of institutional, ideological, and partisan commitments form a basic context within which presidents operate, help structure their strategic options, and provide a first cut on the set of constraints and opportunities facing a given political leader. Presidents may be either supportive of or opposed to these established sets of commitments and, if opposed, may or may not have the political resources to significantly alter the inherited regime.[56] Presidents may be positioned to reconstruct the inherited constitutional order, in which case they will seek to maximize their own interpretive authority. More likely, they will operate within that established order, whether in affiliation with or in opposition to the dominant regime. In such cases they will be forced to share the interpretive task with the courts and will have a variety of reasons to defer to judicial authority. When the political debate begins to focus on the "constitutional baseline" itself, judicial authority becomes more tenuous and other political actors make stronger claims to interpretive primacy. When the baseline is itself fairly stable and constitutional debates become more diffuse and focused on more marginal disputes, the political incen-

[54] Ackerman, *We the People*, 1:59.
[55] Skowronek, *The Politics Presidents Make*, 34.
[56] This basic framework draws on Skowronek's more general analysis of presidential leadership. See generally, ibid., 33–58.

tives to displace the primary interpretive authority of the Court are weak. Presidents rarely confront these strategic situations in their pure form. They are better understood as ends on a continuum than boxes that individual presidents occupy. They are useful starting points, however, in thinking about how the Court fits into the presidential effort to manage the conflicting demands of political leadership.

A very few presidents are well situated to reconstruct the established order along new lines. These presidents come to office opposed to the established regime but at a time when that order is weak and collapsing. As a result, these presidencies are primarily concerned with destroying the last vestiges of the old regime and articulating the foundations of the new one. Presidential political authority is maximized through the confluence of the presidential capacity to disrupt existing political relations and the shaky legitimacy of the status quo. The key question during these moments is who will take control over the future direction of the polity. Overpowering competing institutions and actors is a prerequisite for presidential success.

The reconstructive task leads presidents to politicize constitutional meaning. As a consequence, reconstructive presidents are likely to deny judicial supremacy and reject the idea that the Court is the ultimate expositor of constitutional meaning. Historically, these are the presidents who have asserted the authority to ignore the Court's constitutional reasoning and act upon their own independent constitutional judgments. In other words, reconstructive presidents tend to be departmentalists. The list of presidents who have adopted such a stance is a familiar one, and includes Thomas Jefferson, Andrew Jackson, Abraham Lincoln, Franklin Roosevelt, and less strongly Ronald Reagan. The judicial authority to settle disputed constitutional meaning wanes as a concurrent presidential authority to reconstruct the inherited constitutional order waxes. This situation is examined in more detail in chapter 2.

Reconstructive presidents are relatively rare. Few presidents have the desire or authority to challenge inherited constitutional and ideological norms and attempt to construct a new political regime. Far more common are affiliated leaders, who rise to power within an assumed framework of goals, possibilities, and resources.[57] Affiliated leaders are primarily concerned with continuing, extending, or more creatively reconceptualizing the fundamental commitments made by an earlier reconstructive leader.

---

[57] Skowronek distinguishes between two types of affiliated leaders, those in a politics of articulation and those in a politics of disjunction. As we will see, that distinction is relevant to judicial authority as well. But I find the differences between affiliated leaders to be less important than their similarities for purposes of examining the logic of their relationship to the Court.

They are second-order interpreters. They interpret the inherited regime, not the constitutional order itself—that is, they interpret the interpretations of the reconstructive leader. They are the workaday practitioners of constitutional politics, concerned with clarifying what the constitutional regime is and working out its momentary problems rather than with specifying what it should be.

The political situation of an affiliated leader both limits his own interpretive authority and creates opportunities for other institutions, most notably the judiciary, to assert their own interpretive authority. An affiliated Court can be expected to articulate the constitutional commitments of the dominant coalition. To that extent, the judiciary is an important asset to the dominant coalition. The Court can help enforce and extend those commitments, perhaps in ways that are not readily available to legislative leaders who must cope with fractious coalitions and crowded agendas. Somewhat differently, an affiliated Court draws on sources of authority similar to those of an affiliated president. When the inherited regime is collapsing under the force of a reconstructive president's challenge, then the Court is vulnerable. When the regime itself is resilient, however, the Court's interpretive authority can be a source of strength. When constitutional politics is primarily interpretive rather than creative, the Court can lay claim to a larger space of operations. Even so, the dominant political coalition's support for judicial authority is contingent. Operating too far outside the framework of regime commitments would put the Court in danger of losing its political support. Within that framework, however, the Court has substantial autonomy to shape its own agenda and elaborate constitutional meaning. This situation is examined further in chapter 3.

Reconstructive presidents are not the only leaders who manage to come to power while opposing the dominant regime. Nonetheless, not every oppositional president is as well positioned to remake the inherited order as Jefferson, Jackson, Lincoln, and Roosevelt were. These other oppositional presidents, who "preempt" a continuing partisan order, come to office with relatively little authority and few resources with which to significantly increase their authority. The regime that they oppose is still vibrant, popular, and resilient to pressure. The preemptive situation is one of sharp constraints. Preemptive presidents have unusually wide latitude in conducting their office in the sense that their oppositional status carries few partisan commitments or political expectations that they must achieve during their administration. The preemptive president is fortunate to be elected and complete his term of office without incident; other priorities take a backseat to this minimalist imperative. Preemptive presidents are distinguished by coming to power in a context of little ideological or political support. The more "political" and politically responsive the institution, the less likely it is to be a reliable ally to the president. The very features that make the old regime resilient remove possible political resources from an oppositional president, and the continued strength of the old regime insures that such presidents cannot expect to advance their oppositional agenda very directly.

For oppositional political leaders, the Court is both a potential constraint and a potential means for overcoming constraints. Preemptive presidents are likely to find themselves in disagreement with much of the substance of the Court's output, just as they are likely to disagree with other political actors affiliated with the dominant regime. Oppositional leaders are likely to face more immediate obstacles than the relatively distant threat of judicial review, however, and they are unlikely to have either the motive or the resources to mount a serious challenge to judicial authority. They may even have reasons to attempt to bolster judicial authority. In a generally hostile political environment, a relatively independent judiciary can be an asset to an oppositional president. Unable to assume a leadership role in construing the Constitution, the president can at least hope to influence the courts as they exercise their interpretive responsibilities and may look to the judiciary as a potential ally in the president's struggle against the numerous more partisan foes. Judicial supremacy may be the favored choice of oppositional presidents simply because the alternatives are either unavailable or even less attractive. This situation is examined in chapter 4.

Over time the federal judiciary seems to have gained more authority over constitutional interpretation. As it has become evident that judicial supremacy is more often a help than a hindrance to political leaders, judicial supremacy has become more prominent and secure. The general political environment has also evolved in such a way that the logic of deference to judicial authority has itself become more prevalent. The strategic calculations of the professional politician of the twentieth century increasingly emphasized the value of recognizing judicial authority, even as the judiciary built political resources of its own. This broader developmental tendency is explored in chapter 5.

Conclusion

Constitutional theory is often treated in the same formalistic manner as constitutional law. The implications of the Constitution are developed as logical implications of an abstract text. Judicial interpretive authority is posited as absolute, ahistorical, and politically effective. At the same time, sensible claims on behalf of the utility of judicial review for maintaining constitutional forms have been transmogrified into a demand for judicial supremacy. The ultimate exposition of constitutional meaning by the Supreme Court is deemed a necessary and sufficient condition for sustaining constitutionalism. All that remains is to determine how the Court should interpret the text. Constitutional maintenance becomes a bloodless and technical enterprise best conducted by the legal intelligentsia.

This vision of constitutional maintenance is neither desirable nor realistic. Constitutional maintenance is above all a political task. As such, it must be considered in political terms. Constitutions cannot survive if they are too politically costly to maintain, and they cannot survive if they are too distant from normal political concerns. Constitutions are made real by being constantly embraced and reenacted by citizens and government officials. The Court cannot stand outside of politics and exercise a unique role as guardian of constitutional verities. The crucial problem is not that judicial interpretations cannot remain "objective" and "neutral" and sealed off from political considerations. The more fundamental problem is that the Court's judgments will have no force unless other powerful political actors accept the importance of the interpretive task and the priority of the judicial voice. Constitutional law rests within a larger field of constitutional politics, and the scope and substance of constitutional law will be shaped by that politics.

The Court must compete with other political actors for the authority to define the terms of the Constitution. For the Court to compete successfully, other political actors must have reasons for allowing the Court to "win." The president, among others, must see some political value in deferring to the Court and helping to construct a space for judicial autonomy.[58] Judicial supremacy makes the strongest claims on other political institutions. It asserts that the Court has a role not only in applying the law of the Constitution to specific disputes between individual parties but also in defining the content of the nation's most fundamental values and the appropriate workings of the most basic structures of governance. This

---

[58] The process started early. In 1765, the royal governor of the colony of Massachusetts Bay, Francis Bernard, was presented with the Boston Memorial declaring the Stamp Act unconstitutional and calling on the governor to block its implementation in the colony. Before the governor's council, Samuel Adams and James Otis argued that acts of Parliament that violated English liberties were void and could be disregarded. After they had presented their case, Bernard responded, "The arguments made use of, both by Mr. Adams and you, would be very pertinent to induce the Judges of the Superior Court to think the Act of no validity, and that therefore they should pay no regard to it; but the question with me is, whether that very thing don't argue the impropriety of our intermeddling in a matter which solely belongs to them to judge of in their judicial department." Even though the governor was not elected, he was accountable in other ways and torn between the demands of the colonists and the demands of the authorities in London. Under the circumstances, he too saw the advantage of passing the buck to the courts. Josiah Quincy, *Reports of the Cases argued and adjudged in the Superior Court of Judicature* (Boston: Little, Brown, 1865), 206.

is a strong claim to make, and we can easily imagine why other political actors might not wish to accede to such a claim. We can easily imagine presidents dismissing the authority of the Court and ignoring its opinions, if not its decisions. We can easily imagine a Court reduced to political subservience, inactive in the exercise of its power of review and incapable of acting independently. But judicial supremacy has grown and become more secure over time. Despite occasional voices of dissent, crucial government officials have generally supported the judiciary and recognized its claim to being the ultimate interpreter of constitutional meaning.

The American judiciary has been able to win the authority to independently interpret the Constitution because recognizing such an authority has been politically beneficial to others. Relative judicial independence and authority can help elected political officials overcome a variety of political dilemmas that they routinely encounter. In particular, the authority of the federal judiciary is rooted in concerns for electoral success and coalitional maintenance and the complications for political action created by the American constitutional system of fragmented power. Within boundary constraints set by other political actors, the judiciary has enjoyed significant autonomy in giving the Constitution meaning.

The judicial authority to interpret the Constitution is neither absolute nor stable. The judiciary has been able to sustain its claims to interpretive predominance primarily because, and when, other political actors have had reasons of their own to recognize such claims. Powerful political figures have often found such reasons and have determined that judicial supremacy has been in their own best interests. Occasionally, political leaders reject the Court's claims for its own superiority and have advanced their own claims for interpretive authority. Constitutional authority has not been distributed once and for all by either the text or history. Constitutional authority, both substantive and interpretive, is dynamic and politically contested. The judiciary is an important player in this constitutional process, but it is not the only player. Challenges to judicial authority in part show the vibrancy of our constitutional system, as various political figures grapple with the requirements of the Constitution and try to reach a compelling understanding of our most fundamental values and commitments. If the voice of the judiciary is often primary in our dialogue over constitutional meaning, it is not the only voice that speaks in the name of the Constitution and sometimes not the best.

TWO

The Construction of Constitutional Regimes

IN THE EARLY TWENTIETH CENTURY, scholars and commentators began to speak of "judicial supremacy." This is not surprising timing. It was during this period, when the *Lochner* Court was in full swing, that the "higher law" features of the American constitutional system became most evident.[1] It was not until the twentieth century that a specific term, judicial review, was coined to refer to the judicial invalidation of laws on the grounds of their being contrary to the requirements of the Constitution.[2] The power of judicial review had long been recognized and occasionally exercised, but it was not until the turn of the century that the Court routinely played this role and seemed to review the actions of the coordinate legislative branch as if it were a mere administrative agency or subordinate court.[3]

Perhaps most notably, political scientist Charles Grove Haines entitled his 1914 book critically examining the history of judicial review *The American Doctrine of Judicial Supremacy*. Haines began, "One of the axioms of political theory and governmental practice is that there must be in every state a supreme authority whose determinations are final and not subject to any recognized higher power." This supreme authority would be "the very essence of the state."[4] Identifying where supremacy lay within a political system would clarify the basic nature of that political system and the locus of political power. It could provide the basis for distinguishing and categorizing the various governments of the world.

---

[1] See, e.g., Edward S. Corwin, "The 'Higher Law' Background of American Constitutional Law," *Harvard Law Review* 42 (1928): 149.

[2] Edward S. Corwin, "The Establishment of Judicial Review," *Michigan Law Review* 9 (1910): 102. Competing terms to describe the phenomenon were being suggested at the same time, including *judicial supremacy, judicial veto,* and *judicial nullification.* Charles Grove Haines, *The American Doctrine of Judicial Supremacy* (New York: Macmillan, 1914), 16n2.

[3] This was the original context for the term *judicial review,* as legislatures provided for judicial examination of administrative actions to insure their conformity with the law. See, e.g., John Den, et al. v. The Hoboken Land and Improvement Company, 59 U.S. 272, 283 (1855); Frank Goodnow, "The Administrative Law of the United States," *Political Science Quarterly* 19 (1904): 115; Thomas Reed Powell, "Judicial Review of Administrative Action in Immigration Proceedings," *Harvard Law Review* 22 (1908): 360.

[4] Haines, *American Doctrine,* 1.

Haines found that the state and federal governments of the United States seemed to be in a class by themselves. In this country alone had a constitution imposing written limitations on the government been established and the judiciary given "the extraordinary power . . . to say what the law is," including the law of the Constitution. "Thus the judiciary, a coordinate branch of the government, becomes the particular guardian of the terms of the written constitution." The rest of the government is "held within the bounds of authority as understood and interpreted by the judicial power," for the "judiciary has the sole right to place an authoritative interpretation upon the fundamental written law."[5] For "most practical purposes the judiciary exercises supreme power in the United States," which was then leading to popular controversy and such common denunciations as "judicial legislation" and "judicial oligarchy."[6]

The controversy over this peculiar American doctrine only seemed to grow, until the storm finally broke in 1937 with President Franklin D. Roosevelt's dramatic challenge to the Court and the judicial withdrawal from the struggle over the New Deal. Political scientist Edward Corwin had been one of the most insightful, and critical, commentators on the Court and its understandings of the Constitution in the years leading up to Roosevelt's battle with the Court. Although a Republican, Corwin had in fact been an advocate of and advisor to the Roosevelt administration, and had been involved in the planning and promotion of the president's proposal to "reorganize" the federal judiciary. The following year he attempted to justify that effort with a remarkable historical and theoretical treatise titled *The Court Over the Constitution*, informed by "the fresh perspective afforded by the New Deal" and interested in examining how judicial review could be made into, in the words of the subtitle, "an Instrument of Popular Government."[7]

In that book, Corwin suggested an innovative reconceptualization of the doctrine of judicial review. In particular, he suggested a distinction between a "juristic" conception, in which the courts are the proper authority to interpret the Constitution because of their special competence in the field, and a "departmentalist" conception. Departmentalism would hold that constitutional interpretation is not peculiar to the courts, but rather that each of the three coordinate branches has an equal responsibility and authority to interpret. Whenever each branch acts, it necessarily exercises an interpretive power. The question is not whether the nonjudicial branches will interpret the Constitution, but "what deference are they

---

[5] Ibid., 5.

[6] Ibid., 11.

[7] Edward S. Corwin, *Court over Constitution* (Princeton: Princeton University Press, 1938), vii.

required by the Constitution to pay relevant judicial versions of the Constitution, when such are available?"[8] Departmentalism refuses to recognize the "transubstantiation whereby the Court's opinion of the Constitution . . . becomes the very body and blood of the Constitution."[9] "Finality of interpretation is hence the outcome—when it exists—not of judicial application of the Constitution to the decision of cases, but of the continued harmony of views among the three departments."[10] The judicial interpretation of the Constitution "is final for the case in which it is pronounced, it is not final against the political forces to which a changed opinion may give rise," whether in the judiciary itself or in the other branches of government.[11] Though the professional bar could be expected to support judicial interpretation, the "driving power" behind the departmentalist conception had "always been *Presidential leadership.*"[12]

Corwin ultimately turned this departmentalist theory in support of Roosevelt, arguing that the Court's rulings against the New Deal had "thrust forward the political aspect of the Court's role in constitutional interpretation as never before." Under such circumstances, it was entirely appropriate that the president challenge the Court's constitutional interpretation directly rather than seek a constitutional amendment. For those "who deny the necessary identity of the judicial version of the Constitution with the Constitution," the juristic insistence on the amendment route "simply begs the question whether the Constitution needs amending."[13]

The case for the departmentalist conception of constitutional interpretation has been built as much on historical precedent as on theoretical analysis. Corwin was the first to point to what has become a standard list of presidents who articulated the departmentalist themes. In addition to Franklin Roosevelt, that list has traditionally included Thomas Jefferson, Andrew Jackson, and Abraham Lincoln.[14] More recently, the Reagan administration struck some of those themes as well. For Corwin and others

---

[8] Ibid., 15.

[9] Ibid., 68.

[10] Ibid., 7 (emphasis omitted).

[11] Ibid., 61.

[12] Ibid., 69.

[13] Ibid., 80, 80n84.

[14] See, e.g., Robert Scigliano, *The Supreme Court and the Presidency* (New York: Free Press, 1971), 23–50; John Agresto, *The Supreme Court and Constitutional Democracy* (Ithaca: Cornell University Press, 1984), 78–95, 116–38; Murphy, "Who Shall Interpret?" 409–12; Sanford Levinson, *Constitutional Faith* (Princeton: Princeton University Press, 1988), 39–43; Susan R. Burgess, *Contest for Constitutional Authority* (Lawrence: University Press of Kansas, 1988), 1–27; Fisher, *Constitutional Dialogues*, 233–47; Easterbrook, "Presidential Review," 906–11; Michael Stokes Paulsen, "The *Merryman* Power and the Dilemma of Autonomous Executive Branch Interpretation," *Cardozo Law Review* 15 (1993): 84–98; Steven G. Calabresi, "Caesarism, Departmentalism, and Professor Paulsen," *Minnesota Law Review* 83 (1999): 1421. See also Kramer, *The People Themselves.*

primarily concerned with establishing the consistency of departmentalism with the American constitutional tradition, these cases have been most useful as precedents. It is notable, however, that these presidents alone have made such appeals. "When [nondepartmentalist] presidents disagree with the constitutional decisions of the federal courts, they appoint judges, endorse constitutional amendments to overturn disfavored decisions, or flog the decisions from the bully pulpit of the White House." They "act *as if* the opinions of the federal judiciary have special priority in the interpretation of the Constitution" and do not ordinarily claim the authority to act on their own independent understandings of the Constitution.[15] Those few departmentalist presidents are different, and we are left with the question of why and what it means for American constitutionalism.

This pattern requires no particular explanation for those legal scholars interested in advocating the case for the departmentalist conception of constitutional interpretation. The important point for them is that prominent officials have over the course of American history repeatedly voiced the theory. Merely listing a series of decontextualized quotations from these presidents, however, may lose important information that would help not only to justify departmentalism but also to explain these episodes of presidential challenge to judicial authority. Understanding the political rationale for such presidential challenges will clarify why the authority to give meaning to the Constitution has at times shifted away from the judiciary and to the political branches of government and how the American constitutional order develops. Before exploring that political rationale, it is useful to briefly review these presidential challenges to judicial supremacy and a prominent political account of them.

PRESIDENTIAL CHALLENGES TO JUDICIAL AUTHORITY

Presidents have been the most prominent and most important challengers to the judicial authority to settle constitutional meaning, though they have not been alone in doing so. Before considering the reasons for these challenges and how these challenges fit into the larger pattern of presidential relationships with the Court, it is worthwhile to establish that these few presidents have been correctly identified as making departmentalist claims (there will be opportunities to consider the extent to which other presidents have made similar claims in later chapters).

Thomas Jefferson was the first president to explicitly embrace the departmentalist theory, and explained and defended it at greatest length.

---

[15] Geoffrey P. Miller, "The President's Power of Interpretation: Implications of a Unified Theory of Constitutional Law," *Law and Contemporary Problems* 56 (1993): 42.

The Jeffersonians had come to power challenging the authority of the federal judiciary. Responding to fears of war abroad and domestic opposition at home, the Federalist Congress passed the onerous Alien and Sedition Acts in 1798, which were vigorously enforced by party loyalists in the executive and judicial branches. Organizing resistance where they could, the growing Jeffersonian opposition turned to the states. Resolutions penned by Jefferson and James Madison attacking the constitutionality of the acts were passed by the legislatures of Kentucky and Virginia, respectively. In doing so, they asserted the authority of the states to pass judgment on the constitutionality of federal legislation. Jefferson's Kentucky Resolution denied that any branch of the federal government could be the "exclusive or final judge" of the powers delegated to that government by the Constitution. As the members of the federal compact, each of the states had "an equal right to judge for itself" whether the Constitution had been violated and how violations should be remedied.[16] When a number of Federalist-controlled state legislatures responded by asserting the supremacy of the federal judiciary to resolve constitutional disputes, Madison penned a Report on the Resolutions for the Virginia legislature in 1799. To the objection that "the federal judiciary is to be regarded as the sole expositor of the Constitution, in the last resort," Madison responded that judicial supremacy was inadequate to the preservation of the Constitution since "the judicial department also may exercise or sanction dangerous powers beyond the grant of the Constitution."[17]

Jefferson subsequently turned his attention away from the states and toward the elected branches of government, and particularly the president, as interpreters of the Constitution. Upon assuming the presidency, Jefferson asserted the authority to act on his own understanding of constitutional requirements. As the chief executive, Jefferson wrote, "I affirm that [sedition] act to be no law, because in opposition to the constitution; and I shall treat it as a nullity, wherever it comes in the way of my functions."[18] It was in fact his "duty to arrest its execution at every stage," and therefore he "discharged every person under punishment or prosecution under the sedition law."[19] In response to various correspondents and the

---

[16] Thomas Jefferson, *The Writings of Thomas Jefferson*, ed. Paul Leicester Ford, 10 vols. (New York: G. P. Putnam's Sons, 1896), 7:292.

[17] James Madison, *The Writings of James Madison*, ed. Gaillard Hunt, 9 vols. (New York: G. P. Putnam's Sons, 1900–1910), 6:351. Madison later qualified this argument by noting that the states were not taking direct action to enforce their constitutional views, backing off Jefferson's stronger suggestion that the states had the authority to take remedial action against the federal government Ibid., 402. In Congress, Madison had earlier denied that the judiciary had greater authority than the other branches to settle constitutional disputes. *Annals of Congress* (17 June 1789), 1:519–21.

[18] Jefferson, *Writings*, 8:58n1.

[19] Ibid., 309n1.

reception of the Court's *Marbury* opinion, Jefferson elaborated on his understanding of constitutional interpretation and judicial authority, arguing that the departments of government must be "co-ordinate and independent of each other." The Constitution has given "no control to another branch" of the decisions of one branch, and ultimately "each branch has an equal right to decide for itself what is the meaning of the Constitution."[20] That judges could be "the ultimate arbiters of all constitutional questions" was "a very dangerous doctrine indeed."[21] Far better that the "co-ordinate branches should be checks on each other" and be "equally independent in the sphere of action assigned to them."[22] Judges could interpret the Constitution only "*for themselves.*"[23]

Andrew Jackson later echoed Jefferson's argument. The *locus classicus* for Jackson's departmentalism is the message accompanying his veto of the rechartering of the Second National Bank in the summer of 1832, which was among his most prominent and important acts and statements. In that message, Jackson argued that the "Congress, the Executive, and the Court must each for itself be guided by its own opinion of the Constitution. Each public officer who takes an oath to support the Constitution swears that he will support it as he understands it, and not as it is understood by others." The interpretations of the Constitution offered by the judicial branch were not authoritative, but only entitled to "such influence as the force of their reasoning may deserve."[24] Jackson was less blunt in his handling of the Cherokee cases. As part of a series of conflicts involving the Court, the state of Georgia, and the Cherokee tribe, the Marshall Court in 1832 struck down a state statute requiring the licensing of all whites in Cherokee territory as in tension with a superior national statute and treaties.[25] Though Jackson may not have declared, "John Marshall has made his decision, now let him enforce it," it was common in the contemporary press that the president might refuse to enforce the Court's decision based on his theory of the independence of the coordinate branches and given

[20] Jefferson, *The Writings of Thomas Jefferson*, ed. Andrew A. Lipscomb, vol. 11 (Washington, DC: Thomas Jefferson Memorial Association, 1903), 213, 214; Jefferson, *Writings*, ed. Ford, 10:141.

[21] Jefferson, *Writings*, ed. Ford, 10:160.

[22] Ibid., 8:311n1.

[23] Ibid., 9:517.

[24] Andrew Jackson, *Presidential Messages, Addresses and State Papers*, ed. Julius Miller, vol. 3 (New York: Review of Reviews, 1917), 995, 996. Roger Taney, the presumed author of Jackson's veto message, emphasized a qualification of that departmentalist theme some three decades later. In an 1860 letter to Martin Van Buren, Taney wrote that Jackson "was speaking of his rights and duty, when acting as part of the Legislative power [in exercising the veto], and not of his right or duty as an Executive officer." Quoted in Charles Warren, *The Supreme Court in United States History*, 3 vols. (Boston: Little, Brown, 1922), 2:223.

[25] Worcester v. Georgia, 31 U.S. 515 (1832).

his hostility to both Marshall and the Indians.[26] As it developed, the president was never formally required to execute an order of the Court in that case, but he publicly stated his disinclination to do so.[27] Before the Court had even ruled, Jackson had informed interested parties that "on mature reflection" he had satisfied himself that the state had acted within its constitutional authority and the president "has not authority to interfere."[28] Similarly, in 1831 Jackson told Congress that it did not have the authority over Indian tribes residing within a state and could not give the president the authority to "make war upon the rights of the States," a constitutional argument that he elaborated in a letter to his secretary of war.[29] After the Court's decision in *Worcester*, Jackson wrote, "[T]he decision of the supreme court has fell still born and they find it cannot coerce Georgia to yield to its mandate."[30] Jackson was happy to enlist the courts in support of his own policies, such as revenue collection in the resistant South Carolina, and he refrained from throwing his own weight behind the numerous judicial reform measures backed by his supporters, but he was clear that the Court's constitutional understandings were not authoritative for the other branches of the national government.

Abraham Lincoln offered yet another variation on the departmentalist theme. Lincoln developed this position at length in responding to the *Dred Scott* decision in his 1858 "debates" with Stephen Douglas. Lincoln noted, "I do not propose to disturb or resist the [Court's] decision" as it applied to Dred Scott and his family. But he would not make the Court's constitutional understanding "a rule of political action, for the people and all the departments of the government." Adding "something to the authority in favor of my own position," Lincoln rehearsed at length Jefferson's and Jackson's departmentalist theories.[31] He repeated and adhered to that understanding upon gaining the White House. Central to the Court's holding in *Dred Scott* was the argument that free blacks were not citizens under the Constitution. In the course of its daily business the Lincoln administration was faced with the question of whether or not to adhere to the Court's understanding of citizenship and chose to break

---

[26] For discussion, see Warren, *Supreme Court*, 2:216–21.

[27] For discussion of the administration's actions and obligations in the Cherokee cases, see Richard E. Ellis, *The Union at Risk* (New York: Oxford University Press, 1987), 30–32, 112–20; Edwin A. Miles, "After John Marshall's Decision: Worcester v. Georgia and the Nullification Crisis," *Journal of Southern History* 39 (1973): 519.

[28] Quoted in Richard P. Longaker, "Andrew Jackson and the Judiciary," *Political Science Quarterly* 71 (1956): 345n9.

[29] Quoted in Ibid., 346.

[30] Andrew Jackson, *The Correspondence of Andrew Jackson*, ed. John Bassett, vol. 4 (Washington, DC: Carnegie Institute, 1929), 430.

[31] Abraham Lincoln, *Abraham Lincoln*, ed. Roy P. Basler (New York: Da Capo, 1990), 418.

from the Court. Federal statute required, for example, that the masters of coastal trading ships be American citizens, raising the "question whether or not colored men can be citizens of the United States . . . and therefore competent to command American vessels."[32] Lincoln's attorney general, Edward Bates, wrote a lengthy formal opinion providing a detailed rebuttal to Chief Justice Roger Taney's argument against black citizenship. That opinion became the basis for the subsequent decisions by the administration, on encouragement from abolitionist Republican legislators, to begin granting passports and patents to blacks.[33] Congress and the president likewise enacted legislation abolishing slavery in all federal territories and the District of Columbia, directly rejecting the Court's specific argument that the federal territories had to be open to slavery and with Lincoln noting that he "never doubted the constitutional authority of Congress" to take such action.[34]

Lincoln was less public about his reasoning when faced with state and federal habeas corpus writs for civilians held by the military during the Civil War. When Chief Justice Taney concluded that Congress alone had the authority to suspend the writ of habeas corpus, the military refused to comply with his orders, the president disregarded the papers Taney transmitted to him, and Lincoln explained to Congress his understanding of presidential authority during a rebellion.[35] His attorney general subsequently issued a formal opinion stating, "[T]he president and the judiciary are coordinate departments of government, and the one not subordinate to the other," and empowered "to act out its own granted powers, without any ordained or legal superior possessing the power to revise and reverse its action."[36] Even after passage of a congressional statute continuing the suspension of habeas corpus, the War Department issued an order instructing military officers to cite presidential authority for refusing to honor such writs.[37]

---

[32] "Citizenship, November 29, 1862," in *Official Opinions of the Attorneys General of the United States*, vol. 10 (Washington, DC: Government Printing Office, 1868), 382 (emphasis omitted).

[33] *The Works of Charles Sumner*, 15 vols. (Boston: Lee and Shepard, 1870–83), 5:498, 6:144. Bates's opinion not only rejected Taney's judicial opinion in *Dred Scott*, but also the opinion of earlier attorneys general who were called upon to interpret the same and similar statutory provisions. For a discussion, see H. Jefferson Powell, *A Community Built on Words* (Chicago: University of Chicago Press, 2002), 171–76.

[34] Abolition of Slavery Act (Territories), ch. 112, 12 Stat. 432 (1862); Abolition of Slavery Act (District of Columbia), ch. 54, 12 Stat. 376 (1862); Lincoln, *Abraham Lincoln*, 640.

[35] Lincoln, *Abraham Lincoln*, 600–601. For discussion, see Scigliano, *Supreme Court and Presidency*, 39–44; Daniel Farber, *Lincoln's Constitution* (Chicago: University of Chicago Press, 2003), 157–63, 177–99.

[36] "Suspension of the Privilege of the Writ of Habeas Corpus, July 5, 1861," in *Opinions of the Attorneys General*, 10:85, 77.

[37] Scigliano, *Supreme Court and Presidency*, 42.

Franklin Roosevelt reached similar conclusions about the relative authority of the Court and the president in interpreting the Constitution. The argument was made most famously as Roosevelt sought to justify his Court-packing plan. Given his immediate object of getting the Court to accept the presidential understanding of the Constitution, Roosevelt broke from the traditional rhetoric of three independent branches. Instead, he "described the American form of Government as a three horse team provided by the Constitution to the American people." The people would find that "two of the horses are pulling in unison today; the third is not," and the people could rightfully "expect the third horse to pull in unison with the other two."[38] The Court was misreading the Constitution, or perhaps not reading it at all. As a result, the "balance of power between the three branches of the Federal Government, has been tipped out of balance by the Courts," and Roosevelt declared, "[I]t is my purpose to restore that balance."[39] Unlike lawyers, "[T]he lay rank and file of political parties . . . have respected as sacred *all* branches of their government. They have seen nothing *more* sacred about one branch than about either of the others."[40]

In earlier addresses prior to his proposal to reorganize the judiciary, Roosevelt had hearkened back to the examples of Jefferson, Jackson, and Lincoln. Speaking in Little Rock, Roosevelt reminded his audience that Jefferson "had the courage, the backbone, to act for the benefit of the United States without the full and unanimous approval of every member of the legal profession." Roosevelt was in fact twisting history a bit to make his point, for the example he used of Jefferson's courage was the Louisiana Purchase, about which Jefferson himself had substantial constitutional qualms. Nonetheless, Roosevelt cast Jefferson as justifying the constitutionality of the purchase against the lawyerly doubters, "and, my friends, nobody carried the case to the Supreme Court."[41] Similarly, Andrew Jackson was willing to buck the "so-called guardian groups of the Republic," in order to realize an "era of a truer democracy." The "American doctrine" that emerged from the Jacksonian presidency was that "the American people shall not be thwarted from their high purpose to remain the custodians of their own destiny."[42]

Roosevelt's most direct appeal to Lincoln and the authority of departmentalism came in a speech he prepared but never had to deliver. At the very outset of the Roosevelt administration as Congress and the Treasury

---

[38] Franklin D. Roosevelt, *Public Papers and Addresses of Franklin D. Roosevelt*, ed. Samuel I. Rosenman, 6 vols. (New York: Random House, 1938), 6:123, 124.

[39] Ibid., 6:133.

[40] Ibid., 6:365.

[41] Ibid., 5:196.

[42] Ibid., 5:198.

debated the lawfulness of paying federal "gold-clause contracts" with greenbacks, the *New York Times* declared that the "Supreme Court will be the final arbiter."[43] After the Court heard the case, prominent political columnist Arthur Krock reported that Washington was aflame with speculation about the Court's actions and the possible responses, with the "prevailing opinion" being that a majority of the justices would recognize "that the public welfare requires" upholding the repeal of the gold clause and that a Court that only "assumed, but did not specially acquire from the Constitution, the right to hold Congressional statutes invalid" could be "relied upon" to see its duty in this case.[44] In preparation for an adverse ruling from the Court, Roosevelt had a speech drafted quoting Lincoln's First Inaugural, declaring that "vital questions affecting the whole people" could not be "fixed by decisions of the Supreme Court" unless "the people will have ceased to be their own rulers." Though (presumably) the majority of the justices "have decided these cases in accordance with the letter of the law as they read it," the president had an obligation "to

[43] Turner Catledge, "Gold-Bond Clause Awaits Court Test," *New York Times*, 7 May 1933, xx2. Editorializing on the congressional debate, the *Times* observed that Congress was proposing to do nothing more than "legislate a lawsuit" since legislative backing would add nothing to the question "until the Supreme Court had passed upon it." "If," *New York Times*, 28 April 1933, 16. It later more strongly warned that if the federal government were willing "to violate its plighted word to its own citizens" by suspending gold payments, then Congress and the president might equally leave an adverse decision "of the Supreme Court hanging in the air as a mere *brutum fulmen*." "Able to Repudiate," *New York Times*, 31 May 1933, 16.

[44] Arthur Krock, "In Washington: Gold Case Crowds All Other Topics Into the Background," *New York Times*, 15 January 1935, 18. Professor John George of Rutgers published a long letter in the *Times* complaining, "Just now there is entirely too much talk of the Supreme Court being the final judge of law in the United States," and reviewing the various ways, from amendment to Court-packing, by which an adverse ruling on the gold clause could be vitiated. John George, "High Court Ruling Not Final," *New York Times*, 27 January 1935, E9. On the very day the justices met in conference to discuss the case, congressmen and administration officials publicly discussed options to circumvent a negative decision. "Quick Action on Gold Due if U.S. Loses," *Washington Post*, 13 January 1935, 1. In anticipation of the decision, Attorney General Homer Cummings denied to the press that the president planned to put the nation under martial law if the Court ruled against the administration's position, but did assure them, "We are ready for any emergency." Special to the *New York Times*, "Cummings Says We Are Ready on Gold," *New York Times*, 8 February 1935, 2. A few days later, however, the *Times* editorialized that while the Court's decision was still unknown, "there is no difference of opinion on one point. It is that whatever the judges decide the country will accept." The American people now "expect it to be the acknowledged arbiter in great public questions arising under the law and the Constitution . . . when the Court has finally spoken, acquiescence in its rules and obedience to its command will be instinctive with American citizens and will come as a matter of course from all our authorities." "One Point Not Doubtful," *New York Times*, 13 February 1935, 18. See also David Glick, "Strategic Retreat and the 1935 Gold Clause Cases: Upholding the New Deal to Challenge the New Deal," unpublished paper.

protect the people of the United States to the best of his ability." Roosevelt could not "stand idly by and . . . permit the decision of the Supreme Court to be carried through to its logical, inescapable conclusion" to the detriment of the country and in disregard of the best understanding of the legal obligations of the government and debtors.[45] The day after the Court announced its decision, Krock pointed to the fact that government officials "behaved like worried schoolboys when the master is marking their examination papers" as evidence that Roosevelt was no dictator and to rebut Justice McReynold's declaration that the Constitution was "gone."[46] The very next day, however, he broke the news of Roosevelt's undelivered speech on the front page of the *Times* and declared that its delivery would have been "the most sensational and historic episode of constitutional history of the United States" since Andrew Jackson refused to enforce the Cherokee decision.[47] Krock concluded his report by noting that many had reminded the administration that the "specific power" of judicial review could not be found in the text of the Constitution but was merely an "evolution of the personal beliefs of Chief Justice Marshall" and that the occasion may yet arise, "before the New Deal has been completed," that would "bring the President to the radio to make, in revised form, the speech he has now laid aside."[48]

Most recently, Ronald Reagan has questioned the authority of the judiciary to settle contested constitutional meaning. He insisted that "the issue of abortion must be resolved by a democratic process," and called for Congress to pass legislation "to restore legal protection to the unborn" despite the Court's declaration that such laws were unconstitutional.[49] Edwin Meese, Reagan's attorney general, prominently drew the "necessary distinction between the Constitution and constitutional law," and

[45] Roosevelt, *F.D.R.: His Personal Letters*, ed. Elliott Roosevelt, vol. 3 (New York: Duell, Sloan and Pearce, 1950), 459. Roosevelt apparently also threatened to defy an adverse Court decision involving a military trial of saboteurs during World War II. Scigliano, *Supreme Court and Presidency*, 49. In his speech, Roosevelt did not specify how he would block the implementation of the Court's decision. After initially suggesting the possibility of following Ulysses Grant's example of packing the Court after an unfavorable ruling on paper currency, Robert Jackson proposed an assertion of sovereign immunity from suits to recover claims based on gold clauses. Robert H. Jackson, *That Man* (New York: Oxford University Press, 2003), 66.

[46] Arthur Krock, "In Washington: Supreme Court Exploded Dictatorship Illusion," *New York Times*, 20 February 1935, 18.

[47] Arthur Krock, "Roosevelt Speech Ready in Case He Lost on Gold," *New York Times*, 21 February 1935, 1.

[48] Ibid., 4. Krock later expanded on this point, clearly relaying the administration's belief that the public would support it over the Court if battle lines had to be drawn. Krock, "Gold Ruling Effects Weighed at Capital," *New York Times*, 24 February 1935, E3.

[49] Ronald Reagan, *Public Papers of the Presidents of the United States: Ronald Reagan, 1983* (Washington, DC: Government Printing Office, 1982–), 876.

insisted that judge-made constitutional law did not determine the meaning of the Constitution. Constitutional law is merely "what the Supreme Court says about the Constitution," not the authoritative Constitution itself. Citing the examples of Jefferson, Jackson, and Lincoln, Meese denied the authority of judicial precedents for resolving political debates over constitutional meaning and insisted that "constitutional interpretation is not the business of the Court only, but also properly the business of all the branches of government."[50] The Reagan administration likewise adopted the position of executive "nonacquiescence" in cases in which the executive branch believed a statute was unconstitutional or in cases of disagreement among the circuit courts as to the meaning of the Constitution, though this assertion of executive interpretive authority was tempered by deference to the holdings of the Supreme Court.[51] For the Reagan administration, Meese's effort to distinguish the Constitution from constitutional law not only set up the possibility of ignoring the Court but more importantly of making room for presidential leadership in correcting the Court's reading of the Constitution and establishing an alternative constitutional vision that could guide the nation in the future. The Court did not deserve automatic deference. It was possible to take our constitutional cues from elsewhere.

Departmentalist presidents are substantively important in their own right and significant for normative theories of constitutional interpretation, though for empirical theorizing about presidential-judicial relations they are somewhat *sui generis*. It should be noted that these cases of presidential assertion of independent authority to interpret the Constitution are directed toward the Court. This focus does not cover cases of executive departmentalism aimed at Congress, as when Andrew Johnson asserted the right to disobey the Tenure of Office Act, in order to bring the constitutional dispute into the courts, or the practice of Bill Clinton and other recent presidents of issuing signing statements expressing constitutional doubts about legislation and pledging to administer the law accordingly. Likewise, Richard Nixon is traditionally not included in the list of departmentalist presidents. Though critical of various court decisions and aggressive in litigation, Nixon did not claim the authority to act contrary to the Court's interpretation of constitutional meaning. Notably, Nixon quickly complied with the Court's ruling to turn over subpoenaed docu-

[50] Edwin Meese, "The Law of the Constitution," *Tulane Law Review* 61 (1987): 981, 982, 985.

[51] See Samuel Estreicher and Richard L. Revesz, "Nonacquiescence by Federal Administrative Agencies," *Yale Law Journal* 98 (1989): 679; Deborah Maranville, "Nonacquiescence: Outlaw Agencies, Imperial Courts, and the Perils of Pluralism," *Vanderbilt Law Review* 39 (1986): 471. Unsurprisingly, the judiciary reacted negatively to this argument. See, e.g., Lear Siegler, Inc. Energy Prods. Div. v. Lehman, 842 F.2d 1102, 1117–26 (9th Cir. 1988).

ments to the special prosecutor, despite his attorney's equivocation at oral arguments.[52] Such cases, however, are useful in indicating that presidential challenges to judicial authority are best regarded as existing at one end of a continuum, along which lesser assertions of presidential constitutional authority can be arrayed.[53]

Some Approaches to Understanding Presidential Challenges to Judicial Authority

It is not uncommon for presidents and politicians generally to complain about the Court. It is uncommon for presidents to claim that judicial understandings of the Constitution do not have the authority to bind the coordinate branches and that presidents have an independent authority to interpret the Constitution for themselves and to act on those interpretations in carrying out their own constitutional responsibilities. The ability of modern constitutional theorists to point to examples of such presidential claims in American history may help demonstrate that such arguments are not completely innovative and unprecedented. This does not, however, help us understand why judicial authority has been challenged in this way, why it has been challenged so rarely, or how we should evaluate such challenges.

For many constitutional scholars, such challenges seem quite dangerous. Although some of our most celebrated presidents have embraced departmentalist theories, this has often been seen as a flaw within their presidencies rather than a model to be emulated. Their challenges to judicial authority may be seen as detracting from, rather than contributing to, the greatness of their presidencies. Presidential challenges to judicial authority seem particularly threatening, given that the executive is potentially the "most dangerous branch" since the presidency possesses both force and will and exerts its influence both at the beginning and the end

---

[52] During the oral arguments for *United States v. Nixon*, Justice Thurgood Marshall asked "Well, do you agree that [the issue of executive privilege] is before this Court, and you are submitting it to this Court for decision?" Nixon's attorney, James St. Clair, responded, "This is being submitted to this court for its guidance and judgment with respect to the law. The President, on the other hand, has his obligations under the Constitution." Quoted in Alexander and Schauer, "On Extrajudicial Constitutional Interpretation," 1364n22.

[53] James Monroe, for example, sent messages to both Congress and the justices of the Supreme Court detailing his views on the unconstitutionality of internal improvements. The fact that he was told in an informal capacity that the majority of the justices did not share his understanding did not stop him from exercising his veto power against what he took to be unconstitutional federal appropriations.

of the legal process.[54] Such challenges to judicial authority are often seen as posing basic threats to the rule of law and constitutionalism.

The theoretical critique of departmentalism converges with a prominent empirical explanation for these episodes of presidential challenge. The normative defense of judicial supremacy against these presidential assertions does not itself make any claims about why these particular presidents make such claims. Like its proponents, the critics of departmentalism are more concerned with its theory than with its historical practice. A political explanation for this historical pattern can be easily derived, however, from a few prominent precepts about American politics.

Robert Jackson, Franklin Roosevelt's attorney general and eventual Supreme Court nominee, provided the core of such an explanation at the end of his examination of "the struggle for judicial supremacy." Jackson argued that the party system has tended "to separate the judiciary from the elective branches and to place them in opposition." Although the party system "often serves to bridge the constitutional division between the executive and legislative branches," that "inducement to cooperation has at all critical times operated in reverse between the judiciary and the elective branches of government." When the dominant party has, in effect, "appointed all the judges," then there will be no important differences between the branches. "But at every turn in national policy where the cleavage between the old order and the new was sharp, the new President has faced a judiciary almost wholly held over from the preceding regime." These partisan differences have "been an estranging influence between the Court and the great Presidents, Jefferson, Jackson, Lincoln and Franklin D. Roosevelt."[55]

This basic argument was given more systematic form in a pioneering article by Robert Dahl. Though Dahl was also working in the shadow of Roosevelt's struggle with the Court, he had the benefit of observing the operation of the New Deal Court on which Jackson served, and Dahl was interested in a slightly different question. Dahl set out to examine the empirical basis for the common claim that Court "stands in some special way as a protection of minorities against tyranny by majorities," or from a different perspective that the Court "supports minority preferences against majorities" in opposition to "popular sovereignty and political equality."[56] Dahl himself thought this quite unlikely. Given the stability of national lawmaking coalitions and the regularity of presidential ap-

[54] Paulsen, "The Most Dangerous Branch," 217.

[55] Robert H. Jackson, *The Struggle for Judicial Supremacy* (New York: Vintage, 1941), 314, 315.

[56] Dahl, "Decision-Making in Democracy," 282, 283.

pointments to the Court, it could be expected that "the policy views dominant on the Court are never for long out of line with the policy views
dominant among the lawmaking majorities of the United States."[57] Examining the Court's history of striking down congressional statutes, Dahl
concluded that "except for short-lived transitional periods when the old
alliance is disintegrating and the new one is struggling to take control of
political institutions, the Supreme Court is inevitably a part of the dominant national alliance."[58] To Dahl, the New Deal and the New Deal Court
were indicative of a larger pattern. Courts that lag behind rapid electoral
change are obstructive, but the appointment process soon leads to judicial
quiescence as the reconstituted Court accepts and legitimates the actions
of the political branches.

This simple and intriguing hypothesis seemed to readily explain not
only the judicial behavior that concerned Dahl, but also the political challenges to the Court that Robert Jackson, Edward Corwin, and others had
observed. Judicial independence should make itself felt in the willingness
of judges to exercise their veto over disfavored policies and in the success
of judges in imposing their policy agenda on other officials. It would not
be surprising if political frustration with the judicial obstruction, however
temporary, would lead to court-curbing efforts to overcome judicial resistance. In particular, presidents who come to power through "realigning"
or "critical" elections should face holdover courts, and Jefferson, Jackson, Lincoln, and Roosevelt could be seen as the beneficiaries of such
critical elections.

Unfortunately, Dahl's simple hypothesis has not borne up well under
scrutiny. Subsequent empirical analyses of Dahl's thesis have generally
failed to confirm his findings.[59] In terms of the number of judicial invalidations of federal law, the New Deal era is anomalous rather than represen-

---

[57] Ibid., 285.

[58] Ibid., 293.

[59] See generally Richard Funston, "The Supreme Court and Critical Elections," *American
Political Science Review* 69 (1975): 795; Jonathan D. Casper, "The Supreme Court and
National Policy Making," *American Political Science Review* 70 (1976): 50; Bradley C.
Canon and S. Sidney Ulmer, "The Supreme Court and Critical Elections: A Dissent," *Ameri-
can Political Science Review* 70 (1976): 1215; Roger Handberg and Harold F. Hill Jr.,
"Court Curbing, Court Reversals, and Judicial Review: The Supreme Court versus Con-
gress," *Law and Society Review* 14 (1980): 309; Gregory A. Caldeira and Donald J.
McCrone, "Of Time and Judicial Activism: A Study of the U.S. Supreme Court, 1800–
1973," in *Supreme Court Activism and Restraint*, ed. Stephen Halpern and Charles Lamb
(Lexington, MA: Lexington Books, 1982); William Lasser, "The Supreme Court in Periods
of Critical Realignment," *Journal of Politics* 47 (1985): 1174; John B. Taylor, "The Supreme
Court and Political Eras: A Perspective on Judicial Power in a Democratic Polity," *Review
of Politics* 54 (1992): 345.

tative. So-called lagging courts have not been uniquely active in the exercise of judicial review.[60] In addition, the Court has been active during periods of relative electoral stability, when the judiciary should be firmly under the control of the dominant coalition and presumably passively endorsing the work of its coalition partners in Congress. If passivity is what politicians want from the Court, then rather than acting as a reliable partner of elected officials, the Court would often seem to be an independent and disruptive force in politics.

This framework for understanding judicial review also has theoretical complications. Dahl suggested that judges behave like policymakers elsewhere in the government, obstructing the policies they dislike. But Dahl ignored the unique institutional environment that mediates the ready linkage of judicial policy preferences with the incidence of judicial invalidation. Court action is shaped by such institutional commitments as precedent, doctrinal analysis, the constitutional text, and the mechanics of litigation.[61] Electorally driven policy innovation will not necessarily provoke judicially relevant problems, regardless of the partisan feelings of holdover judges. Judicial review is not readily analogous to a policy veto. The implications of electoral change for judicial action depend heavily on the particular substance of dominant institutional and policy commitments, which are not easily captured in such formal analyses of partisan transitions.[62] For example, to the extent that judicial review expresses judicial policy preferences, it is asymmetric.[63] Judicial review is more useful for hampering the expansion of government than for hampering the reduction of government, regardless of any policy disagreements between

[60] Dahl's model suggests other hypotheses beyond the obstruction/deference pattern. For a critique of the hypothesis that the Court can legitimate newly dominant majorities, see David Adamany, "Legitimacy, Realigning Elections, and the Supreme Court," *Wisconsin Law Review* 1973 (1973): 790. For a comprehensive consideration of the thesis that the Court acts as a catalyst for realignments, see John B. Gates, *The Supreme Court and Partisan Realignment* (Boulder, CO: Westview Press, 1992).

[61] Rogers M. Smith, "Political Jurisprudence, the 'New Institutionalism,' and the Future of Public Law," *American Political Science Review* 82 (1988): 89; Howard Gillman, "The Court as an Idea, Not a Building (or a Game): Interpretive Institutionalism and the Analysis of Supreme Court Decision-Making," in *Supreme Court Decision-Making*, ed. Cornell W. Clayton and Howard Gillman (Chicago: University of Chicago Press, 1999); Keith E. Whittington, "Once More Unto the Breach: Post-Behavioralist Approaches to Judicial Politics," *Law and Social Inquiry* 25 (2000): 601.

[62] See, e.g., Wallace Mendelson, "The Politics of Judicial Supremacy," *Journal of Law and Economics* 4 (1961): 175; Arnold Paul, *Conservative Crisis and the Rule of Law* (Ithaca: Cornell University Press, 1960).

[63] Mark A. Graber, "The Jacksonian Origins of Chase Court Activism," *Journal of Supreme Court History* 25 (2000): 17.

the Court and the elected branches.[64] The expansionist political program of the New Deal Democrats is not representative of periods of electoral transition. Thomas Jefferson, Andrew Jackson, and Ronald Reagan all came to power hoping to cut back the national government. A like-minded Court could be a help in that project, but a hostile Court cannot easily be much of a hindrance. Moreover, simply knowing how often the Court has invalidated federal legislation does not establish the political importance or salience of the Court's actions and the laws that were invalidated. To the extent that subsequent scholars have followed Dahl's lead in simply counting how many laws have been invalidated by the Court, an important dimension of interbranch tensions has been overlooked.[65]

The inadequacy of Dahl's model and measures of judicial activism still leaves us not only with the problem of explaining judicial behavior, but also with the lingering problem of explaining political reactions to the Court. We are left with his core intuitive insight into the American historical experience—that elected officials are periodically in conflict with the Court—but without his ready explanation for that conflict, an unusually obstructionist judiciary. For those who would follow Dahl's logic, elected officials, with the exception of Franklin Roosevelt, seemed to have attacked the Court without political justification. David Adamany, for example, suggests that these political challenges to the Court occur because the new majorities are "harboring deep hostility toward the Court" because of its earlier decisions and "resent . . . that they cannot immediately place their own men in the desirable seats of judicial authority." These presidents and their supporters hysterically overreact to the Court, "inspiring internal disunity" and becoming "diverted from [their] program of substantive policies" by a pointless "quarrel."[66] The explanation for such presidential challenges turns from the political to the psychological, a failure of "emotional intelligence" on the part of individual officeholders.[67]

---

[64] This point can be complicated, however. As the Rehnquist Court has shown, judicial review can be used to obstruct the federal government's efforts to constrain the state governments. The judicial power to interpret statutes, rather than simply void them, suggests another mechanism for the judiciary to pursue its distinct policy goals and one that can be used to expand, as well as restrict, government. See, e.g., Casper, "National Policy Making," 56; R. Shep Melnick, *Between the Lines* (Washington, DC: Brookings Institution, 1994).

[65] It is notable that in the New Deal period that motivated Dahl, incidence of judicial review and significance of judicial review were conflated. The Court was both very active and acting on politically important issues. Dahl and others have made the sensible assumption that the exercise of judicial review is intrinsically important. It may well be the case, however, that judicial review can be exercised in a fashion that is not particularly politically salient.

[66] Adamany, "Supreme Court's Role," 245, 246.

[67] Fred I. Greenstein, *The Presidential Difference* (New York: Free Press, 2000), 6.

Dahl framed conflicts between political actors and the courts in terms of divergent policy preferences. One alternative is to reframe those conflicts in terms of substantive disputes over constitutional meaning. Although political scientists have been quick to accept Dahl's portrait of judges as policymakers, there is an intuitive appeal to regarding them as at least as concerned with the perceived constitutional transgressions of political majorities as with their policy agenda. Rather than judges stooping to battle elected officials over policy, perhaps elected officials rise up to battle judges over the Constitution. Refocusing on the constitutional issues involved in these conflicts, and not just the policy obstructions, may clarify why these conflicts occurred and what was at stake in these disputes.

Bruce Ackerman offers a theory of constitutional change that moves in that direction. He posits a number of "constitutional moments" over the course of American history in which political actors alter the Constitution by unconventional methods and launch a new constitutional regime.[68] For Ackerman, such presidential challenges to the Court signal a political interest in transforming the Constitution, a transformation that would be complete if political officials were able to win large and sustained electoral mandates for their constitutional proposals and force other institutions to accede to their wishes. Eschewing formal constitutional amendments through regular Article V procedures, transformative leaders can effectively amend the Constitution by overcoming the institutional obstructions to their constitutional proposals. Although Ackerman recognizes Jefferson's and Jackson's conflicts with the judiciary, this process of constitutional transformation is most fully realized in Roosevelt's triumph over the Court in 1937. Ackerman judges the Jeffersonian and Jacksonian projects as insufficiently sweeping, insufficiently productive of judicial doctrine, and substantively too decentralizing and libertarian to be significant constitutional moments initiating new constitutional regimes, but they are part of a pattern of constitutional politics.[69]

Ackerman's attention to constitutional politics is extremely helpful, but it ironically remains too wedded to judicial supremacy. Ackerman does not question the central claim of judicial supremacy, that the courts are the authoritative interpreters of the Constitution. Although Ackerman does not provide an elaborated theory of constitutional interpretation, he works with an implicit assumption that the courts faithfully preserve the Constitution until political actors demonstrate the authority to amend that higher law.[70] A striking feature of Ackerman's approach is his argu-

---

[68] Ackerman, *We the People.*

[69] Ibid., 1:71–78.

[70] For a critique of Ackerman for his lack of an interpretive theory, see Robert Justin Lipkin, *Constitutional Revolutions* (Durham: Duke University Press, 2000), 28–76.

ment that apparent judicial mistakes in constitutional interpretation, including most notably *Dred Scott* and *Lochner,* were in fact the correct interpretations of the Constitution as it existed at the time. Disagreement with those decisions suggested only the need to amend the Constitution. The Constitution appears to have a determinate, if not necessarily obvious, meaning, which the judiciary affirms and enforces through constitutional law. Political attacks on the Court are not challenges to judicial interpretive authority, but rather signals to the electorate that an unconventional constitutional amendment is being proposed. Constitutional politics is concerned with making new higher law, not with interpreting the existing law.

Ackerman provides a clear political account of conflict with the Court, and one that has the appealing feature of recognizing elected officials as constitutional agents. Two difficulties with this account are particularly relevant for present purposes, however. First, Ackerman's emphasis on an amendment model of constitutional change is theoretically limiting and historically problematic.[71] In particular, Ackerman never seriously grapples with the question of how these elected officials understood and presented their own actions. This problem infects his extended discussion of the passage of the Reconstruction amendments, where he ignores the extent to which the Reconstruction Congress was committed to a legislative supremacy within the normal constitutional framework as well as how they understood and justified the irregularities in the process creating the Reconstruction amendments. More immediately, it infects his discussion of Roosevelt and the New Deal. He does not explore the administration's own thinking about how best to respond to the Court's challenge to the New Deal, including its debates over whether to pursue an Article V amendment and whether Roosevelt's fundamental problem was with the Constitution as it existed or simply with the Court itself. Unlike earlier Progressives, the Roosevelt administration ultimately decided to question the fidelity of the *Lochner* Court, not the acceptability of the written Constitution. Like his predecessors, Roosevelt challenged judicial supremacy and repeatedly offered a distinctive interpretation of the Constitution as more faithful to the constitutional inheritance than the one asserted by the judiciary.

Although a unanimous Court lined up against the administration in some embarrassing defeats such as the May 1935 *Schechter* and *Humphrey* cases striking down the National Recovery Act and limiting the presidential removal power, the New Dealers knew from early on that the Court was more generally sharply divided on the constitutionality of social legislation and that everything turned on the swing vote of Justice

---

[71] For one alternative approach to constitutional politics, see Whittington, *Constitutional Construction.*

Owen Roberts.[72] Three months earlier, the administration had won some close cases, and Roosevelt wrote, "I shudder at the closeness of five to four decisions in these important matters." Senator George Norris was more proactive: "These five to four Supreme Court decisions on the constitutionality of congressional acts it seems to me are illogical and should not occur in a country like ours."[73] When Justice Roberts swung the other way on the Railroad Retirement Act in early May, the Department of Justice began to investigate "the question of the right of the Congress, by legislation, to limit the terms and conditions upon which the Supreme Court can pass on constitutional questions."[74] The press was soon reporting rumors that Roberts would make a presidential run in 1936.[75] Prominent legal scholars Felix Frankfurter, Henry Hart, and Thurman Arnold, among others, took to the media to denounce Roberts as entering a "mental darkroom" and lacking "common sense," "taking debaters' points" with a "combination of pure fantasy and legal syllogisms with little persuasive power." The apparent solidification of a narrow conservative majority on the Court had convinced many New Dealers that "the menace of the Supreme Court" hung "over all legal attempts to solve the social problems that are crowding upon us."[76] Dissenting Justice Harlan Fiske Stone, later Roosevelt's choice as chief justice, characterized the decision to sympathetic legal scholar Thomas Reed Powell as "the worst performance on the Court in my time."[77] Attorney General Homer Cummings declared, "I tell you, Mr. President, they mean to destroy us."[78]

For those who had been long engaged in the Progressive critique of the *Lochner* era jurisprudence, it was clear that the primary fault was in the Court rather than in the Constitution. That still left the immediate question of what was to be done, of course, and options under active consideration ranged from corrective constitutional amendments to some form of legislative court-curbing. A veteran of previous amendment battles, Roosevelt was skeptical of the Article V route that faced obstructions in the states and still left interpretive authority in the courts. Strategic and ideological considerations came together in the reconstructive posture.

---

[72] Humphrey's Executor v. United States, 295 U.S. 602 (1935); A.L.A. Schechter Poultry Corporation v. United States, 295 U.S. 495 (1935). Roosevelt was shocked by the three unanimous opinions that were handed down against him on 27 May 1935, asking, "[W]here was Ben Cardozo?" Stanley Reed, FDR's solicitor general at the time, had thought that *Humphrey* "couldn't be lost." Quoted in William E. Leuchtenburg, *The Supreme Court Reborn* (New York: Oxford University Press, 1995), 89, 64.

[73] Quoted in Leuchtenburg, *The Supreme Court Reborn*, 88.

[74] Leuchtenburg, *The Supreme Court Reborn*, 89.

[75] Ibid., 43–44.

[76] Quoted in ibid., 46–47.

[77] Quoted in ibid., 48.

[78] Quoted in ibid., 92.

Standing on three decades of Progressive constitutional scholarship and agitation, Roosevelt consciously insisted that the Constitution did not need to be amended. It needed to be more favorably interpreted.[79] The courts needed to be able to "recognize and apply the essential concepts of justice in the light of the needs and the facts of an ever-changing world."[80] The Framers had intentionally and appropriately used "phrases which flexible statesmanship of the future, within the Constitution, could adapt to time and circumstance." It was an "unending struggle" to "preserve this original broad concept of the Constitution" against those who would "shrivel" it. Some of the justices "have sought to *read* into the Constitution language which the framers refused to *write* into the Constitution," but the president asked the American people to "give their fealty to the Constitution *itself* and not to its misinterpreters."[81] In a May 1935 press conference Roosevelt compared the recent decisions of the Court to its actions in the *Dred Scott* case, but reassured reporters that the mistake could be corrected without the necessity of a constitutional amendment.[82] In pitching the nation back to the "horse-and-buggy age," the Court had not only neglected to interpret "the Constitution in light of these new things that have come to the country" but had also ignored its own prior decisions, "the whole tendency" of which had been to view the Constitution "in the light of present-day civilization."[83]

The second difficulty with Ackerman's account of constitutional politics is that it does not extend its political analysis far enough. Ackerman is particularly enlightening in explaining the political rationale for carrying the debate onto the constitutional dimension. Elected officials do not deliberate on the Constitution because they are particularly high-minded but because they have immediate political needs that gradually draw them into constitutional disputes. In these moments of constitutional politics, Ackerman provides a political explanation for why the judiciary is challenged. He has not, to this point, provided a similar political explanation for the presumably more deferential behavior of elected officials at other times or for the behavior of judges at any time. The possibility of judicial politics or the judiciary as an active agent of constitutional development creates severe problems for his normative and historical narrative, and Ackerman takes pains to marginalize it. The preser-

---

[79] In a 1932 campaign address, Roosevelt suggested a similar instinct in connection with his earlier career. In New York, reformers "had to go about amending the Constitution" in order to pass workmen's compensation, but the fault was in "the courts, thinking in terms of the Seventeenth Century, as some courts do." Roosevelt, *Public Papers and Addresses*, 1:774.

[80] Ibid., 6:55.

[81] Ibid., 6:363, 366, 367.

[82] Ibid., *Papers*, 4:222.

[83] Ibid., 209, 210.

vationist role of the judiciary is generally assumed to be politically unproblematic. In keeping with the assertion of the Court in *Cooper,* Ackerman seems to assume that the principle that the Court is "supreme in the exposition of the law of the Constitution" has "ever since [*Marbury*] been respected by this Court and the Country."[84] That assumption remains problematic, and the political foundations of judicial supremacy need to be laid bare.

Constitutional Authority in Political Time

These presidential challenges to the judicial authority to determine constitutional meaning can be better understood if they are placed within their particular political context and the political tasks that these presidents have faced. Since constitutional theory has generally proceeded on the assumption that constitutional meaning, including the determination of the institutional authority to settle constitutional disputes, is a matter of abstract reasoning, departmentalist claims have been treated as logical conclusions from fundamental postulates about constitutional text and structure.[85] The correctness of that reasoning can then be readily abstracted from any immediate political context. A more developmental approach would suggest that claims about constitutional meaning arise out of particular political contexts and are only comprehensible when considered in that context. The central question to be answered is why these presidents made such challenges and why they attracted substantial political support in so doing.

The traditionally recognized departmentalist presidents are notable for the ambition of their political projects, as well as for their conflicts with the courts. These presidents are distinctive in their authority to act to remake the inherited political system. In his examination of presidential leadership, Stephen Skowronek has emphasized the extent to which presidential action depends upon a prior claim to authority.[86] Before an individual occupies the presidency, the political agenda is already partially determined through commitments previously made by the candidate, the president's party, and the president's predecessors. In addition, presidents are not free to act as they choose on the agenda that they do face. Skowronek suggests that the authority to act is derived from the political regime, the "commitments of ideology and interest embodied in the preexisting institutional arrangements."[87] Depending on how the president relates to

---

[84] Cooper v. Aaron, 358 U.S. 18 (1958).
[85] E.g., Paulsen, "The Most Dangerous Branch," 217.
[86] Skowronek, *The Politics Presidents Make.*
[87] Ibid., 34.

this larger political order—his claim to political authority to supplement his claim on the inherent resources of his office—some strategic options become easier, while others become more difficult to pursue. The concept of political time describes the pattern formed by the presidential relationship to political authority, the intersection of the vitality of the regime and the president's relationship to it.

Reconstructive presidents periodically emerge in opposition to weak regimes. Their authority in office is rooted in their antagonism to existing commitments, allowing them to gain prestige precisely through their efforts to shatter the inherited constitutional order. Presidents such as Abraham Lincoln and Franklin Roosevelt achieve "greatness" through their ability to tear down the inherited but discredited regime and raise up a new one in their own image. They "reconstruct" the nation by reinterpreting its fundamental commitments. Because their leadership task is foundational, they are called upon to reconsider basic substantive political values and reconfigure existing institutional arrangements. The political strength of these substantive claims enhances their own authority to act and thus the institutional stature of the presidency. Lincoln became a powerful president because of the political support that he could muster behind his political vision, and his presidency became historic as a consequence of the constitutional depth and political success of that vision.

An important feature of this model of political time is the relative rarity of reconstructive presidents. Few presidents have either the inclination or the support to mount such a political effort. The political authority that falls to these presidents is not readily available to their successors. If presidential challenges to judicial supremacy are fundamentally connected to the politics of reconstruction, then the nature of the threat to constitutionalism that many critics of coordinate constitutional interpretation raise has to be reevaluated. A "Euclidean" approach to constitutional theory can neither explain the historic assertion of departmentalist claims nor recognize their limited scope.[88] Although these historic episodes of presidential attacks on the Court are familiar, they have not been adequately integrated into constitutional theory. Our historical experience with presidential challenges to judicial supremacy needs to be situated within the broader context of these administrations and their political efforts.

RECONSTRUCTIVE PRESIDENCIES AND CONSTITUTIONAL AUTHORITY

In order to address the relationship of the judiciary to the reconstructive presidency, the political order being shattered and recreated by those pres-

---

[88] Paulsen, "The Most Dangerous Branch," 226.

idents must be reconsidered. At times, Skowronek suggests that presidential efforts to recast the dominant regime are somehow significant for an understanding of the constitutional order. He notes briefly, for example, that these reconstructive presidents "have reset the very terms and conditions of constitutional government" and that their struggles "have penetrated to the deepest questions of governmental design and of the proper relations between state and society."[89] But his explicit discussion of political regimes renders them essentially partisan, oriented around relatively narrow differences of policy and constituency. The Constitution enters most directly into his discussion as an important background condition for the emergence of reconstructive politics. The "constitutional ordering of institutional prerogatives . . . frames the persistent pattern of political disruption."[90] By creating a system of separated powers, the Constitution insures that presidents will struggle with other actors for control over the government. As part of that basic institutional design, the Constitution arms each president with the "same basic prerogatives of the presidential office," such as the pardoning and veto powers.[91] Although Bruce Ackerman uses the term "constitutional politics" to refer to the political effort to remake the effective set of fundamental values and formal powers, Skowronek uses the same term merely to refer to the presidential exploitation of available powers in pursuit of other, nonconstitutional goals.[92] When he speaks of presidents keeping or recasting the "political faith," he is inevitably speaking of coalitional policy platforms.[93] He does find the Court to be an increasing impediment to presidential goals, but the judiciary in this sense is just part of the generally "thickening" institutional environment, and Skowronek offers no particular theory of presidential-judicial conflict and attributes no special significance to it.[94]

The constitutional politics of reconstructive presidents extends beyond the instrumental use of available institutional resources and formal powers. Constitutional meaning is not fixed. The president cannot uncontroversially claim the authority of his office, for the nature of the office is itself often in dispute.[95] Moreover, the regimes that presidents attempt

[89] Skowronek, *The Politics Presidents Make*, 39, 38.
[90] Ibid., 9.
[91] Ibid., 12.
[92] Ackerman, *We the People*, 1:7; Skowronek, *The Politics Presidents Make*, 12.
[93] Skowronek, *The Politics Presidents Make*, 12.
[94] Ibid., 75.
[95] This feature of presidential politics is not emphasized here. Skowronek recognizes that the presidential office develops over time and discusses, for example, Jackson's expansion of the veto power and Lincoln's constitutional innovations in prosecuting the Civil War. More often, however, he distinguishes institutional innovation from constitutional continuity, creating some unresolved tensions for his historical analysis.

to structure, and which in turn structure presidential action, are deeply entangled with the constitutional order as they understand it. This feature of reconstructive politics makes the Court particularly relevant and insures presidential conflict with the judiciary. For these presidents, fellow partisans are not the only threats to their authority, for their authority claims are constitutional as well as partisan. Because reconstructive presidents are attempting to restructure inherited constitutional understandings, they find the judiciary to be an intrinsic challenge to their authority, even absent the contemporaneous exercise of judicial review. The heightened constitutional sensitivity of these presidents is likely to make any contemporary judicial actions unusually salient, far out of proportion to what might be expected simply looking at the volume of judicial activity.

At least as fundamental as any judicial policy obstruction, however, is the judiciary's constant engagement with constitutional meaning. For political leaders with reconstructive ambitions, the ongoing judicial elaboration of the constitutional inheritance necessarily frustrates that ambition and potentially calls into question the very legitimacy of substantive presidential actions. The assertion of "judicial omniscience in the interpretation of the Constitution" will itself seem quite arrogant and shocking to political leaders who sought and gained power in order to advance radically different constitutional understandings.[96] As a result, judicial authority within the constitutional system should be expected to vary with political time as well.[97] The president and the judiciary compete over the same constitutional space, with the authority of presidents to reconstruct the inherited order supplanting judicial authority to settle disputed constitutional meaning.

In order to develop this dimension of reconstructive politics, the constitutional concerns of these presidents must be emphasized. The connections between their conflicts with the Court and other actors must be developed, and the logic of the politics of technique that Skowronek finds as characteristic of late regime leaders must be extended to the legal sphere. This section develops several relevant features of reconstructive politics and their consequences for the separation of powers. These historical episodes are not unfamiliar, but they are sharply at odds with the assumptions of judicially centered theories of constitutionalism.

These historical episodes of presidential challenge to the judicial authority to determine constitutional meaning are best understood as part

---

[96] Harlan Fiske Stone, quoted in Leuchtenburg, *The Supreme Court Reborn*, 48.

[97] It might be noted that judicial authority appears to vary with "secular time" also, as discussed in chapter 5. See also Caldeira and McCrone "Time and Judicial Activism"; Mark Silverstein and Benjamin Ginsberg, "The Supreme Court and the New Politics of Judicial Review," *Political Science Quarterly* 102 (1987): 371.

of political time and as an aspect of the president's reconstructive stance, rather than in the terms of currently available accounts. In particular, existing accounts of such presidential-Court conflicts posit that these presidents are engaged in the majoritarian rejection of limits of their policy preferences and demonstrate a targeted hostility toward an obstructionist judiciary. Neither claim provides an adequate interpretation of these events. In addition to advancing the specific institutional claim that presidents have a right to engage in coordinate construction of constitutional meaning, reconstructive presidents can be expected to articulate a more general and substantive vision of the Constitution. The judiciary is unlikely to be the only adversary that the president will face, and presidential challenges to judicial supremacy are likely to be linked to presidential assaults on other political enemies who challenge presidential leadership. Departmentalist claims are also likely to be accompanied by a politicization of constitutional meaning that displaces the legalistic discourse favored by the Court. The reconstructive perspective calls attention to the positive contribution these presidents have made to American constitutionalism and to the dynamics of American constitutional development.

Visions of the Constitution

Reconstructive presidents are most concerned with establishing their own substantive vision of the constitutional order. Conflict with the Court is merely a by-product of this primary focus. Existing approaches to presidential challenges to judicial supremacy often view them in purely instrumental terms, legal ploys designed to overcome policy conflicts between the president and the Court. Such approaches overlook the substantive political vision that reconstructive presidents seek to realize. Particular conflicts with the courts are contingent outcomes of this constitutive effort. Departmentalism is implicit in the reconstructive posture, rather than the legitimating theory for attacks on the Court. Reconstructive presidents need not be hostile to courts per se or judicial review in general. For most presidents, there may be occasional disagreements with the Court and efforts to alter the trajectory of constitutional law, but there is no crisis of, or challenge to, judicial authority. For reconstructive presidents, however, establishing a contested vision of the constitutional order is central to their political task.

Reconstructive politics shifts the institutional locus for the debate over constitutional meaning, as the examples of Jefferson and Roosevelt make clear. The challenge to judicial authority mounted by these presidents did not sweep constitutional principles from the public sphere, as many modern advocates of judicial supremacy tend to assume. Rather, a de-emphasis on the judicial interpretation of the Constitution simply accompanied an increased focus on constitutional meaning on the part of the president. Whereas the judiciary usually emphasizes the constitutional constraints on government power, reconstructive presidents draw inspiration from the Constitution for their positive vision of how political power should be used. In presidential hands, the Constitution becomes an ideal to be realized in political practice rather than a set of rules that hamper political action. The symbol of the Constitution is employed to legitimate presidential actions. The policies of the administration are portrayed as not merely consistent with but as *products of* the Constitution. As architects of fundamental political change, reconstructive presidents appeal to the Constitution to help legitimate their enterprise. The substantive vision of the Constitution that these presidents offer is explicitly different from the interpretations and practices of their immediate predecessors, but these presidents insist that theirs is an effort to save the Constitution from the mishandling of their immediate predecessors and the Court itself.

For Thomas Jefferson and his followers working within the republican paradigm, the "Revolution of 1800" meant saving the Constitution from the Federalists' centralizing and monarchical tendencies. Jefferson had left Washington's administration as a result of disagreements over the constitutional and policy wisdom of presidential policies. The subsequent administration of John Adams and his congressional supporters pursued even more aggressively an effort to expand the power of the national government. The Republican Party began in opposition to what was seen as the Federalists' constitutional heresy. But for Jefferson, unlike some future presidents, those apparent constitutional errors were still of recent vintage. The revolution required less the adoption of a whole new set of policies than the reversal of recent Federalist initiatives and the prevention of future drift, "the inviolable preservation of our present federal constitution."[98] The Jeffersonians feared that the Constitution was being strangled in its cradle, and extraordinary means such as the formation of an organized political party were necessary to preserve it from a cabal of aristocratic conspirators. For the Jeffersonians, Federalist policies fostered corruption within the republic, using public resources to support private privilege through such instruments as protectionist tariffs and excise taxes. At the same time, "more disposed to coerce than to court" the public, the Federalists were using the state apparatus to consolidate their own power through such actions as the expansion of the judiciary and the passage of the Alien and Sedition Acts.[99]

Jefferson insisted on a return to first principles: "a wise and frugal government which shall restrain men from injuring one another" and be dom-

---

[98] Jefferson, *Writings*, ed. Ford, 7:327.
[99] Jefferson, *Writings*, ed. Ford, 7:447.

inated by the legislature was the "sum of good government."[100] Believing that the citizenry "agreed in ancient whig principles," it was Jefferson's task merely to "define and declare them" to provide "the ground on which we could rally" to resist the enemies of the Constitution.[101] For his supporters, Jefferson's ascension to office meant that "the Revolution of 1776 is now and for the first time arrived at its completion," as "the issue of which rested the liberty, Constitution, and happiness of America" was resolved.[102] Jefferson's constitutional task after the election was primarily negative, uprooting as many of the invidious institutions introduced by the Federalists as advisable. Some were retained, most notably the national bank that Madison had fought in Congress and Jefferson had fought in the cabinet during the Washington administration as unwise and grossly unconstitutional.[103] Many others were dismantled. Those parts of the hated Alien and Sedition Acts that had not expired by their own terms were repealed, and those who had been prosecuted were pardoned and their fines reimbursed with interest. A host of internal taxes instituted by the Federalists were immediately repealed, and the military and its budget were slashed. Cost-cutting efforts were undertaken in the domestic budget, with some general tightening of the appropriations process, in order to reduce government and ease the burden of the public debt. The Judiciary Act of 1801 was repealed, eliminating both Federalist judges and the federal judicial presence in the countryside.[104] The mobilization of the late 1790s began an extensive process of specifying the true meaning of the Constitution and identifying constitutional errors. Federalist politicians and publicists, as well as the Court, were frequent targets of criticism, as the Jeffersonians sought to teach their constitutional values and consolidate their dominance in American politics.

Even at this early date, however, Jeffersonian constitutionalism was not simply a return to the pristine Constitution before the Federalist fall. The Jeffersonian Constitution carried different inflections and emphases than it had before, developed through the interaction of inherited principle, changing circumstance, and response to Federalist actions. Themes of de-

---

[100] Jefferson, *Writings*, ed. Ford, 8:3.

[101] Thomas Jefferson, *The Writings of Thomas Jefferson*, ed. H. A. Washington, 9 vols. (New York: John C. Riker, 1853–56), 4:386.

[102] Quoted in Lance Banning, *The Jefferson Persuasion* (Ithaca: Cornell University Press, 1978), 270.

[103] Stanley Elkins and Eric McKitrick, *The Age of Federalism* (New York: Oxford University Press, 1993), 224–40; Currie, *The Constitution in Congress*, 1:78–80.

[104] See generally Forrest McDonald, *The Presidency of Thomas Jefferson* (Lawrence: University Press of Kansas, 1976), 41–52; Leonard D. White, *The Jeffersonians* (New York: Macmillan, 1956); Richard E. Ellis, *The Jeffersonian Crisis* (New York: Norton, 1971), 19–107, 233–84; Drew R. McCoy, *The Elusive Republic* (New York: Norton, 1980).

mocracy, free speech, agrarianism, and frugality were more prominent in the reconstruction of the Constitution than they had been previously. The president called upon the nation "to retrace our steps and to regain the road which alone leads to peace, liberty, and safety," recovering the "creed of our political faith" and the "text of civil instruction."[105] The Jeffersonian interpretation of the Constitution built on an existing tradition, but it did so selectively. Jefferson provided a sweeping vision of constitutional principles and their political implications, not detailed textual analysis of the founding document. Even as John Marshall in the judiciary worked to make constitutional interpretation seem more technical and apolitical in cases such as *Marbury*, the Jeffersonians in the public arena emphasized the contested nature of constitutional meaning and the need for a broad-based campaign to win support for their constitutional vision.

Franklin Roosevelt's understanding of the crisis of his times and the appropriate response to it was quite different from Jefferson's, but the two presidents shared a concern with recovering the Constitution as a foundation of and guide for their politics. If Jefferson feared that the Constitution had become a "mere thing of wax" in the hands of his opponents, Roosevelt and his allies complained that the Constitution had become a "straitjacket" as implemented by his foes.[106] Like Jefferson, Roosevelt thought the Constitution was more than merely a set of constraints on government. It was a normative ideal toward which political actors should strive. In an important 1932 campaign speech to the Commonwealth Club, Roosevelt contended that predatory government was overcome by two commitments: one to "limitations on arbitrary power," but the other to "the rise of the ethical conception that a ruler bore a responsibility for the welfare of his subjects."[107] In pledging himself "to a new deal for the American people," Roosevelt continually emphasized that the administration, the Democratic Party, and the U.S. government should be dedicated to "the greatest good to the greatest number of our citizens."[108] Government had the obligation and the power to secure "economic and social security" for "the great mass of our people."[109] Quoting Chief Justice Edward White, Roosevelt insisted that the Constitution should not be viewed as being "a barrier to progress instead of being the broad highway through which alone true progress may be enjoyed."[110] Although Roosevelt's particular conflicts with the Court centered on legal

---

[105] Jefferson, *Writings*, ed. Ford, 8:5.

[106] Jefferson, *Writings*, ed. Ford, 10:141; "Unshackling the Tax Power," *New Republic*, 30 January 1935.

[107] Roosevelt, *Public Papers and Addresses*, 1:745.

[108] Ibid., 1:659, 650.

[109] Ibid., 6:361.

[110] Ibid., 3:421.

restrictions that hampered the administration's policies, the president also drew upon the Constitution to create positive authority for the New Deal. The Constitution was flexible enough to allow Roosevelt's actions, and progressive enough to call for such actions.

The "New Deal" was more than a slogan for a particular list of policies. The New Deal was the realization of Roosevelt's constitutional vision, an effort to achieve "greater freedom [and] greater security for the average man."[111] As such it was tied less to the particular policy approach embodied in the "First" New Deal or the "Second" New Deal, than to the general commitment to positive popular government. In realizing that commitment, Roosevelt was generally less proactive than reactive. His initial proposals embodied in such First New Deal legislation as the National Industrial Recovery Act were largely more ambitious versions of the government-business cooperation efforts favored by his predecessor.[112] Having committed the government to progressive ends, however, the Roosevelt administration did struggle to be responsive to the cacophony of competing pressures and interests that commitment had helped unleash, resulting in legislation such as the Wagner Act and the Social Security Act.[113] At the same time, Roosevelt aggressively sought to shape the popular image of the Republicanism he intended to displace. Despite many apparent similarities at the policy level, Roosevelt maximized the apparent ideological divisions between the New Deal and the old order, portraying his opponents as Social Darwinists, reactionaries, and tories. Roosevelt denounced "Republican leaders" as "false prophets" who had "failed in national vision." In their place, Roosevelt called upon his followers to "constitute ourselves prophets of a new order" that would "restore America to its own people."[114]

One of Roosevelt's central political tasks was to articulate a constitutional order consistent with the social demands of the modern age. In his speech to the Commonwealth Club during his first presidential campaign, Roosevelt declared that "faith in America . . . demand[s] that we recognize the new terms of the old social contract."[115] His language here is significant. The political task is to reinterpret the old, to reconcile the new political commitments with the inherited constitutional order, not simply to claim legitimacy on completely new grounds. The particular new terms

[111] Ibid., 3:422.
[112] See, e.g., Ellis Hawley, "Herbert Hoover and Modern American History: Sixty Years After," in *Herbert Hoover and the Historians*, ed. Mark M. Dodge (West Branch, IO: Herbert Hoover Presidential Library Association, 1989).
[113] For an overview, see Colin Gordon, "Rethinking the New Deal," *Columbia Law Review* 98 (1998): 2029.
[114] Roosevelt, *Public Papers and Addresses*, 1:658–59.
[115] Ibid., 1:756.

that Roosevelt hoped to recognize required "the development of an economic declaration of rights, an economic constitutional order."[116] A mature nation would abandon the "jungle law of the survival of the so-called fittest" in order to implement a "philosophy of social justice through social action."[117] But such social justice was merely "an expression, in concrete form, of the human rights" perpetuated "by the adoption of the Constitution of the United States."[118] The New Deal was the appropriate realization of the Constitution's aspirations and commitments in the context of a new political economy.

Government as an instrument of social justice was not only to secure human rights, however, it was also to democratize government. Roosevelt's New Deal elaborated the promise of a government working for the "general welfare" of the whole people, including the "forgotten man at the bottom of the economic pyramid."[119] The government was to be the custodian of the whole people and responsive to the whole people. Such efforts were understood to protect democratic forms of government against either reactionary or radical threats and to better realize the democratic promise of the constitutional inheritance itself. Roosevelt's reconstruction of constitutional authority served the dual purpose of loosening the constraints on government power and of reframing the positive responsibilities of government.[120] Just as Jefferson's vision of good government required political officials to prevent citizens from injuring one another and nothing more, so Roosevelt's vision required officials to "cure . . . these evils of society" and nothing less.[121]

[116] Ibid., 1:752.

[117] Ibid., 4:771.

[118] Ibid., 4:385.

[119] Ibid., 1:625. Roosevelt was drawing on a vibrant tradition of reformist constitutional thought. William E. Forbath, "Caste, Class, and Equal Citizenship," *Michigan Law Review* 98 (1999): 1, 23–76.

[120] Lincoln and Reagan shared with Roosevelt this concern with establishing the new terms of the old order. In contrast, Jefferson and Jackson primarily emphasized the need to save the Constitution from imminent threat of subversion. For the later presidents, the problems facing the constitutional order are long-standing, not imminent. The true Constitution had to be recovered, but it could not simply be saved. For Roosevelt, this required shedding the immature philosophy of social Darwinism. For Lincoln, the promissory note of the Declaration of Independence's egalitarianism had to be repaid and the temporary compromise with slavery had to be abandoned. Garry Wills, *Lincoln at Gettysburg* (New York: Simon and Schuster, 1992); James M. McPherson, *Abraham Lincoln and the Second American Revolution* (New York: Oxford University Press, 1991). For Reagan, the excesses of modern liberalism had to be purged from government and society in "a Second American Revolution of hope and opportunity" in order to "renew the meaning of the Constitution" and "restore constitutional government" so that free individuals could reap the rewards of their own efforts. Ronald K. Muir Jr., "Ronald Reagan: The Primacy of Rhetoric," in *Leadership in the Modern Presidency*, ed. Fred I. Greenstein (Cambridge: Harvard University Press, 1988), 260.

[121] Jefferson, *Writings*, ed. Ford, 9:197; Roosevelt, *Public Papers and Addresses*, 4:423.

Pervasive Presidential Conflict

Constitutional analyses of presidential-judicial conflicts often take them in isolation. The Court is portrayed as the sole obstruction to an otherwise dominant governing majority, and these departmentalist presidents single out the judiciary as a particular object of scorn and criticism. As a consequence, the judiciary is imagined to be uniquely vulnerable to presidential aggressions, a lonely bastion of constitutionalism under siege by feckless politicians. These clashes with the judiciary, however, are part of a more general pattern of pervasive conflict that characterizes these administrations. Conflicts with the courts are only a single skirmish within the larger presidential offensive to establish his authority to remake American politics, as more detailed consideration of Jackson and Roosevelt demonstrates.

Andrew Jackson's veto of legislation to recharter the Second Bank of the United States is the focal point for much of the analysis of his challenge to the judiciary. Jackson was in part faced with the difficulty that the veto power had traditionally, though not uniformly, been exercised on constitutional, not policy, grounds. A constitutional objection to the bank bill was complicated, however, by the Supreme Court's earlier acceptance in *McCulloch v. Maryland* of an implied congressional power to incorporate the bank.[122] In order to veto the bank bill, Jackson would have to reject the Court's authority to settle the constitutional issue. Jackson argued that the president must be guided by his "own opinion of the Constitution" and defend it "as he understands it, and not as it is understood by others."[123] The Supreme Court "ought not to control the coordinate authorities of this Government." As far as Jackson was concerned, it was the legislature's "abandonment of the legitimate objects of Government" that posed "most of the dangers" to the republic. The president rejected both Chief Justice John Marshall's specific constitutional reasoning and the Court's authority to bind the other departments to its particular understanding of constitutional requirements. Jackson's hostility to the Marshall Court was often intense, and when the Court became an obstacle to his own political goals, he was prepared to ignore it.[124]

---

[122] McCulloch v. Maryland, 17 U.S. 316 (1819).

[123] Andrew Jackson, in *A Compilation of the Messages and Papers of the Presidents*, ed. James D. Richardson, 20 vols. (New York: Bureau of National Literature, 1897), 3:1145.

[124] Efforts to minimize Jackson's conflict with the Court depend primarily on Jackson's rejection of the doctrine of nullification, which challenged judicial authority to define the Constitution vis-à-vis the states. Jackson's support for the judiciary against the nullifiers, however, was highly contingent and expressed his commitment to nationalism, not his respect for judicial authority. Jackson's departmentalist logic is not readily bounded, and the hostility of the Jacksonians more broadly to the courts is undeniable. Paulsen, "*Merryman* Power," 81. Cf. Longaker, "Jackson and the Judiciary," 341; Fisher, *Constitutional Dia-*

Although Jackson's argument has clear implications for judicial authority, it must also be understood in the context of more pervasive political conflict. Jackson had not singled out the judiciary for particular assault. The Court as an institution was at most a sideshow to the main event. The veto message itself is indicative of this broader context. The rejection of judicial supremacy was a necessary step in Jackson's argument, but the main target of his ire was the bank and its Whig supporters. This was the element Senator Thomas Benton, a Jacksonian leader, emphasized in commenting on the president's first message to Congress, which invited early legislative consideration of the bank and its constitutionality. In throwing down that gauntlet, the president was "rising above precedent and judicial decisions, going back to the constitution and the foundation of a party on principle," as no "mere politician" would do. Going "to the words of the constitution, and not to the interpretations of its administrators," the president opposed the "latitudinarian construction . . . which would enable Congress to substitute its own will . . . for the words of the constitution, and do what it pleased under the plea of 'necessary.' " It was the "leading politicians friendly to the bank" who pushed Jackson into using his veto power.[125]

The Court may have enabled Congress to violate the Constitution in this way of thinking, but it was the bank and its conspirators who were prepared to do the violating. The Court had only made it more necessary for the president to step forward and do his duty to the Constitution. The "rich and powerful," Jackson argued, were seeking to "bend the acts of governments to their selfish purposes," and Congress was willing to oblige them, arraying "section against section, interest against interest." Jackson could not speculate on what "interest or influence, whether public or private, has given birth to this act," but he could assure Congress and the American people that those interests and influences had not found their way into the executive branch. "Rich men have not been content with equal protection and equal benefits," and Congress was willing to "shake the foundations of our Union" in order "to gratify their desires."[126] If the Court was going to enable perfidious congressmen, the president would have to be willing to interpose his own veto.

Moreover, the veto message was a campaign document as well as a communiqué to Congress.[127] The authority it claimed for the president

---

logues, 238–41. But Jackson's willingness to employ the courts in his battle against the nullifiers does emphasize the contingent, political nature of the conflict. The Court is part of reconstruction politics—not the object of irrational hatred.

[125] Thomas Hart Benton, *Thirty Years' View*, vol. 1 (New York: D. Appleton, 1865), 224, 225, 227.

[126] Jackson, in Richardson, *Messages and Papers*, 3:1153.

[127] Robert V. Remini, *Andrew Jackson and the Bank War* (New York: Norton, 1967), 80–100.

was not only against the Court, but more importantly also against his electoral opponents. Jackson concluded his July 1832 veto message by simply stating, "I have now done my duty to my country," and leaving it up to "my fellow-citizens" to sustain him.[128] Jackson's posture as independent constitutional interpreter not only authorized him to reject the proposed legislation, but it also fed his claim on the votes of the citizenry. It was both his willingness to do his duty in the face of opposition and the content of his substantive constitutional vision that made him deserving of popular support. An isolated focus on the judiciary has tended to portray the veto as a serious challenge to judicial review, but a broader perspective indicates that judicial review was at best an incidental concern. The primary purpose of the message was to rally support for Jackson's substantive constitutional vision against all of his opponents, from private interests to congressional leaders. Most directly, the president's veto denied the conclusive authority of Congress to define the extent of its own powers. With his veto, Jackson was challenging legislative supremacy as well as judicial supremacy, and those institutional claims were specifically tied to a particular substantive vision that helped establish and legitimate Jackson's stance.

Franklin Roosevelt's Court-packing plan is similarly taken as an exemplar of presidential conflict with the judiciary, but it too must be placed in the context of the reconstructive president's more general conflicts and struggles for political authority. His Court-packing rhetoric linked that effort to similar battles the administration was waging against the forces of paralysis and reaction elsewhere. Just months after his 1936 reelection, the president proposed legislation to enable him to nominate an additional justice for each sitting justice over the age of seventy, to a total of fifteen, giving Roosevelt an immediate majority on a reconstituted Court. A bipartisan Senate Judiciary Committee report ultimately denounced the plan as an "invasion of the judicial power" requiring such an emphatic rejection that "its parallel will never again be presented to the free representatives of the free people of America."[129] Despite such vocal opposition, a scandalized press and Congress, and a fortuitously timed switch in the Court's majority, the plan nearly passed, and before his sudden death from a heart attack the Senate majority leader claimed to have the necessary votes.[130] Roosevelt himself expressed surprise at the tumult, ask-

---

[128] Jackson, in Richardson, *Messages and Papers*, 3:1154.

[129] Senate Committee on the Judiciary, *Reorganization of the Federal Judiciary*, 75th Cong., 1st sess., 1937, S. Rept. 711, 10, 23.

[130] Leuchtenburg, *The Supreme Court Reborn*, 132–62; Michael Nelson, "The President and the Court: Reinterpreting the Court-Packing Episode of 1937," *Political Science Quarterly* 103 (1988): 267; Gregory A. Caldeira, "Public Opinion and the U.S. Supreme Court: FDR's Court-Packing Plan," *American Political Science Review* 81 (1987): 1139. See also

ing if "some people really believe that we did not mean it" when he had warned in November that "we had only just begun to fight."[131] Although his surprise at the reaction to his Court-packing plan was disingenuous—he had prepared the plan in secret to heighten its dramatic effect—his bewilderment at the political dilemma it created is more understandable. The Court-packing plan was consistent with his larger rhetorical message of late 1936 and early 1937, and indeed with the themes of his entire presidency. For the president, his attack on the Court was of a piece with his attack on numerous other opponents.

To the president, the Court was allied with a broad array of entrenched and elite interests that would have to be overcome in order to achieve the new constitutional order that Roosevelt envisioned. As opposition to the New Deal built, the president declared in a 1936 campaign address that "organized money" were "unanimous in their hate for me—and I welcome their hatred. I should like to have it said of my first administration that in it the forces of selfishness and of lust for power met their match. I should like it said of my second Administration that in it these forces met their master."[132] Mastering those forces of selfishness required democratizing the government, in both form and substance. The president warned another audience that some "would like to turn the conduct of Government over to a selected, self-chosen few. I would rather leave it in the hands of what we call the democracy of the United States."[133] Popular government should also serve the good of the people, promoting justice "for the great masses" and abandoning a philosophy of "indifference" that did not "promote the general welfare" but only benefited the few.[134]

In his 1937 annual message to Congress, Roosevelt's challenge to the Court was direct as he defended his own reading of the Constitution as better than that offered by the Court. The president's own constitutional studies had convinced him that the "vital need is not an alteration of our fundamental law, but an increasingly enlightened view with reference to it." The text should be given a "liberal interpretation" so as to be an

---

Kevin J. McMahon, *Reconsidering Roosevelt on Race* (Chicago: University of Chicago Press, 2004), 61–96.

[131] Roosevelt, *Public Papers and Addresses*, 6:114. Roosevelt's opponent in the 1936 election, Alf Landon, had persistently complained that the president had refused to say what such a fight meant. "And what are the intentions of the President with respect to the Constitution? Does he believe changes are required? If so, will an amendment be submitted to the people, or will he attempt to get around the Constitution by tampering with the Supreme Court? The answer is: No one can be sure." "The Texts of Governor's Landon's Addresses at Madison Square Garden and Over the Radio," *New York Times*, 30 October 1936, 16.

[132] Roosevelt, *Public Papers and Addresses*, 5:568–569.

[133] Ibid., 5:478.

[134] Ibid., 5:280, 568.

"instrument of progress."[135] The Court had been "asked by the people to do its part in making democracy successful," and Roosevelt contended that the people had "a right to expect" the Court to allow the use of "legitimately implied" powers for the "common good."[136] Although the president initially justified his Court-packing plan on the basis of increased efficiency, he soon turned to a political defense, arguing that he needed a Court that would "enforce the Constitution as written," or more to the point, justices "who will bring the Court to a present-day sense of the Constitution."[137] A "reinvigorated, liberal-minded Judiciary" would not "override the judgment of the Congress on legislative policy."[138] Forcing the Court to recognize presidential authority to construct the terms of the Constitution in the interest of and at the behest of the people at large was essential to realizing the promise of democracy in America.

A central theme of Roosevelt's presidency was the need to unleash the political power created by the Constitution to promote the welfare of the people. In recent years, he argued, the power of the government to do good for the whole people had been allowed to atrophy. Private interests who hoped to gain at the expense of the common good had thrown up obstacles to reform that exploited constitutional forms to defeat constitutional purposes. From his perspective, the Court's flawed interpretations of the Constitution could not be readily corrected by constitutional amendment because a small number of self-interested state legislatures could, and had before, blocked the ratification of progressive amendments. Even Congress itself was resistant to change. As part of his 1936 reelection campaign, Roosevelt organized pro-reform groups such as the Labor Nonpartisan League that could circumvent Democratic Party regulars and mobilize progressive support behind the president and his priorities. After his reelection, he actively sought, but failed to achieve, a purge of conservative legislators from the Democratic Party and Congress. Roosevelt's attorney general, Homer Cummings, wrote in his diary that behind "all of these fights, including the Supreme Court fight, there lies the question of the nomination of 1940, and the incidental control of party destinies."[139] Critics of the New Deal might denounce Roosevelt as some kind of "Caesar or Napoleon," but he assured his supporters, those critics preferred to lodge government power the hands of a "select" and "educated class, of a class which is, and knows itself to be, deeply interested in the security of property and the maintenance of order." Against this

[135] Ibid., 5:639.
[136] Ibid., 5:641.
[137] Ibid., 6:126, 127.
[138] Ibid., 6:133, 129.
[139] Quoted in Sidney M. Milkis, *The President and the Parties* (New York: Oxford University Press, 1993), 81.

select class of the old order, the president found his anchor in "democracy—and more democracy."[140] The president's war against the power brokers had many fronts.

Roosevelt's Court-packing plan was announced just two months after the unveiling of his proposal to reorganize the executive branch. The judiciary was not the only obstruction to be cleared away, and the two proposals were rhetorically linked as necessary to save democracy from crisis and elite rule. The reorganization plan, known as the Brownlow Report, sought to draw policymaking into the executive departments and to develop administrative controls under direct supervision of the president, addressing a widespread concern that rapid growth had left the government fragmented and uncoordinated. As with the Court-packing plan, Roosevelt saw the Brownlow Report as a vehicle for adapting the Constitution to the requirements of a new age.[141] Roosevelt introduced his proposal as a fight to save democracy. Reform was necessary "unless it be said that in our generation national self-government broke down and was frittered away in bad management. Will it be said 'Democracy was a great dream, but it could not do the job?' "[142] Both continuing economic crisis and political resistance to the New Deal made such questions quite pressing, especially given the implicit example of events in Europe. Presidential authority, he argued, had to be expanded to overcome bureaucratic resistance to policy goals. Executive reorganization would in turn allow the government to overcome political resistance from private interests. The "freedom of self-government" depended on "an effective and efficient agency to serve mankind and carry out the will of the Nation."[143] The Constitution designated the president as the agent of the nation, and he must have "the authority commensurate with his responsibilities under the Constitution."[144] As the report asserted, "the President is a political leader—leader of a party, leader of the Congress, leader of a people," and "the President alone" constitutionally possessed "the whole executive power of the Government of the United States."[145] Congress eventually approved executive-branch reorganization, but only in a form significantly diluted from what the president had wanted.

---

[140] Roosevelt, *Public Papers and Addresses*, 6:331.

[141] Roosevelt reportedly regarded the Brownlow committee as doing the work of a "constitutional convention." John A. Rohr, *To Run a Constitution* (Lawrence: University Press of Kansas, 1986), 136.

[142] Roosevelt, *Public Papers and Addresses*, 5:669.

[143] Ibid., 5:669.

[144] Ibid., 5:673.

[145] *Report of the President's Committee on Administrative Management* (Washington, DC: Government Printing Office, 1937), 31, 2.

The obstacles to presidential authority were legion, and the judicial challenge was one of many that such reconstructive presidents had to overcome in order to lay claim to their right to define the future of American governance.[146] Departmentalism was not an isolated and idiosyncratic theory adopted by these presidents. It was an aspect of their general political posture. What is most notable about these presidents is not their hostility to the judiciary, but their struggle against a variety of competitors for the authority to interpret the Constitution's meaning in a new historical context. These presidents recognized that there were many voices in the political arena advocating different readings of the nation's constitutional traditions, and their reconstructive efforts were aimed at establishing their own voice and vision as paramount. Departmentalism is neither the exclusion of the judicial voice nor the rejection of the last barrier to majoritarian political power. It is part of the presidential recognition of an ongoing struggle for political authority among the many competing institutions within the Founders' fragmented constitutional system.

Technique versus Ideology

An important aspect of this presidential effort to shift institutional authority over the Constitution is the reconceptualization of the nature of the Constitution and the judiciary. Within the politics of reconstruction, the judiciary is portrayed as itself highly politicized.[147] Whether because constitutional renewal is a political task or because the judiciary has allowed itself to become politicized, the reconstructive president asserts the need to reclaim control over the nation's constitutional future. The judicial claim to authority is forfeited through a demonstration that its project is an essentially political one. For reconstructive presidents, judicial authority is undercut not by the countermajoritarian problem but by the substantive nature of judicial action in that historical moment. Judicial authority

[146] Although Jefferson's partisan opponents were easily vanquished, he faced continuing resistance to his project from his ideological base, domestic economic interests, and foreign agents. McCoy, *The Elusive Republic*; McDonald, *Presidency of Thomas Jefferson*, 75–160. Lincoln, of course, faced severe challenges to his constitutional vision from the southern states, partisan foes, and internal divisions within his own party. Skowronek, *The Politics Presidents Make*, 198–227. Reagan struggled with a powerful opposition party and "liberal special interests." Ronald Reagan, *Public Papers, 1988–89*, 1619. The reconstructive effort required challenging the authority of a myriad of opponents for all of these presidents.

[147] Of course, some political actors are always likely to regard the judiciary as politicized. E.g., Alan Westin, "The Supreme Court, the Populist Movement, and the Campaign of 1896," *Journal of Politics* 15 (1953): 3; William G. Ross, *A Muted Fury* (Princeton: Princeton University Press, 1994). The key question is whether dominant political actors take up such arguments, or whether such claims remain the province of a marginal few dissenting from a vital political regime.

is undermined by the perception that the courts are addressing nonjudicial problems and behaving in a nonjudicial fashion. They are behaving politically. These presidents have not generally framed the problem of judicial authority in the terms favored by modern academic theory (which were borrowed in turn from radical Populist writers), as a problem of judicial resistance to untrammeled majority rule. Presidential authority does not depend on the elimination of judicial review, but rather on the appropriate delimitation of the sphere of judicial action. The judiciary retains authority to act, but only where its decisions can be truly regarded as "legal." The distinction between law and politics is not fixed, however. The meaning of purely legal action is itself politically constructed. During these reconstructive moments, the understood sphere of legality is substantially reduced, and the realm of politics is correspondingly expanded. These presidents attempt to move the line dividing those issues appropriately settled by judicial action from those requiring political resolution. For political leaders in a reconstructive posture, these constitutional disputes are essentially political, and it is the president, not the courts, who must speak for the Constitution.

The abortion debate has recently exposed such a dynamic at work in the contrasting positions of Jimmy Carter and Ronald Reagan. As a political outsider and born-again southerner, Carter faced a particularly daunting task of maintaining an increasingly frayed party coalition, while also keeping faith with the political image and concerns that brought him to the presidency in the first place. The Court placed abortion on the national agenda, but its position was consistent with that of the progressive wing of the Democratic Party (as well as the embattled liberal wing of the Republican Party). As abortion polarized Democrats, the Carter administration could not take a clear position on the issue.[148] Party stalwarts were committed to the Court's resolution of the abortion question, even as Carter's own conservative and evangelical characteristics appealed to pro-life voters. As a consequence, when pressed on how he could "support abortion" in a 1980 press conference, Carter deferred to the Court. Not only did the president distinguish sharply between his personal beliefs on the issue and his politically salient policy stance, but he also denied his own power to take action on the issue at all. For Carter, the optimal political strategy was to maximize the judicial authority to resolve the issue and remove abortion from the political arena. Thus, he insisted that "I'm personally against abortion," but he noted, "[A]s President I have taken an oath to uphold the laws of the United States as interpreted by

---

[148] The polarization extended into the White House itself. See Andrew R. Flint and Joy Porter, "Jimmy Carter: The Re-emergence of Faith-Based Politics and the Abortion Rights Issue," *Presidential Studies Quarterly* 35 (2005): 28.

the Supreme Court of the United States. So, if the Supreme Court should rule, as they have, on abortion and other sensitive issues contrary to my own personal beliefs, I have to carry out, in accordance with my solemn oath and my duties as President, the ruling of the Supreme Court."[149] In this policy area, the president portrayed himself as a mere executive officer, not as a political agent. The presidential duty, as he portrayed it, was both clear and rigidly administrative.[150] As a private citizen, Carter might disagree with the substance of the Court's decision. But as a constitutional officer and political representative, the president supported the Court and was powerless to resist it.

Although not central to his reconstructive effort, Ronald Reagan offered a radically different view of the abortion debate. Benefiting from a relatively united party and a consistent political profile, Reagan's political authority and electoral future were enhanced by politicizing the issue. Reagan's political authority derived from a conservative base that expected him to emphasize the political mutability of the status quo on abortion. Thus, unlike Carter, who emphasized that his hands were tied by the courts that had sole authority to interpret the law, Reagan insisted that "the issue of abortion must be resolved by our democratic process. Once again I call on Congress to make its voice heard against abortion on demand and to restore legal protection for the unborn."[151] Whereas Carter portrayed abortion as a legal issue about which he could have only personal views, Reagan insisted that abortion was a political issue about which policy should be made. The range of vehicles for politicizing the issue was wide, and some posed a more direct challenge to judicial authority than did others. Thus, Reagan not only supported direct legislative action to overturn *Roe*, but also supported constitutional amendments to the same effect and various policies that restricted access to abortion procedures and arguably subverted the spirit of *Roe*.

Similarly, the Court's abortion rulings helped motivate Reagan's attorney general to endorse the views of earlier reconstructive presidents on the authority of the Court. "Constitutional interpretation is not the business of the Court only," Edwin Meese argued, "but also properly the business of all branches of government."[152] As a result, the administration contended that "incorrect" judicial rulings were entitled to no broader application than to the immediate parties in the single case. The president would not disobey the Court, but he would not adopt its interpretation

---

[149] Jimmy Carter, *The Public Papers of the Presidents of the United States: Jimmy Carter, 1980* (Washington, DC: Government Printing Office, 1982), 2354.

[150] See also Graber, "The Nonmajoritarian Difficulty," 46–50.

[151] Reagan, *Public Papers, 1983,* 876.

[152] Meese, "Law of the Constitution," 985.

of the laws either. Without sufficient congressional support to threaten judicial independence, the president's efforts were as much or more about political authority as policy achievement. In this case, the judiciary served as a useful foil for Reagan to establish his oppositional credentials. Reagan's position taking on the abortion issue was a sharp departure from that of previous administrations, but Republicans did not have to bear the policy consequences of their strongly pro-life stance.[153] Undermining the judicial monopoly on constitutional reasoning and fostering an alternative constitutional discourse that delegitimated the Court was part and parcel of Reagan's rhetorical effort as president.[154]

Central issues of government are redefined during reconstructions such that they become objects of choice rather than faith. In that context, their very importance militates against judicial determination of the results. Abraham Lincoln was the most assertive on this point, contending in his First Inaugural that "if the policy of government, upon vital questions, affecting the whole people, is to be irrevocably fixed by the decisions of the Supreme Court . . . the people will have ceased to be their own rulers."[155] It was the very importance of the slavery issue that necessitated its democratic resolution. If self-government is to be meaningful, then it is precisely the most fundamental, the most vital political questions that must be subject to democratic decision. Moreover, the variability of the outcome emphasized the political character of the issue; policy choice implied political jurisdiction. Lincoln's ringing endorsement of the politicization of the slavery issue contrasts sharply with his predecessor's careful effort to depoliticize the same. Four years earlier, James Buchanan had argued that "differences of opinion" on this issue were "happily, a matter

[153] Neal Devins, *Shaping Constitutional Values* (Baltimore: Johns Hopkins University Press, 1996), 56–148. The succeeding administration of George H. W. Bush retreated to Carter's line. See, e.g., George H.W. Bush, "Remarks and a Question-and-Answer Session with the Mount Paran Christian School Community in Marietta, May 27, 1992," *Public Papers of the Presidents of the United States: George Bush, 1989–93* (Washington, DC: Government Printing Office, 1990–), *1992*, 830 ("[W]ell, of course, this is a matter that is enshrined in law. My position, as you say, is publicly stated. And I think the matter now is in the courts. . . . But that matter is being adjudicated in the courts right now. But my position is clear. I think it's correct. And there's room for a lively debate out there; you get plenty of argument on it"); Bush, "Statement on the Supreme Court Decision on Abortion [*Casey*], June 29, 1992," *Public Papers, 1992*, 1032 ("I am pleased with the Supreme Court's decision. . . . My own position on abortion is well-known and remains unchanged").

[154] It is significant that the Reagan administration was both forced to and willing to adopt a departmentalist stance on the abortion issue, even though abortion was not central to the administration's policy objectives. Reagan chose to politicize the Court, but much of Reagan's reconstructive project could be accomplished without running afoul of judicial doctrine, eliminating the necessity of a Rooseveltian showdown with the Court.

[155] Lincoln, *Abraham Lincoln*, 585–86.

of but little practical importance," for "it is a judicial question, which legitimately belongs to the Supreme Court of the United States."[156] It was the president's duty, along with that of all good citizens, to "cheerfully submit" to the Court's decision. Although "under our system there is a remedy for all mere political evils in the sound sense and sober judgment of the people . . . this question of domestic slavery is of far graver importance than any mere political question." As a consequence, Buchanan called upon "every Union-loving man . . . to suppress this agitation."[157] It was precisely because of the importance of the slavery issue that Buchanan contended that it had to be depoliticized. Lincoln's conclusions were radically different from Buchanan's because his situation was radically different. Lincoln's own authority as the prophet of a new constitutional order was enhanced by drawing slavery firmly into the political realm and inviting the agitation that Buchanan desperately sought to hold at bay. Lincoln possessed the authority to address the slavery issue; Buchanan emphatically did not. As a consequence, Buchanan sought to bolster the authority of the Court in order to preserve the little authority that might still be available to him, while Lincoln undermined the Court in order to claim constitutional authority for himself.[158]

The hollowness of Buchanan's effort illustrates of the larger dilemma that presidents and judges share in such a vulnerable situation. The old formulas no longer have the ideological force to command authority. The ready claim that slavery was settled as a matter of inherited law was increasingly implausible. Both antislavery constitutional theories and increasingly strained legislative efforts to compromise the slavery issue highlighted the fact that the status quo was contingent and discretionary. President Buchanan's and Chief Justice Taney's claims that their hands were tied by the requirements of the Founders' Constitution were met with derision rather than sympathy or relief. The meaning of the Constitution in regard to slavery was obviously and politically in dispute, and the Court could add little by simply taking sides. The fact that it was "taking

---

[156] James Buchanan, *The Works of James Buchanan*, ed. John Bassett Moore, 12 vols. (Philadelphia: J.B. Lippincott, 1908–11), 10:106.

[157] Ibid., 10:109.

[158] It should be emphasized that Buchanan and Lincoln also differed in their relation to the substantive rulings of the Court. Buchanan could afford to elevate judicial authority, and Lincoln was forced to undermine it, as a consequence of the Court's proslavery ruling. Departmentalism emerges out of contingent political situations, not the intrinsic beliefs of individual occupants of the office. Notably, for Buchanan defending the Court was a favored alternative to defending slavery directly. Regardless of judicial actions, the Democrat Buchanan was required to be proslavery, but his preference was not to have to talk about slavery at all, and he hoped that the Court could provide him the cover to shift politics away from the slavery issue.

sides" on a political controversy was too nakedly apparent to quell the losers in the dispute.[159]

Lincoln did not deny that slavery was a constitutional issue, but he insisted that its resolution was the political task of the current people.[160] From the perspective of the political forces that buoyed Lincoln, the Court was merely part of a "slave power conspiracy" that sought to remove the decision from the people while hiding behind the Constitution. Though Lincoln granted that "we cannot absolutely *know* that all these exact adaptations are the result of preconcert," the consistency of the actions of Democratic senators, presidents, and justices made it "impossible not to *believe* that [they] worked upon a common *plan*."[161] The Constitution did not require *Dred Scott*; the political commitments of the slave power did. Once inherited legal formulas sound empty and "mechanical," judicial authority is poised to be overthrown. As the Republicans contended, under such circumstances the Court is entitled to no more respect than "a majority of those congregated in any Washington bar-room."[162] The Court had made a choice about America's constitutional future. But that was a choice, the Republicans insisted, that the Court had no right to make.

Within the politics of reconstruction, the judiciary's posited "legal" solutions seem like political assertions. Judicial judgments are construed as assertions of judicial will, and as a consequence they are attacked politically by those with greater claims to the authority to make such decisions. Unsurprisingly, the analysis of the legal realists was particularly supportive of the New Deal critique of the Court. Felix Frankfurter and Henry Hart characterized the Court's opposition to the New Deal as "petty" and filled with "intellectual frivolity," appealing only to "the Bar Association gallery while leaving the substance of the matter untouched."[163] Similarly, Thurman Arnold denounced the Court's opinions as "dry as a common-law pleading," with a "complete lack of common sense" and "little persuasive power," making "bland assumptions" that "must shock any realistic mind."[164] Separately, Arnold wrote that the public must "have faith in institutions of legal learning as guaranties that principles, forgotten in the wickedness of a political world, are being constantly refined and made

---

[159] On this problem, see generally Martin Shapiro, *Courts* (Chicago: University of Chicago Press, 1981), 1–35.

[160] Lincoln, *Abraham Lincoln*, 403.

[161] Ibid., 377.

[162] Quoted in Barry Friedman, "The History of the Countermajoritarian Difficulty, Part One: The Road to Judicial Supremacy," *New York University Law Review* 73 (1998): 428n385.

[163] "A Dred Scott Decision," *New Republic*, 22 May 1935, 34.

[164] "The Court Rules Out Security," *Nation*, 22 May 1935, 588.

more useful for the world of tomorrow."[165] In repeating the "old incantations," the Court could no longer sustain that faith.[166]

Roosevelt saw the Court as both political and partisan. On the eve of his first election, Roosevelt departed from his prepared text in order to assert that "the Republican Party was in complete control" of the courts.[167] Once in office, Roosevelt downplayed the particularly partisan nature of the dispute in order to emphasize the broader question of who would control America's "constitutional destiny."[168] It "is not going to be a partisan issue. . . . it is a question for national decision on a very important problem of Government."[169] If democracy were to succeed, then the president had to have the power to "appoint Justices who will act as Justices and not as legislators."[170] The Jeffersonians had similarly asserted that the judiciary had abandoned its appropriate legal tasks and entered into politics. The courts had become, they contended, a mere outpost of the electorally banished Federalist Party, "and from that battery all the works of republicanism are to be beaten down and erased."[171] The reconstructive attack on the judiciary is not an attack on judicial independence per se, but on what is understood to be the inappropriate politicization of the courts by those who have lost the authority to speak for the people.

THE JUDICIARY IN THE POLITICS OF RECONSTRUCTION

The judiciary serves not only as a target for presidential attacks in these instances. The courts also serve as political agents helping to create the

[165] Thurman Arnold, *The Symbols of Government* (New Haven: Yale University Press, 1935), 52.

[166] Robert G. McCloskey, *The American Supreme Court*, 4th ed. revised by Sanford Levinson (Chicago: University of Chicago Press, 2004), 207.

[167] Roosevelt, *Public Papers and Addresses*, 1:837.

[168] Ibid., 6:130.

[169] Ibid., 4:221. See also Edward S. Corwin, "President and Court: A Crucial Issue," *New York Times*, 14 February 1937, 21 ("[I]t is the president's evident belief that the court has become a political body . . . a superlegislature").

[170] Roosevelt, *Public Papers and Addresses*, 6:129. See also Jackson, *Struggle for Judicial Supremacy*.

[171] Jefferson, *Writings*, ed. Washington, 4:424–25. Similarly, the Jacksonians thought the courts were ravaged by "political bias" and had subverted constitutional principles of limited government through their rulings, which required a political response to restore the judiciary to its proper sphere. Warren, *Supreme Court*, 2:112–145, 189–239. Complaints about the politicization of the judiciary, and comparisons with the *Dred Scott* and *Lochner* Courts, were basic to Reaganite constitutional theory, which likewise sought to return the courts to the realm of mere law. Robert H. Bork, *The Tempting of America* (New York: Free Press, 1990); Meese, "Law of the Constitution," 979.

reconstructive situation in the first place. Presidents are not the only order-shattering actors on the political stage.[172] The Court has also tended to exacerbate the crisis of the old regime by pushing forward with its inherited and evolving political agenda even in the face of increasing tensions within the dominant political coalition. The judiciary provides only a temporary refuge for adherents to the old order as judicial action widens existing fissures and creates opportunities for a reconstructive leader to exploit.[173] Likewise, the Court must make its own calculations as to how to preserve its authority in the face of presidential attack.

The judicial challenge is to the president's legitimacy, as well as to his policies. Courts that have lagged the electoral returns have not always been activist courts, though they have often been provocative. The Court has not always played the obstructionist role associated with the Hughes Court during the first New Deal.[174] Nonetheless, the judiciary has been active in building its own authority to construe constitutional meaning, advancing its position as the authority of elected officials wanes, and retrenching when reconstructive leaders take the offensive. Often the crucial judicial move has not come in response to newly elected political forces, but rather has come as the Court seeks to consolidate inherited constitutional understandings in the late stages of a declining regime.[175] In this context, Roosevelt's "problem" was not simply with the Court's obstruction of New Deal legislation, but was also, and perhaps more fundamentally, with the vision of the constitutional order that the Court had been articulating over the previous decades.

As the above cases already suggest, the Court is an important actor in structuring the reconstructive situation. Presidents such as Thomas Jefferson or Abraham Lincoln were not intrinsically hostile to the judiciary. Thomas Jefferson's relationship with the Court would undoubtedly have been more cordial had he been able to appoint Spencer Roane to be chief justice rather than been faced with Adams's lame-duck appointment of John Marshall. Likewise, James Buchanan's and Abraham Lincoln's responses to the Court may have been reversed had the Court in *Dred Scott* stretched to endorse abolitionist William Goodell's vision of the Constitution rather than John C. Calhoun's. But if Jefferson and Lincoln had felt

[172] Skowronek argues that presidents cannot help but be order-shattering, but that in the context of reconstruction that destructive effect is both intentional and strategically helpful. The Court also finds itself shattering received orders, but it is less clear that the effect is ever either intentional or helpful for the Court.

[173] See also Gates, *Partisan Realignment*, 169.

[174] It can be argued that the obstructionist nature of the Hughes Court has been generally overstated. See Barry Cushman, *Rethinking the New Deal Court* (New York: Oxford University Press, 1998).

[175] See also Gerard N. Magliocca, *One Turn of the Wheel* (Lawrence: University Press of Kansas, forthcoming).

no threat from the Court, they also would not have been reconstructive leaders. The reconstructive stance emerges from the interaction of the political situation and presidential goals. The Court helps shape that political situation, in these cases by cementing constitutional understandings at odds with those of the ascending administrations. Even absent specific knowledge of case outcomes, presidents such as Buchanan could be confident in the Court's role as a coalition partner. Both prior judicial appointments and earlier doctrinal developments indicated the relative safety of the Court for those affiliated leaders in the late stages of the regime.

The Court can be expected to help advance the goals of the old order.[176] As Dahl noted, regular appointments of judges by elected officials generally help keep the courts in line with mainstream political opinion. As noted here, in addition to making policy and courting constituents, political actors help articulate a constitutional vision, and affiliated justices are likely to share that constitutional vision and help implement it directly. Affiliated political actors can be expected to invite judicial intervention into political struggles, secure in the knowledge that the Court will intervene on their behalf.[177] The Court need not regard itself as partisan in such situations, for the constitutional understandings shared by those affiliated with the regime will be entrenched and assumed. Lincoln may have seen the Taney Court as an arm of the "slave power conspiracy" and Roosevelt may have seen the Hughes Court as simply "Republican," but to the justices their actions were simply in defense of the Constitution as they understood it.

In the context of transitional periods, however, such actions can have politically destabilizing effects. Judicial authority is strong at these moments precisely because regime authority is weak. The judiciary often finds itself making the controversial decisions that the elected officials cannot make, or at least would prefer to avoid making. Buchanan would not have needed to defer to the Court if he could have reconciled his competing political commitments on his own, or if he could have kept slavery off the national agenda entirely. He needed the Court to offer a technical resolution to the slavery issue, precisely because any explicitly political effort at resolution could be expected to tear the Democratic Party apart, as Buchanan's intervention in "Bleeding Kansas" later that year demonstrated when Stephen Douglas and other Northern Democrats decisively broke from the administration when it embraced the controversial proslavery Lecompton constitution favored by the Southern Democrats.[178]

[176] Dahl, "Decision-Making in Democracy," 284–86; Lucas A. Powe Jr., *The Warren Court and American Politics* (Cambridge: Harvard University Press, 2000), 485–501.

[177] Graber, "The Non-Majoritarian Difficulty," 37–61.

[178] Kenneth M. Stampp, *America in 1857* (New York: Oxford University Press, 1990), 295–322.

But as Lincoln emphasized, a retreat into the politics of technique is unlikely to be successful in the long term, even if it is the only strategic move remaining for these hollowed-out regimes. Thus, Chief Justice Taney echoed President Buchanan's rhetoric in emphasizing the legal necessity of the *Dred Scott* decision. Like Buchanan, Taney disavowed the political significance of his personal views, contending, "It is not the province of the court to decide upon the justice or injustice, the policy or impolicy of these laws." But this disavowal reinforced the duty of the Court "to interpret the instrument as [the Founders] have framed it, with the lights we can obtain on the subject, and to administer it as we find it, according to the true intent and meaning when it was adopted."[179] Justice John Catron asserted that such an unsettling controversy "*must* ultimately be decided by the Supreme Court," and in correspondence he urged the president to reinforce that view in his annual message to Congress and the nation.[180] Similarly, the "*Lochner*-era" Court struggled to apply long-held constitutional principles to increasingly vigorous social and legislative challenges. For the justices who would eventually be denounced as "old men," reasserting inherited understandings was consistent with both the ideological commitments of the Republican Party and the neutral application of the law.[181] As fissures within the governing coalition grow wider, and the hold of that coalition on elective office grows weaker, the Court is increasingly called upon to defend the old order. Not only are affiliated politicians likely to shift policies to the judicial arena for resolution, but legislation and decisions percolating up through the judicial hierarchy are also likely to emphasize the disputed issues.[182] As the old regime collapses, the judiciary is likely to be both a visible defender of the old order and one that survives electoral turnover. As a consequence, it is a likely target for a reconstructive leader seeking to dismantle the previous regime.

Even if the Court does not become an activist obstruction to the policy success of the reconstructive president, it will remain a threat to the new regime's stability and legitimacy. The departmentalist stance undermines the Court's authority to challenge the new regime. The president reclaims the authority of the Constitution by delegitimating the supremacy of the Court. The presidential emphasis on his own authority to define constitutional meaning, however, is often accompanied by more immediate efforts to restructure judicial power. During these periods, the Constitution and

---

[179] Dred Scott v. Sandford, 60 U.S. 393, 405 (1857).

[180] Buchanan, *Works*, 10:106. Significantly, Justice Benjamin Curtis disagreed. See Keith E. Whittington, "The Road Not Taken: *Dred Scott*, Constitutional Law, and Political Questions," *Journal of Politics* 63 (2001): 365.

[181] Howard Gillman, *The Constitution Besieged* (Durham: Duke University Press, 1993).

[182] Gates, *Partisan Realignment*, 169–183.

the courts are of relatively high political salience. The decisions that the Court makes (or has recently made) go to the heart of the central political disputes of the period, and political actors are likely to react with a far greater intensity to those decisions than to the average exercise of the judicial power to interpret the Constitution. The Court and its actions may be subject to sustained, high-level political attention. Reconstructive presidents have signaled their willingness to ignore or curb the Court, not just their disagreement with its decisions. The weapons used to attack the Court have varied, from the Jeffersonian elimination of judgeships to Roosevelt's efforts to pack the Court, but they have been consistent features of reconstruction politics. The authority of the reconstructive president to remake the political landscape results in unusually close ties between the White House and Congress. Although such unity does not guarantee legislative success, it does enhance the likelihood of serious court-curbing efforts. Moreover, such efforts have generally proven successful in forcing judicial accommodation to political pressure, even without the actual restriction of judicial power.[183] For the Marshall Court, the judicial response included the exercise of the "passive-aggressive virtues" as the Court exploited opportunities to enhance its authority without running afoul of Jeffersonian priorities.[184] In the New Deal context of greater judicial activism and a more activist legislative agenda, judicial retreat and ultimate co-optation was the only viable outcome.[185] Judicial independence may insulate the judiciary from normal political pressures, but the extraordinary circumstances of reconstructive politics are more likely to necessitate strategic adjustments by the Court.[186] When challenged by the politically powerful and active posture of the reconstructive leader, judicial options have been severely constrained and judicial authority has only been maintained by accommodating the new order.

The Court does not exist outside of political time, but rather both helps determine political time and occupies a position within it. Through its actions, the Court has acted as a catalyst for change. It has provided a temporary shelter for politically besieged presidents, even as it has sharpened the political crisis by reemphasizing the crumbling consti-

---

[183] Stuart S. Nagel, "Court-Curbing Periods in American History," *Vanderbilt Law Review* 18 (1965): 925; Rosenberg, "Judicial Independence," 378–83.

[184] Graber, "The Passive-Aggressive Virtues," 67.

[185] Leuchtenburg, *The Supreme Court Reborn*, 132–236.

[186] E.g., Jack Knight and Lee Epstein, "On the Struggle for Judicial Supremacy," *Law and Society Review* 30 (1996): 87; Ackerman, *We the People*, 2:255–382; Keith E. Whittington, "Legislative Sanctions and the Strategic Environment of Judicial Review," *International Journal of Constitutional Law* 1 (2003): 446. Cf. Jeffrey A. Segal, "Separation of Powers Games in the Positive Theory of Congress and the Courts," *American Political Science Review* 91 (1997): 28.

tutional construct of the old order. In doing so, the Court helps create
the political situation within which reconstructive leaders can emerge.
The Taney Court could articulate the proslavery underpinnings of the
Democratic regime in a way that Buchanan could not, but in doing so it
handed Lincoln the platform he needed to make his bid to restructure the
political landscape. In the wake of these electoral and ideological crises,
the Court has proven vulnerable. It has found its options severely limited,
and it has maintained a diminished authority by giving ground to the
reconstructive leader.

CONTEST FOR AUTHORITY

These cases of presidential-judicial conflict follow the patterns of behavior expected by the political time model as consistent with struggles for
political authority. Application of this approach to interbranch relations
raises a number of suggestive implications for an understanding of the
separation of powers and of constitutional theory more broadly. Establishing a link between departmentalist presidents and the political time
model also suggests the need to reconceptualize departmentalist theory to
take into account its cyclical appearance. In doing so, constitutional theory must be made more dynamic in order to take into account the historical operation of political institutions.

Reconsideration of the reconstructive presidencies makes sense of our
historical intuitions of judicial-presidential conflict. Such conflict was real
and explicable in political terms, but it did not turn on the quantification
of judicial activism or an immediate disagreement between the branches
on policy goals. The constitutionalist perspective emphasizes the struggle
for authority that is also part of the political realm, and the utility of that
dimension for fully understanding political events. The judiciary and the
presidency are not simply static entities with potentially conflicting preferences. They are also competing and dynamic institutions struggling for
the authority to define the nature of the political regime. The basis for that
authority is granted in the Constitution, but the extent of that authority is
subject to historical action. The politics of reconstruction hinges on the
ability of the president to bolster his authority to define the new regime
and to wrest control over the definition of the constitutional order from
other political actors, including the judiciary. This contest for authority
determines presidential power to reshape the political future and judicial
authority to intervene in political affairs.

These conflicting authority claims arise naturally from the competing
drives of these political institutions in the constitutional system, and are
exacerbated by the unusually strong claims of the reconstructive leader.

The judiciary's implicit challenge to presidential authority creates an opening as well as a threat for reconstructive presidents. In the course of establishing their own constitutional vision, these presidents must necessarily shatter previously established constitutional understandings laid down by the Court. Taney was a threat to Lincoln not because of what he might do, but because of what he had already done. For Lincoln to succeed he not only needed to avoid the judicial veto, he also needed to replace Taney's constitutional logic with his own. The Taney Court's actions in the 1850s were immediately helpful to Lincoln, sharpening the division between the rising Republican Party and the existing political power-holders and encouraging the further articulation of Lincoln's alternative vision of America's constitutional future. Such presidents need to reemphasize the distinction between judicial pronouncements and the Constitution itself, in order to create the space for them to impose their own gloss on that foundational text.

The role of the Court in the American constitutional system also creates an opportunity for these presidents, for it may be used as a foil to enhance the president's own authority. Given their unique authority position within political time, reconstructive presidents are strengthened by opposition. These leaders come to power with a mandate to remake politics. Encountering resistance from defenders of the old order only serves to revive that basic mandate. Politically isolated, judges make a particularly good representative of the old, discredited commitments and entrenched interests. As those most directly speaking in constitutional terms, the courts are likely suspects in the subversion of the inherited Constitution, and conflict with the courts is a useful platform for articulating the president's own constitutional vision. Judicial authority to define constitutional meaning is likely to be weakest when contested by presidents armed with such a powerful mandate.

The historical use of departmentalist arguments indicates that departmentalism appears not as a basic prerogative of the presidential office, but rather as a structurally dependent resource. Not every president has access to the claims of authority that a Jefferson or a Lincoln had, and as a consequence the departmentalist logic does not apply to every president. Andrew Jackson was not wrong in his advocacy of departmentalism, but his position relative to the Constitution is not universally shared. James Buchanan could not look to Jackson as a model for the everyday power of the presidency on this point, even though he could benefit from Jackson's efforts in redefining and expanding the use of the president's veto or his removal power over executive officers. Departmentalism emerges as an extraordinary feature of the constitutional structure, not as an ordinary part of normal politics.

The presidents with the authority to invoke the departmentalist logic are also particularly well positioned to foster the political consensus needed to restructure constitutional meaning. One of the enduring objections to departmentalism is the threat of legal and constitutional chaos that might follow in the wake of the acceptance of coordinate interpretation of the Constitution. If there were no hierarchy of interpreters, it is thought, then the constitutional order would collapse under the weight of conflicting and irresolvable interpretations.[187] This criticism gains its force, however, by being made in an ahistorical, apolitical context. If it is true, as Edward Corwin argued, that the finality of constitutional meaning is the outcome of the "continued harmony of views among the three departments," then the success of departmentalism ultimately turns on the ability of the relevant political actors to achieve such a consensus.[188] The alignment of elected officials in the politics of reconstruction tends to isolate the Court and enhance the effectiveness of the departmentalist stance. Reconstructive presidents are notable for their expansive authority to remake the political environment in their own image, resolving conflict through their own political actions rather than through judicial dictate. Although departmentalism may well lead to deadlock for more constrained leaders, for reconstructive presidents deadlock only becomes the opportunity for reorienting and expanding their own claims to authority.[189] The reconstructive authority is not boundless. These presidents encountered a variety of obstacles to implementing their constitutional vision, and they adjusted their efforts accordingly. Political actors are routinely constrained by their political surroundings, as subsequent chapters will discuss. The expectation that departmentalism will lead to political chaos assumes that political actors will press their claims regardless of the consequences, which is of course not true. Presidents have challenged judicial authority for specific and limited purposes, and have depended on the support of allies in the legislature, the executive branch, and the electorate to make their challenge meaningful.

---

[187] E.g., Alexander and Schauer, "On Extrajudicial Constitutional Interpretation," 1371–85; Erwin Chemerinsky, *Interpreting the Constitution* (Westport, CT: Praeger, 1987), 96.

[188] Corwin, *Court over Constitution*, 7.

[189] This also supplies the answer to the presumably knockdown question: What if Richard Nixon had simply refused to produce the tapes in response to court order. The answer is most likely the same as the outcome if Nixon had refused to resign—he would have been impeached. The waxing of congressional and judicial authority mirrored Nixon's lack of authority. Nixon was "forced" to obey the Court's order because Nixon was no Lincoln—he did not have the authority to put forward departmentalist claims plausibly. Although Nixon cannot be decisively placed in political time here, he has been neither traditionally regarded as a "departmentalist" president nor classified by Skowronek as reconstructive. For analysis of Nixonian conflicts as primarily defensive and legalistic, see also Whittington,

Such a political reconstruction of the constitutional order may still raise normative concerns regarding the types of values being advanced by presidents. The mere fact that political actors are reconstructing the constitutional regime does not mean that they are reconstructing it for the better. The difference between Andrew Jackson's and John Marshall's approach to Indian claims highlights this concern. From a modern perspective, the Court's attitude toward the Indians may well be preferred to Jackson's.[190] Other presidential conflicts with the Court, such as Lincoln's or Roosevelt's, belie any ready valorization of the judiciary's Constitution, however. Especially in these moments of conscious and active reconsideration of basic constitutional principles, it is not clear that the judiciary systematically provides substantively preferable results. In the context of substantial political disagreement about the content of our constitutional inheritance, the supremacy of the judiciary in resolving those disagreements poses its own significant normative difficulties. Normative examinations of the value of judicial review should take account of such historical instances of constitutional politics.[191]

Contextualizing departmentalist theory in this fashion has a significant implication for constitutional theory more broadly. Specifically, departmentalist practice suggests the need to recognize the dynamic nature of the Constitution, which in turn requires recognizing the relationship between politics and the Constitution. The deductive reasoning of traditional constitutional theory draws from a model of the Constitution as a purely legal text. Constitutional interpretation provides dichotomous absolutes—an action is either constitutionally permissible or it is not, an interpretation is either correct or it is wrong. Although aspects of the text operate in this fashion, the Constitution is also a political document.[192] As such, constitutional meaning emerges from the integration of political events and textual authority. Constitutional theory has created an either-or choice between departmentalist and juristic conceptions of constitutional review. In practice, however, the Constitution has not presented that stark choice. Under certain conditions, departmentalism becomes available. In most circumstances, presidents lack the authority to lay claim to such a power.

In most circumstances, presidents cannot plausibly act in the name of "the people themselves" in constitutional disputes. Presidential authority

---

Constitutional Construction, 158–206; L. H. LaRue, *Political Discourse* (Athens: University of Georgia Press, 1988).

[190] On the Indian cases as John Marshall's effort to challenge Jackson's constitutional warrants, see Gerard N. Magliocca, "Preemptive Opinions: The Secret History of *Worcester v. Georgia* and *Dred Scott*," *University of Pittsburgh Law Review* 63 (2002): 487.

[191] Cf. Waldron, *Law and Disagreement*.

[192] Stephen M. Griffin, *American Constitutionalism* (Princeton: Princeton University Press, 1996), 13–58.

under the Constitution cannot simply be claimed; it must be constructed. At the same time, conflicts between divergent political institutions, such as the president and the judiciary, have been significant to forcing constitutional development and shaping our constitutional understandings and practices.[193] The Constitution is not "updated" through judicial action and deliberation alone. Constitutional meaning emerges through the interaction of competing actors with distinct goals and missions. Even without such explicit constitutional mechanisms as Canada's "notwithstanding clause," which allows legislation to go into effect notwithstanding conflicting constitutional requirements, political officials can and do engage the Court over constitutional meaning. Political leaders concerned with reconstructing the constitutional order have mustered both the will and the means to open basic constitutional issues to political consideration. In doing so, they do not claim the right to act against the Constitution. They have asserted the right to read the Constitution for themselves.

An additional set of implications relevant to theorizing about judicial independence and the justification for judicial review should be made explicit. Robert Dahl's conclusion that the Court is rarely capable of acting as a countermajoritarian institution has been more recently echoed. Gerald Rosenberg, for example, has argued that the judiciary is least likely to resist political initiatives precisely "when it is the most necessary" to do so, when the Court's interpretations are being challenged.[194] The example of the reconstructive presidents, however, suggests that the normative lessons to be drawn from such conflicts are not so clear. The normative literature on judicial review has generally assumed that the Court alone is the "forum of principle" in the American system and that political action merely reflects unconsidered policy desires.[195] This substantive judgment requires further consideration. Judicial retreat in the face of the presidential offensive is only problematic if the judiciary is clearly identified with correct constitutional values. If, however, constitutional principles are themselves being contested by the various branches of government, then it makes little sense to favor automatically the judiciary's preferred interpretation. Again, the assumption that the Taney Court was a better guardian of the Constitution than Lincoln may depend on misplaced comparisons with other moments in political time and on the assumption that there is no politics of authority but only a politics of interest and policy preference. That the Court is sometimes more principled than elected of-

---

[193] See also Karen Orren and Stephen Skowronek, "Beyond the Iconography of Order: Notes for a 'New Institutionalism,' " in *The Dynamics of American Politics*, ed. Lawrence C. Dodd and Calvin Jillson (Boulder, CO: Westview Press, 1994).

[194] Rosenberg, "Judicial Independence," 394.

[195] E.g., Dworkin, *Matter of Principle*, 9–102.

ficials does not demonstrate that the Court is always more principled, or that its principles are necessarily correct. Judicial authority to interpret the Constitution waxes and wanes. Taking seriously the authority claims of other political actors suggests that such variation may be highly appropriate as elected officials occasionally adopt a leadership role in determining contested constitutional meaning.

This analysis also suggests that judicial authority is at its weakest when the judiciary is perceived to be highly politicized. The waning of judicial authority within political time is marked by a number of features. The above analysis indicates the occasional presidential challenge to judicial supremacy. To take another measure, the introduction of bills to restructure and rein in the judiciary is also periodic, with leadership support for such measures and their relative success most likely to come during these same reconstructive periods.[196] Such efforts are consistent with the unwillingness on the part of elected officials to defer to the judiciary in its efforts at constitutional interpretation. Such activism on the part of the elected officials reflects both substantive disagreement with the Court and an increasing belief that the judiciary is not engaged in a functionally unique task. It is precisely the denial of the ready identification of the Court and the Constitution that feeds these challenges to judicial authority. A seemingly politicized judiciary is fair game for political intervention. Judicial authority to act independently of other government officials depends on the belief that the courts are genuinely engaged in a task that is the "proper and peculiar province of the courts," as Alexander Hamilton claimed.[197] The political evaluation of and response to the courts depends on the perceived character and importance of judicial action, not its frequency.

[196] Nagel, "Court-Curbing Periods," 927.

[197] Hamilton, Madison, and Jay, *The Federalist Papers*, 467. See also Sylvia Snowiss, *Judicial Review and the Law of the Constitution* (New Haven: Yale University Press, 1990); Keith E. Whittington, "Reconstructing the Federal Judiciary: The Chase Impeachment and the Constitution," *Studies in American Political Development* 9 (1995): 55.

THREE

The Reconstruction of Judicial Authority

IN CHAPTER 2 we saw the political logic of presidential claims of departmentalism. Presidents assert greater authority to interpret the Constitution, and correspondingly attempt to displace the authority of the courts to do the same, when they seek to reconstruct the inherited constitutional regime. The Supreme Court provides a useful foil to such presidents, who may well go out of their way to proclaim their coordinate interpretive authority. The political leader's need to cut a new constitutional path puts him at odds with the institutional pretenses, as well as the substantive pronouncements, of the judges. The reconstructive leader must establish his own warrants to say what the constitutional law is, and that requires, among other things, supplanting competing interpreters. The puzzle for chapter 2 was in understanding the relatively rare political circumstances in which departmentalist rhetoric is asserted.

This and the following chapter address a different kind of puzzle, the political logic for the reconstruction and preservation of judicial authority. Although it goes against our routine experience in modern American politics, it is not surprising that political leaders would sometimes challenge judicial authority. Understanding such challenges is still normatively and empirically complicated, but such challenges are generally consistent with the expectation that political actors will seek to undermine the power and authority of those with whom they disagree. The more common situation, in which political actors defer to judges and even seek to bolster their authority to render controversial constitutional decisions, is also the more puzzling.

The constitutional inheritance left by the reconstructive leader is often ambiguous and incomplete, though the central features of the constitutional vision laid out by the reconstructive leader are often clear enough. There could be no question that Lincoln had stood for inviolable union and the end of chattel slavery or that Roosevelt had created a new governmental commitment to social welfare. They had claimed the authority to set the nation on a new constitutional path, and in the process they had rejected key aspects of the preexistent constitutional tradition. The implications and possible extensions of those fundamental decisions made during the reconstructive period, however, are often less clear. The mid-nineteenth-century Republican embrace of free labor ideology and the "extension of the power of the union over the persons of the individual citizens, through the action of the federal courts" could easily underwrite the activity of the *Lochner* Court as it encountered, and helped construct, industrialization and the nationalization of the market at the end of the nineteenth century and the beginning of the twentieth, but other political actors would have, and did, develop those materials differently.[1] The New Deal's egalitarianism and concern for the "forgotten man" could readily be turned against the South's racial caste system, but Roosevelt himself refused to do so, and southern Democrats succeeded in writing racial conservatism into the heart of the progressive legislative program.[2] The steps leading to *Lochner* and *Brown*, for example, were available moves within the reconstructed constitutional order inherited by the judges and politicians that supported them, but they were not dictated by what had come before.

In articulating the meaning of the new constitutional regime, its interpreters must make choices—while denying that any choices are being made. Unlike the reconstructive leader, who speaks on behalf of a relatively united and dominant political coalition against a collapsing political order, those who articulate an established regime must wrestle with a more fractious coalition that is no longer united against a common foe. The warrants of authority claimed by any given affiliated leader are less certain and less expansive. Such leaders have only limited authority to remake the inherited regime. Their responsibility is to extend their inheritance, but they must be, in Skowronek's terms, "orthodox innovators."[3] The innovative quality of their leadership must be sublimated and masked behind their claims of orthodoxy. The rhetoric of bold constitutional choices made on behalf of a mobilized citizenry must give way to a rhetoric of faithful adherence to the choices already made. Skowronek's study of presidential leadership details how the disruptive quality of presidential action has repeatedly undermined claims of faithful adherence. Constitutional interpretation has raised similar difficulties. In leading the national-

---

[1] The quote is from the "Address of the Republican National Convention, 1831," in *History of American Presidential Elections, 1789–1968*, ed. Arthur M. Schlesinger Jr., vol. 1 (New York: Chelsea House, 1971), 563. On Republican Party ideology, see Eric Foner, *Free Labor, Free Soil, Free Men* (New York: Oxford University Press, 1970); Gillman, *The Constitution Besieged*, 33–99; John Gerring, *Party Ideologies in America, 1828–1996* (New York: Cambridge University Press, 1998), 57–124.

[2] On the New Deal and race, see Harvard Sitkoff, *A New Deal for Blacks* (New York: Oxford University Press, 1978); Ira Katznelson, Kim Geiger, and Daniel Kryder, "Limiting Liberalism: The Southern Veto in Congress, 1933–1950," *Political Science Quarterly* 108 (1993): 283; Ira Katznelson, *When Affirmative Action was White* (New York: Norton, 2005); Robert C. Lieberman, *Shifting the Color Line* (Cambridge: Harvard University Press, 1998); Forbath, "Caste, Class," 1.

[3] Skowronek, *The Politics Presidents Make*, 41–42.

ist reformers against more conservative Republicans in a congressional debate over the constitutionality of internal improvements in which all sides claimed the Jeffersonian mantle, Henry St. George Tucker opined, "In the construction of this Constitution, there is not, there cannot be, a system of orthodoxy. Agreeing, as we do, in principle, there must always be a variety in the application. . . . Sir, with these things before your eyes ["the various shades of opinions on the question before us"], who shall pretend to say what is orthodoxy—what is heterodoxy?"[4] It is the classic task of judges within the Anglo-American tradition, however, to be orthodox innovators, to render new decisions and lay down new rules that can be explicated as a mere working out of previously established legal principles. As Alexander Hamilton phrased the traditional wisdom, the politician exerts will, but the judge exercises judgment. Within the politics of articulation, the judge has a natural advantage.

Political actors are not normally expected to increase the power of competing decision-makers. Power is the central attraction of politics. Making decisions is the vital task of politics. Increasing the authority of some to make important decisions regarding political matters necessarily decreases the power of others. Shifting the right to render authoritative decisions regarding contested constitutional meaning from presidents and legislators to judges increases the power of the latter at the expense of the former. Elected officials would not be expected to acquiesce in that transfer of authority unless they were to receive something in return.

It might be particularly expected that political actors would attempt to retain power in their own offices rather than see it flow to judges exercising the power of judicial review. The authority to determine constitutional meaning, and thereby the authority to determine the constitutional validity of government policy, seems particularly zero-sum, directly pitting potential interpreters against one another for the authority to have the final word. The most notable consequence of the judicial authority to "look into" the Constitution is the judicial warrant to review laws for their consistency with the Constitution and to strike down those that are, in the opinion of the judge, unconstitutional.[5] Increasing the authority of judges to engage in constitutional interpretation means, among other things, empowering them to exercise a veto over the work of elected officials. It would seem unlikely that political actors would voluntarily provide judges with such a weapon or contribute to a political environment in which judges might use such a weapon. And yet they have done just that.

[4] *Annals of Congress*, 15th Cong., 1st sess. (13 March 1818), 32:1323.
[5] Marbury v. Madison, 5 U.S. 137, 179 (1803).

Robert Dahl argued that politicians would be especially unlikely to tolerate judicial review when they had a firm grip on political power. At least in the federal government of the United States, judges are chosen by a political process that links them to other government officials. A successful political coalition can be expected to select only its friends for judicial offices. A reasonably stable political majority can soon expect to face a judiciary staffed largely by its allies. The judiciary is "inevitably part of the dominant national alliance."[6] At that point, "[T]he Court of course supports the major policies of the alliance."[7] Given the politics of the appointment process, Dahl posited, "it would be most unrealistic to suppose that the Court would, for more than a few years at most, stand against any major alternatives sought by a lawmaking majority."[8] At least when the Court is affiliated with the leading politicians, it should remain generally passive. The affiliated leader could expect the Court to eagerly stamp its approval on legislative measures and refrain from challenging the constitutional assertions of elected officials.

Bolstering judicial authority to resolve disputes about constitutional meaning may nonetheless be useful to affiliated leaders. There are several potential benefits to affiliated leaders of enhanced judicial authority. These benefits arise from the particular institutional features of the courts. Even when judges are likely to agree with the affiliated leader on the meaning of the Constitution, it may be useful to have judges play a leading, if not predominant, role in articulating that constitutional vision. In the case of reconstructive leaders, presidents want to wrest that leadership role away from the Court precisely because those presidents want to alter accepted constitutional understandings. By contrast, affiliated leaders are interested only in maintaining and extending a constitutional vision that has already been established. The task of maintenance is fundamentally different from the task of reconstruction. Not only does maintenance not require the same level of personal engagement as does reconstruction, but maintenance may actually be easier to accomplish if conducted by judges. Constitutional maintenance creates its own distinctive set of problems of political management, and bolstering judicial authority may often help solve those problems.

One problem of regime maintenance is administrative, or supervisory. This is a problem of control. Political leaders must not only set the direction of the ship of state, but must also insure that the ship stays on course. The fragmented nature of the American political system creates particular

[6] Dahl, "Decision-Making in Democracy," 279, 293.

[7] Ibid., 293.

[8] Ibid., 285. "Mr. Roosevelt's difficulties with the Court were truly exceptional . . . Mr. Roosevelt had unusually bad luck." Ibid.

problems of regime maintenance. There are many points of access for oppositional figures to influence policy and advance divergent constitutional values. Within the national government itself, legislators and executive-branch officials have substantial independence to resist the direction of affiliated leaders. Perhaps more fundamentally, American federalism provides completely independent governments and opportunities for oppositional political leadership. Affiliated leaders in the national government often have limited leverage over state officials. State governments are autonomous policymakers, capable of expressing divergent political preferences and implementing them at the local level. As political leaders in their own right, state officials may have the warrants to express alternative constitutional visions and challenge national officials for the authority to define the constitutional future. At least in the context of disputes over constitutional meaning, as opposed to policy or politics, affiliated leaders may often be able to displace the actions of others when they run afoul of the officially accepted Constitution. Monitoring the actions of competing officials and enforcing compliance with the established regime are time-consuming tasks that can distract from other political goals, however. Reinforcing the authority of a friendly judiciary to identify constitutional violations and discipline violators frees affiliated political leaders of some of the burdens of regime maintenance.

A second problem of regime maintenance is one of will. Political actors are buffeted by many competing demands, not all of which can be satisfied simultaneously. It is often tempting to sacrifice constitutional values, or long-term principles and commitments, to immediate political pressures. To the extent that constitutional values are abstract, they may be pushed aside by political considerations that are more concrete. To the extent that constitutional commitments are most important in the long term, they may be obscured by the short-term demands of the electoral calendar or the policy agenda. To the extent that political goods are plural, constitutional concerns must compete with others and may sometimes be found of secondary importance. Bolstering the authority of judges to hear and resolve disputes over constitutional meaning may insure affiliated political leaders against a failure of will when faced with particular controversial decisions. Increasing the authority of judges may help affiliated leaders share the responsibility for constitutional maintenance.

Judicial independence creates both opportunities and obstacles for constitutional regime maintenance from the perspective of the affiliated leader. It is precisely the apparent independence of the courts from elected officials that opens the possibility of judges sharing responsibility for constitutional maintenance. Because judges are relatively sheltered from the political concerns of elected officials, they can be expected to focus more tightly on constitutional commitments and recall the basic values of the regime with which they are affiliated. Moreover, because judges are separated from elected officials, the latter can also be plausibly sheltered from responsibility for the former's more controversial decisions. Judicial independence also creates risks for the affiliated leader, however. Judges cannot be easily controlled and may not be reliable agents of elected officials. They may well emerge as competitors for leadership of the constitutional regime. The judicial focus on constitutional matters may at other times seem myopic to elected officials, who might prefer that some decisions not be made in the manner or at the time that the judges make them. For the affiliated leader, encouraging the growth of judicial authority carries risks as well as potential benefits.

As was noted in chapter 1, presidents face a variety of constraints while pursuing their leadership tasks. Even as the affiliated leader attempts to advance a substantive agenda and strengthen a political coalition, he faces obstacles that threaten both. The potential presidential agenda strains the legislative and administrative calendar. Presidential and congressional powers are themselves limited. Political coalitions are diverse and sometimes fragile, and the broader political environment is not always hospitable. The judicial authority to interpret constitutional meaning can assist the affiliated leader in managing these constraints.

Winning a Friendly Judiciary

The starting point for judicial authority to be favored by the affiliated leader is the assumption that the courts are relatively friendly. Three mechanisms help insure that this assumption is a reasonable one: appointments, political supports, and contextual supports. The first is probably the most important. The independence of the courts insures that judges will not simply be the faithful agents of elected officials, but the political appointment process by which federal judges are selected links them to dominant electoral coalitions. Affiliated leaders will expect to place likeminded judges on the bench and can expect that earlier affiliated leaders did the same. If so, then judicial understandings of the Constitution are likely to be broadly convergent with political understandings.

A prerequisite for such convergence, however, is that the political regime have a coherent constitutional component. The mere participation of elected politicians in the selection of judges is not sufficient to create a reliably convergent judiciary. It is not an unreasonable assumption that provided a lever by which to affect the future course of the judiciary in the form of a political selection process, that elected officials will grasp that lever and use it. But other scenarios are not unreasonable as well. One can imagine, for example, a system in which elected officials did not take much interest in judicial appointments or try very hard to install judges that might agree with them. Such a system would not meet Dahl's expectation that president and senators will select judges primarily for "their basic attitudes on fundamental questions of public policy," but it may not be completely naive.[9] Dahl in fact rhetorically stacks the deck in favor of his thesis by asserting that presidents are unlikely to appoint individuals "hostile" to the president's views on public policy or "whose stance on key questions [is] flagrantly at odds" with the political majority.[10] Of course that degree of obliviousness to the ideological character of judicial nominees seems unlikely, but then that is not a very rigorous test. Presidents may avoid appointing "hostile" justices, but that does not insure that they will appoint particularly like-minded justices either. It is often asserted that the Senate, at least, should avoid evaluating judicial nominees on ideological grounds, but instead should limit itself to matters of judicial and legal "merit." Elected officials may express general preferences on the substantive features of an ideal judicial candidate, but presidents and senators seem generally reticent about highlighting in public the substantive political views of individual candidates for judicial office or demanding that candidates make their particular views known. Abraham Lincoln famously explained, "We cannot ask a man what he will do, and if we should, and he should answer us, we should despise him for it." From this circumstance, however, Lincoln concluded that "we must take a man whose opinions are known," and there is substantial evidence that modern senators take ideology into account in confirming nominees at least to the Supreme Court.[11]

Those involved in the appointments process may still not use that process to secure like-minded judges even if they would otherwise prefer to have individuals with agreeable political views on the bench. Presidents and senators suffer from limited resources and competing political desires. Securing the ideological conformity of judges is not always the highest priority of those who control judicial appointments. As Sheldon Goldman has noted in his thorough account of federal judicial selection, "There has been a constant tension between patronage, merit, and policy-ideology considerations in the appointments process. The balance struck has differed from administration to administration," though these differ-

---

[9] Ibid.

[10] Ibid., 284.

[11] Lincoln quoted in George S. Boutwell, *Reminiscences of Sixty Years in Public Affairs*, vol. 2 (New York: McClure, Phillips, 1902), 29. On Senate voting, see Jeffrey A. Segal, Charles M. Cameron, and Albert D. Cover, "A Spatial Model of Roll Call Voting: Senators, Constituents, Presidents, and Interest Groups in Supreme Court Confirmations," *American Journal of Political Science* 36 (1992): 96; Lee Epstein and Jeffrey A. Segal, *Advice and Consent* (New York: Oxford University Press, 2005), 85–116.

ences are not random.[12] Of course, judicial selections may not be a primary concern of a presidential administration at all. This is probably particularly the case when important political conflicts with the judiciary are not expected and other political concerns seem more pressing. Indeed, these will often be the circumstances of the affiliated leader.

Reconstructive presidents understand that the composition and character of the courts is highly salient to their overall political ambitions, and therefore they can expect to take some care in selecting justices when presented with the opportunity, at least relative to the issues that matter to the president. For Franklin Roosevelt, acceptance of the New Deal was the clear litmus test for any judicial nomination. The president could be expected to insist on this degree of conformity, but then other less immediately pressing constitutional and legal issues, such as the views of nominees on civil liberties or racial civil rights, were likely to be of only secondary concern.[13] For rather different reasons, Ronald Reagan entered office with a distinct and detailed judicial agenda, and his administration was highly organized to identify judicial candidates who would fit that rather demanding substantive profile. Administration officials were tasked with planning for Supreme Court vacancies from the moment Reagan assumed office, and judicial ideology was the starting point for administration deliberations. Abraham Lincoln was clear in his wish for nominees who would "sustain what has been done in regard to emancipation and the legal tenders" and "who would be a correct and faithful expositor of the principles of his Administration and policy after his Administration shall have closed."[14] As Charles Sumner reminded Lincoln from the Senate, "[F]rom this time forward the Constitution must be interpreted for liberty."[15] For those with a reconstructive constitutional agenda, achieving ideological convergence on the courts obviously matters and is likely to shape the judicial selection process.[16]

For those political leaders who can be fairly confident in their constitutional assumptions, who are affiliated with an established and resilient

[12] Sheldon Goldman, *Picking Federal Judges* (New Haven: Yale University Press, 1997), 359.

[13] Robert Harrison, "The Breakup of the Roosevelt Supreme Court: The Contribution of History and Biography," *Law and History Review* 2 (1984): 165. Cf. McMahon, *Reconsidering Roosevelt on Race*.

[14] Boutwell, *Reminiscences of Sixty Years* 2:29; Gideon Welles, *Diary of Gideon Welles*, vol. 2 (Boston: Houghton Mifflin, 1911), 184.

[15] Charles Sumner, *Memoir and Letters of Charles Sumner*, ed. Edward L. Pierce, vol. 4 (Boston: Roberts Brothers, 1893), 208.

[16] See also, Goldman, *Picking Federal Judges*, 4. Andrew Jackson likewise vowed to nominate a judicial candidate only "if his principles of the Constitution are sound, and well fixed." Quoted in Kermit L. Hall, *The Politics of Justice* (Lincoln: University of Nebraska Press, 1979), 5.

constitutional regime, judicial ideology is likely to be less pressing. An overriding concern with judicial ideology in such circumstances is more likely to be dependent on the particular inclinations of the individuals in office. Judicial selection in those administrations may be an afterthought, subject to little systematic consideration or organizational planning. In such circumstances, judicial vacancies may primarily be seen by presidents and senators as opportunities to reward personal loyalists, win favor with valuable constituencies, or score symbolic victories. The temptation to trade ideological reliability for other political goods is a constant one in the appointments process. Even Ronald Reagan was willing to compromise ideology in order to fulfill a campaign promise and score political points by selecting the first female justice to fill his first precious vacancy on the Court. The administration was even willing to swallow its concerns about Sandra Day O'Connor's reliability on the abortion question in order to meet its goal of appointing a woman.[17] On the other end of Pennsylvania Avenue, despite the heightened salience in recent years of ideology in the nomination and confirmation of Supreme Court justices, senators compromised their ideological commitments when evaluating Clarence Thomas and his widespread support among black voters in 1991.[18] With little apparent interest in the Court, Harry Truman and Lyndon Johnson were seemingly content generally to use judicial vacancies as rewards for faithful service by political intimates, such as Tom Clark and Abe Fortas. Such men may have been well known to the presidents who nominated them, but there is little evidence that their substantive policy views about matters likely to come before the Court were central to their selection.[19] One reason why it is difficult to pack the Court is because it is difficult for presidents and senators to develop and sustain the will to do so given the myriad competing demands of political leadership.[20]

[17] David A. Yalof, *Pursuit of Justices* (Chicago: University of Chicago Press, 1999), 135–41.

[18] L. Marvin Overby, Beth M. Henschen, Michael H. Walsh, and Julie Strauss, "Courting Constituents? An Analysis of the Senate Confirmation Vote of Clarence Thomas," *American Political Science Review* 86 (1992): 997; Vincent L. Hutchings, "Political Context, Issue Salience, and Selective Attentiveness: Constituent Knowledge of the Clarence Thomas Confirmation Vote," *Journal of Politics* 63 (2001): 846.

[19] Nonetheless, in part for reasons noted below, the selection of political intimates may still produce a politically convergent judiciary. Truman's appointees for the Supreme Court, for example, proved to be a remarkably cohesive bloc on the Court. Stefanie A. Lindquist, David A. Yalof, and John A. Clark, "The Impact of Presidential Appointments to the U.S. Supreme Court: Cohesive and Divisive Voting within Presidential Blocs," *Political Research Quarterly* 53 (2000): 795.

[20] Patronage demands were particularly heavy in the nineteenth century, when Supreme Court appointments were often treated along with other offices as a reward for party ser-

Even when filling positions of importance, presidents may not demonstrate a sharp understanding of and a single-minded focus on the policy consequences of an appointment. It has been reported, for example, that Jimmy Carter took relatively little interest in the selection of the chairman of the Federal Reserve Board and was most concerned with making a selection that would be satisfying to the financial community.[21] Although in hindsight the choice of Paul Volcker in 1979 to head the Federal Reserve may have been one of the most important economic and political decisions that the Carter administration made, it is not evident that the decision was made with particular deliberation as to Volcker's conformity with administration preferences on monetary policy. A political appointments process provides opportunities, but it does not guarantee that the process will be effectively used to bring the two institutions into alignment.

The ability of presidents and senators to secure like-minded appointments for the judiciary also requires that "like-minded" be a meaningful category for the purposes of judicial selection. It requires, for example, that politics be at least partly organized around constitutional disagreements. Political allies must be defined in part by shared constitutional understandings, rather than by, for example, personal loyalties or shared economic interests. In short, there needs to be a constitutional regime with which to be affiliated. In fact, American politics generally tends to be organized in this fashion, with political actors sorting themselves into ideologically coherent coalitions. There may be periods of transition and tension, as for example when abortion first became a significant political issue. Though the new issue of abortion initially cut across existing partisan divides, the two major parties and their supporters soon became identified with opposing sides of that issue and integrated their respective views on abortion with their other ideological commitments.[22] As a consequence of this sort of ideological organization, a like-minded judicial candidate can be expected to be agreeable not just on one issue but across a range of issues. On matters of importance, the points of agreement among fellow partisans are likely to swamp the points of disagreement.

---

vice. See Richard D. Friedman, "The Transformation in Senate Response to Supreme Court Nominations: From Reconstruction to the Taft Administration and Beyond," *Cardozo Law Review* 5 (1983): 26–36, 51; Michael J. Gerhardt, *The Federal Appointments Process* (Durham: Duke University Press, 2000), 50–68.

[21] William Greider, *Secrets of the Temple* (New York: Simon and Schuster, 1987), 22–23, 45–47.

[22] Greg Adams, "Abortion: Evidence of Issue Evolution," *American Journal of Political Science* 41 (1997): 718. The likelihood of this holding true rests on some assumptions, and it remains in the end only probabilistic, not a certainty. Republican judges who predate the consolidation of the party on a given issue such as abortion (like Ford's John Paul Stevens)

In fact, affiliated leaders have generally been successful at placing like-minded judges on the bench. Although legal credentials are presumably distributed evenly across the political spectrum, presidents overwhelmingly select members of their own party for the federal bench, with presidents such as Franklin Roosevelt and Ronald Reagan drawing nearly all their judicial nominations from the ranks of their own parties.[23] Roosevelt and Reagan, moreover, went beyond partisan affiliation to specifically identify judicial candidates who shared the president's own reconstructive constitutional understandings.[24] After initially relying on Democratic senators to identify candidates for positions on the circuit courts, Roosevelt soon began to nominate lawyers from within his own administration and law school professors who had supported his Court-packing plan.[25] Even when judicial selections are made with partisan goals such as coalitional maintenance, rather than specifically policy goals, in mind, the effect is often similar given the ideological affinity of fellow partisans.

When presidents do reach across party lines for their nominee, ideological affinity is usually a key consideration. The Republican William Howard Taft, for example, named three conservative southern Democrats to the Court, including the promotion of sitting associate justice Edward White to chief justice. White had been an ally of the conservative president Grover Cleveland, who had named him to the Court. Despite his Democratic background and failing health, Chief Justice White did not retire and give Woodrow Wilson the chance to name his successor. Taft, at least, believed that White was holding the seat for him and communicated as much to Wilson's successor, Warren Harding.[26] White died soon after the return of the Republicans to the White House, and Taft received the nomination for which he had lobbied. Taft later successfully urged Harding to appoint Pierce Butler to the Court. With only two Democrats left on the Court, Harding was anxious "to avoid the accusation of being unduly partisan," and the 1922 midterm elections had eaten away the once large Republican majorities in the two houses of Congress.[27] Given the ideological divisions within the Republican Party at the time, Taft observed that

---

or are outside the electoral core of the party (like New Hampshire's David Souter) are likely to be less reliable on that issue than other judicial candidates drawn from the party ranks.

[23] David M. O'Brien, *Judicial Roulette* (New York: Priority Press, 1988), 194, 37.

[24] Goldman, *Picking Federal Judges*, 360.

[25] Rayman L. Solomon, "The Politics of Appointment and the Federal Courts' Role in Regulating America: U.S. Courts of Appeals Judgeships from T.R. to F.D.R.," *American Bar Foundation Research Journal* 1984 (1984): 323–27.

[26] Henry F. Pringle, *The Life and Times of William Howard Taft*, vol. 2 (New York: Farrar and Rinehart, 1939), 954–55.

[27] David J. Danelski, *A Supreme Court Justice is Appointed* (New York: Random House, 1964), 43*.

it was preferable to look "for conservatives rather than Republicans" for the Court and assured the president that Butler "is a Democrat of the Cleveland type."[28] In his own way, Theodore Roosevelt had thought similarly, explaining to Henry Cabot Lodge that the right kind of Democrat could merit appointment to the Court because "the *nominal* politics . . . has nothing to do with his action on the bench. His *real* politics are all important"; "I want on the bench a follower of Hamilton and Marshall and not a follower of Jefferson and Calhoun."[29] A rather different situation arose when the Democratic justice Lucius M. Q. Lamar died a few weeks before the inauguration of the Democratic president-elect Grover Cleveland in 1893. The lame-duck incumbent Republican, President Benjamin Harrison, unsurprisingly wanted to grab the opportunity to entrench another Republican on the Court, but his informants in the Senate advised him that the united Democrats, who would also be taking control of the Senate in the next session, would never allow it. Determined not to leave the vacancy to his successor and "preferring a Republican's Democrat to a Democrat's Democrat," Harrison nominated Howell Jackson, a former Democratic senator and sitting circuit court judge who was said to be "really of the political school of Marshall and Hamilton."[30] Taken by surprise, the Republican Senate quickly confirmed Harrison's choice, who was sworn into office the same day as President Cleveland.

Political supports for the judiciary complement this appointment mechanism. Most significantly, Congress can through statute affect the structure and operation of the federal courts. In what Howard Gillman has called "political entrenchment in the judiciary," elected officials have sometimes sought to empower courts to take positive action on a variety of fronts, including the constitutional. By manipulating the size, structure, jurisdiction, and status of the federal judiciary, legislators can help constitute a programmatically friendly judiciary.[31]

[28] Quoted in Walter F. Murphy, "In His Own Image: Mr. Chief Justice Taft and Supreme Court Appointments," in *1961 Supreme Court Review*, 171, 172.

[29] Theodore Roosevelt, "To Henry Cabot Lodge, September 4, 1906," in *Selections from the Correspondence of Theodore Roosevelt and Henry Cabot Lodge, 1884–1918*, ed. Henry Cabot Lodge, vol. 2 (New York: C. Scribner's Sons, 1925), 228; Roosevelt, "To Henry Cabot Lodge, September 12, 1906," in *Selections from the Correspondence*, 2:231. In the end, Roosevelt was talked out of his plan to nominate Democratic state judge Horace Lurton, who was instead nominated by Taft several years later. Roosevelt eventually chose his reliable attorney general, William Moody, for the vacancy.

[30] Quoted in Friedman, "Transformation in Senate Response," 40.

[31] Howard Gillman, "How Parties Can Use the Courts to Advance Their Agendas: Federal Courts in the United States, 1875–1891," *American Political Science Review* 96 (2002): 521. See also Ran Hirschl, "The Political Origins of Judicial Empowerment through Constitutionalization: Lessons from Four Constitutional Revolutions," *Law and Social Inquiry* 25 (2000): 91; John M. DeFigueiredo and Emerson H. Tiller, "Congressional Control of

The most famous effort along these lines was also the least successful. Proposals for judicial reform, especially ending the circuit-riding duties of the Supreme Court justices, had been made in the 1790s, but it did not become a priority for the Federalists until they lost both the Congress and the presidency in the elections of 1800.[32] The hastily passed Judiciary Act of 1801 reduced the size of the Supreme Court from six justices to five, effective "from and after the next vacancy that shall happen," reorganized and expanded the federal trial courts, and vastly expanded the jurisdiction of the federal courts "to the full limit of constitutional power."[33]

The Judiciary Act of 1789 had left the federal courts stretched thin and relied heavily on the state courts to hear and resolve cases involving federal questions, including the constitutionality of federal laws.[34] After the passage of the Virginia and Kentucky resolutions and the rise of Jeffersonian sentiments in a number of states, Alexander Hamilton became a leading proponent of judicial reform. Linking the expansion of the federal courts to the expansion the federal army, Hamilton called for "vigorous measures" while the Federalists still possessed "all the constitutional powers." It would, he observed, "be an unpardonable mistake if they do not exert them to surround the Constitution with more ramparts and to disconcert the schemes of its enemies."[35] Treasury Secretary Oliver Wolcott explained to a congressional leader, "[T]here is no way to combat the state opposition but by an efficient and extended organization of judges."[36] After the election, a correspondent urged Hamilton forward on "the policy of the federal party *extending the influence of our Judiciary*; if neglected by the federalists, the ground will be occupied by the enemy in the very next session of Congress."[37] At the urgent request of Federalist congressmen, President Adams nominated John Marshall to fill the newly opened position of chief justice before "passage of this bill [the Judiciary

---

the Courts: A Theoretical and Empirical Analysis of Expansion of the Federal Judiciary," *Journal of Law and Economics* 39 (1996): 435.

[32] James Madison was already complaining about the Judiciary Act of 1789 and hoping that it would "speedily undergo a reconsideration" while it was still being debated in Congress. Quoted in Felix Frankfurter and James M. Landis, *The Business of the Supreme Court* (New York: Macmillan, 1928), 5.

[33] Judiciary Act of 1801, *U.S. Statutes at Large* 2 (1845): 89, § 3; Frankfurter and Landis, *Business of Supreme Court*, 25. On the Judiciary Act, see Kathryn Turner, "Federalist Policy and the Judiciary Act of 1801," *William and Mary Quarterly*, 3rd series, 22 (1965): 3.

[34] The Judiciary Act of 1789 provided for the appeal to the U.S. Supreme Court of cases in which the state courts had declared federal laws unconstitutional. Judiciary Act of 1789, *U.S. Statutes at Large* 1 (1845): 85–86, § 25.

[35] Quoted in Turner, "Federalist Policy," 9.

[36] Quoted in Turner, "Federalist Policy," 10.

[37] James Gunn, quoted in Frankfurter and Landis, *Business of Supreme Court*, 26.

Act of 1801] even by one Branch of the Legislature."[38] The Senate glee-fully confirmed Marshall's appointment before sending forward for the president's signature the bill that would eliminate the next seat that would become vacant on the Court. With only a month to go before Jefferson's inauguration, the president and the Senate worked literally to the last moments of his administration in "filling these [lower court] Seats with federal characters."[39]

Among the first orders of business for the Jeffersonians was the Repeal Act of 1802, which returned the federal courts to the form and dimensions established in 1789 and in the process eliminating Adams's "midnight judges."[40] The new administration's stance toward the Court was sug-gested in James Monroe's advice to now–President Jefferson, "[T]he best way to prevent [a conflict with the Supreme Court] is to take a bold atti-tude and apparently invite it."[41] The justices declined to fight the adminis-tration over the repeal.[42]

Though unsuccessful themselves in the face of the Jeffersonian recon-struction of the constitutional order, the Federalists pointed the way for future politicians to align the courts with their interests. The Jeffersonians and Jacksonians were content with leaving a substantial role for the state judiciaries and did not significantly alter the basic judicial framework es-tablished by the First Congress. The Federalist vision would have to await the ascent of the more nationally minded Republicans. During the Civil War and Reconstruction, Congress acted to reduce the importance of the South in the makeup of the federal judiciary and enhance federal jurisdic-tion over some limited civil rights cases. More broad-based reform, how-ever, came when the lame-duck Republican Congress passed the Jurisdic-

[38] Secretary of Navy Benjamin Stoddert (relaying the advice of Federalist congressmen), quoted in Turner, "Federalist Policy," 18–19.

[39] Senator William Bingham, quoted in Turner, "Federalist Policy," 19.

[40] Repeal Act of 1802, *U.S. Statutes at Large* 2 (1845): 132. For a discussion of the Repeal Act, see Ellis, *The Jeffersonian Crisis*, 36–68.

[41] Quoted in Ellis, *The Jeffersonian Crisis*, 60. Monroe was urging here that a provision of the Repeal Act that postponed the next session of the Supreme Court be dropped since it would suggest an administration fear of confrontation with the Court and "tended to put at repose the republicans, and relieve from further apprehension the federalists." Nonethe-less, the provision for postponement was kept.

[42] Ellis, *The Jeffersonian Crisis*, 60–68. The Federalist congressional caucus urged the judges to resist the repeal. In successfully urging his fellow justices to return to their circuit-riding duties and implicitly to accept the legitimacy of the Repeal Act, however, Marshall pointed out the obvious: "The consequences of refusing to carry the law into effect may be very serious." Quoted in Ellis, 61. Acting in its official capacity, the Court later upheld the Repeal Act, concluding that "the question is at rest and ought not now to be disturbed." Stuart v. Laird, 1 Cranch (5 U.S.) 299, 309 (1803).

tion and Removal Act of 1875, returning to the federal courts the broad jurisdiction that they would have enjoyed under the Judiciary Act of 1801. The Republicans were particularly concerned with protecting national commercial interests from localist and agrarian measures being adopted in the states in the West and the South, and Congress made it easy for businesses to remove cases filed in the state courts but touching on national economic issues to the federal courts for resolution.[43] The Republicans lost only the House of Representatives in the election of 1874, guaranteeing that their judicial reform would not suffer the statutory reversal endured by the Federalists at the opening of the nineteenth century. The relatively secure Republican control over the Senate and presidency through the late nineteenth century, even with the return of the southern Democratic electorate, gave them further opportunities to add to the Republican numbers on the federal bench.[44] By the time the postbellum Democrats first regained the White House in 1885, 92 percent of the federal bench was occupied by Republicans.[45]

This tactic of expanding the federal judiciary during periods of unified government in order to create new vacancies has become the norm. Congressional majorities shower judicial vacancies on presidents of their own party and deny them to presidents of the other party. Nearly every congressional expansion of the federal bench since the Civil War has been passed when the same party occupied both Congress and the White House.[46]

As the rush of new litigation swamped the federal courts in the latter nineteenth century, Democratic suggestions that federal jurisdiction be rolled back to more manageable levels were countered by Republican proposals that new judges be added to handle the increased workload.[47] As

[43] Gillman, "Parties Can Use Courts," 515–19; Stanley I. Kutler, *Judicial Power and Reconstruction Politics* (Chicago: University of Chicago Press, 1968), 154–60; William M. Wiecek, "The Reconstruction of Federal Judicial Power, 1863–1875," *American Journal of Legal History* 13 (1969): 333; Edward A. Purcell, *Litigation and Inequality* (New York: Oxford University Press, 1992), 15–25.

[44] The Republican tilt in the Gilded Age Senate and presidency was secured in part by the admission of a number of thinly populated but safely Republican western states. Charles W. Stewart III and Barry R. Weingast, "Stacking the Senate, Changing the Nation: Republican Rotten Boroughs, Statehood Politics, and American Political Development," *Studies in American Political Development* 6 (1992): 223.

[45] Deborah J. Barrow, Gary Zuk, and Gregory Gryski, *The Federal Judiciary and Institutional Change* (Ann Arbor: University of Michigan Press, 1996), 30.

[46] Ibid., 36–37, 55–56. Prior to Richard Nixon, presidents under divided government were virtually shut out from appointing judges to fill new positions. In the final decades of the twentieth century, Democratic Congresses created a small number of vacancies to be filled by Republican presidents. This was counterbalanced to some degree by the gift to Jimmy Carter of "the largest omnibus judgeship bill in the history of the federal judiciary." Ibid., 85.

[47] Frankfurter and Landis, *Business of Supreme Court*, 80–93.

one Democratic House member from Illinois complained in 1884, "There is a theory that is attempted to be maintained by those who favor centralization of Federal power, that the Federal courts are the safeguards of the rights of the people; that in these courts alone the ultimate rights and liberties of the citizen can be maintained."[48] A few years later in 1890, when the Supreme Court held that the Constitution required judicial scrutiny of state railroad rate regulation in order to protect property rights, the Farmers' Alliance of Minnesota denounced the decision as the destruction of rights "by a squad of lawyers sitting as a supreme authority high above Congress, the President and people," but New York's *Commercial and Financial Chronicle* cheered the Court and the opening of a grand new "epoch in the industrial and constitutional history of the country."[49] At the same time the political logjam was being broken as Republicans regained control of the House of Representatives, along with the Senate and presidency, in the 1888 elections and finally agreed to the formation of a new circuit court of appeals in the 1891 Evarts Act before they again had to turn over the House to the opposition.[50]

As this illustration from the late nineteenth century indicates, congressional supports for a friendly judiciary take several forms. The timely expansion of the federal bench can create openings for ideologically reliable co-partisans to be entrenched in the judicial branch.[51] The alteration of federal jurisdiction and judicial structure can direct the flow of litigation to politically favored venues and encourage judges to take aggressive action in their handling of such cases. In the case of the business friendly Republicans of the Gilded Age, creating institutional opportunities was sufficient for corporations and their attorneys to take advantage. In other instances, favored litigants and litigation can be more actively encouraged, for example as the Great Society did by the presidential creation of the Legal Services Program that put a variety of constitutional cases benefiting the poor in front of the sympathetic justices of the late Warren

---

[48] Representative Samuel Moulton, quoted in ibid., 85n135.

[49] Quoted in Richard F. Bensel, *The Political Economy of American Industrialization, 1877–1900* (New York: Cambridge University Press, 2000), 335. The case was Chicago, Milwaukee and St. Paul Railway Company v. Minnesota, 134 U.S. 418 (1890).

[50] Frankfurter and Landis, *Business of Supreme Court*, 93–102; Gillman, "Parties Can Use Courts," 520–21.

[51] Sometimes the contraction of the bench can have the same effect, as when the Federalists tried to deny a Supreme Court vacancy to Thomas Jefferson and the Reconstruction-era Republican Congress successfully denied a Supreme Court vacancy to Andrew Johnson by temporarily shrinking the Supreme Court from ten justices (where it had been set in 1863) to seven (in 1866). Congress set the number of justices at the current level of nine as soon as Johnson left office in 1869. Friedman, "Transformation in Senate Response," 22–25; Kutler, *Judicial Power*, 48–63.

and early Burger Courts or by the legislative establishment of private rights of action and financial incentives for civil litigation.[52]

Equally important, elected officials can protect friendly courts from court-curbing legislation, allowing the Court to be activist with little fear of political reprisal. As noted in chapter 2, congressional court-curbing proposals are most frequently associated with the politics of reconstruction, but they are not absent, only less successful, in the politics of affiliation. In the late nineteenth century, the Republican-controlled Senate was the graveyard of Democratic proposals to retrench federal jurisdiction. In the early twentieth century, Progressives responded to the *Lochner* Court by frequently proposing a variety of court-curbing measures that were promptly buried in conservative congressional committees.[53]

Another, more ephemeral, form of political support for a friendly court is what is known in the financial world as "jawboning." Jawboning, or moral suasion, is one of the tools often attributed to public officials for affecting economic actors, such as presidential rhetoric geared toward persuading corporate and labor leaders not to raise prices and wages in an inflationary period or Federal Reserve Board appeals to member banks to alter their lending behavior. In some cases, jawboning can be seen as simple signaling of a policymaker's willingness to employ more forceful tools to achieve some desired aim, as when legislators hold public hearings to urge the entertainment industry to develop content ratings for television shows and video games, or else. In other cases, the moral suasion itself can be effective in reshaping issues and altering opinions.

In the judicial context, jawboning can either encourage the Court to take action, or continue to take action, in a particular direction or bolster judicial authority generally. In the twentieth century, the most direct encouragement to judicial action took the form of briefs submitted by members of the executive and legislative branches, as well as state and local governments, in individual cases, as well as direct litigation of cases by the executive branch. The amicus curiae brief submitted by former military officers in the University of Michigan affirmative action case urging the Court to uphold the constitutionality of race-conscious university admission policies in order to maintain a diverse officer corps caught the atten-

[52] Susan E. Lawrence, *The Poor in Court* (Princeton: Princeton University Press, 1990); Jeremy Rabkin, *Judicial Compulsions* (New York: Basic Books, 1989); Charles R. Epp, *The Rights Revolution* (Chicago: University of Chicago Press, 1998), 59–61; Karen O'Connor and Lee Epstein, "Bridging the Gap Between Congress and the Supreme Court: Interest Groups and the Erosion of the American Rule Governing Awards of Attorney Fees," *Western Political Quarterly* 38 (1985): 238.

[53] Ross, *A Muted Fury*; Nagel, "Court-Curbing Periods," 925.

tion of the justices.[54] As Mary Dudziak has detailed, high-level members of the executive branch were active interlocutors with the Court as it heard the racial desegregation cases of the mid–twentieth century, breaking from the executive's prior practice of intervening only when the federal government had a direct involvement with the individual case at issue. Harry Truman's Justice Department in particular urged the Court to take action on racial segregation for the sake of effective American "moral leadership" abroad in the midst of the Cold War.[55] Elected officials can also encourage appropriate judicial action through less direct but more public statements. The Kansas-Nebraska Act of 1854, the last great compromise act dealing with slavery in the territories before the Civil War, included a provision simply granting territorial legislative power over "all rightful subjects of legislation consistent with the Constitution of the United States."[56] The provision prompted one senator to quip that Congress had enacted a lawsuit, not a law.[57] In the congressional debate, Mark Graber has observed, legislators "virtually begged the Supreme Court to decide the constitutional status of slavery in the territories."[58]

Jawboning can also take more general form, as elected officials seek to boost judicial authority to decide contested constitutional issues and encourage the judges to be active partners in constructing the constitutional regime. The audience for such appeals consists of both judicial and nonjudicial actors. Nonjudicial actors are encouraged to defer to the decisions of the courts and to take their disputes into the courts for resolution. Judicial actors are encouraged to exercise their authority in a manner consistent with the expectations of the speaker and are provided some information as to what a politically acceptable range of decisions might be. We have already encountered examples of such efforts. The Federalist response to Jeffersonian protests against the Alien and Sedition Acts pointed to the federal courts as the only appropriate tribunals for pronouncing on the constitutional validity of those congressional actions. Federalist judges knew their duty, and were encouraged to do it.

[54] Consolidated Brief of Lt. Gen. Julius W. Becton, Jr., et al., Grutter v. Bollinger, 71 U.S.L.W. 4498 (2003). Linda Greenhouse, "The Supreme Court: Affirmative Action; Justices Look for Nuance in Race-Preference Case," *New York Times*, 2 April 2003, A1; Grutter v. Bollinger, 539 U.S. 306, 331–32 (2003). In this case, the Department of Justice filed a brief against the Michigan plan.

[55] Mary L. Dudziak, *Cold War Civil Rights* (Princeton: Princeton University Press, 2000), 90–102.

[56] Kansas-Nebraska Act, U.S. *Statutes at Large* 10 (1855): 279.

[57] Senator Thomas Corwin, quoted in Wallace Mendelson, "Dred Scott's Case—Reconsidered," *Minnesota Law Review* 38 (1953): 16, 20.

[58] Graber, "The Non-Majoritarian Difficulty," 35, 46.

Opponents of the administration were instructed to give themselves up to judicial ministrations. The Federalist press singled out for particular praise those judges who fell most in line with political expectations, and it exhorted the others to follow suit.[59] A wider range of politicians celebrated the Supreme Court as the ultimate constitutional arbiter of the slavery question in the 1850s, with proslavery forces and their sympathizers, James Buchanan among them, expressing particular willingness to entrust the issue of slavery in the territories to the justices.[60] In 1857 newly elected President Buchanan expressed privately to the justices "the desirableness at this time of having an expression of the opinion of the court on this troublesome question" and was informed in turn that the opinions being written in the *Dred Scott* case would in fact address "the powers of Congress" to regulate slavery in the territories.[61] So forewarned, President Buchanan followed the urgings of the justices in the majority and used the prominent platform of his inaugural address to feature an appeal to "all good citizens" to "cheerfully submit" to the judicial settlement, "whatever this may be." Even so, Buchanan went on to praise the "happy conception" of "popular sovereignty," by which territorial legislatures would set their own policies on slavery and "decide their own destiny for themselves, subject only to the Constitution of the United States."[62]

Contextual supports provide a third mechanism for linking the beliefs of the justices with those of other actors within the constitutional regime. The first of these might be termed "sociological." Critics of legal formalism, such as Mark Tushnet, have argued that judges behave in a relatively predictable fashion not because legal rules have a deterministic force that can control adjudicative outcomes but because of the sociological context within which judges operate. At the extreme, he has argued, "we know that no judge will in the near future" reach "the conclusion that the Con-

---

[59] Warren, 1922, 1:166; James Morton Smith, *Freedom's Fetters* (Ithaca: Cornell University Press, 1956), 384.

[60] In regard to the view that slaves might be taken into free territories and legally held there, then–Secretary of State Buchanan wrote in 1849, "Upon this theory the question must be settled by the Judiciary." Quoted in Philip Auchampaugh, "James Buchanan, the Court and the Dred Scott Case," *Tennessee Historical Magazine* 9 (1929): 231, 233.

[61] Justice Robert Grier, quoted in ibid., 236, 237.

[62] Buchanan, *Works*, 10:106, 105, 107. Buchanan's praise of the power of the territorial legislatures in the popular sovereignty scheme appears to have been consistent with what his correspondents had told him of the *Dred Scott* decision, that it would invalidate the power of Congress to create free territories as it had done in the Missouri Compromise of 1820. It was inconsistent, however, with some of Taney's dicta in *Dred Scott*. Dred Scott v. Sandford, 60 U.S. 393, 451 (1857). Cf. Don E. Fehrenbacher, *The Dred Scott Case* (New York: Oxford University Press, 1978), 314 (suggesting that Buchanan knew about Taney's coming references to popular sovereignty).

stitution requires socialism" only because we know that no one who would be regarded as a serious and right-thinking lawyer and potential judicial candidate in the contemporary United States would entertain such interpretive possibilities.[63] On a variety of important questions, the people who become judges are likely to share the beliefs and predispositions of other officials affiliated with the regime.

Federal judges are drawn from a sociologically particular pool of candidates. Sometimes that pool is even further structured by sociologically relevant considerations, such as the nineteenth-century practice of appointing Supreme Court justices to represent each of the geographically organized judicial circuits. In the antebellum period, this had the effect of insuring that a majority of the justices would be from the slaveholding South. Even a random draw of qualified individuals from such a pool could have been expected to produce a Court with distinctive and predictable attitudes about race and slavery.[64] Throughout American history, Supreme Court justices in particular have been drawn from the ranks of the economically well-off.[65] They have also reflected elite legal training and professional success. Until the mid–twentieth century, judges were white males. Of course, individuals with such backgrounds are entirely capable of dividing on many of the issues that have mattered in American politics. But the shared social context of many judges and other political actors and government officials increases the likelihood of a shared perspective as well. When Republican presidents in the late nineteenth and early twentieth century elevated the "nonpolitical" criteria of accomplishment and stature within the legal profession to a central place in judicial selection, the consequent search led them to successful corporate attorneys in good standing with the conservative bar association. Such judicial candidates could also be counted on to be sympathetic to the constitutional commitments of the Republican regime and unsympathetic to emerging radical movements. In the late twentieth century, survey research has indicated "regular and substantial differences in political tolerance between samples of the general public and various political elites and community lead-

[63] Mark V. Tushnet, "Following the Rules Laid Down: A Critique of Interpretivism and Neutral Principles," *Harvard Law Review* 96 (1983): 781, 823.

[64] Of course, on many issues, party ideology may matter as much or more than regional background. See, e.g., John R. Schmidhauser, "Judicial Behavior and the Sectional Crisis of 1837–1860," *Journal of Politics* 23 (1961): 615.

[65] John R. Schmidhauser, "The Justices of the Supreme Court: A Collective Portrait," *Midwest Journal of Political Science* 3 (1959): 1; Kermit L. Hall, "The Children of the Cabins: The Lower Federal Judiciary, Modernization, and the Political Culture, 1789–1899," *Northwestern University Law Review* 75 (1980): 423; Sheldon Goldman and Thomas P. Jahnige, *The Federal Courts as a Political System*, 2nd ed. (New York: Harper & Row, 1976), 66–74.

ers."[66] Both the selective recruitment of relatively tolerant individuals and the adult socialization of judicial candidates in law and politics insures that they will tend to share with national political officials a broad commitment to, and understanding of the meaning of, civil liberties. In recent decades, a commitment to the aggressive judicial protection of individual rights is central to the professional identity of potential judges, whether of the Left or the Right.[67]

Contextual factors are also likely to lead judges to respond to events and developing issues in ways that are in keeping with, and help define, the broad commitments of the regime. Judges are subject to many of the same shifts in public mood and political and social circumstances that affect elected officials. A. V. Dicey observed of British judges in the nineteenth century that they were, "of course, influenced by the beliefs and feelings of their time, and are guided to a considerable extent by the dominant current of public opinion."[68] Likewise Justice Benjamin Cardozo pointed out that judges "do not stand aloof on these chill and distant heights. . . . The great tides and currents which engulf the rest of men do not turn aside in their course and pass the judges by."[69] Judges are neither immune from the social pressures of public opinion nor insulated from public debates on constitutional issues.[70] In racist times, judges are likely

---

[66] John L. Sullivan, Pat Walsh, Michael Shamir, David G. Barnum, and James L. Gibson, "Why Politicians Are More Tolerant: Selective Recruitment and Socialization Among Political Elites in Britain, Israel, New Zealand and the United States," *British Journal of Political Science* 23 (1993): 51.

[67] See also Thomas M. Keck, "From *Bakke* to *Grutter*: The Rise of Rights-Based Conservatism," in *The Supreme Court and American Political Development*, ed. Ronald Kahn and Ken I. Kersch (Lawrence: University Press of Kansas, 2006).

[68] A. V. Dicey, *Lectures on the Relations Between Law and Public Opinion in England During the Nineteenth Century* (London: Macmillan, 1905), 361. Dicey went on to observe: "But whilst our tribunals, or the judges of whom they are composed, are swayed by the prevailing beliefs of a particular time, they are also guided by professional opinions and ways of thinking which are to a certain extent independent and possibly opposed to the general tone of public opinion." Ibid., 362.

[69] Benjamin N. Cardozo, *The Nature of the Judicial Process* (New Haven: Yale University Press, 1921), 168.

[70] William Mishler and Reginald S. Sheehan, "The Supreme Court as a Countermajoritarian Institution? The Impact of Public Opinion on Supreme Court Decisions," *American Political Science Review* 88 (1993): 87; Roy B. Flemming and B. Dan Wood, "The Public and the Supreme Court: Individual Justice Responsiveness to American Policy Moods," *American Journal of Political Science* 41 (1997): 468; J. W. Peltason, *58 Lonely Men* (Urbana: University of Illinois Press, 1971), 3–13, 244–54; Ronald Kahn, "Institutional Norms and Historical Development of Supreme Court Politics: Changing 'Social Facts' and Doctrinal Development," in Gillman and Clayton, *Supreme Court in American Politics*, 43–59; Kevin T. McGuire and James A. Stimson, "The Least Dangerous Branch Revisited: New Evidence on Supreme Court Responsiveness to Public Preferences," *Journal of Politics* 66 (2004): 1018.

to reflect the culturally dominant racial beliefs.[71] When national elites are concerned that property rights are in danger, then the judiciary is likely to be sympathetic to those concerns.[72] Judges too were affected by Pearl Harbor and willing to believe that the military needed to take drastic measures to secure the Pacific coast in time of war, including imposing a curfew on, and then removing to internment camps, resident aliens and American citizens of Japanese origin.[73] When only the legislative obstruction of southern representatives blocked federal civil rights bills in the 1950s, the views of the justices were in keeping with national public sentiment and executive branch officials that racial segregation in the states was an embarrassment—but that little that the federal government did was inconsistent with the requirements of racial equality.[74] The justices feel social shifts such as the rise of the women's movement in the 1960s and 1970s, just as other officials, and members of the general public, do.[75]

Favoring Activism

It is fairly clear how and why government officials would make active use of a friendly judiciary outside the context of constitutional interpretation. In the late 1790s, the Federalists wanted a reliable and powerful federal judiciary that could project national power into the backcountry and put resisters in jail, or the hangman's noose. Standard principal-agent models of delegation indicate the trade-offs to be made between control and expertise, rules and discretion.[76] When it is too difficult for legislators to

[71] Michael J. Klarman, *From Jim Crow to Civil Rights* (New York: Oxford University Press, 2003); Girardeau A. Spann, *Race Against the Court* (New York: New York University Press, 1993), 19–35.

[72] Paul, *Conservative Crisis*; Gillman, *The Constitution Besieged*, 1–100.

[73] Hirabayashi v. United States, 320 U.S. 81 (1943); Korematsu v. United States, 323 U.S. 214 (1944). See Alpheus T. Mason, *Harlan Fiske Stone* (New York: Viking, 1956), 672–81.

[74] Klarman, *Jim Crow*; Dudziak, *Cold War Civil Rights*, 79–114; Powe, *Warren Court*, 27–37; Richard A. Primus, "*Bolling* Alone," *Columbia Law Review* 104 (2004): 975.

[75] Michael J. Klarman, "Rethinking the Civil Rights and Civil Liberties Revolutions," *Virginia Law Review* 82 (1996): 1, 9–10; Lee Epstein and Joseph F. Kobylka, *The Supreme Court and Legal Change* (Chapel Hill: University of North Carolina Press, 1992); Mark Tushnet, "The Burger Court in Historical Perspective: The Triumph of Country-Club Republicanism," in *The Burger Court: Counter-Revolution or Confirmation?* ed. Bernard Schwartz (New York: Oxford University Press, 1998), 207–8; Ronald Kahn and Susan Dennehy, "New Historical Institutionalism, Precedential Social Constructs, and Doctrinal Change: Gender Discrimination in the Twentieth Century," unpublished paper.

[76] See, e.g., David E. M. Sappington, "Incentives in Principal-Agent Relationships," *Journal of Economic Perspectives* 5 (1991): 45; Paul R. Milgrom and John Roberts, *Economics, Organization, and Management* (Englewood Cliffs, NJ: Prentice-Hall, 1992); Oliver E. Williamson, *The Mechanisms of Government* (New York: Oxford University Press, 1996);

define what business practices to outlaw, antitrust legislation is written with only broad standards that empower executive officials and judges to make the crucial decisions in light of the facts of the individual case and their own expert knowledge.[77] Although judicial "agents" cannot easily be sanctioned by their legislative "principals" if their performance fails to meet expectations, in the statutory context the legislature can readily tighten the rules by which judges operate and reduce the slack, or formal room for the exercise of discretion, in the relationship.[78] In the criminal law context, for example, judges are given discretion in sentencing when legislators desire individualized judgment and lose that discretion when legislators prefer "tough on crime" mandatory sentences. Judges may gain some additional independence in exercising their legal authority by exploiting political disagreements among legislators that might hamper their ability to respond to unexpected judicial actions. Regardless of the original legislative intent behind the Civil Rights Act of 1964, for example, the courts might extend the law to address sexual harassment in the workplace or to approve affirmative action programs knowing that it would be difficult to form a legislative majority to reverse those judicial decisions or even knowing that contemporary legislative majorities would favor such developments.[79]

The rationale for making active use of a friendly judiciary in the context of judicial review is less evident. Dahl provided the most obvious expectation: when it comes to exercising the judicial veto over legislation, allied officials expect a friendly Court to be passive. Packing the courts means taking the judicial veto out of the policymaking game. But the Supreme Court has often been activist when it might reasonably be expected to be friendly. Perhaps the Court was really "unfriendly" after all, but the last section gives us reason to doubt that this would be the case. We need to identify reasons why elected officials might favor an activist Court that is willing to use the power of judicial review. There are many.

Terry M. Moe, "The New Economics of Organization," *American Journal of Political Science* 28 (1984): 739; Jonathan Bendor, Ami Glazer, and Thomas Hammond, "Theories of Delegation," *Annual Review of Political Science* 4 (2001): 235.

[77] The inability to legislators to agree on more specific standards often also plays a role in such delegations, of course. See, e.g., George I. Lovell, *Legislative Deferrals* (New York: Cambridge University Press, 2003).

[78] The limited options for sanctioning federal judges do have consequences for the tolerance of legislators for independent judicial review, however. See Whittington, "Legislative Sanctions," 446.

[79] See, e.g., William N. Eskridge Jr., "Reneging on History? Playing the Court/Congress/President Civil Rights Game," *California Law Review* 79 (1991): 613; William N. Eskridge Jr., "Overriding Supreme Court Statutory Decisions," *Yale Law Journal* 101 (1991): 331; William N. Eskridge Jr. and John Ferejohn, "Virtual Logrolling: How the Court, Congress, and the States Multiple Civil Rights," *Southern California Law Review* 68 (1995): 1545.

Regime Enforcement

The easiest judicial role for affiliated leaders to embrace, and perhaps the most important, is one of regime enforcement against constitutional outliers. The American political system is highly fragmented. It provides ample opportunities for electoral minorities to nonetheless exercise political power. Particularly notable is the American federal structure, which allows members of the out-party to consolidate and exercise governmental power over limited geographic jurisdictions. The independence of state and local governments from the national government is a source of ferment and resistance within the constitutional regime that national political officials might seek to establish. It was this very difficulty that led many advocates of constitutional reform in the 1780s, including James Madison, to seek a stronger national government with a more effective capacity for disciplining subnational political actors.[80] At the Philadelphia convention, Madison was unable to win his favored proposal, a congressional veto over state policies. The Supreme Court's power of judicial review of the constitutionality of state statutes is the primary mechanism available to the federal government for supervising the independent state governments.[81]

For the affiliated leader, enhancing judicial authority to define and enforce constitutional meaning provides an efficient mechanism for super-

---

[80] Jack N. Rakove, *Original Meanings* (New York: Vintage, 1996), 51–53, 197–98; Lance Banning, *The Sacred Fire of Liberty* (Ithaca: Cornell University Press, 1995), 43–75.

[81] A century later, James Bryce observed that a congressional veto "would have provoked collisions with them [the states]. The disallowance of a state statute, even if it did really offend against the federal Constitution, would have seemed a political move, to be resented by a political countermove. . . . But by the action of the courts the self-love of the state is not wounded, and the decision declaring one of their laws invalid is nothing but a tribute to the higher authority of that supreme enactment to which they were themselves parties, and which they themselves desire to see enforced against another state on some not remote occasion." James Bryce, *The American Commonwealth*, vol. 1 (Indianapolis: Liberty Fund, 1995), 228–29. Bryce's conclusion probably could not have been drawn much earlier. Just a few years before, the *Nation* celebrated a decision blocking a Virginia effort to repudiate part of its state debt as "the first victory of the Supreme Court over a really recalcitrant and angry State . . . [and] the first absolutely peaceful triumph of the Constitution and its honest principles over the narrowness, bitterness, and often dishonesty of local popular will, and as such they form an epoch in American constitutional history. It is the triumph of the regular power of the national Government over the irregular power of the State." "Virginia Coupon Bonds," *Nation*, 11 February 1886, 121. One observer questing for a new role for the Court in the aftermath of the New Deal noted, "It is not keener vision or larger knowledge which sustains the Court's exercise of power [against the states]; it is rather, that as the structure of government now goes, there is no other agency to which the task can be entrusted." Walton H. Hamilton and George D. Braden, "The Special Competence of the Supreme Court," *Yale Law Journal* 50 (1941): 1319, 1355.

vising and correcting those who might fail to adhere to the politically preferred constitutional vision. The affiliated leader supports judicial activism because he does not expect it to be used against himself. This aspect of judicial review is often obscured by standard treatments of its "counter-majoritarian" nature. Dahl's own analysis of judicial review, with its expectation of a deferential Court, proceeded as if the United States had a unitary rather than federal political system and only treated the Court's handling of congressional statutes.[82] Similarly, when Alexander Bickel labeled judicial review a countermajoritarian institution, he focused on the fact that unelected judges rejected the work of elected legislators but did not consider by whom the legislators were elected.[83] When contemporary conservatives questioned whether recent judicial decisions mean the "end of democracy," the cases they had in mind generally dealt with state laws, and they did not stop to question the extent of their popular support.[84] The populist complaint against judicial review may or may not be a reasonable one, but it elides the institutional dynamics that the separation between national and state governments opens up.

In fact, most of the laws struck down by the U.S. Supreme Court as unconstitutional have been the products of state and local governments, not the federal government. Over the course of its history, the Court has invalidated state and local laws in nearly 1,100 cases, while voiding congressional statutes in just over 150 cases.[85] Oliver Wendell Holmes probably spoke for many justices when he proclaimed, "I do not think the United States would come to an end if we lost our power to declare an Act of Congress void. I do think the Union would be imperiled if we could not make that declaration as to the laws of the several States."[86] In the nineteenth century it was common to regard the federal judiciary as a nationalizing institution, reflecting national interests and perspectives against the states. By the end of the nineteenth century that angle of vision on the Court had largely been displaced by others. But especially when "national interests" are given a more substantive, partisan shading—as in the form of constitutional regimes—then the national dimension of judicial review takes on continued relevance.

[82] Dahl bracketed the "ticklish question of federalism" in his analysis since he did not think that the judicial protection of "the rights of national majorities against local interests" was an important rationale for judicial review. Dahl, "Decision-Making in Democracy," 282.

[83] Bickel, *The Least Dangerous Branch*, 17.

[84] Mitchell S. Muncy, ed., *The End of Democracy?* (Dallas: Spence Publishing, 1997).

[85] Congressional Research Service, *The Constitution of the United States of America, Analysis and Interpretation* (Washington, DC: Government Printing Office, 2002, 2004).

[86] Oliver Wendell Holmes, "Speech at a Dinner of the Harvard Law School Association of New York, February 15, 1913," in *Collected Legal Papers* (New York: Harcourt, Brace, 1921), 295–96.

The Supreme Court has often used the power of judicial review to bring states into line with the nationally dominant constitutional vision. In his comprehensive analysis of state statutes and constitutional provisions invalidated by the Supreme Court from the Jacksonian era through 1964, John Gates found that the Court was particularly likely to act against "states whose partisan character is different from the dominant majority on the Court or from regions which evidence ideological incongruence between the state and national party organizations."[87] In the late nineteenth and early twentieth centuries, judicial review by a conservative Court was primarily exercised against "regions where populism [and later progressivism] had made strong inroads."[88] In the mid–twentieth century, invalidated state laws emerged mostly from Republican states and the ideologically isolated South.[89] Political losers at the national level can often pursue their constitutional and policy proclivities in various state governments, but throughout its history the Supreme Court has stood ready to "expand the scope of conflict" by pulling those policies back into the national arena for ultimate resolution.[90]

The Court first built its relative authority to define constitutional meaning through its inspection of actions of the states. Although *Marbury* famously invalidated a provision of a congressional statute while censuring presidential action, the Court's constitutional caseload in the early nineteenth century was largely generated by the states. After striking down its first state law in 1809, it averaged over six such actions per decade from then until secession. In doing so, the Court found political advantage in upholding national supremacy, resolving interstate disputes, and securing the constitutional understandings favored by national political officials. The Court hardly escaped controversy, and its decisions often met resistance in the states during those decades, but even so its authority and ambition steadily grew.[91] Despite these occasional acts of state defiance, the Court's authority "was accepted as legitimate, in almost all the states, almost all the time, and on almost all issues."[92] The judicial historian Charles Warren concluded that by the late 1840s, "the Court may be said to have reached its height in the confidence of the people of the country."[93]

[87] John B. Gates, "Partisan Realignment, Unconstitutional State Polities, and the U.S. Supreme Court: 1837–1964," *American Journal of Political Science* 31 (1987): 259, 260.

[88] Gates, *Partisan Realignment*, 67.

[89] See ibid.; Powe, *Warren Court*, 485–500.

[90] E. E. Schattschneider, *The Semi-Sovereign People* (Hinsdale, IL: Dryden Press, 1975), 1–11.

[91] Leslie Friedman Goldstein, *Constituting Federal Sovereignty* (Baltimore: Johns Hopkins University Press, 2001), 19–33.

[92] Ibid., 32.

[93] Warren, *Supreme Court*, 2:480.

The Jeffersonians were disappointed that the Court under Chief Justice Marshall and his predecessors did not stand as a firm barrier against the expansion and abuse of federal powers, but instead seemed to facilitate them. Although Jefferson and Madison had argued, while in the opposition in 1798, that the judicial authority to interpret the Constitution could not be exclusive or ultimate and that the states had the authority to evaluate the constitutionality of federal laws, they were more generally favorably disposed to judicial authority. Jefferson had criticized Madison's original constitutional proposal of creating a congressional veto over state laws as "mend[ing] a small hole by covering the whole garment," and suggested instead empowering a federal judiciary to invalidate only those laws that conflicted with the Constitution or superior federal law.[94] Jefferson had later advocated a federal bill of rights to Madison on the grounds that it would put "the legal check . . . into the hands of the judiciary."[95] In the mid-1790s, Jeffersonian Virginians were the ones who sought to test the constitutionality of the federal carriage tax in court, with John Taylor, who would soon introduce the Virginia Resolution in the state legislature, urging the federal circuit court to begin "deciding constitutional cases, like other judicial cases—independently of political influence, upon free discussion, and without a risqué of any disagreeable consequence to the party propounding them."[96] Even in 1798, Jefferson reassured a correspondent that "upright judges, would protect you from any exercise of power unauthorized by the Constitution of the United States."[97]

Having accepted the device, Madison became the stauncher advocate of judicial authority.[98] Madison was particularly moved, as many were,

[94] Jefferson, "To James Madison, March 19, 1787," in *The Works of Thomas Jefferson*, ed. Paul Leicester Ford, 12 vols. (New York: G. P. Putnam's Sons. 1904–5), 5:284. On Jefferson and judicial review, see David N. Mayer, *The Constitutional Thought of Thomas Jefferson* (Charlottesville: University Press of Virginia, 1994), 257–94. On Madison, see Jack N. Rakove, "Judicial Power in the Constitutional Theory of James Madison," *William and Mary Law Review* 43 (2002): 1513.

[95] Jefferson, "To James Madison, March 15, 1789," in *Works*, ed. Ford, 5:461.

[96] Robert P. Frankel Jr., "Before *Marbury* : *Hylton v. United States* and the Origins of Judicial Review," *Journal of Supreme Court History* 28 (2003): 1, 6.

[97] Thomas Jefferson, "To Archibald H. Rowan, September 26, 1798," in *Works*, ed. Ford, 8:448.

[98] When the Pennsylvania governor wrote to recently inaugurated President Madison looking for a way out of an impasse over the state's refusal to comply with a federal judge's order in a long-simmering Revolutionary War–era prize case, Madison took a hard line: "The Executive of the U. States, is not only unauthorized to prevent the execution of a Decree sanctioned by the Supreme Court of the U. States, but is expressly enjoined by Statute, to carry into effect any such decree, where opposition may be made to it. It is propitious circumstance therefore, that whilst no legal discretion lies with the Executive of the U. States to decline steps which might lead to a very painful issue, a provision has been made by the Legislative Act transmitted to you, adequate to a removal of the existing difficulty." Madi-

by the prospect of internecine violence and the promise of the judiciary as a way of securing union and preserving the peace.[99] In the *Federalist*, Madison held up the Supreme Court "as the tribunal which is ultimately to decide" the limits of state and federal power. Every effort would be made to insure the Court's impartiality and independence in resolving such issues, but regardless, "some such tribunal is clearly essential to prevent an appeal to the sword and a dissolution of the compact."[100] Decades later, Madison continued to affirm those early views despite the Court's doctrinal missteps. At least in those cases "not of that extreme character" the Court was "the authority constitutionally provided for deciding controversies concerning the boundaries of right and power."[101] The alternative to such a "peaceful and effectual" system was likely to be "the sword."[102] "Without losing sight" of Jeffersonian departmentalism, the retired Madison explained to a correspondent, "it may always be expected that the judicial bench, when happily filled, will . . . most engage the respect and reliance of the public as the surest expositor of the Constitution."[103]

---

son, "To Simon Snyder, April 13, 1809," in *The Papers of James Madison*, ed. Robert A. Rutland and Thomas A. Mason, vol. 1 (Charlottesville: University Press of Virginia, 1984), 114. In response to Pennsylvania's actions a leading Republican paper, the *Philadelphia Aurora*, distinguished this episode from earlier Jeffersonian battles with the judiciary: "[H]ere is a point at which the independence of the Judiciary, in its strict and constitutional sense, exists and demands to be supported and maintained." Quoted in Warren, *Supreme Court*, 1:379. Pennsylvania quickly backed down, and the influential *Richmond Enquirer* drew the lesson for the future (referencing the Chase impeachment), "The true doctrine is this: let the decisions of the Federal Courts be paramount, but as a pledge that these decisions should not entrench upon the sovereignty of the States or the provisions of the Constitution, let the Judges be more responsible in all impeachments." Quoted in Warren, 1:387. Madison expressed relief when Pennsylvania backed down "without the threatened collisions of force. It is bad eno' as it is; but a blessing compared with such a result." Madison, "To Caesar Rodney, April 22, 1809," in *Papers*, 1:131. The immediate case at issue was U.S. v. Peters, 9 U.S. 115 (1809). On the politics surrounding the case, see Gary D. Rowe, "Constitutionalism in the Streets," *Southern California Law Review* 78 (2005): 401.

[99] On the Constitution as a "peace pact" among the states, see David C. Hendrickson, *Peace Pact* (Lawrence: University Press of Kansas, 2003); Daniel Deudney, "The Philadelphia System: Sovereignty, Arms Control, and Balance of Power in the American States-Union, Circa 1787–1861," *International Organization* 49 (1995): 191.

[100] Hamilton, Madison, and Jay, *The Federalist Papers*, No. 39, 245, 246.

[101] James Madison, "To Joseph C. Cabell, August 16, 1829," in *Writings*, 9:342–43. See also Madison, "To N. P. Trist, December 1831," in *Writings*, 9:471–77; Ibid., "To M. L. Hurlbert, May 1830," in *Writings*, 9:374; Ibid., "To Spencer Roane, May 6, 1821," in *Writings*, 9:56–59; Ibid., "To Thomas Jefferson, June 27, 1823," in *Writings*, 9:143.

[102] Madison, "To Joseph C. Cabell, September 7, 1829," in *Writings*, 9:348.

[103] James Madison, "To Mr. ——, 1834," in *Letters and Other Writings of James Madison*, vol. 4 (Philadelphia: J. B. Lippincott, 1865), 350. Madison made it clear that he favored this outcome, noting: "It is the Judicial department in which questions of constitutionality, as well as legality, generally find their ultimate discussion and operative decision: and the

Other Jeffersonians were similarly supportive of the Court once past the initial reconstructive conflicts of the Jefferson administration.[104] By the 1810s and 1820s, many shared Madison's interest in a judicial tribunal that could peacefully resolve interstate and federal-state disagreements. In reporting the Court's opinion upholding the seizure of a Massachusetts ship caught trading with the enemy during the War of 1812, the primary Madisonian newspaper urged New England and "fair and honest merchant[s]" to fall in line with the war effort and recognize the Court as "a branch of the Government which it is important to hold in due veneration, and whose decisions are entitled to the highest respect."[105] President James Monroe was a lifelong friend of Chief Justice Marshall and frequently sent copies of his addresses and writings to the justices. New York senator Rufus King observed to Monroe, who was deliberating on a judicial appointment, "No other nation has a tribunal so powerful, conclusive and independent," since it decides "all questions arising under the Constitution, which by restricting or enlarging the power of the States or the Union may disturb the nice and complicated balance of our political system."[106] William Wirt, Monroe's respected attorney general, dismissed the "few exasperated portions of our people" who, responding to "local irritations," favored "narrowing the sphere of action of that Court and subduing its energies." The "far greater number . . . wish to see it in the free and independent exercise of its constitutional powers, as the best means of preserving the Constitution itself."[107] Before the Court itself in

---

public deference to and confidence in the judgment of the body are peculiarly inspired by the qualities implied in its members; by the gravity and deliberation of their proceedings; and by the advantage their plurality gives them over the unity of the Executive department, and their fewness over the multitudinous composition of the Legislative Department." Ibid., 349–50.

[104] Cf. Kramer, *The People Themselves*, 138–69.

[105] *National Intelligencer*, quoted in Warren, *Supreme Court*, 1:429, 430. The case was *The Aurora*, 12 U.S. 203 (1814).

[106] Rufus King, quoted in Warren, *Supreme Court*, 2:52. For further context of Monroe's deliberations, see G. Edward White, *The Marshall Court and Cultural Change, 1815–1835* (New York: Oxford University Press, 1991), 307–18.

[107] William Wirt, quoted in John Pendleton Kennedy, *Memoirs of the Life of William Wirt*, vol. 2 (Philadelphia: Lea and Blanchard, 1850), 134. Virginia Senator James Barbour similarly rose to the Court's defense in the Senate, just weeks before being tapped by John Quincy Adams to serve as secretary of war, arguing that "if ever the time should come, which God avert, that this branch of government, in which was deposited the peace and tranquility of the Union, should commence destroying the rights of the states, and prostrating their independence, instead of the little murmur of excitement that was now occasionally heard, they would hear the voice of the whole nation, swelling as it advanced, till it had announced that the people had felt this oppression committed on their rights, and were about to take decisive measures." But if, "after forty years, it is found that the power of this court has not been abused, they might reasonably expect that it would not be hereafter." *Register of Debates*, 18th Cong., 2nd sess. (15 February 1825), 585.

1824, Wirt asserted that the constitutional framers would deserve praise if they had done "nothing else than to establish this guardian tribunal, to harmonize the jarring elements of our system." The attorney general insisted, "It is the high province of this Court to interpose its benign and mediatorial influence" to "extirpate the seeds of anarchy" and stave off "civil war," by, in this case, striking down New York's steamship monopoly.[108] When the Court acceded to the administration's request, newspapers across the country and political spectrum "rejoiced over the destruction of the obnoxious steamboat Monopoly."[109]

Wirt's belief in the Court's ability to "interpose your friendly hand" to end political and constitutional controversy echoed Marshall's own beliefs. In his *McCulloch* opinion in 1819, the chief justice observed the bank controversy that pitted "a sovereign State" against the "legislature of the Union" and involved the "most interesting and vital parts" of the Constitution affecting the "great operations of the government," and determined that the issue must be decided, and be "decided peacefully." If the bank issue were to be decided peacefully, Marshall declared, "by this tribunal alone can the decision be made. On the Supreme Court of the United States has the Constitution of our country devolved this important duty."[110] As Marshall later elaborated in a pseudonymous defense of his opinion, for judges alone is "their paramount interest . . . public prosperity." Indeed, "[I]f we were now making, instead of a controversy, a constitution, where else could this important duty of deciding questions which grow out of the constitution, and the laws of the union, be safely and wisely placed."[111] The Court was not the first to interpret the Constitution's relevance to the Bank of the United States, but Marshall insisted that it should be the last. In the post–New Deal context, *McCulloch* is often read as a deferential decision upholding congressional authority. In the context of the time, however, *McCulloch* was decidedly activist, but the activism was directed against the states on behalf of the national constitutional regime.[112]

Like many of the Marshall Court's decisions during this period, *McCulloch* was well calculated to enhance judicial authority by aligning the Court with other national actors.[113] The sweeping nationalist vision ex-

---

[108] Gibbons v. Ogden, 22 U.S. 1, 229 (1824).

[109] Warren, *Supreme Court*, 2:72.

[110] McCulloch v. Maryland, 17 U.S. 316, 400, 401 (1819).

[111] John Marshall, "A Friend of the Constitution," in *John Marshall's Defense of McCulloch v Maryland*, ed. Gerald Gunther (Stanford, CA: Stanford University Press, 1969), 212, 208.

[112] See also Whittington, "The Road Not Taken," 365.

[113] See especially Graber, "Federalist or Friends," 229. See also Michael J. Klarman, "How Great were the 'Great' Marshall Court Decisions?" *Virginia Law Review* 87 (2001): 1111.

pressed in Marshall's opinion met with fierce denunciation "by the democracy in Virginia," as Marshall reported to Justice Joseph Story, but by 1819 the national Jeffersonians had accepted both the constitutionality of the bank and the necessity of judicial intervention against state obstruction of its operation.[114] As Wirt explained when urging the Court to act in the *McCulloch* case, the Monroe administration considered the bank issue long-since settled, "ratified by the voice of the people, and sanctioned by precedent."[115]

In reaching the result widely desired in national political circles, Marshall seized the opportunity to express a broad view of federal power that was consistent with the emerging group of "National Republicans" but at odds with the more orthodox states-rights Jeffersonianism defended in the elected branches. Madison spoke for many Jeffersonians in complaining about "the general and abstract doctrine interwoven with the decision of the particular case" common in Marshall's opinions even when "the occasion did not call for" it.[116] Although bolstering the authority of the Court to engage in constitutional enforcement against the states, the more strict constructionist-minded Jeffersonians feared that Marshall's opinions "break down the landmarks intended by a specification of the Powers of Congress."[117] Here, judicial authority would have to be bounded by the recognition that there were "limitations and exceptions to its efficient character" and that the Court did not have the right of "exclusively ex-

---

[114] John Marshall, quoted in Warren, *Supreme Court*, 1:515. Marshall wrote similarly to Bushrod Washington, observing that the administration and its allies "have no objection to a decision in favor of the Bank since the good patriots who administer the government wished it, and would probably have been offended with us had we dared to have decided otherwise, but they required an obsequious, silent opinion without reasons." Quoted in Dwight Wiley Jessup, *Reaction and Accommodation* (New York: Garland, 1987), 196.

[115] McCulloch, v. Maryland, 17 U.S. 316, 353. President Monroe expressed this view directly to Secretary of State John Quincy Adams and future Bank of the United States president Nicholas Biddle. John Quincy Adams, *Memoirs of John Quincy Adams*, ed. Charles Francis Adams, vol. 4 (Philadelphia: J. B. Lippincott, 1875), 499; Harry Ammon, *James Monroe* (New York: McGraw-Hill, 1971), 467–68. The Court was widely expected to render the decision that it did in the *McCulloch* case, and days after the case was argued a bill to repeal the bank charter was soundly defeated in the House of Representatives (the advocates of repeal focused more on policy than constitutional issues). Warren, *Supreme Court*, 1:509; *House Journal*, 15th Cong., 2nd sess., 25 February 1819, 308.

[116] Madison, "To Spencer Roane, September 2, 1819," in *Writings*, 8:447. See also Madison, "To Spencer Roane, May 6, 1821," in *Writings*, 9:56; Jefferson, "To Spencer Roane, September 6, 1819," in *Works*, ed. Ford, 12:136; John Randolph, "To Dr. Brockenbrough, March 3, 1824," in Hugh A. Garland, *Life of John Randolph of Roanoke*, vol. 2 (1854), 212 (of the *Gibbons* opinion, "It contains a great deal that has no business there, or indeed anywhere. . . . A judicial opinion should decide nothing and embrace nothing that is not before the Court").

[117] Madison, "To Spencer Roane, September 2, 1819," in *Writings*, 8:448.

plaining the Constitution."[118] Congress would have to be convinced through extrajudicial means, including the presidential veto and "sound arguments & conciliatory expostulations addressed both to Congress & to their Constituents," to "abstain from the exercise of Powers claimed for them by the Court."[119]

In the early nineteenth century, political efforts to encourage and support judicial enforcement of the regime's constitutional commitments against dissident states were as much a matter of preserving the union and preventing violence as they were of bringing outliers into line with national constitutional norms. Especially after the sectional tensions of the Missouri Compromise and the South Carolinian nullification crisis, national political leaders were eager to direct constitutional disputes into the courts for settlement.[120] The federal judiciary could plausibly claim to be an impartial tribunal for resolving disputes pitting states against states and states against individuals. Its impartiality was subject to greater question in the case of disputes between the national and state governments, but, as Madison warned, "as some such Tribunal is a vital element, a sine qua non, in an efficient & permanent Govt. the Tribunal existing must be acquiesced in, until a better or more satisfactory one can be substituted."[121] By the time of Lincoln's election, the Court was no longer a

[118] Madison, "To Spencer Roane, May 6, 1821," in *Writings*, 9:62; Jefferson, "To Judge Spencer Roane, September 6, 1819," in *Works*, ed. Ford, 12:137.

[119] Madison, "To Spencer Roane, May 6, 1821," in *Writings*, 9:59. On Jeffersonian and Jacksonian presidential vetoes enforcing a more limited conception of congressional power, see Whittington, "The Road Not Taken," 374–77; Graber, "Naked Land Transfers," 73, 111–12. See also Graber, "Jacksonian Origins," 17.

[120] See, e.g., Senator Lewis Cass, *Congressional Globe*, 33rd Cong., 2nd sess., 17 January 1855, 298 ("[M]y desire is to have a judiciary dependent on moral, and not physical force. I repeat, it is a great moral spectacle to see the decree of the Judges of our Supreme Court on the most vital questions obeyed in such a country as this. . . . They have stopped armed men in our country"). On the Jacksonian appointments to the Supreme Court, Benjamin Wright remarked, "[T]he most significant fact is that all were lawyers and all held it as a cardinal principle of politics that the Court was the final arbitral authority." Benjamin F. Wright, *The Growth of American Constitutional Law* (Chicago: University of Chicago Press, 1967), 57.

[121] James Madison, "To N. P. Trist, February 15, 1830," in *Writings*, 9:355. In response to a call from Pennsylvania for the creation of an "impartial tribunal to determine disputes between the general and state governments," the Virginia legislature observed in 1810, as Madison no doubt believed as well, that such "a tribunal is already provided by the Constitution of the United States, *to wit*: the Supreme Court, more eminently qualified to decide the disputes aforesaid in an enlightened and impartial manner than any other tribunal which could be created." "Resolution of the Legislature of Pennsylvania, April 3, 1809," in *State Documents on Federal Relations*, ed. Herman V. Ames (Philadelphia: University of Pennsylvania, 1900), 48; "Reply of the General Assembly of Virginia to Pennsylvania, January 25, 1810," in ibid., 49. For an example of the doubts about the Court's adequacy for this purpose, see John C. Calhoun, "To Frederick W. Symmes, July 26, 1831," in *The Papers of*

plausible means of preventing "anarchy & disunion," though this goal had been an important force for building judicial authority and cabining "popular constitutionalism" up to that time.[122]

In the postbellum years, suppression of substantive outliers became more salient. Despite the desire to keep the Court on a short leash to avoid "another *Dred Scott*," or worse, during the Civil War and Reconstruction, congressional Republicans soon empowered the judiciary to extend federal influence into the conquered South.[123] A series of ad hoc extensions of jurisdiction for the federal courts operating in the South culminated in the Jurisdiction and Removal Act of 1875, which gave the judiciary the power to hear all cases involving federal questions from across the country. With a reconstituted membership, the Reconstruction-era Court was "more vigorous in its condemnation of state legislation than at any time since Marshall's most active years."[124]

John C. Calhoun, ed. Clyde N. Wilson, vol. 11 (Columbia: University of South Carolina Press, 1978), 423 ("The Judges are, in fact, as truly the Judicial Representatives of this united majority, as the majority of Congress itself, or the President, is its legislative, or executive representative. . . . Nor will the tenure by which the Judges hold their office . . . materially vary the case. Its highest possible effect would be to *retard* and not *finally* to *resist*, the will of a dominant majority"); ibid., "To Virgil Maxcy, September 1, 1831," in *Papers*, 464 ("The question is in truth between the people & the supreme court. . . . I hold him a shallow statesman, who, after proper examination, does not see, which is most in conformity to the genius of our system and the most effective & safe in its operation"); ibid., "To James Hamilton, Jr., August 28, 1832," in *Papers*, 625 ("the high authority, claimed for the Supreme Court, to adjust such controversies" has been unable to settle even "a single question, of a political character, which has ever been agitated"). On the competing constitutional claims in the nullification crisis, see Whittington, *Constitutional Construction*, 72–112.

[122] Madison, "To N. P. Trist, December 1831," in *Writings*, 9:476. On "popular constitutionalism" and its development over time, see Kramer, *The People Themselves*, ch. 6.

[123] See Friedman, "Transformation in Senate Response," 5–21.

[124] Wright, *Growth of Constitutional Law*, 82. The Court struck down ten state laws in 1867 alone, more than double the number voided in any previous year. On the eve of the *Dred Scott* decision, Republican representative Benjamin Stanton had unsuccessfully proposed reorganizing judiciary to give "all sections of the Confederacy their equal and just representation to the Supreme Court of the United States." Stanton argued that "the Supreme Court is the ultimate arbiter of all questions arising upon the Constitution and the laws of the United States, and, therefore, should be so constituted as to command the confidence of the whole people in all sections of the country." With the South's disproportionate influence on the Court, "its decisions can have no moral power, and cannot command the confidence of the people." Stanton would admit that the Court "is the final arbiter in every case which it decides, because there is no appeal from it," but Stanton would "not surrender any individual opinion to the decision of the Court" and would "deny the principle on which that decision was founded, and say it was not law." Only a representative Court could "give a construction to the Constitution" that Stanton would recognize "as the true one." *Congressional Globe*, 34th Cong., 3rd sess., 12 December 1857, 300. Stanton urged the Democratic House to reorganize the judiciary now, "voluntarily, and with a good grace,

The final version of the Fourteenth Amendment had moved the authorization of congressional enforcement of its terms from the first section to the fifth, allowing the amendment's guarantees of equality and liberty against the state governments to stand on their own footing as direct commandments subject to judicial interpretation and application. As one Republican congressman explained to his colleagues, "[N]ow, when we have the power in this Government, the power in this Congress, and the power in the States to make the Constitution what we desire it to be, I want to secure those rights against accidents, against the accidental majority of Congress." The definition and enforcement of those constitutional securities would not be left "to the caprice of Congress."[125] As congressional attention and commitment wavered after Reconstruction, "[T]he Court— a small, cohesive institution whose function is to respond to precise questions with a single answer that a majority of its members support—had become the amendment's main interpreter."[126] As economics became the most salient feature of the Republican constitutional regime, the Court was in the vanguard of enforcing its requirements.

A primary constitutional and legal project of the late nineteenth century was the "judicial construction of a national market," and the courts moved aggressively to strike down state "legislative barriers ["to the consolidation of the national market"] almost as fast they were erected."[127] With an eye on national policymakers, the Court wielded the "dormant" commerce clause to keep states in line with "matters of national concern."[128] The Court would enforce the general constitutional rule, leaving it to Congress "to indicate such exceptions as in its judgment a wise discretion may demand under particular circumstances" but "[i]ts nonaction in such cases . . . is a declaration of its purpose that the commerce . . . shall be free."[129] Congress cooperated by being "remarkably restrained," leaving the definition of the constitutional scope of state regulatory action to the courts.[130] When the "corporations uniformly fell back

---

and not postpone it until you have no longer the power of resistance." Ibid., 301. The judicial reorganization was accomplished by the Republican Congress in 1862.

[125] Representative Giles Hotchkiss, *Congressional Globe*, 39th Cong., 1st sess., 28 February 1866, 1095. See also William E. Nelson, *The Fourteenth Amendment* (Cambridge: Harvard University Press, 1988), 142–47.

[126] Nelson, *The Fourteenth Amendment*, 149.

[127] Bensel, *Political Economy*, 321.

[128] Kutler, *Judicial Power*, 127. Kutler points out that this meant using judicial discretion since it "often operated without the benefit of asserted [legislative] national policy," and that sometimes required leaving the disputed state policy in place if it was "unlikely that Congress would fill the void left by the invalidation of state regulation." Kutler, 126.

[129] Lyng v. Michigan, 135 U.S. 161, 167 (1889); Webber v. Virginia, 103 U.S. 344, 351 (1880).

[130] Bensel, *Political Economy*, 348.

on their constitutional guaranties . . . [and] sought shelter behind the Constitution of the United States" from the ravages of various locally influential farmers' movements, the Court, after some initial hesitation, stood ready to extend constitutional protection to them.[131] By the final decades of the nineteenth century, "the legislatures of the States . . . [were] subject to the superintendence of the judiciary" as the Court elaborated the economic liberties it found in the Constitution and the Fourteenth Amendment, and talk of the "centralizing tendencies in the Supreme Court" was commonplace.[132]

The Court received plenty of encouragement to seize the lead in implementing these constitutional understandings. Although reformist elements made few inroads in the national government during these decades, they were able to set policy in a number of states. Conservatives called for the courts to intervene to stop the menace. Christopher Tiedeman, in the preface of his influential treatise on the limits of the constitutional authority of the states, called for "a full appreciation of the power of constitutional limitations to protect private rights against the radical experimentation of social reformers."[133] This view was echoed across the country by the increasingly organized and vocal legal profession, which found strong support in the national legislature and executive. The 1890 centennial celebration of the Supreme Court, suggested by President Benjamin Harrison, presided over by former president Grover Cleveland, and sponsored by the New York Bar Association, featured speakers emphasizing the "imperative duty of the court to enforce with a firm hand every guarantee of the constitution" and the value of "an independent judi-

---

[131] C. F. Adams, Jr., "The Granger Movement," *North American Review* 120 (1875): 394, 413. The early movement to address barriers to interstate commerce helped beget the later movement to create substantive barriers to state interference with the rights of property. The Court introduced its substantive due process and right to contract doctrines in just such cases. E.g., Smyth v. Ames, 169 U.S. 466 (1898) (striking down a state-imposed railroad rate as a deprivation of property without due process of law); Allgeyer v. Louisiana, 165 U.S. 578 (1897) (striking down a state ban on out-of-state marine insurance as an unconstitutional interference with "an ordinary calling or trade").

[132] "Notes of Recent Decisions: Regulation of Railway Fares," *American Law Review* 24 (1890): 516, 521 (emphasis omitted); Fred Perry Powers, "Recent Centralizing Tendencies in the Supreme Court," *Political Science Quarterly* 5 (1890): 389. On developments in this period, see Warren, *Supreme Court*, 3:463–90; Gillman, *The Constitution Besieged*, 61–146; Owen M. Fiss, *Troubled Beginnings of the Modern State, 1888–1910*, vol. 8 of *History of the Supreme Court of the United States* (New York: Macmillan, 1993); William F. Swindler, *The Old Legality, 1889–1932*, vol. 1 of *Court and Constitution in the Twentieth Century* (Indianapolis: Bobbs-Merrill, 1969); John E. Semonche, *Charting the Future* (Westport, CT: Greenwood Press, 1978).

[133] Christopher G. Tiedeman, *A Treatise on the Limitations of Police Powers in the United States* (St. Louis: F. H. Thomas Law Book Co., 1886), viii.

ciary" as "the true and final custodian of the liberty of the subject."[134] The nationwide 1901 centennial celebration of the appointment of John Marshall to the Court was organized by the American Bar Association and largely used to celebrate the power of courts to interpret and enforce the Constitution, the American innovation that threw off "the doctrines and theories engendered by the French Revolution—the supreme and uncontrollable right of the people to govern."[135] Future-justice Joseph R. Lamar observed in 1902 that society was "voluntarily referring [to the judiciary] the solution of the new problems and the difficult questions of this age."[136]

The activism of the Warren Court in the mid–twentieth century was likewise largely directed at the states and is best understood in the context of regime elaboration and enforcement. In placing the Warren Court in "historical and political perspective," Mark Tushnet, for example, observes that "[o]n the ideological level the Warren Court fully participated in the grand sweep of political liberalism that pervaded the political system, in various guises, from the New Deal to the Reagan Revolution."[137] Although the 1954 *Brown* decision dramatically launched Earl Warren's tenure as chief justice, it reflected the developments of the Vinson Court, and the distinctive Warren-era did not truly emerge until the 1960s.[138] In 1961, the Supreme Court struck down more state laws than in any year since the 1920s, and over the remaining years of Warren's tenure the Court nullified state laws at an annual rate three times as high as during Warren's first years. When President Kennedy had the opportunity to replace two of the more conservative members of the early Warren Court (Charles Whittaker and Felix Frankfurter) in the spring of 1962, he consulted with core members of the liberal wing of the Court on the selection

[134] Stephen J. Field, "The Centenary of the Supreme Court of the United States," *American Law Review* 24 (1890): 351, 367; Edward J. Phelps, quoted in Arnold M. Paul, *Conservative Crisis and the Rule of Law* (New York: Harper & Row, 1969), 64. Field had been chosen by the justices to speak on behalf of the Court. It is interesting to note that even in 1890, Field gave substantial attention to the historically unprecedented "spectacle" that "controversies between States . . . shall be submitted to the peaceful and orderly modes of judicial procedure for settlement"; "no provision of the constitution can be mentioned more honorable to the country or more expressive of its Christian civilization." Field, 360.

[135] John F. Dillon, introduction to *John Marshall*, ed. John F. Dillon, vol. 1 (Chicago: Callaghan, 1903), xviii. See also Davison M. Douglas, "The Rhetorical Uses of *Marbury v. Madison*: The Emergence of a 'Great Case,'" *Wake Forest Law Review* 38 (2003): 375, 398–403; Michael Kammen, *A Machine That Would Go of Itself* (New York: Vintage, 1986), 209–13.

[136] Joseph R. Lamar, quoted in Friedman, "Transformation in Senate Response," 59.

[137] Mark Tushnet, "The Warren Court as History: An Interpretation," in *The Warren Court in Historical and Political Perspective*, ed. Mark Tushnet (Charlottesville: University of Virginia Press, 1993), 3.

[138] See also Klarman, *Jim Crow*; McMahon, *Reconsidering Roosevelt on Race*.

of their new colleagues before settling on Byron White and Arthur Goldberg.[139] Through long personal acquaintance the Kennedy brothers thought White was someone "who generally agreed with your views of the country" and was "basically an activist," but he proved to be a "blunt instrument" on the Court.[140] Goldberg in particular, having told his wife that he "intended to be an activist judge," proved to be the key vote in solidifying a liberal majority, and the president made an appearance at his swearing in and the opening of the Court's 1962 term.[141] As Scot Powe concluded in his history of the Warren Court, by the time White and Goldberg assumed their place on the bench, the mainstream criticisms of the Court had largely died down and the Court had "found friends in high places. . . . The best description of the period is that all three branches of government believed they were working harmoniously to tackle the nation's problems" and the Court was "reaching results that conformed to the values that enjoyed significant national support in the mid-1960s."[142]

Although Warren had personally favored the perennial Adlai Stevenson for the Democratic nomination in 1960, Kennedy proved to be a strong supporter of the Warren Court and the judiciary's constitutional authority. It was well known that relations between Eisenhower and Warren had turned chilly by the end of the former's administration, and Kennedy entered office determined to cultivate the good feelings of the chief justice and his brethren. As an initial gesture of good will, the president invited Warren to sit with him in the reviewing stand for his inauguration pa-

[139] Warren and William O. Douglas tried to douse Robert Kennedy's desire to name circuit court judge William Hastie to be the first black justice on the Court, warning the attorney general that Hastie "wasn't liberal enough," "opposed to all the measures we are interested in . . . completely unsatisfactory," and "very conservative." Yalof, *Pursuit of Justices*, 236n44; Schwartz, *Super Chief*, 428. Nonetheless, Yalof concludes that Kennedy did not have any particular selection criteria, "ideological or otherwise," for choosing justices. Yalof, 80. Generally, the administration looked for "a judge who is a careful liberal, . . . liberal yet cautious." Deputy Attorney General Nicholas Katzenbach, quoted in Goldman, *Picking Federal Judges*, 163.

[140] Robert Kennedy, quoted in Randy L. Sowell, "Judicial Vigor: The Warren Court and the Kennedy Administration," Ph.D. diss., University of Kansas, 1992, 230 ("generally agreed"); unnamed friend, quoted in Anthony Lewis, "Byron White Gets Whittaker's Seat on the Supreme Court," *New York Times*, 31 March 1962, 10 ("activist"); Sowell, 148 ("blunt instrument").

[141] Powe, *Warren Court*, 211; Schwartz, *Super Chief*, 445–46. The importance of the appointments was highlighted by the immediate change of majorities in several cases argued before the resignations but not issued until after the replacements. See Schwartz, 449–57. Former justice Sherman Minton later wrote to Frankfurter of the latter's successor, "Mr. J. Goldberg is a walking Constitutional Convention! Wow what an activist he is!" Schwartz, 446.

[142] Powe, *Warren Court*, 214, 215.

rade.[143] Kennedy reportedly assured Warren that he would supply the public support for the Court's decisions that the previous administration was disinclined, for reasons of constitutional form and legal substance, to offer.[144] They soon developed a "warm relationship," with Kennedy making frequent appearances at the weekly gatherings of Warren and his clerks (a practice sustained by President Lyndon Johnson). On Warren's seventy-third birthday, Kennedy sent a congratulatory message thanking Warren for the "dignity and wisdom of your judicial leadership" and concluding that "in a very real sense we are all your students."[145] When asked at a press conference about proposals to amend the Constitution to weaken the Court, Kennedy was clear that the Court "is one of the most important protections of individual rights and one of the most important securities for we have for an amicable settlement of disputes" and expressed pleasure that such "efforts will come to nothing."[146] According to one Warren biographer, "For Warren personally, few things were more gratifying than the Kennedy support for the Court and the constant deference which the President displayed toward the Chief Justice."[147] Lyndon Johnson was similarly deferential. Johnson had exercised visible leadership in the Senate in 1958 to help turn back a measure to deprive the Court of jurisdiction over national security cases after a series of Court decisions favoring Communist litigants.[148] As president, Johnson showered affection on Warren, whom he called "the greatest Chief Justice of them all."[149]

Like the Republican Court of the late nineteenth and early twentieth centuries, the Warren Court's constitutional leadership extended regime commitments beyond the issues central to the initial reconstruction (race in the case of the Republicans, economics in the case of the New Deal). The Warren Court's efforts extended across a wider range of more loosely connected issues than did the earlier Court's, however. The "civil rights and civil liberties revolutions" of the Warren era, nonetheless, were cen-

---

[143] Schwartz, *Super Chief*, 390, 388.

[144] Sowell, "Judicial Vigor," 130.

[145] Schwartz, *Super Chief*, 63; John F. Kennedy, quoted in Schwartz, 390, 391.

[146] Kennedy, "The President's News Conference of May 8, 1963," in *Public Papers of the Presidents of the United States: John F. Kennedy, 1963* (Washington, DC: Government Printing Office, 1964), 375.

[147] Schwartz, *Super Chief*, 491. Warren later said that Kennedy's death "was like losing one of my own sons." Quoted in John D. Weaver, *Warren* (Boston: Little, Brown, 1967), 300.

[148] Walter F. Murphy, *Congress and the Court* (Chicago: University of Chicago Press, 1962), 196–223; Robert A. Caro, *Master of the Senate*, vol. 3 of *The Years of Lyndon Johnson* (New York: Vintage, 2002), 1030–33.

[149] Lyndon B. Johnson, quoted in Schwartz, *Super Chief*, 583. On Johnson's personal catering to Warren, see Schwartz, 581–83.

trally concerned with enforcing the evolving constitutional understandings of the "Democratic political order" against resistant states.[150] Though a critical electoral and legislative component of the New Deal coalition, the South emerged as a hindrance to the consolidation of "American liberalism" early in Franklin Roosevelt's administration and remained so through the Great Society, obstructing both the programmatic ambitions of the New Deal liberalism and its reach into the domestic affairs of the southern states.[151] The political weight of southern Democrats, acutely felt by Roosevelt and his successors, did not directly impinge on the justices. Overviewing the Court's constitutional jurisprudence, Powe concluded that "the dominant motif of the Warren Court is an assault on the South as a unique legal and cultural region" that was "designed to force the South to conform to northern—that is, national—norms."[152] The enforcement of the racial civil rights commitments embraced by national Democratic officials propelled the Court not only in its explicit racial desegregation cases but also in many of its pioneering civil liberties cases, especially in regards to free speech and criminal justice. Relatedly, the Court's innovations on obscenity and religion were largely targeted at the South and a handful of localities that were predominantly Catholic. Such decisions were welcomed by mainstream Protestants and post–Vatican II Catholics, who rushed to defend the Court against conservative critics.[153] Of course, the classic instance of regime enforcement against state outliers came in *Griswold v. Connecticut*, where the Court articulated a new constitutional right to privacy in order to strike down Connecticut's unique and rarely enforced ban on contraceptives.[154]

Division of Labor

Political officials are willing to give away powers when those powers do not matter to them. Power is to some extent a primary good (politicians simply want to be powerful), but it is foremost an instrumental good

---

[150] Klarman, "Rethinking Revolutions," 1; David Plotke, *Building a Democratic Political Order* (New York: Cambridge University Press, 1996).

[151] See Plotke, *Democratic Political Order*; James T. Patterson, *Congressional Conservatism and the New Deal* (Lexington: University of Kentucky Press, 1967); Milkis, *President and the Parties*; Katznelson, Geiger, and Kryder, "Limiting Liberalism," 283; Forbath, "Caste, Class," 1; William E. Forbath, "The New Deal Constitution in Exile," *Duke Law Journal* 51 (2001): 165; Alan Brinkley, *The End of Reform* (New York: Knopf, 1995).

[152] Powe, *Warren Court*, 490.

[153] See, e.g., ibid., 361–63; Klarman, "Rethinking Revolutions," 46–62.

[154] Griswold v. Connecticut, 381 U.S. 479 (1965). On the limited national effects of the Supreme Court's review of state statutes, see also Thomas A. Schmeling, "That Dreadful Class of Evils: Supreme Court Countermajoritarianism in Cases Invalidating State Laws, 1880–2003," unpublished paper.

(politicians want power to accomplish other ends). To the extent that giving away some relatively unimportant power can advance other goals, political actors will be willing to make that exchange. Of course, the power to define constitutional meaning is not an unimportant power. From a political perspective, however, that interpretive authority might be used to achieve relatively low-salience political goals. Judicial authority may be bolstered by political officials if they expect that courts will largely operate around the political margins. Elected officials can then husband their resources to go after bigger political game.

This pattern is somewhat familiar from the legislative context. Since there is a glut of demand on the time of modern legislators, they must prioritize. Even activities that could, on balance, be regarded as politically profitable could be pushed aside by a legislator determined to invest his limited time in activities with even higher returns. Thus, legislators may invest a marginal unit of their time in the fund-raising needed for conducting electoral campaigns at the "wholesale" level rather than the neighborhood canvassing needed for conducting electoral campaigns at the "retail" level. They may invest a marginal unit of time in constituency service rather than bureaucratic oversight.[155] They may take on issues that are newsworthy and of evident relevance to constituents rather than those that are dull and esoteric. They may spend time deciding how to cast a vote when the issue is an important one, but rely on cues from others when the vote is likely to have little personal consequence.[156] Legislators will preserve decision making in their own hands when there are substantial political benefits to be accrued from rendering a decision themselves, but may leave the decision to others when the issues have low political salience.

Elected officials may tolerate and even favor judicial authority when the courts operate in issue areas of relatively low political salience. An informal division of labor can easily develop in which elected officials are seen to render decisions that will win political plaudits while judges toil over decisions that are deemed unworthy of legislative attention. This obviously does not describe many of the constitutional issues that we most associate with judicial review, but that is true almost by definition. The Court's most celebrated and reviled decisions are precisely on high-salience issues, but these are relatively few and far between. The more routine constitutional activity of the Court, especially before the creation

---

[155] See, e.g., Morris P. Fiorina, *Congress: Keystone of the Washington Establishment*, 2nd ed. (New Haven: Yale University Press, 1989); Mathew D. McCubbins and Thomas A. Schwartz, "Congressional Oversight Overlooked: Police Patrols versus Fire Alarms," *American Journal of Political Science* 28 (1984): 165.

[156] On decisional shortcuts adopted by legislators, see John W. Kingdon, *Congressmen's Voting Decisions*, 3rd ed. (Ann Arbor: University of Michigan Press, 1989).

of the discretionary docket in the early twentieth century, is substantially less remarkable. The majority of the state and federal policies invalidated by the Court in John Gates's study, for example, were not salient to the core issues driving the politics of the period in which they were rendered.[157] Oliver Wendell Holmes once admitted the Court was quiet, but that it was the "quiet of a storm center."[158] While this is clearly true, both sides of the comment have to be noted. The Court occasionally unleashes political storms, but most of the Court's work goes unreported in the media and unnoticed by the general public.[159] Even Supreme Court justices generally work in the kind of obscurity that would make an elected representative feel faint. Legislators can afford to tolerate independent judicial decision-making when the alternative is spending additional time on those issues themselves. Legislators may gain political benefit by taking positions on some of the more high-profile constitutional issues that the Court addresses, but legislators who might consider encroaching on the Court's constitutional territory are likely to find little political credit to be claimed there.[160] Courts can build authority by specializing in the type of issues that complement the agenda of other political actors.

Mark Graber has uncovered a particularly clear case of such a division of labor between Congress and the Supreme Court in the early nineteenth century. The standard narrative of the pre–Civil War Court is that it only exercised the power of judicial review against a federal statute twice, once in *Marbury*, where it invalidated a provision of the Judiciary Act of 1789 in order to escape a conflict with the executive, and once, a half century later, in *Dred Scott*, where it disastrously waded into the slavery dispute by invalidating the already superseded Missouri Compromise (though with widely recognized implications for the ongoing slavery debate). Graber has helped fill in the historical and political gap between these

---

[157] Gates, *Partisan Realignment*, 170. These numbers are only suggestive for my purposes. Most notably, Gates is using "salient" in a somewhat different sense than I am using it here, since he is concerned with salience of partisan divisions and the organization of electoral politics rather than salience to public attention, though the two are clearly related. There is also significant variation over time in the Court's focus on salient issues.

[158] Holmes, "Speech at a Dinner," 292.

[159] Elliot E. Slotnick and Jennifer A. Segal, *Television News and the Supreme Court* (New York: Cambridge University Press, 1998); Richard Davis, *Decisions and Images* (Englewood Cliffs, NJ: Prentice-Hall, 1994); Ethan Katsh, "The Supreme Court Beat: How Television Covers the U.S. Supreme Court," *Judicature* 67 (1983): 6.

[160] David Mayhew classically argued that electorally minded politicians would focus their activities where there were opportunities for persuasively claiming credit to constituents for good results. David R. Mayhew, *Congress: The Electoral Connection* (New Haven: Yale University Press, 1974), 52–61, 121–32 ("Credit claiming is highly important to congressmen, with the consequence that much of congressional life is a relentless search for opportunities to engage in it").

two cases by examining more closely the Court's routine work during the intervening decades. Numerous cases in which the Marshall and Taney Courts imposed "constitutional limits on federal power" have escaped historical notice because the justices on those Courts often operated "through statutory misconstruction and neglect" rather than by ostentatiously declaring a law unconstitutional.[161] This stylistic difference and its historiographical significance is of less immediate relevance than the substantive content and institutional implications of those cases.

In the early decades of the nineteenth century, the Court built support for its constitutional authority by taking action that other political actors would be willing, even eager, to support. We have already observed that this dynamic was in place in the numerous and high-profile cases in which the Court struck down state laws. Perhaps more surprisingly, it also operated in cases in which the Court turned its attention to acts of Congress. The Marshall Court was not about to invalidate the Bank of the United States, of course, but it was interested in preventing Congress from violating what the justices regarded as vested property rights, specifically in cases of disputed land claims that made up much of the federal judiciary's business at that time. Unlike the state property rights cases, these federal cases were rarely controversial as to basic constitutional principles or their application. The interests affected by these decisions were relatively small, and the underlying factual and legal questions at issue were often complicated. But "these politically inconsequential cases" involving "politically uninteresting matters" were the bread and butter of the Court's early constitutional jurisprudence involving Congress and helped routinize the judicial authority to define constitutional requirements.[162]

In the early nineteenth century, the state, territorial, and federal governments were busily granting publicly held lands to private parties for settlement and development. The process was often messy, however, and multiple claimants sometimes appeared for the same parcel of land.[163] Though state and federal legislatures and executive officials sometimes attempted to settle these disputes on their own by extending new grants to specific individuals, the federal judiciary insisted on its ultimate authority to arbitrate these disputes. On the basis of "general principles," the Court asserted, "it is incontestable that a grantee can convey no more than he possesses."[164] Disputed claims could be litigated, and if the Court deter-

---

[161] Graber, "Naked Land Transfers," 113. See also Keith E. Whittington, "Judicial Review of Acts of Congress," unpublished paper.

[162] Graber, "Naked Land Transfers," 78.

[163] For an analysis that places these cases in the context of an "informational model of judicial review" by which legislators tolerate judicial review that results in concededly better policy outcomes, see Whittington, "Legislative Sanctions," 450–53.

[164] Sampeyreac v. United States, 32 U.S. 222, 241 (1833).

mined that an earlier claimant in fact had legal title, then, regardless of legislative determinations, "the second grant" would be "inoperative."[165] Though not firmly rooted in the constitutional text, the "general principles which are common to our free institutions" that the Court asserted in these cases were indeed commonly held, and Congress frequently recognized in statute the constitutional limits on the legislative fixing of property rights that the Court was enforcing.[166] In these and other cases of low political salience, the antebellum Court actively claimed authority to define and enforce constitutional meaning against Congress and the states, and litigants appeared to urge the Court to use that authority.[167] Rather than invest the time and resources that would be needed to handle these matters themselves, legislators acceded to the Court's claims.

Overcoming Gridlock

It has already been noted that the American political system is highly fragmented. This is true within the national government as well as across the federal system. Unlike the strongly majoritarian political systems adopted in some countries, in which narrow electoral majorities are capable of grasping the fairly unitary and centralized levers of governmental power, the political system of the United States puts obstacles in the way of exercising power.[168] Within the national government, the United States has a relatively strong legislature with an independent executive. The legislature itself is constitutionally divided, and those chambers are further fragmented by internal rules, such as the Senate filibuster and the committee system, that distribute power to multiple actors. Often to the great frustration of affiliated leaders, the American system

---

[165] Mayor of New Orleans v. United States, 35 U.S. 662, 731 (1836). This also applied to titles originally derived from foreign countries that had once controlled the territory. "[W]hen a party, holding such a complete title, is encroached upon, he should find protection in the judicial tribunals." Doe ex dem. Barbarie v. Eslava, 50 U.S. 421, 445 (1850).

[166] Fletcher v. Peck, 10 U.S. 87, 139 (1810). On the relevant statutory and treaty language, see Graber, "Naked Land Transfers," 91–98.

[167] The Court offered nonobvious interpretations of federal statutes so as to render them "consistent with the Constitution" in a variety of cases relating to the jurisdiction of courts and the transition between territorial and state governments. Graber, "Naked Land Transfers," 106–12. Although I do not explore the relationship here, the expansion of judicial authority through these cases in the early nineteenth century resembles Dan Carpenter's analysis of "the forging of bureaucratic authority" by executive-branch entrepreneurs in the late nineteenth and early twentieth centuries. Daniel P. Carpenter, The Forging of Bureaucratic Autonomy (Princeton: Princeton University Press, 2001).

[168] Arend Lijphart, Patterns of Democracy (New Haven: Yale University Press, 1999); G. Bingham Powell Jr., Elections as Instruments of Democracy (New Haven: Yale University Press, 2000).

facilitates obstructionism and makes political action difficult without widespread support.[169]

As discussed in the previous chapter, reconstructive leaders seek to draw constitutional authority to themselves and overthrow the interpretive claims of the courts. The interpretive actions of the reconstructive leader lay the ground for new types of government policy and action. The task of reconstructing constitutional understandings is often accompanied by unilateral presidential action and legislative effort to instantiate the new constitutional order. The reconstructive leader is backed by a relatively united political coalition that helps support and advance the constitutional and political project.

Affiliated leaders, while part of a dominant political coalition, face different obstacles. The legacy of the reconstructive act is up for grabs, and there are likely to be a multitude of affiliated actors seeking to assert their own understanding of the fundamental commitments of the regime and their leadership of it. Indeed, the justices themselves jostle for position amidst that crowd. Articulating, and acting upon, constitutional orthodoxy in the context of affiliated politics requires the ability to marshal the necessary political resources, hold together a fractious coalition, and find the tactical and strategic openings that can be exploited.[170]

The Court can sometimes move forward on the constitutional agenda where other political officials cannot. The Court benefits from the fact that it can be inspired by the constitutional vision but operates outside the jumble of legislative and electoral politics. The Court has a relatively streamlined decision-making process and has the power of unilateral action.[171] Where coalition leaders might be constrained by the needs of coalition maintenance and demands of the legislative process, judges have a relatively free hand. They can sometimes move boldly in areas where

[169] On the supermajoritarian character of the American political and constitutional system, see Keith Krehbiel, *Pivotal Politics* (Chicago: University of Chicago Press, 1998); Charles M. Cameron, *Veto Bargaining* (New York: Cambridge University Press, 2000); Keith E. Whittington, "Extrajudicial Constitutional Interpretation," 773, 835–44.

[170] On the political structure of the politics of affiliation, see Skowronek, *The Politics Presidents Make.*

[171] The ability of presidents to also take unilateral action is receiving renewed attention from political scientists. See, e.g., Terry M. Moe and William G. Howell, "The Presidential Power of Unilateral Action," *Journal of Law, Economics, and Organization* 15 (1999): 132; Kenneth R. Mayer, *With the Stroke of a Pen* (Princeton: Princeton University Press, 2001); Phillip J. Cooper, *By Order of the President* (Lawrence: University Press of Kansas, 2002); William G. Howell, *Power Without Persuasion* (Princeton: Princeton University Press, 2003). There are, of course, limits to what the judiciary can achieve by acting unilaterally as well. See, e.g., Gerald Rosenberg, *The Hollow Hope* (Chicago: University of Chicago Press, 1991); David A. Schultz, ed., *Leveraging the Law* (New York: Peter Land, 1998); McCann, "Supreme Court Matters."

coalition leaders are hobbled. To the extent that a friendly judiciary can cut through legislative gridlock to achieve results consistent with regime commitments, affiliated leaders have both an incentive to support judicial authority and a limited capacity to take action to sanction or reverse the decisions that the Court makes. The same gridlock that hampers positive action by elected officials also constrains their responsiveness to judicial actions.

The famed legislative apportionment decision of 1962 is an example of the Court cutting through the "political thicket."[172] Chief Justice Warren later regarded *Baker v. Carr* as "the most important case of my tenure on the Court."[173] As governor of California, Warren had contributed to the preservation of malapportioned and gerrymandered legislative districts, which he later admitted "was frankly a matter of political expediency."[174] "But I saw the situation in a different light on the Court. There, you have a different responsibility." From that perspective, he came to believe that he "was just wrong as Governor."[175] The Court's willingness to intervene in the field was an abrupt departure from the traditional understanding of apportionment being a legislative and deeply political prerogative.

Others on the Court shared Warren's sense of the momentous significance of the case, but for quite different reasons. A bitter dissenter in the case, Frankfurter thought the decision was "bound to stimulate litigation by doctrinaire 'liberals' and the politically ambitious" that could only damage the Court in the long run. His ally John Marshall Harlan agreed and appealed to the swing justices not to open the door to such cases in which partisan politics and interest were so much on the surface. "Today," he noted, "state reapportionment is being espoused by a Democratic administration; the next time it may be supported (or opposed) by a Republican administration. Can it be that it will be only the cynics who may say that the outcome of a particular case was influenced by the political backgrounds or ideologies of the then members of the Court . . . ?"[176] But Congress, Warren countered, had already pushed the justices into serving as "the referee" in state elections.[177] Justice Tom Clark had initially planned to write a dissent in the case, emphasizing that nonjudicial remedies were available to address the malapportioned districts in Tennessee that were immediately at issue. After conducting the research

[172] I borrow here, of course, from Justice Felix Frankfurter. Colegrove v. Green, 328 U.S. 549, 556 (1946).

[173] Earl Warren, *The Memoirs of Earl Warren* (Garden City, NY: Doubleday, 1977), 306.

[174] Ibid., 310.

[175] Earl Warren, quoted in Schwartz, *Super Chief*, 411.

[176] Felix Frankfurter, quoted in Schwartz, *Super Chief*, 413; John Marshall Harlan, quoted in Schwartz, 414.

[177] Earl Warren, quoted in Schwartz, *Super Chief*, 416.

for his opinion, however, Clark had to report to Frankfurter that he had changed his mind and would be joining the majority, "I am sorry to say that I cannot find any practical course that the people could take in bringing this about except through the Federal courts."[178] Solicitor General Archibald Cox had emphasized the same point in his oral arguments as a friend of the Court: "Either there is a remedy in the Federal court or there is no remedy at all."[179]

The Court's willingness to extend constitutional principles to cover legislative apportionment was welcomed by liberals, who had long favored reapportionment but had been stymied in the political process. The New Deal had pulled urban voters firmly into the Democratic coalition, and the malapportionment of the era overwhelmingly favored more conservative rural voters over more liberal urban voters. After Roosevelt's initial landslide victory, the *Nation* crowed, "For seventy-five years the Republicans have dominated the Northern and Eastern States through rotten-borough provisions in the State constitutions. . . . [But now] the day of retribution has come."[180] But the day had not yet come, and a decade later it could only complain, "[T]he present gerrymandering of state districts amounts to supporters of the New Deal being denied equal voice with its opponents."[181] Both the constitutional principle and the political consequences of judicial intervention were in line with the liberal regime.[182] In the last years of the Eisenhower administration, Anthony Lewis of the *New York Times* had prominently pointed to the federal courts as the only institu-

[178] Tom Clark, quoted in Schwartz, *Super Chief*, 423.

[179] "U.S. Asks High Court Review of Tennessee Apportionment," *New York Times*, 20 April 1961, 25. "If a Federal court takes jurisdiction, that in itself will generate great forces for change. . . . The theory of legitimacy, a solemn adjudication that the Constitution had been violated, carries great weight with the people of this country." Archibald Cox, quoted in Anthony Lewis, "High Court Scans Urban-Vote Case," *New York Times*, 23 April 1961, 47. This view was shared by academic experts on the issue. See, e.g., Robert B. McKay, *Reapportionment* (New York: Twentieth Century Fund, 1965), 67; Robert G. Dixon, *Democratic Representation* (New York: Oxford University Press, 1968), 137–38.

[180] Orville Welsh, "The Democratic Revolution," *Nation*, 30 November 1932, 523.

[181] Richard L. Neuberger, "Our Gerrymandered States," *Nation*, 1 February 1941, 127.

[182] The perceived relationship between political opposition to black civil rights and legislative malapportionment should not be overlooked. In explaining political resistance to desegregation to a British audience, Harvard's Paul Freund observed, "[T]he strength of the resistance movement is more largely in the state capitals and rural areas whose representation predominates in state government than in the major cities." Paul A. Freund, "Storm over the Supreme Court," *Modern Law Review* 21 (1958): 345, 355. See also Klarman, *Jim Crow*, 415. Relatedly, voting rights cases arising out of the South confronted the Court with the tangled relationship between the drawing of electoral jurisdictions and the limitation of black voting power. Gomillion v. Lightfoot, 364 U.S. 339 (1960). Kennedy's solicitor general, Archibald Cox, later reported, "The issue of reapportionment is dramatically linked to the Negroes' effective use of the right to vote." Quoted in Sowell, "Judicial Vigor," 539.

tion politically capable of correcting "this growing evil of inequitably apportioned legislative districts" and exhorted them to take the lead. "A vacuum exists in our political system; the federal courts have the power and the duty to fill this vacuum."[183] Taking a cue from the Supreme Court's boldness in *Brown*, federal district judge Frank McLaughlin, a Truman appointee and former New Deal congressman, declared that legislative inaction on reapportionment in Hawaii had gone on for too long: "The time has come, and the Supreme Court has marked the way, when serious consideration should be given to a reversal of the traditional reluctance of judicial intervention in legislative reapportionment. The whole thrust of today's legal climate is to end unconstitutional discrimination. It is ludicrous to preclude judicial relief when a main-spring of representative government is impaired."[184] While senator, John F. Kennedy had published a magazine article calling legislative apportionment "deliberately rigged" and "shamefully ignored"; the only result of "this basic political discrimination," he argued, was the "frustration of progress."[185] By then, the *Nation* could see the possibility of a "civil-liberties battle" over legislative apportionment being fought in the courts, and liberal interest groups such as the AFL-CIO, American Civil Liberties Union, and Americans for Democratic Action were early participants in apportionment litigation.[186] Even as friends of the Kennedy administration such as James MacGregor Burns bemoaned the "old cycle of deadlock and drift" that killed "most of Mr. Kennedy's bold proposals," the *Nation* pointed to malapportionment as the linchpin of the conservative coalition's legislative power and encouraged the courts to pull it out. Doing so was expected not only to aid Democrats over Republicans but also, pointedly, to strengthen the hands of liberal Democrats and the expense of conservative Democrats.[187]

---

[183] Anthony Lewis, "Legislative Apportionment and the Federal Courts," *Harvard Law Review* 71 (1958): 1057, 1059. Lewis concluded that the "evidence is overwhelming that neither Congress nor the state legislatures could be relied on to ensure equitable representation, indeed that there are virtually insurmountable, built-in obstacles to legislative action." Ibid., 1058–59.

[184] Dyer v. Abe, 138 F.Supp. 220, 226 (D. Hawaii 1956) (footnote omitted).

[185] John F. Kennedy, "The Shame of the States," *New York Times Magazine*, 18 May 1958, 12, 37, 38.

[186] Roscoe Fleming, "America's Rotten Boroughs," *Nation*, 10 January 1959, 26; Richard C. Cortner, *The Apportionment Cases* (Knoxville: University of Tennessee Press, 1970), 71, 130, 145, 207, 244. Kennedy himself was initially more reluctant to involve the courts, explaining to one correspondent in 1958, "I can see great harm coming to the Supreme Court if it were to enter into this complex and hotly disputed area." Quoted in Sowell, "Judicial Vigor," 350.

[187] James MacGregor Burns, *The Deadlock of Democracy* (Englewood Cliffs, NJ: Prentice-Hall, 1963), 1; John J. Lindsay, "The Underprivileged Majority," *Nation*, 10 March 1962, 208.

The Kennedy campaign concentrated on the urban vote, and once in the White House the administration encouraged the Court to intervene in *Baker v. Carr* and voiced its support after the decision was announced.[188] Attorney General Robert Kennedy immediately hailed the decision as a "landmark in the development of representative government." He went on to observe that prior to the decision "the democratic process has been distorted" and required an "effective judicial remedy," and New York senator Kenneth Keating praised the Court for entering an area that had been "long neglected."[189] Publicly, the president endorsed the Court's decision and reminded the American people that the administration had in fact encouraged it. "Quite obviously," John Kennedy asserted, "the right to fair representation and to have each vote counted equally is, it seems to me, basic to the successful operation of a democracy." It had been "impossible for the people involved to secure adequate relief through the normal political processes." Although it was the "responsibility of the political groups to respond to the need," when no relief was forthcoming "then of course it seemed to the Administration that the judicial branch must meet a responsibility."[190] Privately, he elaborated to former secretary of state Dean Acheson, "[T]he legislatures would never reform themselves and . . . he did not see how we were going to make any progress unless the Court intervened."[191] Administration officials subsequently claimed credit for winning the result in *Baker*, and it remained active in subsequent reapportionment litigation.[192] Two years later, in another reapportionment case, Harlan complained, "[T]hese decisions give support to a current mistaken view of the Constitution and the constitutional function of this Court. This view, in a nutshell, is that every major social ill in this country can find its cure in some constitutional 'principle,' and that this Court should 'take the lead' in promoting reform when other branches of government fail to act."[193] For the affiliated leader, this view might be "current," but it is hardly politically "mistaken." From the White House down, liberals turned to the Court in order to displace entrenched conservative legislators who could not be defeated by other means, and they

---

[188] Solicitor General Archibald Cox proved the most reluctant within the Kennedy Justice Department to urge the Court to take this course. Sowell, "Judicial Vigor," 360–65, 386–406.

[189] "Capital is Split on Apportioning," *New York Times*, 28 March 1962, 1, 22.

[190] "Transcript of the President's News Conference on Domestic and World Affairs," *New York Times*, 30 March 1962, 12. Kennedy's extemporaneous remarks focused more on the substance of the decision and the judicial role in reapportionment than did the more cautious statement prepared by the White House before the press conference. Sowell, "Judicial Vigor," 376–83.

[191] Quoted in Schwartz, *Super Chief*, 425.

[192] Sowell, "Judicial Vigor," 383–84.

[193] Reynolds v. Sims, 377 U.S. 533, 624 (1964) (Harlan, J., dissenting).

contributed to the political and intellectual climate that would lend support and legitimacy to the Court taking that unprecedented step.

The classic case of turning to the courts in this fashion is racial civil rights in the postwar period. For liberals during the Roosevelt and Truman administrations, racial civil rights suffered from a gridlock problem arising from within the Democrats' own electoral coalition. Decades of political neglect and the Great Depression nonetheless tore the black vote loose from the party of Lincoln. As blacks continued to migrate north and became an important part of the voting constituency of northern Democrats, black civil rights became an increasingly salient issue for northern liberals and national party leaders. Even so, the pivotal role of southern Democrats in the New Deal legislative and electoral coalition stymied progress on the issue. Southern Democrats were not only important members of the New Deal electoral and legislative coalition, but they had disproportionate influence in congressional committee and chamber leadership. They were an insurmountable obstacle to civil rights legislation. FDR rebuffed requests from the NAACP to put civil rights and violence against blacks on the political agenda. The president explained,

> I did not choose the tools with which I must work. . . . I've got to get legislation passed by Congress to save America. Southerners, by reason of the seniority rule in Congress, are chairmen or occupy strategic places on most of the Senate and House committees. If I come out for the anti-lynching bill now, they will block every bill I ask Congress to pass to keep America from collapsing. I just can't take the risk.[194]

The pressures on the party were intense and made electoral calculations difficult for party leaders. By 1940, the Roosevelt administration recognized the importance of the black vote in the North, with one memo concluding that it "may well become the decisive factor in the Presidential election in most of these states" and the Democratic Party could not assume that the black vote that had swung behind FDR in 1936 would continue to vote Democratic.[195] Truman was famously advised by his aides in preparation for the 1948 campaign, "A theory of many professional politicians is that the northern Negro voter today holds the balance of power in Presidential elections for the simple arithmetical reason that the Negroes not only vote in a bloc but are geographically concentrated

[194] Quoted in Walter White, *A Man Called White* (New York: Viking, 1948), 169–70. To advocates of more direct federal action on race, Roosevelt counseled patience and caution. See, e.g., Arthur M. Schlesinger Jr., *The Politics of Upheaval* (Boston: Houghton Mifflin, 1960), 434–35.

[195] "Statement in Support of Proposed Negro Plank," quoted in Kevin J. McMahon, "Constitutional Vision and Supreme Court Decisions: Reconsidering Roosevelt on Race," *Studies in American Political Development* 14 (2000): 20, 26.

in the pivotal, large and closely contested electoral states such as New York, Illinois, Pennsylvania, Ohio and Michigan. This theory may or may not be absolutely true, but it is certainly close enough to the truth to be extremely arguable."[196] Hubert Humphrey rose to prominence in the 1940s stumping for a "real, liberal Democratic party" and for black civil rights as the issue by which the party would excommunicate the southern conservatives.[197] For programmatic postwar liberals, black civil rights were a natural extension of the New Deal constitutional order, but the southern veto in Congress (and the risky calculation about the reliability of the white southern Democratic vote) limited the elaboration and instantiation of this conception of liberal constitutionalism by elected officials.

Harry Truman demonstrated that the president had some unilateral power to assert this understanding.[198] In speaking to the NAACP in 1947, the president welded the quest for black civil rights to the New Deal project launched by Franklin Roosevelt.

> We must keep moving forward, with new concepts of civil rights to safeguard our heritage. The extension of civil rights today means, not protection of the people against the Government, but protection of the people by the Government. . . . Every man should have the right to a decent home, the right to an education, the right to adequate medical care, the right to a worthwhile job, the right to an equal share in making public decisions through the ballot, and the right to a fair trial in a fair court. . . . we can no longer afford the luxury of

[196] James Rowe Jr., "The Politics of 1948, September 18, 1947," in *Documentary History of the Truman Presidency*, ed. Dennis K. Merrill, vol. 14 (Bethesda, MD: University Publications of America, 1995), 36. They were grossly wrong, however, in asserting, "It is inconceivable that any policies initiated by the Truman administration no matter how 'liberal' could so alienate the South in the next year that it would revolt." Ibid., 30. See also Barton J. Bernstein, "The Ambiguous Legacy: The Truman Administration and Civil Rights," in *Politics and Policies of the Truman Administration*, ed. Barton J. Bernstein (Chicago: Quadrangle Books, 1970); Donald R. McCoy and Richard T. Ruetten, *Quest and Response* (Lawrence: University Press of Kansas, 1973); William Berman, *The Politics of Civil Rights in the Truman Administration* (Columbus: Ohio State University Press, 1970).

[197] Jennifer A. Delton, *Making Minnesota Liberal* (Minneapolis: University of Minnesota Press, 2002), 120.

[198] This route had been tentatively explored by the Roosevelt administration. McMahon, "Constitutional Vision," 27–48; Risa L. Goluboff, "The Thirteenth Amendment and the Lost Origins of Civil Rights," *Duke Law Journal* 50 (2001): 1609. These initial explorations of executive action on civil rights, however, were more concerned with the rights of labor than the rights of blacks until the pressures of World War II brought about a "convergence of race and labor." Risa L. Goluboff, "The Work of Civil Rights in the 1940s: The Department of Justice, the NAACP, and African American Agricultural Labor," Ph.D. diss., Princeton University, 2003; Daniel Kryder, *Divided Arsenal* (New York: Cambridge University Press, 2000). See also Philip A. Klinkner with Rogers M. Smith, *The Unsteady March* (Chicago: University of Chicago Press, 1999), 161–201.

a leisurely attack upon prejudice and discrimination. There is much that State and local governments can do in providing positive safeguards for civil rights. But we cannot, any longer, await the growth of a will to action in the slowest State or the most backward community. Our National Government must show the way.[199]

Denied statutory authority for a permanent Federal Employment Practices Commission, Truman created an advisory committee on civil rights that produced a much publicized report, "To Secure These Rights," that called for a host of new laws. In presenting the report to Congress, the president insisted,

> The Federal Government has a clear duty to see that Constitutional guarantees of individual liberties and of equal protection under the laws are not denied or abridged anywhere in our Union. That duty is shared by all three branches of the Government, but it can be fulfilled only if the Congress enacts modern, comprehensive civil rights laws, adequate to the needs of the day.[200]

To no one's surprise, Congress refused the call to "strengthen the organization of the Federal Government" for this purpose, but facing pressure from the left, the president cautiously ordered the desegregation of the military and allowed the inclusion of a strong civil rights plank in the 1948 Democratic platform.[201]

The federal courts were an obvious alternative vehicle for elaborating this dimension of the new constitutional regime. In the president's second term, Truman's primary White House aide on civil rights, Stephen Spingarn, outlined the strategy in a memo proposing to more than double the size of the civil rights section of the Justice Department. The additional lawyers would not only show "that the administration meant business in the civil rights field," but their work "would offset the legislative defeats in this field which we are likely to receive."[202] In a campaign address in Harlem, the president explained, "I went ahead and did what the President can do, unaided by the Congress," which included sending the Department of Justice to the Supreme Court to win a decision outlawing

---

[199] Harry Truman, "Address Before the National Association for the Advancement of Colored People, June 29, 1947," in *Public Papers of Presidents of the United States: Harry S. Truman, 1945–1952/53* (Washington, DC: Government Printing Office, 1961–66), *1947*, 311–12.

[200] Harry Truman, "Special Message to Congress on Civil Rights, February 2, 1948," in *Public Papers, 1948*, 122.

[201] Ibid. See Harry Truman, "Executive Order 9981: Establishing the President's Committee on Equality of Treatment and Opportunity in the Armed Services," *Federal Register* 13 (26 July 1948): 4313.

[202] Stephen Spingarn, quoted in Berman, *Politics of Civil Rights*, 165–66.

racial covenants.[203] Back in Harlem four years later, while stumping for Democratic presidential nominee Adlai Stevenson and blaming Republicans for the defeat of civil rights legislation, Truman again emphasized, "This fight of ours cannot stop just because we have been blocked in the United States Congress," and highlighted a longer list of actions that his administration had urged the Supreme Court to take.[204] John P. Frank, a Yale law professor and active participant in the desegregation litigation, noted in 1951 that the Court had generally become more of an "onlooker rather than a spirited participant in the controversies of the American scene," but he thought racial civil rights was a notable exception. In this area, Congress was "constantly urged to act, [but] never acted." "While filibusters have stopped racial equality legislation," he observed admiringly and hopefully, "they could not block the racial equality movement in the executive and judicial departments."[205] Although *Brown v. Board of Education* met with strong disapproval in the South and its reasoning left much to be desired in the opinion of many academics and judges, it was hailed by both the public and elites outside the South as substantively right, and even overdue.[206] Harvard law professor Charles Fairman pointed out that "constitutional rights [must] stand" even when Congress was "recreant. . . . Of this, at any rate, we can be certain: it would be utterly out of accord with the purpose of the 39th Congress, which framed the [Fourteenth] amendment, that the right of Negroes should be left to the mercy of a Congress organized in disregard" of the efficacy of black voting rights in the South. Members of Congress had failed to act on what was "their own responsibility"; the Court "merits our confidence and

[203] Truman, "Address in Harlem, New York, Upon Receiving the Franklin Roosevelt Award, October 29, 1948," in *Public Papers, 1948*, 924.

[204] Truman, "Address in Harlem, New York, Upon Receiving the Franklin Roosevelt Award, October 11, 1952," in *Public Papers, 1952–1953*, 798. The *Nation* likewise reported, "Since de-segregation of schools by Congressional action appears remote while the filibuster is available in the Senate, those looking beyond . . . temporary palliatives . . . are placing their hope on court action." Phineas Indritz, "Racism in the Nation's Capital," *Nation*, 18 October 1952, 356. After the 1952 election, the Truman Justice Department submitted an *amicus* brief in *Brown v. Board of Education* urging the Court to rule segregation unconstitutional, emphasizing the damage racial injustices in the United States were doing to American foreign policy efforts abroad. Berman, *Politics of Civil Rights*, 232–34; Dudziak, *Cold War Civil Rights*, 91–102.

[205] John P. Frank, "Court and Constitution: The Passive Period," *Vanderbilt Law Review* 4 (1951): 400, 401, 407.

[206] On the reaction to *Brown*, see Barry Friedman, "The Birth of an Academic Obsession: The History of the Countermajoritarian Difficulty, Part Five," *Yale Law Journal* 112 (2002): 153; William G. Ross, "Attacks on the Warren Court by State Officials: A Case Study of Why Court-Curbing Movements Fail," *Buffalo Law Review* 50 (2002): 483.

support" for stepping into the breach.[207] Entrenched and disproportionately powerful southern conservatives had gridlocked Congress. The Court became the alternative.

Position Taking and Blame Avoidance

Legislators are driven by a desire to win reelection. Leaders of legislative coalitions must facilitate and accommodate that drive. This is not to suggest that legislators are literally single-minded seekers of reelection. Legislators do have other goals and desires that influence their behavior, including such goals as producing good public policy and advancing a personal career, but reelection is often a prerequisite to the pursuit of other goals and it looms large in the calculations of members of legislatures. A variety of features of legislative politics, from direct features of electoral campaigning and constituent communication and services to legislative behavior and organization, are shaped by the reelection imperative.

Among the activities that legislators find electorally useful is what David Mayhew has called position taking. Mayhew defined such activity as "public enunciation of a judgmental statement on anything likely to be of interest to political actors."[208] Such statements need not cause anything to happen. The point is simply to align the public image of the legislator with the sentiments of the constituents.[209] This effort at image adjustment can take many forms, including press releases, letters to constituents, paid advertising, public appearances, interviews, writings, roll call votes, bill sponsorships, floor speeches, and activity at legislative hearings. There are many ways for legislators to create a public record on a given issue, and they creatively seek out ways of doing so.

Coalition leaders routinely abet this activity. The organization of Congress provides an infrastructure for position taking by individual legislators. "Franking" privileges allow members of Congress to send mail to their constituents free of charge, and Congress provides staff and technical

---

[207] Charles Fairman, "The Supreme Court, 1955 Term—Foreword: The Attack on the Segregation Cases," *Harvard Law Review* 70 (1956): 83, 85, 84. See also, Robert J. Harris, "The Constitution, Education, and Segregation," *Temple Law Quarterly* 29 (1956): 432 (Congress was "powerless" due to the "atrophy of the fifth section of the fourteenth amendment as a result . . . [of] the Senate filibuster and the seniority rule in the organization of congressional committees, either of which is sufficient barrier to legislative implementation of the fourteenth amendment. If the fourteenth amendment is to have meaning, the Court must provide it"); Freund, "Storm over Supreme Court," 351 ("Congress had left it to the court to develop the content of the equal protection guarantee. To announce now that the responsibility rested in truth on Congress would have been something of an Alphonse-Gaston game, with no one going through the door").

[208] Mayhew, *Congress*, 61.

[209] "The position itself is the commodity." Ibid., 62.

resources to assist members in speaking to the media.[210] The chamber floor and the *Congressional Record* are made available as platforms for any remarks a member might care to make. Myriad committees and subcommittees offer ample opportunities for individual members to exercise "leadership," and they are afforded the right to hold hearings on almost any subject. Presidents take care to amplify and lend credibility to the position taking and credit claiming of the members of their legislative coalition. Congressional leaders make sure to organize legislation and schedule roll call votes that will allow members to present themselves in the best possible light. Effective coalition leaders create opportunities for their members to engage in position taking, and they assist in lending plausibility to the credit-claiming activity of legislators who wish not only to take politically advantageous positions on the issues but also to claim credit for causing the government to take actions desired by constituents.[211]

The flip side of position taking and credit claiming, however, is issue and blame avoidance. Every act of position taking is inherently risky; some constituents might not like the position that the legislator is taking. As a consequence, politicians are particularly enthusiastic about taking positions on issues that are clearly safe either by virtue of the issue itself (e.g., "motherhood and apple pie" issues) or of the relevant constituency (e.g., proslavery congressmen in the antebellum South). They are substantially less enthusiastic about being pinned down on issues for which the electoral ramifications are not yet clear or are known to be negative. Elected officials are more likely to meet those issues with studied ambiguity or a strategic silence.[212]

The uncertainty facing the politician increases as the electorate becomes more diverse. As Madison recognized, smaller electorates are likely to be

---

[210] Position taking on national and local issues is the biggest component of congressional newsletters and press releases. Diana Evans Yiannakis, "House Members' Communication Styles: Newsletters and Press Releases," *Journal of Politics* 44 (1982): 1049, 1062.

[211] Credit claiming is "acting so as to generate a belief in a relevant political actor (or actors) that one is personally responsible for causing the government, or some unit thereof, to do something that the actor (or actors) considers desirable." Mayhew, *Congress*, 52–53. Such presidential gestures as invitations to Rose Garden bill-signing ceremonies and presentations of pens used to sign bills into law are obviously designed to lend plausibility to favored legislators' claims of responsibility for changing the law.

[212] See, e.g., Kenneth A. Shepsle, "The Strategy of Ambiguity: Uncertainty and Electoral Competition," *American Political Science Review* 66 (1972): 555; Benjamin I. Page, *Choices and Echoes in Presidential Elections* (Chicago: University of Chicago Press, 1978); Amihai Glazer, "The Strategy of Candidate Ambiguity," *American Political Science Review* 84 (1990): 237; Alberto Alesina and Alex Cukierman, "The Politics of Ambiguity," *Quarterly Journal of Economics* 105 (1990): 829; Martin Thomas, "Issue Avoidance: Evidence from the U.S. Senate," *Political Behavior* 13 (1991): 1; David R. Jones, "Position Taking and Position Avoidance in the U.S. Senate," *Journal of Politics* 65 (2003): 851.

less diverse, which allows representatives in turn to be fairly confident in taking positions on issues, even fairly extreme ones. Members of the House of Representatives from antebellum South Carolina or Massachusetts had no difficulty taking a position on slavery, for example. National coalition leaders such as candidates for the presidency or Speaker of the House, however, were in a much more difficult political situation and consequently preferred to fudge the slavery issue.[213]

A critical task for the coalition leader is to shield individual legislators and the coalition as a whole from having to take clear positions on politically risky issues. In some cases, this can be accomplished simply by keeping the issue off the political or legislative agenda. Excluding slavery from national politics was a key goal of the architects of the Second Party System during the early Jacksonian period. Both Whigs and Democrats understood that the slavery issue threatened to tear apart their national coalitions and so preferred to orient politics around less politically threatening economic issues, such as tariffs and banking. Of course, opposition leaders may have an incentive to focus attention precisely on those issues so as to disrupt existing coalitions and encourage broader realignments, as the sectionally based Republican Party did with slavery in the 1850s. When the issue cannot be avoided completely, as with tax increases, legislative pay raises, and budget retrenchment, however, it must be finessed.[214]

Effective political leaders find the means for achieving the policy results that they want while protecting legislators from any political backlash that might result from those policies (and insuring that legislators reap any political rewards that might result). As Doug Arnold has explained, voters can only hold legislators accountable for their past performance if they can follow a "traceability chain" between the actions of the legislator and policy outcomes. When the policy is a popular one, legislators strive to "strengthen" the traceability chain (they engage in highly visible position taking). When the policy is unpopular, they take steps to "weaken" or "break" it.[215] Coalition leaders can manipulate the timing of unpopular votes, for example, so that legislators need not cast too many at once or too close to an election. They can avoid putting the unpopular actions of individual legislators on the record. They can bundle legislative proposals

---

[213] On this antebellum dynamic, see Mark A. Graber, *Dred Scott and the Problem of Constitutional Evil* (New York: Cambridge University Press, 2006); Jeffery A. Jenkins and Charles Stewart III, *Fighting for the Speakership* (Princeton: Princeton University Press, forthcoming).

[214] See R. Kent Weaver, "The Politics of Blame Avoidance," *Journal of Public Policy* 6 (1986): 371; Paul Pierson, *Dismantling the Welfare State?* (New York: Cambridge University Press, 1994).

[215] R. Douglas Arnold, *The Logic of Congressional Action* (New Haven: Yale University Press, 1990), 47–51, 100–105.

so as to avoid separate votes on unpopular items.[216] They can create complex and indirect mechanisms for implementing unpopular policies, such as automatic cost-of-living increases for congressional salaries.[217] They can delegate unpopular policy decisions to others, such as bureaucrats or special commissions, allowing legislators to avoid blame themselves while shifting blame to others.

Position taking is fundamentally about taking actions without policy consequences. In order to take an electorally advantageous position, politicians need only posture, not achieve results. Legislators on the losing side of an issue still score political points with their constituents by taking the "right" stance, even if the policy outcome goes against the preferences of the voters. Because legislators also have policy preferences of their own, as well as longer-term concerns about how voter attitudes might be affected by real events, they cannot simply take the electorally popular position. Sometimes legislators believe taxes need to be raised despite voter hostility. If legislators could simply posture without consequence, then they could always vote against taxes, but their responsibility for policy outcomes constrains their position taking. The more pivotal a legislator's vote becomes to determining policy outcomes, then the more the value of the substantive policy outcome must be weighed against the value of the position taking. When legislators know that a president will veto a given piece of legislation, for example, they may be free to vote in favor of it in order to satisfy constituents (or perhaps, some particular group of constituents). When the threat of a presidential veto is removed, however, legislators may be forced to switch their own votes in order to prevent an undesired bill from becoming law.

Independent and active judicial review generates position-taking opportunities by reducing the policy responsibility of the elected officials. They may vote in favor of a bill that they personally dislike secure in the knowledge that it will never be implemented. State statutes regulating abortion after the *Roe* decision, for example, were often pure symbolism, though they could also play a more productive role in pressing the Court to refine its doctrine or in filling in the lacuna left by the judicial decisions.[218] More subtly, the judicial backstop allows legislators to focus on some dimen-

---

[216] Even better, they can bundle proposals so as to allow legislators to record a negative vote against some unpopular item while nonetheless securing the desired outcome through less visible provisions. Legislators may be allowed to vote on an amendment to a foreign aid bill cutting funding to some unpopular country, only to later wipe out the result with an amendment granting the president discretion to restore funding as circumstances dictate. Ibid., 106.

[217] See R. Kent Weaver, *Automatic Government* (Washington, DC: Brookings Institution, 1988).

[218] See, e.g., Devins, *Shaping Constitutional Values*; Epstein and Kobylka, *Supreme Court and Legal Change*, 203–98.

sions of the proposed policy (the most optimistic and politically popular) while downplaying others (the constitutionally subversive and treacherous). Legislators even gain a political windfall when the courts actually act to strike down the popular law. The visibility of the exercise of judicial review creates another opportunity for legislators to publicize their position on the issue, this time by bewailing the Court's actions.

It is possible that the existence of judicial review encourages legislators to behave less responsibly than they otherwise would. Mark Tushnet has called this the problem of "judicial overhang." The promise of judicial review may promote legislative irresponsibility and distort legislative deliberation.[219] As the Supreme Court became increasingly activist in the late nineteenth century, James Bradley Thayer complained that this development "has tended to bereave our legislatures of their feeling of responsibility and their sense of honor. . . . It is a common saying in our legislative bodies when any constitutional point is raised, 'Oh, the courts will set that right.' " The courts "have often assumed a tone that tended to encourage these views," but Thayer warned that such complacency overlooked "how great . . . is legislative power, and how limited is judicial power."[220]

On the other hand, by allowing elected politicians to shift political blame to judges for unpopular actions judicial review may also stiffen the spine of politicians to act on their central ideological commitments. As we saw in chapter 2, for example, the Court's decisions on abortion allowed some politicians, such as Jimmy Carter, to try to have it both ways with voters, by simultaneously proclaiming their pro-life private opinions and their judicially imposed pro-choice public responsibilities. Similarly, as the first Catholic president, John F. Kennedy was acutely conscious of the need to demonstrate his independence from the church while still holding the political support of his fellow Catholics. Before and during his campaign for the presidency, Kennedy emphasized how the Constitution, and the Court's interpretation of it, tied the hands of individual officeholders—to the consternation of religious critics who found him "spiritually rootless and politically almost disturbingly secular."[221] The "Constitution and all its parts—including the First Amendment and the strict separation of church and state," he avowed, necessarily trumped

---

[219] Mark Tushnet, *Taking the Constitution Away from the Courts* (Princeton: Princeton University Press, 1999), 57–65.

[220] James Bradley Thayer, "Constitutionality of Legislation: The Precise Question for a Court," *Nation*, 10 April 1884, 315. See also James Bradley Thayer, "The Origin and Scope of the American Doctrine of Constitutional Law," *Harvard Law Review* 7 (1893): 17.

[221] See Lawrence H. Fuchs, *John F. Kennedy and American Catholicism* (New York: Meredith Press, 1967), 167–68; quote from *Christian Century* associate editor Martin Marty at 168.

"one's religion in private life." For example, "the First Amendment as interpreted by the Supreme Court" left "no question of federal funds being used for support of parochial or private schools."[222] In office he bristled at criticism from Catholic officials of his proposal for federal aid to public schools but not private schools, criticisms that he did not recall being made during the Eisenhower administration. Though he was "extremely sympathetic" to the financial burdens borne by families sending children to parochial schools, a close "reading [of] the cases" raised "serious constitutional questions" that the president could not be expected to ignore. "It is prohibited by the Constitution, and the Supreme Court has made that very clear."[223]

Regardless of whether legislators would be more constitutionally responsible if judicial review did not exist, they can certainly recognize the political opportunities created by the empirical reality of judicial review. The consequence is that the actual exercise of judicial review may not be as unwelcome and hostile to congressional interests as is often assumed, and affiliated leaders have further reason to support the judicial authority to determine constitutional meaning. Some legislative votes are "politically compelling," in that "legislators feel compelled to support certain policy options because their intended effects are popular, irrespective of whether the proposed means will really achieve those ends" or are even necessary.[224] Once a bill that professes to stop violence against women, keep guns out of schools, protect the flag from desecration, or prevent child pornography reaches the floor, legislators are "practically forced to support it."[225] Although legislators may harbor doubts about the policy and constitutional wisdom of such proposals, clear electoral imperatives are likely to drive legislative decision-making. Enhancing the judicial authority to define and enforce constitutional meaning can ease the legislative policy conscience, while allowing legislators to reap the electoral gains of position taking.

The flag-burning controversy of 1989–90 provides an illustration. In June 1989, the Supreme Court overturned the conviction of Gregory Lee Johnson for the "desecration of a venerated object," in this case by burning an American flag outside the 1984 Republican National Convention in Dallas, in violation of Texas state law. The Court held by a five-to-four margin that expressive acts designed "to seriously offend one or more

[222] Quoted in ibid., 165–66.

[223] "The President's News Conference of March 8, 1961," in *Public Papers, 1961*, 156; "The President's News Conference of March 1, 1961," 142–43. See also "The President's News Conference of March 15, 1961," 184; "The President's News Conference of June 27, 1962," in *Public Papers, 1962*, 511.

[224] Arnold, *Logic of Congressional Action*, 77–78.

[225] Ibid., 78.

persons," in the words of the statute, were protected speech under the First Amendment.[226] In the wake of great public outcry, President George H. W. Bush called for a constitutional amendment excluding flag burning from constitutional protection.[227] The Democratic congressional leadership countered with a proposal for a revised federal statute banning flag burning. In October 1989, Congress passed the Flag Protection Act by large margins, replacing a 1968 federal flag-burning statute. In June 1990, the same majority on the Court invalidated the federal statute on the same grounds.[228] Later that month, a flag-burning constitutional amendment failed to receive the necessary two-thirds majority in Congress.

The Court's actions created irresistible position-taking opportunities, and pressures, for legislators. Flag burning was a nonissue before the Court placed it on the political agenda with its 1989 ruling. The political response once the Court made it an issue was immediate and explosive, however. Opinion surveys instantly showed roughly 70 percent of the public disapproving of the decision and supporting a constitutional amendment to ban flag burning.[229] Within a week of the decision, both the Senate and the House had passed, with nearly unanimous support,

[226] Texas v. Johnson, 491 U.S. 397, 399–400 (1989).

[227] Notably, while eventually accepting an effort to substantively alter the result reached by the Court (and employing the standard presidential trope of distinguishing between his "personal" opinion on the substance and his presidential stance on judicial authority), Bush immediately precluded any thought of attacking judicial authority over constitutional interpretation. "I want to comment on the Supreme Court decision about our flag. I understand the legal basis for that decision, and I respect the Supreme Court. And as President of the United States, I will see that the law of the land is fully supported. But I have to give you my personal, emotional response. Flag-burning is wrong—dead wrong—and the flag of the United States is very, very special." George H. W. Bush, "Remarks at a Luncheon Hosted by the New York Partnership and the Association for a Better New York, New York, June 22, 1989," in Public Papers, 1989, 785.

[228] United States v. Eichman, 496 U.S. 310 (1990).

[229] Robert Justin Goldstein, Burning the Flag (Kent, OH: Kent State University Press, 1996), 114. An August 1989 poll found 31 percent of respondents claiming to be less likely to vote for a congressman unwilling to tighten restrictions on flag-burning, 21 percent being more likely, and 44 percent doubting any effect on their vote choice. Far more supporters than opponents of flag-burning restrictions tended to regard the issue as important, however. When offered a choice, most respondents preferred statutory change to a constitutional amendment. ABC/Washington Post Poll, Public Opinion Online, Accession Numbers 0007701–6, August 1989. On the other hand, when not prompted about the issue, survey respondents were very unlikely to name flag-burning as an important issue facing the country, and within six weeks of the Court's decision public interest in the issue was already fading. CBS/New York Times Poll, Public Opinion Online, Accession Number 0021267, July 1989; Gallup Poll, Public Opinion Online, Accession Number 0140682, July 1990; Helen Dewar and Tom Kenworthy, "Support Lags for Amendment to Prohibit Flag Burning," Washington Post, 25 July 1989, A1; Ethan Bronner, "Amendment Losing Ground in Flag Debate," Boston Globe, 27 July 1989, 1.

resolutions condemning the *Johnson* decision, and nearly half the membership of Congress had introduced or co-sponsored resolutions calling for a constitutional amendment on flag burning. The House followed its resolution with a special all-night session of floor speeches denouncing flag burning.[230]

The political situation became more complicated when the president endorsed a constitutional amendment on flag burning and the issue that had been a universal political good for legislators took a partisan turn. Though quick to denounce the *Johnson* decision, Democrats were hesitant to embrace the favored Republican response of amending the Constitution to address it. Given the state of public opinion, a constitutional amendment was likely to win passage in an immediate floor vote. The Democratic congressional leadership sought to shield their caucus members from having to face such a politically compelling vote by moving forward a statutory response instead, in the form of the Flag Protection Act.[231] Though likely to be rejected by the Court, the statute provided another "safe" roll call on flag burning while deflecting the pressure for a vote on an amendment, and it passed with overwhelming majorities.[232] Significantly, far from challenging the Court's authority to determine constitutional meaning, the debate surrounding the Flag Protection Act was framed entirely in terms of designing a statute that might meet the Court's approval, and the act included a provision requiring the Supreme Court to "accept jurisdiction" and provide an expedited review of the statute.[233] By the time the Court struck down the Flag Protection Act a year later, the Democrats had reframed the issue as one of protecting the Bill of Rights from amendment and public passion for the issue had cooled.

[230] State and local officials did not miss the opportunity either. Goldstein, *Burning the Flag*, 114.

[231] When former solicitor general Charles Fried told a House committee that the best congressional response to the *Johnson* decision was to "bravely do nothing," Representative Don Edwards explained, "Your point of view is the correct point of view, but it's such a [political] loser." Quoted in ibid., 158.

[232] Goldstein, *Burning the Flag*, 144–230; Charles Tiefer, "The Flag-Burning Controversy of 1989–1990: Congress' Valid Role in Constitutional Dialogue," *Harvard Journal of Legislation* 29 (1992): 357; Barbara Sinclair, *Legislators, Leaders, and Lawmaking* (Baltimore: Johns Hopkins University Press, 1995), 283–85; Norman Dorsen, "Flag Desecration in Courts, Congress, and Country," *Thomas M. Cooley Law Review* 17 (2000): 417, 427. By controlling the floor, the Democratic leadership insured that the statutory vote was "the only game in town." Representative Douglas Applegate, quoted in Goldstein, 217. At the same time, it allowed Democrats to have it "both ways" and provided them "with the ability to say, 'I can defend the flag and I support the Constitution.'" People for the American Way legislative counsel John Gomperts and anonymous Democratic staffer, quoted in Goldstein, 166, 167.

[233] Tiefer, "Flag-Burning Controversy," 365–68; Goldstein, *Burning the Flag*, 166–83; 18 U.S.C. § 700(d) (1989).

Nonetheless, the well-organized Democratic leadership quickly brought a constitutional amendment to the floor before pro-amendment supporters could mobilize.[234]

The House vote on the amendment is illuminating. Given the two-thirds requirement for passage of a constitutional amendment, 144 negative votes in the House were sufficient to defeat it. Representatives do not cast recorded votes all at once but rather have a window of time within which to cast their votes, during which the current vote total is known. At the time that the 144th negative vote was cast against the amendment, only 163 yes votes had been cast. Of the Republicans voting to that point, 91 percent had voted in favor of the amendment, but only 28 percent of the voting Democrats had done the same. After the defeat of the amendment was assured, however, 124 additional votes were cast, nearly all of them in favor of the amendment. In contrast to the early Democratic votes, 73 percent of the Democrats voting after the decisive vote had been cast voted in favor of it.[235] Democratic legislators from electorally secure districts and whose own constituents did not support the amendment were most likely to vote against it.[236] Once the vote on flag burning had again become purely symbolic, legislators under constituent pressure were free to take the electorally safer position. Although the willingness of the Republicans to raise the stakes of the position taking ultimately complicated the leadership task facing the Democrats, the Court's exercise of the power of judicial review created political opportunities for legislators, in this case by presenting themselves as being opposed to the Court's decision.

Recognizing the importance of position taking to legislative activity puts judicial review in a new light. It is common in the modern Congress for tasks bearing electoral risks or little electoral payoff to be delegated to members whose own electoral prospects are relatively secure. Similarly, affiliated leaders recognize that they face collective action problems when attempting to push forward constitutional regime commitments that run counter, for example, to the immediate electoral pressures of individual legislators. Without coercive mechanisms to enforce voting discipline, coalition leaders have little ability to force legislators to take electoral risks. Independent, but friendly, judges armed with the authority to define and enforce constitutional commitments can help solve this collective action

---

[234] Goldstein, *Burning the Flag*, 299–340; Joan Biskupic, "For Critics of Flag Measure, Advance Work Pays Off," *Congressional Quarterly Weekly Report*, 23 June 1990, 1962. Subsequent efforts to pass a flag-burning amendment were similarly countered with statutory alternatives that provided political cover. Dorsen, "Flag Desecration," 430–33.

[235] David C. King and Richard J. Zeckhauser, "Congressional Vote Options," *Legislative Studies Quarterly* 28 (2003): 387, 400–401.

[236] Edward L. Lascher Jr., Steven Kelman, and Thomas J. Kane, "Policy Views, Constituency Pressure, and Congressional Action on Flag Burning," *Public Choice* 76 (1993): 79.

dilemma. Judicially enforced federalism allows contemporary congressional conservatives to vote for politically attractive measures that nonetheless run contrary to ideological commitments, such as the federalization of criminal punishment for carrying guns near schools or committing violence against women. The Court might, as the Rehnquist Court did, later strike down such laws, allowing legislators to reap the electoral benefits of their position taking while further elaborating the post-Reagan constitutional regime.[237] Similarly, the judicial enforcement of an expansive "liberty of contract" in the late nineteenth and early twentieth centuries freed congressional conservatives to vote for a federal ban on "yellowdog" contracts, in which employees agree not to join a labor union, in the railroad industry. Passed in the wake of the Pullman strike of 1894, the Erdman Act that included the ban also enhanced the power of federal courts to intervene in labor disputes. In rejecting one proposed change to the bill, a Republican senator declaimed against any proposal "which will deprive the courts of the right to do what they consider proper in the case of any citizen or in the case of any corporation in anything which involves great business interests or the rights of the individual concerned."[238] Few of its conservative legislative "supporters" could have been disappointed when the Court later struck down the yellow-dog provisions as unconstitutional.[239] In such cases, judicial authority, even though used against Congress, may be welcomed by affiliated leaders.

An active and independent Court can assume the blame for advancing constitutional commitments that might have electoral costs. The relatively obscure traceability chain between elected officials and judicial action allows coalition members to simultaneously achieve certain substantive goals while publicly distancing themselves from electoral responsibility for the Court and denouncing it for its actions. Elected officials have an incentive to bolster the authority of the courts precisely in order to distance themselves from responsibility for any of its actions. As long as the Court is acting in concert with basic regime commitments, and thus is not imposing serious electoral or policy costs on other affiliated political actors, it may enjoy substantial autonomy in interpreting those commitments.

---

[237] See Keith E. Whittington, "Taking What They Give Us: Explaining the Court's Federalism Offensive," *Duke Law Journal* 51 (2001): 477.

[238] William J. Sewell, quoted in Lovell, *Legislative Deferrals*, 85. Though the bill was endorsed by some unions, the primary critics of the bill were legislators with close ties to labor. Despite the uncertainty about how the law would be implemented by the courts, many of those critics nonetheless accepted the bill, destined for passage, "on the theory that half a loaf is better than no bread." Representative William Sulzer, quoted in Lovell, 94.

[239] Adair v. United States, 208 U.S. 161 (1908). On the Erdman Act's triumph of "symbol over substance," see Lovell, *Legislative Deferrals*, 93–95.

Black civil rights again provides an illustration. Extending the story of the Court's midcentury intervention in behalf of black civil rights, we can now focus less on how the president could turn to the Court to circumvent legislative gridlock and more on how politicians positioned themselves so as to minimize the personal political fallout from the Court's actions. For Democrats, civil rights fell along the central fault line of their existing legislative and electoral coalition, dividing white southern Democrats from more liberal northern Democrats. Both black voters in the North and white voters in the South were increasingly regarded as potentially pivotal in determining the control of the White House, but they put conflicting demands on presidential candidates. The Court as a policymaker was a potential strategic resource for overcoming a fragmented coalition and achieving policy outcomes greatly desired by some constituents. The independence of the judiciary from explicit political control allowed politicians to distance themselves from judicial actions greatly disliked by other constituents, allowing politicians to roll with the judicial punches rather than having to retaliate against them. Feeling pressure from the left and convinced that blacks in the North held a critical swing vote in the presidential election while southern whites were safely in the pocket of the Democratic Party, Truman launched a brief but vigorous rhetorical, administrative, and legislative civil rights campaign in the months preceding the 1948 election. Though his legislative proposals were buried in Congress, the inclusion of a strong civil rights plank in the 1948 Democratic platform provoked a southern walkout. Strom Thurmond's "Dixiecrat" revolt eventually stole thirty-nine electoral votes from Truman in the general election. In the end Truman did not need them, and the short-term result was to spur the president to even greater efforts to court black voters before the election and to propose curbing the Senate filibuster afterwards before bowing to legislative defeat and largely abandoning the issue.[240] In the longer term, Thurmond's challenge showed national leaders that political activism on civil rights carried substantial electoral risks.

The lesson of the Dixiecrat scare was not lost on subsequent presidential aspirants. Though "black activists and their white liberal allies from the programmatic wing of the Democratic party . . . were determined to press their cause even at the risk of disrupting the unity of the national party," others were centrally concerned with coalition maintenance.[241] Factional firebrands such as Hubert Humphrey could dismiss the "hodge-podge of sections held together by a Roosevelt or a Wilson," but other

[240] Berman, *Politics of Civil Rights*, 79–181.

[241] James L. Sundquist, *Dynamics of the Party System*, rev. ed. (Washington, DC: Brookings Institution, 1983), 354. The NAACP complained that Democratic leaders were silent on civil rights after *Brown*. John Frederick Martin, *Civil Rights and the Crisis of Liberalism* (Boulder, CO: Westview Press, 1979), 126.

party leaders saw the fragile New Deal coalition as the only means of national electoral victory.[242] "Programmatic" advances would have to be accomplished through safer means. In 1952, Adlai Stevenson emerged as "the man most likely to hold together the liberal-labor-Southern coalition that Franklin D. Roosevelt built," though black Democratic convention delegates walked off the floor when Alabama senator John Sparkman was selected as the vice presidential candidate.[243] After *Brown* raised the stakes on civil rights, Stevenson remained insistent in 1956 that "where principle and unity conflicted in this matter [of civil rights], he was bound to stand by unity." Though he pledged that he would "act in the knowledge that law and order is the Executive's responsibility" and asserted that it was "the sworn responsibility of the President of this nation to carry out the law of the land" as declared by the Court, he worked to keep the party from explicitly endorsing the *Brown* decision.[244] Stevenson's advisors initially assured him that the Court in *Brown* had ended civil rights as a political issue, but later changed their minds and raised the specter of another Dixiecrat revolt, but of "considerably greater magnitude."[245] Pulled by both sides, Stevenson wailed in frustration during the 1956 primaries, "I had hoped the action of the Court and the notable record of compliance . . . would remove this issue from the political arena," and complained that the Eisenhower administration was not doing enough to make the issue go away faster.[246] In the general election, the "racial backlash to the *Brown* decision fell disproportionately on the Republican incumbent rather than on the Northern leadership of the Democratic Party which had openly welcomed the decision" but did not have to stand for election in the South.[247]

Though not confronting the same internal conflicts as Stevenson and the Democratic coalition, President Dwight Eisenhower took a similar approach to civil rights. Eisenhower had made an impressive showing with white southern voters in 1952 while making no dent in the Demo-

[242] Hubert Humphrey, quoted in Delton, *Making Minnesota Liberal*, 150.

[243] James Reston, "Governor Says 'No,'" *New York Times*, 31 March 1952, 1; Berman, *Politics of Civil Rights*, 217.

[244] Adlai Stevenson (as reported by Arthur Schlesinger Jr.), quoted in John Bartlow Martin, *Adlai Stevenson and the World* (Garden City, NY: Doubleday, 1977), 302, 317. For Stevenson, the Court in *Brown* had done the "inevitable" and had decided "*what* is to be done" and would say when, leaving only the problem of "*how* we will effect this transition in an orderly, peaceful way." On the question of implementation, Stevenson thought the nation should offer "our advice, counsel and help and certainly our understanding to the states in which this is a problem" in order to "work this out without disorder and violence." Quoted in Martin, 289, 131.

[245] Martin, *Crisis of Liberalism*, 125; Harry Ashmore, quoted in Steven M. Gillon, *Politics and Vision* (New York: Oxford University Press, 1987), 97.

[246] Martin, *Adlai Stevenson*, 266.

[247] Richard L. Rubin, *Party Dynamics* (New York: Oxford University Press, 1976), 123.

cratic hold on the black vote, and though supportive of civil rights reform, he favored a gradualist approach. Though the administration made historic gains in civil rights through executive action in its first year of office, it was done "with as little fanfare as possible" and with the president largely invisible.[248] When the Supreme Court in June 1953 ordered a reargument of *Brown v. Board of Education* and invited the new attorney general to participate, the "prevailing attitude" among the Republican appointees at the Justice Department was "Jesus, do we really *have* to file a brief? Aren't we better off staying out of it?"[249] Eisenhower was clearly torn over the decision in *Brown*, concerned especially that forceful immediate desegregation would only damage reform and that the South might respond by abandoning public education, but agreeing that segregation was unjust and unconstitutional.[250] After the *Brown* decision was issued, the president determined only to say, "The Supreme Court has spoken and I am sworn to uphold the constitutional processes in this country; and I will obey," while endorsing the South Carolina governor's call for people to be "calm" and "reasonable." When pressed by a reporter on the political implications of the decision being "brought out under the Republican administration," Eisenhower bristled and denied the connection: "The Supreme Court, as I understand it, is not under any administration."[251] As a close student of Eisenhower's civil rights policy concluded,

[248] Michael S. Mayer, "With Much Deliberation and Some Speed: Eisenhower and the *Brown* Decision," *Journal of Southern History* 52 (1986): 43, 45. See also Robert Fredrick Burk, *The Eisenhower Administration and Black Civil Rights* (Knoxville: University of Tennessee Press, 1984).

[249] Assistant Attorney General William P. Rogers as reported by Philip Elman, quoted in Richard Kluger, *Simple Justice* (New York: Vintage, 1975), 650. See also, Mayer, "With Much Deliberation," 50–51. Eisenhower at first believed that a direct Justice Department statement on the constitutionality of segregation would invade the Court's authority to decide the case, and when persuaded to intervene, the president insisted that the Justice Department not work with civil rights activists in preparing the case out of concern that the administration would appear to be allying with them. Mayer, "With Much Deliberation," 48; Herbert Brownell and John P. Burke, *Advising Ike* (Lawrence: University Press of Kansas, 1993), 194. Behind the scenes that summer, Eisenhower wrote to southern governors that they had a "clear responsibility to show constant progress in the direction of complete justice" if they were to avoid the application of "overriding Federal law and Federal police methods." Quoted in Mayer, "With Much Deliberation," 49, 50. When Brownell suggested that the Court might want to defer the issue of remedies for segregation, the president joked that "perhaps they would defer the matter until the next administration." Mayer, "With Much Deliberation," 59.

[250] See Mayer, "With Much Deliberation," 59–60. On Eisenhower's views on race and civil rights more generally, see Michael S. Mayer, "Eisenhower's Conditional Crusade: The Eisenhower Administration and Civil Rights, 1953–1957," Ph.D. diss., Princeton University, 1984, 189–231.

[251] Dwight D. Eisenhower, "The President's News Conference of May 19, 1954," in *Public Papers of the Presidents of the United States: Dwight D. Eisenhower, 1953–1960/61* (Washington, DC: Government Printing Office, 1958–61), *1954*, 491, 492. The Republican

the "White House strategy consisted of shifting the burden of ending segregation outside areas of specific executive authority to the courts."[252]

Eisenhower's "hidden-hand" style of leadership applies as well to his approach to civil rights as to any other issue area.[253] The president instructed his attorney general at their first meeting, "It's your responsibility, you know, as well as your authority. Now if anything goes wrong, you know who's going to get it, don't you."[254] When pressed by South Carolina governor James Byrnes, to support the *Plessy* doctrine that segregation was constitutional, the president shifted blame to Attorney General Herbert Brownell and the Court: "[I]t became clear to me that the questions asked of the Attorney General by the Supreme Court [in the *Brown* reargument] demanded answers that could be determined only by lawyers and historians. Consequently, I have been compelled to turn over to the Attorney General and his associates full responsibility in the matter"; the "legal aspects of the case" would reflect the "conviction and understanding" of the attorneys in the Justice Department. This was a frequent gambit of Eisenhower's.[255]

This purported deference to legal expertise was consistent with both Eisenhower's personal philosophy and his political strategy. A "sucker

---

Party 1956 platform did endorse *Brown*, however, and Vice President Nixon pointed to the fact that a "Republican Chief Justice" had issued the decision. Richard J. Ellis, *Presidential Lightning Rods* (Lawrence: University Press of Kansas, 1994), 126. When Eisenhower was asked about the "possible reasons" that blacks might switch their support to the Republican Party in 1956, the president did not mention civil rights but simply noted, "I am doing my job well . . . but as far as I am concerned, I am trying to do it for 166 million people, not for any group." Eisenhower, "The President's News Conference of March 21, 1956," in *Public Papers, 1956*, 337. Eisenhower did make some gains among northern black voters in 1956. James L. Sundquist, *Politics and Policy* (Washington, DC: Brookings Institution, 1968), 230; Everett Carll Ladd Jr. and Charles D. Hadley, *Transformations of the American Party System* (New York: Norton, 1975), 112–14, 158.

[252] Mayer, "Eisenhower's Conditional Crusade," 115. The strategy was fairly successful; Eisenhower gained support in the South in the 1956 election, and his approval ratings in the South did not decline until he introduced a civil rights bill into Congress and intervened in Little Rock in 1957. Ellis, *Presidential Lightning Rods*, 127, 128. Initially, however, observers thought the primary effect of Brownell "whooping it up for 'civil rights' in this election year" would be "to cause maximum embarrassment to the Democratic party." *Richmond Times-Dispatch* and *New York Times*, quoted in J. W. Anderson, *Eisenhower, Brownell, and the Congress* (University: University of Alabama Press, 1964), 46. In 1960 Nixon ran slightly behind Eisenhower's numbers in the South, more substantially in the Deep South.

[253] On Eisenhower's leadership style, see Fred I. Greenstein, *The Hidden-Hand Presidency* (New York: Basic Books, 1982).

[254] Herbert Brownell, "From Campaigning to Governance," in *The Eisenhower Presidency*, ed. Kenneth W. Thompson (Lanham, MD: University Press of America, 1984), 168. On Eisenhower's use of advisors as "lightning rods to take the heat on controversial issues," see Ellis, *Presidential Lightning Rods*, 15–32, 122–44 (quote at 15).

[255] Dwight Eisenhower, quoted in Ellis, *Presidential Lightning Rods*, 124. See also, Ellis, 125.

for duty," Eisenhower often emphasized the president's duty to uphold judicial authority in this area, as well as understood constitutional requirements.[256] The president recognized the "plain duty" of the federal government to end racial discrimination "in the areas in which it is clearly responsible." Similarly, in responding to Byrnes's plea that federal facilities not be integrated, the president observed, "I feel that my oath of office as well as my own convictions, requires me to eliminate discrimination within the definite areas of Federal responsibility."[257] When Arkansas governor Orval Faubus called out the National Guard to obstruct a judicial order desegregating Central High School, Eisenhower telegrammed Faubus, "When I became President, I took an oath to support and defend the Constitution of the United States. The only assurance I can give you is that the federal Constitution will be upheld by me by every legal means at my command."[258] Upon sending troops to Little Rock, he explained to the nation that the situation had made the "President's responsibility . . . inescapable." The Court had construed the Constitution to require school desegregation: "Our personal opinions about the decision have no bearing on the matter of enforcement; the responsibility and authority of the Supreme Court to interpret the Constitution are very clear. . . . The very basis of our individual rights and freedoms rests upon the certainty that the President and the Executive Branch of Government will support and insure the carrying out of the decisions of the Federal Courts."[259]

[256] James David Barber, *The Presidential Character*, 3rd ed. (Englewood Cliffs, NJ: Prentice-Hall, 1985), 136. "[F]or Eisenhower, his duty, first and foremost, was to see that the Constitution, and by implication the Supreme Court's interpretation of it, was upheld." Brownell, *Advising Ike*, 200.

[257] Dwight Eisenhower, quoted in Mayer, "Eisenhower's Conditional Crusade," 32, 34. To White House aides, Eisenhower emphasized that these communications were not for publication; "Our job is to convince; not to publicize." Quoted in Greenstein, *The Hidden-Hand Presidency*, 61. When Billy Graham followed up the president's suggestion of meeting with southern ministers but then used Eisenhower's name in urging them to take action on behalf of moderation, the president chastised him. "I, of course, was completely confident that you would hold confidential any suggestions I made; otherwise I could not have written as I did. . . . [I cannot] make specific suggestions as to what anybody, even the clergy, might do in the circumstances," though of course this is exactly what the president was doing in private correspondence and meetings. Quoted in Mayer, 214.

[258] Dwight Eisenhower, "Telegram to the Governor of Arkansas in Response to his Request for Assurance Regarding his Action at Little Rock, September 5, 1957," in *Public Papers, 1957*, 659.

[259] Dwight Eisenhower, "Radio and Television Address to the American People on the Situation in Little Rock, September 24, 1957," in *Public Papers, 1957*, 690. Brownell reports that when Congress moved to repeal federal statutory authority for presidential use of troops to execute judicial orders, the administration did not object since it believed that the president had inherent authority to enforce the Constitution and support the federal courts. Brownell, *Advising Ike*, 222. See also, Herbert Brownell, "President's Power to Use Federal Troops to Suppress Resistance to Enforcement of Federal Court Orders—Little

A year later, the Supreme Court finally heard a case arising out of the Little Rock situation. When pressed for his "personal feeling" on desegregation just days before the Court accepted that case for decision, the president demurred: "I have always declined to do that for the simple reason that here was something that the Supreme Court says, 'This is the direction of the Constitution, this is the instruction of the Constitution'; that is, they say, 'This is the meaning of the Constitution.' The president's oath was merely "to defend the Constitution of the United States. . . . [and] I expect to carry it out." The White House released a formal statement that if the Court's order in that case was frustrated, then "there can be no equivocation as to the responsibility of the federal government in such an event. My feelings are exactly as they were a year ago."[260] Backed by that support, it is little wonder that when the justices heard the case, *Cooper v. Aaron*, they used it as an opportunity to make their boldest assertion of judicial supremacy to that date.[261]

The Supreme Court's leadership on the civil rights issue allowed legislators to play to their individual constituencies by either directing blame at the Court or lining up with it. The reaction of southern legislators was, of course, intense. Most famously, the "Southern Manifesto" signed by most of the federal legislators from the southern states (but the Speaker of the House and the Senate majority leader, both of Texas, were not asked to sign), railed at the "clear abuse of judicial power" in *Brown* that was "in derogation of the authority of Congress" and "substituted [the justices'] personal and political and social ideas for the established law of the land."[262] According to the *Washington Post*, the immediate position

---

Rock, Arkansas," in *Official Opinions of the Attorneys General*, 41:313. While resolutely refusing to discuss the use of troops in public, the administration began researching its authority to use them soon after resistance to *Brown* began to mobilize. Mayer, Eisenhower's "Conditional Crusade," 235–52.

[260] Dwight Eisenhower, "The President's News Conference of August 20, 1958," in *Public Papers, 1958*, 626; Eisenhower, "Statement by the President on Compliance with Final Orders of the Courts, August 20, 1958," in *Public Papers, 1958*, 631. Similarly, in response to the Southern Manifesto, Eisenhower declared that no responsible southern politician would claim to "defy the Supreme Court" because "when we carry this to the ultimate, remember the Constitution, as interpreted by the Supreme Court, is our basic law." Eisenhower, "The President's News Conference of March 21, 1956," in *Public Papers, 1956*, 340. See also Eisenhower, "The President's News Conference of September 5, 1956," in *Public Papers, 1956*, 737 ("The Constitution is as the Supreme Court interprets it; and I must conform to that and do my very best to see that it is carried out in this country").

[261] Cooper v. Aaron, 358 U.S. 1, 18–19 (1958).

[262] *Congressional Record*, 84th Cong., 2nd sess., 12 March 1956, 4515. Even so, the manifesto implicitly accepted the judicial authority to correctly determine constitutional meaning and limited itself to encouraging "all lawful means to bring about a reversal of this decision which is contrary to the Constitution and to prevent its use of force in its implementation," though this had the effect of launching the strategy of "massive resis-

of southern "moderates" on the decision was exemplified by Louisiana senator Russell Long's response: "Although I completely disagree with the decision, my oath of office requires me to accept it as law. Every citizen is likewise bound by his oath of allegiance to his country."[263] The liberal Tennessee senator Estes Kefauver, under attack from segregationists, explained to home state voters that his hands were tied by the Court: "There is not one thing that a member of the United States Senate can do about that decision [*Brown*]—and anyone who tells you that he's going to do something about it is just trying to mislead you for votes."[264] Georgia senator Richard Russell, a Democratic presidential aspirant, went further and tried, in the *Post*'s estimation, "to pin responsibility for the decision directly on the Republican administration."[265] Russell declared that *Brown* was a "flagrant abuse of judicial power" that "demonstrates that the Supreme Court is becoming the political arm of the executive branch," with the attorney general intervening with "pressure groups" while the Court "supinely transposes the words of the briefs filed by the Attorney General and adopts the philosophy of the brief as its decision."[266]

Northern reaction was less intense, but Democrats (as well as Republicans) outside the South positioned themselves with the Court. Joseph Rauh of Americans for Democratic Action unsuccessfully exhorted the party to embrace *Brown*, for "the Supreme Court has pointed the way for the future."[267] Instead, the very last plank of the 1956 party platform "recognize[d] the Supreme Court of the United States as one of three Constitutional and coordinate branches of the Federal Government, superior to and separate from any political party, the decisions of which are part

---

tance" that eventually led to Little Rock. Stevenson responded to the manifesto by praising its emphasis on "legal processes" and disagreeing with its contention that the Court had abused its authority. "Stevenson Differs on Race Manifesto," *New York Times*, 14 March 1956, 34. Eisenhower likewise emphasized the reference to "legal means," and emphasized, "I can never abandon or refuse to carry out my own duty" in the case of an actual effort at "nullification." Dwight Eisenhower, "The President's News Conference of March 14, 1956," in *Public Papers, 1956*, 304.

[263] Robert C. Albright, "Southerners Assail High Court Ruling," *Washington Post*, 18 May 1954, 2.

[264] "Tennessee Race is Growing Heated," *New York Times*, 25 July 1954, 60.

[265] Albright, "Southerners," 2.

[266] Quoted in ibid., 2. Other southern Democrats likewise "held the Administration responsible." Albright, 2. Russell's linkage of the attorney general and the Court was picked up by others. The *Richmond Times-Dispatch*, for example, later complained of a "Warren-Brownell coup," though it also found Eisenhower complicit. After Little Rock, the *Mobile Register* began referring to "the team of Eisenhower and Brownell." Quoted in Ellis, *Presidential Lightning Rods*, 128, 132. Northern congressional Democrats took the opposite tack and tried to separate the Republicans from the Court and *Brown* by attacking the administration for not doing enough to enforce desegregation. See William S. White, "President Scored on Racial Stand," *New York Times*, 17 March 1956, 1.

[267] Quoted in Martin, *Crisis of Liberalism*, 149.

of the law of the land."[268] New Mexico senator Dennis Chavez proclaimed that *Brown* "meets with my entire thinking and approval," while Minnesota senator Hubert Humphrey urged Congress to "catch up with the American spirit," as the Supreme Court had taken "another step in the forward march of democracy."[269] Indeed, northern congressional Democrats in the wake of *Brown* were concerned that "Republicans will move in on their once vast minority group following" and found stronger appeals on the civil rights issue electorally essential.[270]

The Democratic national leadership's concern with being identified with black civil rights continued into the 1960s, however. Even as President Kennedy heaped praise on Chief Justice Warren, he tried to avoid becoming entangled in the civil rights struggle himself. Doing so, the Kennedy brothers feared, would cost the party more votes than it gained, a special concern for a president who barely carried the electorate in 1960 and needed the majority of both white southerners and black voters to do so.[271] Though approving a party campaign platform calling for civil rights legislation, the "administration determined neither to sponsor a civil rights law, issue a sweeping executive order, nor endorse a frontal assault against the segregation system." When violence in the South made it necessary to take action, the administration "kept the president in the background, and stressed the need to uphold the law, rather than the moral right of blacks to use desegregated facilities."[272] The Justice Department advised citizens that civil rights were "individual, private" and "personal" and to be pursued in court with their own attorneys.[273] In anticipation of James Meredith's court-ordered entry into the University of

---

[268] Quoted in Martin, *Crisis of Liberalism*, 150. See also, Gillon, *Politics and Vision*, 99–102.

[269] Albright, "Southerners," 2. See also William S. White, "Manifesto Splits Democrats Again," *New York Times*, 13 March 1956, 1, 14.

[270] Robert C. Albright, "Rest of Party Might Just Write Off the South," *Washington Post*, 1 April 1956, E1. Humphrey, for one, tried to make the case to his colleagues that these votes were essential to retaining Democratic congressional majorities, as well as individual northern seats. Carl Solberg, *Hubert Humphrey* (New York: Norton, 1984), 170.

[271] Paul Frymer, *Uneasy Alliances* (Princeton: Princeton University Press, 1999), 97. See also Carl M. Brauer, *John F. Kennedy and the Second Reconstruction* (New York: Columbia University Press, 1977), 20–30, 40–60.

[272] Allen J. Matusow, *The Unraveling of America* (New York: Harper & Row, 1984), 64, 74.

[273] Burke Marshall, *Federalism and Civil Rights* (New York: Columbia University Press, 1964), 50. Though Kennedy helped constitute the later Warren Court, the desegregation struggle had made lower-court appointments in the South very politically salient, and Kennedy allowed southern senators to dictate his selections there, though efforts were made to exclude clear segregationists. Johnson was rather more aggressive in vetting candidates to make sure that they were "all right on the Civil Rights question." Goldman, *Picking Federal Judges*, 170; see also Goldman, 167–73; Victor S. Navasky, *Kennedy Justice* (New York: Atheneum, 1971), 243–76; Sowell, "Judicial Vigor," 559–63.

Mississippi, both the president and the attorney general echoed their predecessors in emphasizing to Governor Ross Barnett, "[T]he only thing is I got my responsibility. . . . This is not my order, I just have to carry it out."[274] The Ole Miss episode, which eventually required the intervention of federal troops, forced Kennedy to make his first national address on civil rights, in which he informed the nation, "Even though this Government had not originally been a party to the [Meredith litigation], my responsibility as President was therefore inescapable. . . . My obligation under the Constitution is to implement the orders of the court with whatever means are necessary."[275] By the summer of 1963, however, televised images of violence in the streets, the clear weight of northern public opinion, and international pressure forced the administration to reverse course, with the president telling the nation, "We are confronted primarily with a moral issue. It is as old as the scriptures and is as clear as the American Constitution."[276] After Kennedy's death, Johnson went even further, rhetorically and legislatively. No longer able to straddle the divide, the Democratic Party cast its lot with the civil rights movement and accepted the political consequences.[277]

Legitimation

Dahl's article on the role of the Court in the constitutional system was concerned with demonstrating that judicial review would not be used to

---

[274] John F. Kennedy, quoted in Sowell, "Judicial Vigor," 523. See also, Navasky, *Kennedy Justice*, 187–202; Brauer, *Kennedy and Second Reconstruction*, 184–89.

[275] John F. Kennedy, "Radio and Television Report to the Nation on the Situation at the University of Mississippi, September 30, 1962," in *Public Papers of the Presidents of the United States: John F. Kennedy, 1962* (Washington, DC: Government Printing Office, 1963), 726–27. As with Eisenhower, this blame avoidance strategy was only partly successful. The Mississippi state senate subsequently adopted a resolution denouncing "the Kennedy administration and its puppet courts," while Martin Luther King Jr. complained that "President Kennedy had summoned the nation to nothing more positive than a grim obedience to law." Quoted in Sowell, "Judicial Vigor," 531–32.

[276] John F. Kennedy, "Radio and Television Report to the American People on Civil Rights, June 11, 1963," in *Public Papers, 1963*, 469. Earlier in the year, Kennedy had endorsed *Brown* as "both legally and morally right." Kennedy, "Special Message to Congress on Civil Rights, February 28, 1963," in *Public Papers, 1963*, 225. In finally embracing the civil rights cause as his own, Kennedy sacrificed his public approval among white southerners.

[277] In abandoning the increasingly isolated South, the Democratic Party reaped immediate electoral gains. The political fallout as civil rights disputes moved north proved greater and more complicated than initially expected, however. See Frymer, *Uneasy Alliances*, 97–119; Sundquist, *Dynamics*, 352–75; Ladd and Hadley, *Transformations*, 129–77; Edward G. Carmines and James A. Stimson, *Issue Evolution* (Princeton: Princeton University Press, 1989), 27–88.

obstruct the democratic will as represented in congressional majorities. Having made that demonstration to his satisfaction, Dahl suggested at the very conclusion of his article that the "main task of the Court is to confer legitimacy on the fundamental policies of the successful coalition." Since the Court was not using its power of constitutional interpretation to strike down popular legislation and yet must be serving some function within the national policymaking coalition, Dahl posited that the Court must be accomplishing something by upholding legislation, and legitimation appeared to be a likely possibility. Charles Black subsequently expanded on this account, arguing that "the prime and most necessary function of the Court has been that of *validation*, not that of invalidation." By "satisfying the people" that the government has stayed within its limited powers, the Court "has acted as the legitimator of the government" and facilitated voluntary compliance with government decisions.[278]

There are well-known difficulties with the legitimation hypothesis as inherited from Dahl. For judicial legitimation to work in the manner that Dahl and Black presume, the Court's validation of legislation as constitutional would have to be well known to the public and drive the public to be more accepting of those policies than would otherwise be the case. Unfortunately, there is little evidence that the Court has that kind of visibility or influence. The Supreme Court works in relative obscurity, and the general public is more likely to be aware of cases in which the Court strikes down a law than those in which it upholds legislation. Survey respondents generally support the Court as an institution, but they often disapprove of particular decisions that the Court has rendered. There is little evidence that judicial opinions significantly influence public opinion on substantive issues or that the Court can convert opponents of a given policy result. The Court appears to be more likely to reinforce existing cleavages in public opinion than to build consensus behind policies that it validates.[279]

---

[278] Charles L. Black Jr., *The People and the Court* (New York: Macmillan, 1960), 52.

[279] See Walter F. Murphy and Joseph Tanenhaus, "Public Opinion and the United States Supreme Court: A Preliminary Mapping of Some Prerequisites for Court Legitimation of Regime Change," *Law and Society Review* 2 (1968): 357; Walter F. Murphy, Joseph Tanenhaus, and Daniel Kastner, *Public Evaluations of Constitutional Courts* (Beverly Hills: Sage Publications, 1973); Walter F. Murphy and Joseph Tanenhaus, "Publicity, Public Opinion, and the Court," *Northwestern University Law Review* 84 (1990): 985; Thomas R. Marshall, *Public Opinion and the Supreme Court* (Boston: Unwin Hyman, 1989); Charles H. Franklin and Lisa C. Kosaki, "Republican Schoolmaster: The U.S. Supreme Court, Public Opinion, and Abortion," *American Political Science Review* 83 (1989): 751; Gregory A. Caldeira and James L. Gibson, "The Etiology of Public Support for the Supreme Court," *American Journal of Political Science* 36 (1992): 635; Valerie J. Hoekstra and Jeffrey A. Segal, "The Shepherding of Local Public Opinion: The Supreme Court and *Lamb's Chapel*," *Journal of Politics* 58 (1996): 1079; Anke Grosskope and Jeffrey J. Mondak, "Do Attitudes

It seems unlikely that the Court can often extinguish a serious constitutional controversy, at least one rooted in mass opinion.[280] Likewise, it seems dubious that the Supreme Court conferred much-needed legitimacy on Franklin Roosevelt and the New Deal coalition, the case that both Dahl and Black had most immediately in mind. As argued in the previous chapter, Roosevelt was fully capable of constructing his own constitutional warrants for his actions. At the same time, the research to date on the Court and public opinion provides only indirect clues about the capacity of the judiciary to help legitimate the actions of the other branches. Scholars have focused more attention on the sources and robustness of judicial legitimacy than on the legitimating possibilities of the courts. Evidence on the Court's capacity to shift public opinion has mostly centered on public approval of the policy as such, rather than the public's acceptance of the policy as constitutionally legitimate. Given the stability of the American constitutional regime, it is perhaps unsurprising that scholars have not seriously probed the Court's relative contribution to that stability.

Despite the Court's apparent weakness in altering public opinion, it is still quite possible that affiliated leaders support judicial authority out of concern for whatever legitimation the Court might be able to provide. Of course, politicians might be more willing to credit the legitimating power of courts than political scientists have been. Even if affiliated leaders recognize that winning the constitutional seal of approval from the Court provides little direct benefit with the general public, they may well believe

---

Toward Specific Supreme Court Decisions Matter? The Impact of *Webster* and *Texas v. Johnson* on Public Confidence in the Supreme Court," *Political Research Quarterly* 51 (1998): 633; Valerie J. Hoekstra, "The Supreme Court and Local Public Opinion," *American Political Science Review* 94 (2000): 89; Robert H. Durr, Andrew D. Martin, and Christina Wolbrecht, "Ideological Divergence and Public Support for the Supreme Court," *American Journal of Political Science* 44 (2000): 768; Herbert M. Kritzer, "The Impact of Bush v. Gore on Public Perceptions and Knowledge of the Supreme Court," *Judicature* 85 (2001): 32; James L. Gibson, Gregory A. Caldeira, and Lester Kenyatta Spence, "The Supreme Court and the U.S. Presidential Election of 2000: Wounds, Self-Inflicted or Otherwise?" *British Journal of Political Science* 33 (2003): 535.

[280] It may be possible that the Court can settle less salient constitutional disputes. When the Court first decided in *Clinton v. Jones* that presidents did not enjoy immunity from civil proceedings while in office, Anthony Lewis declared, "But when the Court spoke, that was it. The decision reordered nearly everyone's thinking." Lewis, "When the Court Speaks," *New York Times*, 30 May 1997, A29; Clinton v. Jones, 520 U.S. 681 (1997). It is possible that this seemed true at the time. Lewis himself soon changed his mind on this very issue, however. See Lewis, "What Has Gone Wrong," *New York Times*, 2 March 1998, A17 ("Time has made clear how wrong the Court was . . . this country is going to have to rescue the Presidency from that legal swamp"); Lewis, "Paula Jones: Lessons," *New York Times*, 6 April 1998, A23 (The Court's decision was "divorced from reality"); Lewis, "Some Unfinished Business," *New York Times*, 16 February 1999, A19 ("[W]e must correct the folly of the Supreme Court's 1997 decision in the Paula Jones case").

that when it comes to legitimation every little bit helps. Certainly judicial approval will not harm the affiliated leader in his task of winning acceptance for his actions, and the judiciary's willingness to provide that approval is a point in its favor from the perspective of the elected officials from whom the Court wishes to win support.

The legitimating value of the Court may also operate at a more general level than scholars have assumed. While the general public may not follow the fate of individual statutes as they come before the Court, it may be reassured by the knowledge that the judiciary is, distantly and quietly, guarding constitutional boundaries and inspecting the handiwork of Congress. The courts may not so much legitimate a particular statute by upholding it as they indemnify the legislative process and increase public confidence in the governing system. For affiliated leaders, bolstering judicial authority runs the risk that the Court may use that authority to strike down favored statutes, but it may also help win public trust for the regime as a whole.[281]

The primary value of judicial legitimation of the acts of the affiliated leader may not reside in its effects on the general public, however, so much as in the "self-legitimation" of the political elite. As the political theorist Rodney Barker has insightfully suggested, "What characterizes government . . . is not the possession of a quality defined as legitimacy, but the claiming, the activity of legitimation."[282] This activity of legitimation is largely "self-referential or self-justifying" and pursued "with great intensity at the centre of government and with those engaged in the business of government as its principal consumers."[283] The courts provide a forum within which politicians can demonstrate their reasonableness. The constitutional approval of courts is hardly a necessary aspect of that self-legitimating activity, but once a judicial authority to define constitutional meaning is successfully claimed, it becomes another venue for politicians to present themselves as faithful to the fundamental commitments of the regime and as exercising not just power, but legitimate power. To this extent, politicians recognize the authority of judges so that the judges can in turn recognize the authority of the politicians.

---

[281] Certainly there is evidence that the public values the operational characteristics of the courts and finds political authorities employing those procedures to be more legitimate. See Tom R. Tyler, Jonathan D. Casper, and Bonnie Fisher, "Maintaining Allegiance toward Political Authorities: The Role of Prior Attitudes and the Use of Fair Procedures," *American Journal of Political Science* 33 (1989): 629; Tom R. Tyler and Gregory Mitchell, "Legitimacy and the Empowerment of Discretionary Legal Authority: The United States Supreme Court and Abortion Rights," *Duke Law Journal* 43 (1994): 703; Tom R. Tyler, *Why People Obey the Law* (New Haven: Yale University Press, 1992).

[282] Rodney Barker, *Legitimating Identities* (New York: Cambridge University Press, 2001), 4.

[283] Ibid., 13.

Politicians can also withhold this recognition from the courts. State and federal officials can strike at the symbolic status of the Court simply by refusing to show up. President Jefferson backed up his belief that the Marshall Court did not have jurisdiction over the administration's refusal to deliver William Marbury's commission by declining to send a representative to argue the case before the Court. The chief justice understood that this symbolic refusal to recognize the Court's authority in the case was a likely prelude to a more concrete refusal if the Court were to attempt to order the administration to turn over the commission. In these early years, state governments were likewise prone to refusing to recognize the existence of Court proceedings.

By contrast, the actions of the Federalists during the Sedition Act controversy followed the legitimation rationale as Federalists politicians countered the Jeffersonian assertions of the act's unconstitutionality by pointing to its acceptance and enforcement in the courts. We might expect the Federalists to be particularly likely to use the judiciary in this fashion. In an era in which "democracy" was still regarded with distrust and elections bore a limited relationship to governing authority, the conservative Federalists were particularly skeptical of "the people." The validation of the courts held special appeal within their ideology of order. Similarly, in an era in which politics was largely an elite activity and parties were not yet organized to mobilize the masses, the Federalists disdained popular electioneering and were slow to organize their supporters. Though the Jeffersonians were unlikely to be persuaded by the acceptance of the Sedition Act by the Federalist-appointed judges, the validation of those policies by the courts was an important component of the Federalists' own self-presentation as guardians of the republican constitutional order.

For affiliated leaders operating in less turbulent times than the Federalists in the midst of the Sedition Act crisis, the judiciary may help arbitrate among conflicting claims of orthodoxy. As reconstructive leaders in their own right, Jefferson and Roosevelt were neither impressed by judicial denunciations of their constitutional enterprise nor substantially helped by a tardy judicial imprimatur. When the battle for constitutional reconstruction is under way, the claims of judicial neutrality ring hollow. Neutrality is a more plausible stance, and a more fruitful one, when the constitutional questions are less fundamental, the constitutional regime is vibrant, and the primary political challenge is one of managing the multiple interpreters within it. Here the judge comes closer to the arbitrator, minimizing his "permanent crisis" of authority by solidifying its grip on the professional narrative of independence and the neutral application of shared principles.[284]

---

[284] On the "permanent crisis" of modern courts resulting from their unstable role in resolving social conflicts, see Shapiro, Courts, 8.

As the ideological cleavages were just emerging in the new republic, the Federalists could still hope that favorable judicial decisions would shepherd the Jeffersonians back into the fold. The Carriage Tax Act of 1794 riled Virginians who thought Congress was playing too loose with its constitutional taxing authority, and who also happened to own a disproportionate share of the carriages used in the United States. The 1796 *Hylton* carriage tax case arose from the cooperation of the Virginian dissenters and the federal tax authorities, who both hoped to lay the issue before the Court and win a public judgment. Attorney General William Bradford wrote Alexander Hamilton that he was particularly anxious "not only that the act should be supported, but supported by a unanimous opinion of the judges and on grounds that will bear public inspection." Bradford was especially concerned that Hylton's attorney, the Jeffersonian firebrand John Taylor (who would later sponsor the Virginia Resolution of 1798 in the state legislature), "wishes to prevent the Effect of a decision of the Supreme Court on *full argument* would have" by refusing to appear before the Court.[285] Daniel Lawrence Hylton, however, signed an agreement with the government stating that his goal was "merely to ascertain a Constitutional point," and the government found new attorneys for him who would carry the case before the Supreme Court.[286] When the Court validated the Carriage Tax Act, all sides accepted the issue as settled. Similarly, when the Bank of the United States ran afoul of Maryland's protectionist tax on out-of-state banks as the Era of Good Feelings was winding toward an end, the ideologically sympathetic state government entered into "an amicable arrangement" to put a case before the Supreme Court for prompt resolution, on the understanding that "no further steps [would be] taken" against the bank if the Court ruled against the state.[287]

CONCLUSION

Our standard image of judicial review as antidemocratic suggests that elected officials would simply seek, whenever possible, to disarm judges of this weapon. The judicial authority to interpret the Constitution primarily implies the judicial authority to nullify the work of elected officials, and it would therefore be unsurprising to see politicians seeking to subvert the

---

[285] Quoted in Frankel, "Before Marbury," 8.

[286] Hylton had earlier stipulated to a tax bill of two thousand dollars, the amount necessary for the case to fall within the jurisdiction of the federal courts, although he actually owed (and ultimately expected to pay) only sixteen dollars. Warren, *Supreme Court*, 1:147n1.

[287] Governor Charles Ridgley, quoted in Jessup, *Reaction and Accommodation*, 191. Other states more specifically at odds with the bank and not participants in the suit were less acquiescent.

authority of judges and to install judges committed to judicial deference and restraint. We might expect, with Dahl, to see affiliated leaders greeted by a passive Court.

In fact, judges are often activist when their apparent friends occupy the corridors of legislative power. Either presidents and senators are less successful in installing sympathetic individuals on the bench than scholars have generally assumed or judicial passivism is not the unalloyed good for the affiliated leader that it would appear to be on first impression. In fact, affiliated leaders want more from judges than that they simply get out of the way, and even sympathetic judges want to do more than sit on their hands. There are opportunities for activism within the politics of affiliation.

As Stephen Skowronek has noted, even the affiliated leader wants to hold office in his own right. Presidents, among others, want to act on the regime commitments that they have inherited and to advance their own particular understandings of what those commitments entail. They are hemmed in by expectations and constraints. They must sustain and work with an often fractious coalition. They must continue to win elections. They must manage numerous demands on their time and energy within a context of limited resources. They must overcome challenges to their own authority as faithful interpreters of the constitutional and political regime.

Judges can help the affiliated leader manage his leadership task, and as a consequence politicians have an interest in recognizing and building judicial authority. As reviewed in this chapter, judges can take action on the shared agenda of those affiliated with the established regime while reducing the pressures on coalition leaders. The judiciary is an alternative policymaking resource for affiliated leaders that can be used to advance and secure constitutional commitments. The Court is useful not only when it strikes down policies enacted by independent institutions with which the affiliated leader might disagree (state governments controlled by ideological and partisan opponents, most prominently) but even when it rejects policies adopted by Congress itself. Given the various pressures on Congress, laws that are approved by the legislature are not invariably consistent with the constitutional commitments that affiliated leaders would themselves recognize as important.

The courts are not simply the agents of legislators and presidents, however. Judges have their own substantive agendas and priorities, as well, and the constitutional authority that they possess can be wielded independently. While presidents and legislators can signal the judiciary that they would like the courts to resolve or avoid certain disputes, they rarely exercise direct control over outcomes. Although legislative deferrals to the Court certainly occur, it is also the case that the Court can and does act on its own, intervening even when uninvited and perhaps even immediately unwelcome.[288] The politics of affiliation creates a supportive environment for judicial activism, and judges often seize that opportunity to advance their own substantive goals. The federal judiciary enhanced and empowered by the Republicans in the latter nineteenth century, for example, aggressively moved beyond handling corporate bankruptcies and the like to redefine the rights of property in the Constitution. Similarly, the Warren Court of the late 1960s authored an expansionist vision of civil liberties in areas such as criminal justice that were of little prior concern to liberal Democrats.[289] It is perhaps unsurprising that sympathetic legislators would busy themselves with social and economic policies such as tariffs and social security and judges would take particular interest in the common-law rights of property and the due process rights of criminal defendants. Judges take the inheritance of the reconstructive leader and contribute their own distinctive vision to it.

In some cases, the courts are called upon to reconcile competing strands of the inherited regime. The argumentative style of the judicial arena may encourage courts to perform a synthesizing role, weaving together the various strands of the constitutional regime into a more coherent whole. Where legislators may be paralyzed by cross-pressures within their own base of support, judges may be willing to synthesize and prioritize. Ken Kersch has detailed this tendency in the case of the New Deal Court. The Roosevelt reconstruction was particularly concerned with vindicating the rights of labor to organize the workplace in pursuit of a form of industrial democracy, and of course the justices played an important role in facilitating that effort, including through the reworking of free speech doctrine to provide constitutional protection to labor picketing. Almost immediately, however, the early black civil rights movement challenged that resolution as black workers sought legal protection in court from racist labor unions. In defiance of both statute and the Democrats' labor

---

[288] On legislative deferrals, see Graber, "The Non-Majoritarian Difficulty"; Lovell, *Legislative Deferrals*.

[289] The Kennedy administration, for example, had an ambivalent relationship to the Warren Court's criminal justice activism. The administration was, in fact, ahead of the Court on the question of the provision of legal counsel to indigent criminal defendants, proposing, even before the Court addressed the constitutional issue in *Gideon v. Wainwright*, that Congress both solve the federal problem and provide a model for the states to follow. A few months later, Chief Justice Warren volunteered to Attorney General Robert Kennedy to "take the time to help the cause no matter how busy I might be" in relation to the administration's investigation of the problem of bail in cases involving indigent defendants. The Kennedy Justice Department was rather less enthusiastic, however, about the Court's tightening of law enforcement's ability to conduct searches, including wiretaps (on this, Kennedy echoed Franklin Roosevelt's frustration with, and evasion of, an earlier Supreme Court decision limiting the use of wiretaps). Earl Warren, quoted in Sowell, "Judicial Vigor," 602; on Roosevelt, see Jackson, *That Man*, 68–69. See generally Sowell, 573–605.

constituency, the Court promoted black civil rights in the context of such labor disputes and sought to provide a new vision of minority rights within an industrial democracy.[290]

This is not to say that these judicial efforts to hold together the various pieces of a political coalition will necessarily be successful. It is often precisely the difficulty of the political situation that leads affiliated leaders to turn to the courts to assistance. When elected officials cannot act on their own because they have insufficient electoral and legislative support, judges may be tempted, or invited, to step in. Judicial intervention in such cases may only heighten the tensions pressuring coalition leaders, however. The Taney Court's efforts to preserve the Second Party System and sweep slavery back under the rug only intensified Republican agitation and complicated the leadership task of Democratic moderates. The Warren Court's willingness to move forward on racial civil rights only increased the conflicting demands made on national policymakers by both black leaders and southern politicians and did not avert the eventual necessity facing both parties of making a choice between two potential constituencies and their constitutional expectations.

Judicial activism in the context of the politics of affiliation reflects a blend of ambition on the part of judges and stratagem on the part of elected officials. The Court's willingness to strike down legislation does not evidence the judiciary's existence outside of politics so much as it points out the complicated role of the Court within politics. As the previous chapter indicates, judicial authority cannot be assumed but must be constantly nurtured within the political arena. When judicial ambitions are too disruptive to the plans of other powerful political actors, then those ambitions are likely to encounter serious resistance. Under normal circumstances, however, and given a modicum of political sense on the part of the judges, the authority of the Court is likely to actually be enhanced by judicial interventions. In the politics of affiliation, the justices generally swim with the political current, and they can make substantial progress as a result.

---

[290] Ken I. Kersch, *Constructing Civil Liberties* (New York: Cambridge University Press, 2004), 188–233. See also Paul Frymer, "Acting When Elected Officials Won't: Federal Courts and Civil Rights Enforcement in U.S. Labor Unions, 1935–85," *American Political Science Review* 97 (2003): 483.

FOUR

The Judiciary in the Politics of Opposition

NOT ALL OPPOSITIONAL LEADERS who gain power can claim the authority to reconstruct the inherited constitutional order. Their claims on political leadership are more modest and more tenuous. Unlike presidents such as Jefferson, Jackson, Lincoln, and Franklin Roosevelt, who stand in opposition to a vulnerable set of constitutional commitments ready to be toppled over, other oppositional presidents merely "preempt" a continuing partisan and political order. Such oppositional candidates may manage to win election, but they come to office with relatively little authority and few resources with which to increase their authority. The regime they oppose is still vibrant, popular, and resilient to pressure. Such presidents must learn to accommodate themselves to the dominant regime in order to be successful.

Judicial authority to interpret the Constitution within the politics of opposition is likely to be secure, but the relationship between the Court and the president in such situations is hardly idyllic. Reconstructive presidents are likely to disagree with the constitutional understandings of the Court, and they have the ambitions and capacity to displace the judicial authority to interpret the Constitution with their own. Presidents who are more sympathetic with the constitutional understandings of the Court are likely to find reason to support the independent authority of the Court to act on those understandings. Presidents within the politics of opposition are likely to disagree with the Court about what the Constitution means, and we might expect them therefore to express that substantive disagreement by seeking to subvert the judicial authority to say what the Constitution means. Even if oppositional presidents might harbor such transformative ambitions, few are in a position to launch the reconstructive project. Preemptive presidents will instead have to pick their shots. They may encourage others to adopt their own constitutional understandings, but they will have to defer to the Court's judgment as to whether those understandings are to be accepted and made authoritative. Despite their own disagreements with the Court, such presidents may even find reasons of their own to encourage wider support for judicial supremacy in constitutional interpretation.

The politics of opposition is often driven by presidents who have largely accommodated themselves to the commitments of the established regime.

They are reformers within their own party, seeking to transform their party into a loyal opposition to the established regime. These "third-way" politicians are often able to achieve substantial personal electoral success by blurring party distinctions and offering themselves up as a moderate administrator of the consensus ideology, but their personal success does not lay a firm foundation for broader gains for their party.

When the existing regime has been vibrant, oppositional parties have sometimes found a way to win with "me-too" tickets, but candidates with potentially reconstructive ambitions have been crushed. Henry Clay, a Whig Party founder and congressional leader, offered a clear alternative to the Jacksonian Democrats but was trounced at the polls in 1832 and 1844. William Jennings Bryan helped remake the Democratic Party by allying it with the Populists, but in doing so led them into defeat in 1896, 1900, and 1908. Matching Phyllis Schlafly's exhortations that the GOP offer a "choice, not an echo" in 1964, Barry Goldwater famously sang the virtues of extremism and drew the smallest share of the popular vote since Alf Landon was run over by Franklin Roosevelt in 1936.

As was said of Bill Clinton in 1992, successful candidates are more likely to pick the electoral lock that the dominant party holds on the presidency than to break it. Their routes to the White House are seemingly idiosyncratic. In a generally disadvantageous political environment, they often first gain the White House with the benefit of an independent candidate's campaign siphoning critical voters from the historically dominant party. This was most spectacularly true of Woodrow Wilson, who drew fewer votes in 1912 than had three-time Democratic loser William Jennings Bryan, but nonetheless won an electoral college majority as Theodore Roosevelt's Bull Moose shattered the Republican Party. But several others received less dramatic assistance from spoilers as well. The Free Soil run of former Democratic president Martin Van Buren in 1848 helped Whig Zachary Taylor enter the White House with less than 50 percent of the popular vote. Grover Cleveland got an assist from former Republican congressional leader Ben Butler in 1884 and another from Republican-turned-Populist James Weaver and Prohibitionist John Bidwell in 1892. George Wallace took the South away from the Democrats in 1968, allowing Richard Nixon to gain the spoils of an electoral college victory. As the Ross Perot insurgency confounded traditional electoral calculations, Bill Clinton claimed victory in 1992 despite mustering a popular majority in only Arkansas and the District of Columbia. Those six successful candidates averaged a mere 45 percent of the national popular vote.[1]

---

[1] There have been only two other successful campaigns by nonincumbent, "preemptive" candidates. General William Henry Harrison in 1840 and General Dwight Eisenhower in 1952 both won popular majorities.

In other cases, the oppositional party was willing to accept as its standard bearer a military hero with an indistinct partisan history in order to gain a clean win in the presidential election. Even in the midst of economic depression, the Whigs passed over party stalwart Henry Clay in favor of William Henry Harrison, still best known for his three-decade-old military exploits against the Indians and the British and his studied silence on the issues of the day, to oust a stumbling Democratic incumbent in 1840. General Zachary Taylor returned from the Mexican War covered in glory, and the Whigs seized on his bitter falling-out with the Polk administration to ride him to a narrow victory in 1848. The GOP took a similar gamble in courting Dwight Eisenhower to succeed Harry Truman as a "New Republican" rather than as a Democrat in 1952.

Bad luck and necessary political calculation sometimes combined to boost "accidental presidents" into the politics of opposition. Though Zachary Taylor's cabinet resigned *en masse* as Millard Fillmore remade the administration's alliances and policy positions upon Taylor's death, Fillmore was if anything more recognizable as a Whig. On the other hand, when former Democrat John Tyler took over from the deceased William Henry Harrison barely a month into his term of office, the Whigs paid the price for their ticket-balancing stratagems as the new president gutted their legislative program. The "Union Party" did no better when War Democrat Andrew Johnson assumed the presidency from the martyred Abraham Lincoln and promptly waged political war on the Republican leaders in Congress over the shape of Reconstruction.

Having captured the White House, oppositional leaders have not been able to count on a friendly Congress. Divided government is common in this political context, with such preemptive presidents often facing a Congress held by the other party. During the thirteen presidential terms that might be characterized as preemptive, the same party controlled the House as the presidency only 35 percent of the time and the Senate only 31 percent of the time.[2] The House was most commonly lost during the president's term of office.[3] Richard Nixon joined only the ticket of Zachary Taylor and Millard Fillmore in winning the presidency without car-

---

[2] The president's party also controlled both chambers of Congress simultaneously only 27 percent of the time. By contrast, the other forty-two presidential terms featured same-party control of the House 69 percent of the time and of the Senate 86 percent of the time. Following Skowronek, the preemptive presidents are Harrison/Tyler, Taylor/Fillmore, Andrew Johnson, Cleveland, Wilson, Eisenhower, Nixon/Ford, and Clinton. Skowronek, *The Politics Presidents Make*; Stephen Skowronek, "The Risks of 'Third-Way' Politics," *Society* 33 (1996): 32.

[3] Compared to other presidents, such presidents carry far fewer legislative seats with them in the years that they win the White House, and they lose far more seats during midterm elections. See David A. Crockett, "Samson Unbound: Opposition Presidents and the Failure of Party Leadership," *Social Science Journal* 40 (2003): 371.

rying the House, but only Woodrow Wilson and Grover Cleveland were able to work with a friendly House for an entire term (in both cases, their first term of office). Only the Harrison/Tyler administration and the first Wilson administration enjoyed a full term of same-party control of the Senate. By contrast, Taylor/Fillmore, Cleveland (in his first term), and Nixon never shared party affiliation with a Senate majority. Within the politics of opposition, presidents must either learn to work with the other party or go it alone.

Preemptive presidents may have unusually wide latitude in conducting their office, for their oppositional status often carries few partisan commitments or political expectations that they must satisfy during their administration. Richard Nixon may go to China, invent affirmative action, impose price controls, and create the Environmental Protection Agency with few political repercussions. Bill Clinton may "end welfare as we know it," advance free trade, and oversee domestic spending cuts without alienating his partisan base. The preemptive president seeks to be elected and complete his term without incident; other priorities take a backseat to this minimalist imperative.

Preemptive presidents fit uneasily within the dominant order, lacking sufficient support for pursuing an ideological agenda. As accommodationists, they are unlikely to be fully trusted by their own partisans. At the same time, the dominant order may tolerate and even embrace them. Indeed, an administration like Eisenhower's ("middle-of-the-road, creative Republicanism") or Clinton's ("the era of big government is over") can represent the hegemonic strength of the regime.[4] But preemptive success is contingent on respecting the limits and demands of the new political climate. The disasters of Andrew Johnson's resistance to Reconstruction or Clinton's health care reform are cautionary tales about these limits and their demands.

---

[4] Dwight D. Eisenhower, "Remarks to the Republican National Committee Meeting in Chicago, August 27, 1958," in *Public Papers, 1958*, 651; William J. Clinton, "Address Before a Joint Session of Congress on the State of the Union, January 23, 1996," in *The Public Papers of the Presidents of the United States: William J. Clinton, 1993–2001* (Washington, DC: Government Printing Office, 1994–), *1996*, 79. See also Dwight D. Eisenhower, "The Middle of the Road: A Statement of Faith in America, September 5, 1949," in *Dwight D. Eisenhower*, ed. Martin J. Medhurst (Westport, CT: Greenwood, 1993), 136 ("The middle of the road is derided by all of the right and of the left. They deliberately misrepresent the central position as a neutral, wishy-washy one. Yet here is the truly creative area in which we may obtain agreement for constructive social action compatible with basic American principles and with the just aspirations of every sincere American"); Dwight D. Eisenhower, "To Bradford Grethen Chynoweth, July 20, 1954," in *The Papers of Dwight David Eisenhower*, ed. Louis Galambos and Daun Van Ee, vol. 15 (Baltimore: Johns Hopkins University Press, 1996), 1202 ("I believe that the true radical is the fellow who is standing in the middle and battling both extremes").

The continued strength of the old regime ensures that preemptive presidents cannot expect to advance their oppositional agenda very directly. Their supporters in Congress are likely to be in the minority or to be part of an unstable coalition and unable to unite behind a positive agenda. The loyalty of the executive branch is likely to be questioned, as both its defining programmatic mission and the majority of its personnel were put in place by earlier presidents affiliated with the established regime. In extreme cases, the longevity of the administration itself may be threatened by presidential efforts to gain control over or to circumvent an executive branch that was inherited from ideological foes, as in the cases of Andrew Johnson and Richard Nixon.[5] Party and popular support are likely to be thin and unreliable, given the preemptive president's uncertain relationship to dominant policies and powerful constituencies. In short, the very features that make the old regime resilient remove possible political resources from a preemptive president.

Preemptive presidents are the fly in the ointment for the Dahlian story of the place of the courts in national politics. Dahl's simplified history recognizes only two types of presidents, the reconstructive, who shift politics onto a new path, and the affiliated, who walk alongside the courts down that new path. From the judicial side, courts might temporarily attempt to block the policies of the newly emergent majority but will soon settle into a pattern of passive embrace of the work of their co-partisans on Capitol Hill. From the political side, coalition leaders might have incentives to subvert judicial authority during the politics of reconstruction but to build it back up during more normal times. The possibility of preemptive presidents complicates the narrative in at least three ways. By promoting ideologically jarring legislation, oppositional sojourns in Washington might prompt the Court to rouse itself into a renewed exercise of judicial review. Viewing the courts as an instrument of their adversaries, oppositional leaders might attempt to undercut the judicial authority to define the Constitution. Finally, by making judicial nominations of their own, oppositional presidents might call into question Dahl's assumption that a single coherent coalition will dominate the courts and can thereafter count on their friends on the bench. In fact, none of these simple predictions is borne out in the historical practice. The politics of preemption does indeed complicate Dahl's story, but it does not simply replicate the politics of reconstruction on a smaller scale.

---

[5] There was also loose talk in Congress of impeaching John Tyler. Bill Clinton's troubles did not arise from his political exertions, though his impeachment points out the fragile status of preemptive presidents. See also Keith E. Whittington, "Bill Clinton was no Andrew Johnson: Comparing Two Impeachments," *University of Pennsylvania Journal of Constitutional Law* 2 (2000): 422.

The Ambivalent Embrace of the Courts

The preemptive president is likely to be in opposition to the Court and its understandings of the Constitution as well as to other elected officials and the dominant ideology. The Court will primarily be shaped by affiliated leaders, who will generally control appointments. In addition, the Court's basic agenda and constitutional understandings will be defined in terms of the dominant regime. Like other political institutions, the Court will help articulate the tenets of the dominant regime. As a result, preemptive presidents are likely to find themselves in disagreement with much of the Court's output. Like the reconstructive presidents who are more powerful in their opposition to the inherited regime, preemptive presidents are likely to chafe under the Court's constitutional leadership and will often think that the Court is leading in the wrong direction. Unable to pursue the politics of reconstruction, however, the preemptive leader will see little benefit and much danger in the path of maximal resistance and will refrain from issuing a direct challenge to the judicial authority to say what the Constitution means.

Indeed, the judiciary holds open certain possibilities for the preemptive leader. The Court is likely to be sympathetic to the dominant regime, but at the same time it is a relatively autonomous institution. Its membership is less partisan and less involved in daily political struggles than most elected officials. Moreover, a major concern of the Court is articulating and enforcing the constitutional norms of the dominant regime. Given the tenuous nature of most preemptive presidencies, such leaders are unlikely to advance legislation seriously at odds with the fundamental commitments of the dominant regime. To the extent that this is true, the judiciary is not a primary concern of the preemptive leader; he faces more immediate obstacles. The judiciary's constitutional leadership is no threat to the modest aspirations of presidents in the politics of preemption. Likewise, the dominant regime is too resilient for the preemptive president to make significant progress in articulating an alternative constitutional vision. The preemptive president does not have the authority to call into question the foundations of the dominant regime. He cannot seriously challenge the Court's primacy as the more orthodox interpreter of existing constitutional commitments.

In this context, the judiciary may be an important resource to the president. In their political weakness, preemptive presidents may seek alliances with the courts. Despite their particular disagreements with judicial doctrine, preemptive presidents may find themselves attempting to bolster judicial authority in order to save themselves and serve their own interests. In a hostile political environment, the law and the judiciary may be the best defense that a president has. The judiciary's advantage, from the president's perspective, is only comparative. The presidential embrace of judicial authority arises out of political necessity, not sincere enthusiasm. But an appeal for help from the judicial branch may slow or defeat partisan foes of the president who control the legislative branch, the electorate, and other powerful interests.

The judiciary is valuable to the president because of the complicated nature of law. When the regime is strong, the political context is likely to be inhospitable to the preemptive president. Political opponents have few reasons to support the preemptive president and many reasons to oppose him. The relationship between the president and his political opponents is relatively pure in its antagonism. In the political arena, actors are partisan, and the president is on the wrong side. The law is much more ambiguous. The law, especially constitutional law, is likely to have a relatively long history, its origins predating the rise of the currently dominant regime. As a consequence, the law is not a simple reflection of current commitments, but rather contains elements of older and crosscutting concerns and interests. The law is intertemporal and partially incongruent with the current regime, and as such it may provide shelter from the prevailing political winds. There may be resources within the law with that may be exploited by a creative president to resist the momentum of, or open fissures within, the dominant regime.[6]

The preemptive president's interest in bolstering judicial authority reflects the institutional nature of the courts. Preemptive presidents can ally with the courts only to the extent that the courts take the law seriously. The relative insulation of the judiciary from normal political pressures—that is, the relative independence of the judiciary—prevents it from being a mere instrument of the dominant regime. Although judges are likely to be generally sympathetic with the basic assumptions and commitments of an enduring political order, judges are not immediately accountable to electoral and political interests and are less responsive to transitory political pressures. Judges are not immediately involved in the particular disputes that arise between legislators and preemptive presidents, for example. They are rarely appointed with those disputes in mind, and they are likely to have little stake in their outcomes. The institutional role and norms of the judiciary further insulate the courts from partisan pressures. Judges are supposed to worry about the law, and the individuals selected to be judges are usually socialized into that role.

---

[6] See also Orren and Skowronek, "Iconography of Order"; Karen Orren and Stephen Skowronek, "Institutions and Intercurrence: Theory Building in the Fullness of Time," in *Political Order: NOMOS XXXVIII*, ed. Ian Shapiro and Russell Hardin (New York: New York University Press, 1996); Ackerman, *We the People*, 1:140–62.

The particular procedures of the courts reinforce that orientation, putting lawyers, texts, and precedents in the foreground of judicial operations. The daily working environment of judges distinguishes them from their legislative colleagues.[7]

Partisan legislators are notoriously fickle in their views on institutional power, for example. In what some have called "situational constitutionalism," partisan political actors tend to adopt expansive understandings of the power of the institutions that they currently hold and constricted understandings of the institutions that are held by their opponents, and these commitments may sometimes change on a moment's notice. Thus, Jack Rakove suggests that, "there should be nothing surprising about the discovery that a Republican might be a strong advocate of congressional micromanagement of the presidential conduct of foreign policy during the Clinton presidency, but then be a vigorous proponent of executive prerogative during either the Bush I or Bush II administrations."[8] Congressional Republicans confronting Bill Clinton suddenly adopted a broad reading of the impeachment power and trumpeted the legal analysis of Democratic staffers, including Hillary Rodham, who had prepared the case for impeaching Richard Nixon.[9] Liberals in Congress and academia who had spent decades after Franklin Roosevelt's ascension constructing a vision of a powerful president who could make policy unimpeded by a conservative Congress suddenly learned to fear the "imperial presidency" as it was operated by Republicans such as Richard Nixon.[10] Legislators who find themselves in seemingly stable and unified ideological and partisan majorities soon develop an interest in strengthening the rules favoring

---

[7] See also Smith, "Political Jurisprudence," 89; Ronald Kahn, *The Supreme Court and Constitutional Theory, 1953–1993* (Lawrence: University Press of Kansas, 1994); Howard Gillman, "The Court as an Idea, Not a Building (or a Game): Interpretive Institutionalism and the Analysis of Supreme Court Decision-Making," in Clayton and Gillman, *Supreme Court Decision-Making.*

[8] Jack N. Rakove, "Confessions of an Ambivalent Originalist," *NYU Law Review* 78 (2003): 1346.

[9] Richard M. Pious, "The Constitutional and Popular Law of Impeachment," *Presidential Studies Quarterly* 28 (1998): 806; Richard M. Pious, "Why Do Presidents Fail?" *Presidential Studies Quarterly* 32 (2002): 724.

[10] J. Richard Piper, "Situational Constitutionalism and Presidential Power," *Presidential Studies Quarterly* 24 (1994): 584; J. Richard Piper, "Presidential-Congressional Power Prescriptions in Conservative Political Thought Since 1933," *Presidential Studies Quarterly* 21 (1991): 35; William G. Andrews, "The Presidency, Congress, and Constitutional Theory," in *Perspectives on the Presidency,* ed. Aaron Wildavsky (Boston: Little, Brown, 1975); Theodore J. Lowi, "Presidential Power and the Ideological Struggle Over its Interpretation," in *The Constitution and the American Presidency,* ed. Martin L. Fausold and Alan Shank (Albany: SUNY Press, 1991); Louis W. Koenig, "Historical Perspectives: The Swings and Roundabouts of Presidential Power," in *The Tethered Presidency,* ed. Thomas M. Frank (New York: New York University Press, 1981).

majoritarianism and weakening the rights of legislative minorities, such as the filibuster in the Senate or the disappearing quorum in the House.[11] There are advantages to such ideological fluidity, as it facilitates the Madisonian linkage of interest and institution that keeps a system of checks and balances in good working order.[12]

Judges are likely to be somewhat more consistent and less likely to be situational constitutionalists. While Congress may be unwilling to give new statutory grounds for discretionary action by executive-branch officials of the opposite party, judges are likely to recognize the statutory and precedential bases of discretion that the oppositional president has inherited from affiliated administrations.[13] Having embraced broad theories of inherent presidential powers, judges are unlikely to hedge them simply because they are being exercised by oppositional presidents. Given the precedent-setting effects of judicial decisions, the Court cannot readily afford to ignore the long-term and wide-ranging implications of its decisions affecting the current occupant of a government office. The judiciary cannot so easily reverse course when a more friendly figure occupies the Oval Office, and thus must hold the line when executive-legislative battles spill over into the courtroom. When the Court turns back Barry Goldwater's bid to limit Jimmy Carter's authority to terminate a treaty with Taiwan, judges will later spurn Michael Lowry's plea to constrain Ronald Reagan's use of force in the Persian Gulf, Ronald Dellums's effort to prevent George H. W. Bush from going to war with Iraq, Tom Campbell's suit to stop Bill Clinton from conducting air strikes in Yugoslavia, and Dennis Kucinich's request to block George W. Bush's withdrawal from the Antiballistic Missile Defense Treaty.[14] The willingness of judges to look beyond the officeholder and focus on the office makes the judiciary a somewhat better environment for an oppositional president than are more nakedly partisan venues, and gives such presidents reason to support judicial supremacy in the resolution of such constitutional claims rather than risk a legislative dictate. With the circumstances of divided government and the preemptive president being particularly likely to fos-

---

[11] David W. Rohde, *Parties and Leaders in the Postreform House* (Chicago: University of Chicago Press, 1991); Eric Schickler, *Disjointed Pluralism* (Princeton: Princeton University Press, 2001); Sarah A. Binder, *Minority Rights, Majority Rule* (New York: Cambridge University Press, 1997); Norman Ornstein, "Filibuster Redux: Reform is Needed, but Tread Carefully," *Roll Call*, 21 May 2003.

[12] James Madison, No. 51, in Hamilton, Madison, and Jay, *The Federalist Papers*, 322.

[13] On legislative delegation of discretion under unified and divided government, see David Epstein and Sharyn O'Halloran, *Delegating Powers* (New York: Cambridge University Press, 1999).

[14] Goldwater v. Carter, 444 U.S. 996 (1979); Lowry v. Reagan, 676 F.Supp. 333 (D.D.C. 1987); Dellums v. Bush, 752 F.Supp. 1141 (D.D.C. 1990); Campbell v. Clinton, 52 F.Supp.2d 34 (D.D.C. 1999); Kucinich v. Bush, 236 F.Supp.2d 1 (D.D.C. 2002).

ter separation-of-powers conflicts, the possibility of judicial arbitration of these conflicts becomes particularly important.

DOMESTICATED DEPARTMENTALISM

A central feature of the politics of reconstruction for judicial authority is the emergence of presidential theories of departmentalism, or the equal authority of the president to interpret the Constitution. Reconstructive presidents challenge judicial supremacy in order to cast themselves as leaders in creatively articulating the nation's fundamental commitments. Each branch of government must interpret the Constitution for itself, they have insisted, which in particular means that elected officials cannot regard themselves as bound by the constitutional understandings of judges.

The fact that Andrew Jackson's bank veto raised constitutional objections to the bank was not itself surprising. Presidents ever since George Washington had justified the exercise of the presidential veto on the basis of constitutional infirmities with the bill under consideration, and indeed constitutional considerations were the most common basis for exercising the veto in the early republic. The surprising aspect of the bank veto was that it did not take the constitutionality of the bank as having been settled by previous practice and John Marshall's earlier Supreme Court opinion. Instead, Jackson took the Supreme Court's decision as one relevant factor among many, and not an especially important one at that, in determining whether the constitutional question could be taken as resolved. Far from saying what the Constitution meant, Jackson asserted, the Court could merely express an opinion as to what it might mean. The president was obliged to act on his own judgment, regardless of the opinion of the Supreme Court. The president had at least an equal authority as the Court to interpret the Constitution.

Constitutionally based presidential vetoes suggested that the president had an equal authority to Congress to interpret the Constitution. This could also cause some discomfiture. In some instances, it might be argued that in passing a bill Congress had not attempted to advance an authoritative interpretation of the Constitution. Perhaps constitutional objections had not been thoroughly vetted in legislative debates, such that a presidential veto message might be seen not so much as contradicting Congress as raising issues for congressional deliberation. That certainly was not the case with Jackson's bank veto, since the constitutional issues had been front and center ever since a national bank was first proposed during the Washington administration. But it might be the case with others. In the absence of prior constitutional deliberation, a presidential veto might not assert an independent executive authority to define constitutional meaning, only an authority to participate in a constitutional dialogue. In the presence of mature legislative judgment, however, a presidential veto takes on more of the cast of a departmentalist assertion.

In order to see how distinctive the departmentalist claims of the reconstructive presidents might be, and the extent to which presidential discussions of constitutional issues routinely subvert or support the judicial authority to say what the Constitution means, presidential vetoes are a natural place to begin. The presidential consideration of whether or not to veto legislation raises the possibility of challenging how authoritative the constitutional interpretation of other branches of government might be. Although oppositional presidents may seem particularly likely candidates for departmentalist exertions, this section will also give brief consideration to how affiliated presidents have discussed the constitutionality of proposed legislation. As would be expected, oppositional presidents have been far more likely to sound departmentalist themes, but affiliated and preemptive presidents alike have avoided challenging the interpretive authority of the judiciary. Even in staking out the claim that the president could not close his eyes to the Constitution and see only the law, these political leaders have been careful to recognize the superior warrants of the Court to act as the ultimate constitutional interpreter.

The Presidential Veto in the Nineteenth Century

Early consideration of the veto power recognized that it raised questions of constitutional propriety. After the first revolutionary constitutions stripped the governor of a veto power, the Massachusetts constitution of 1780 reintroduced it as a necessary check on legislative power and preservative of the separation of powers. Without "this Weapon of Defence," John Adams argued, the governor "will be run down like a Hare before the Hunters," and the "independence of the executive and judicial departments" would be lost.[15] In explaining the presidential veto in the federal Constitution, Alexander Hamilton recalled this need for an "effectual power of self-defense," but added that the veto "not only serves as a shield to the executive," but also "establishes a salutary check upon the legislative body . . . [and] the effects of faction, precipitancy, or of any impulse unfriendly to the public good." An executive with even "a common share of firmness" would be able, "in a very plain case," to stop the

---

[15] John Adams, "To Elbridge Gerry, November 4, 1779," in John Adams, *The Papers of John Adams*, ed. Robert J. Taylor et al., vol. 8 (Cambridge: Harvard University Press, 1989), 276; Adams, "The Report of a Constitution or Form of Government for the Commonwealth of Massachusetts, October 28–31, 1779," in *Papers*, 242. On the development of the veto power in the early state constitutions, see Marc Kruman, *Between Authority and Liberty* (Chapel Hill: University of North Carolina Press, 1997), 123–30.

public good from being "evidently and palpably sacrificed."[16] Upon seeing the new federal Constitution, Jefferson wrote to Madison from Paris that he liked the inclusion of a presidential veto, though he wished the judiciary had been "invested with a similar . . . power."[17] As secretary of state, Jefferson fretted that Washington was setting a precedent by "non-use of his negative" and finally expressed relief "to have at length an instance of the negative being exercised" on a legislative apportionment bill that Congress had passed "without explaining any principle at all, which may shew it's conformity with the constitution."[18] The veto, he explained to the president, was a shield to "protect against the invasions of the legislature" not only of the executive branch but also of the judiciary and the states.

Even so, it was Jefferson, later known for his departmentalism in pursuing his own politics of reconstruction, who summed up a fairly deferential approach to the veto power in advising Washington on the first bank bill. A "just respect" for the legislature should lead the president to defer unless it "is tolerably clear that [a bill] is unauthorized by the Constitution." The presidential check was to be reserved for those cases where the legislators "are clearly misled by error, ambition, or interest."[19] Washington tended to agree, telling one correspondent that the president should only exercise the veto in "clear and obvious" cases but should defer to the legislature in all "doubtful cases."[20] Given his dominance of Congress during his own administration, Jefferson did not find the need to use the veto power as president.

James Monroe took a highly visible stand for orthodox Jeffersonian constitutional values, exerting presidential prerogatives to bolster and defend inherited understandings. His concern was with congressional backsliding. When President Monroe saw fit to warn Congress in his first state of the union address that long deliberation had led to "a settled conviction in my mind that Congress do not possess the right" to appropriate funds for internal improvements (i.e., roads and canals), a committee formed to

[16] Alexander Hamilton, No. 73, in Hamilton, Madison, and Jay, *The Federalist Papers*, 442, 443, 445.

[17] Thomas Jefferson, "To James Madison, December 20, 1787," in *The Papers of Thomas Jefferson*, ed. Julian P. Boyd, vol. 12 (Princeton: Princeton University Press, 1955), 440.

[18] Thomas Jefferson, "Memoranda of Consultations with the President, March 11–April 9, 1792," in *Papers*, 23:264; Jefferson, "Opinion on Apportionment Bill, April 4, 1792," in *Papers*, 23:375, 370.

[19] Thomas Jefferson, "Opinion on the Constitutionality of a National Bank, February 15, 1791," in *Papers*, 19:279, 280.

[20] George Washington, "To Edmund Pendleton, September 23, 1793," in *The Writings of George Washington*, ed. John C. Fitzpatrick, vol. 33 (Washington, DC: Government Printing Office, 1940), 96.

consider his message reported to the House of Representatives that the president's conclusion should not "be permitted to have any influence on the disposition of Congress to legislate on this interesting subject." The committee did not doubt the legitimacy of the president's adhering to his independent understanding of the Constitution. It merely observed that a "constitutional majority" could override the president's judgment, "however respectable" it might be, and urged that Congress should not refrain from exploring the question on its own and determining whether as much as a third of either chamber agreed with the president's views.[21] As it turned out, they did, and Monroe was able to restrict Congress to the appropriations that he thought constitutional.

Andrew Jackson's use of the veto as an instrument of constitutional reconstruction aroused far more controversy, and his constitutional assertions were intended to be transformative. Monroe felt the need to remove any "uncertainty" about his position on internal improvements precisely because this was an ongoing controversy.[22] By contrast, Jackson was reviving a constitutional debate that had been settled in the previous regime. After losing the battle with Hamilton over the formation of the first bank during the Washington administration and suffering the fiscal humiliations of attempting to fight the War of 1812 without the resources of the bank, the Jeffersonians had made their constitutional accommodations with it. Jackson sought to wipe out those corruptions of the constitutional faith. Henry Clay moaned, "It is cry down old constructions of the Constitution . . . make all Mr. Jefferson's opinions the articles of faith of the new Church."[23] But when the president vetoed Clay's own Maysville Road project as unconstitutional, Jackson expressed regret that the "symmetry and purity of the Government" had been sacrificed as every administration after Jefferson's "adopted a more enlarged construction of the power" of the national government than the "most valuable principles" that Jefferson himself had articulated. Past subversions emphasized "the necessity of guarding the Constitution with sleepless vigilance against the authority of precedents," and he reminded the legislators that "it is the duty of all to look to that sacred instrument instead of the statute book," though he admitted that "individual differences should yield to a well-settled acquiescence of the people and confederated authorities in particular constructions of the Constitution on doubtful points."[24]

[21] James Monroe, "First Annual Message, December 2, 1817," in Richardson, 2:18; *Annals of Congress*, 15th Cong., 1st sess. (December 15, 1817), 452 (Henry Tucker).

[22] Monroe, "First Annual Message," in Richardson, *Messages and Papers*, 2:18.

[23] Henry Clay, "To James E. Conover, May 1, 1830," in *The Papers of Henry Clay*, ed. James F. Hopkins, vol. 8 (Lexington: University of Kentucky Press, 1984), 200.

[24] Andrew Jackson, "Veto Message, May 27, 1830," in Richardson, *Messages and Papers*, 2:485, 487. On the transformative character of Jackson's vetoes, see Gerard N. Magli-

But the standard for "well-settled acquiescence" was clearly very high, for, as Jackson elaborated in his bank veto, "[m]ere precedent is a dangerous source of authority," and he was unwilling to recognize the constitutionality of the bank as settled. The president was still free to support the Constitution "as he understands it" and to form his opinion independently of either the legislators or the judges.[25] In his retirement, Madison took to instructing all sides on the correct understanding of the Constitution, rebuking those who deviated, and trying to save himself from charges of inconsistency. Listening to the debate leading up to the bank veto, he took the Jacksonians to task for "a defiance of all the obligations derived from a course of precedents amounting to the requisite evidence of the national judgment and intention" and asked whether the safer "construction of a constitution" was to be found in the "uniform sanction of successive legislative bodies" or the "opinions of every new Legislature . . . led astray by the eloquence and address of popular statesmen."[26] Daniel Webster, the bank's great advocate, expressed astonishment that the president would refuse to accept "the constitutionality of the bank [as] a settled question." Jackson wanted to assert "a right of individual judgment on constitutional questions," but "hitherto it has been thought that the final decision of constitutional questions belonged to the supreme judicial tribunal. The very nature of free Government, it has been supposed, enjoins this: and our constitution, moreover, has been understood so to provide, clearly and expressly. . . . *The President may say a law is unconstitutional, but he is not the judge.*"[27]

The veto was used, and contested, rather differently when John Tyler occupied the presidency as a Whig and assumed the posture of one neither clearly affiliated with nor clearly oppositional to the Jacksonian regime. The propriety and substance of Jackson's vetoes helped motivate the formation of the Whig Party, and therefore it was all the more shocking when the first term of a Whig presidency brought more such vetoes. As a governor and senator from Virginia, John Tyler had been a wary ally of Jackson's but finally broke from the president during his second term over

occa, "Veto! The Jacksonian Revolution in Constitutional Law," *Nebraska Law Review* 78 (1999): 205.

[25] Jackson, "Veto Message, July 10, 1832," in Richardson, *Messages and Papers*, 2:581, 582.

[26] James Madison, "To Charles J. Ingersoll, June 25, 1831," in *Letters and Other Writings*, 186. See also Madison, "To C. E. Haynes, February 25, 1831," in *Letters and Other Writings*, 165; "To Joseph C. Cabell, May 31, 1830," in *Letters and Other Writings*, 4:86; "To N. P. Trist, June 3, 1830," in *Letters and Other Writings*, 4:87; "To Martin Van Buren, July 3, 1830," in *Letters and Other Writings*, 4:88. On Madison in retirement, see Drew R. McCoy, *The Last of the Fathers* (New York: Cambridge University Press, 1989).

[27] *Register of Debates*, 22nd Cong., 1st sess. (11 July 1832), 1229, 1231, 1232 (Daniel Webster) (emphasis added).

his response to nullification and his withdrawal of the government's funds from the bank without congressional authorization. His inclusion on the 1840 presidential ballot reflected the hope that "[c]o-operation between the Whigs and Conservatives will secure a majority against the Administration," though Tyler's principles were often at odds with those of his erstwhile allies.[28] The Whigs did not publish a platform in 1840 and successfully stole the Democrat's thunder with their "Log Cabin and Hard Cider" campaign of the common man, but late in the campaign Tyler was pressed to declare whether he had renounced his previous strict constructionist commitments. Though equivocating a bit, he finally averred that he had never "departed from the principles of the old Republican Party, in word or deed" and that he remained a "Jeffersonian Republican."[29]

Upon accepting the office of president on Harrison's death, Tyler issued a statement to serve in the stead of an inaugural address expressing the principles to govern his administration. While he notably pledged to abandon Jackson's spoils system and to faithfully enforce existing laws, he called for measures to restore an adequate financial system but promised only to sign such measures that were "in conformity to the Constitution" as indicated by the "fathers of the great republican school." Only strict adherence to the constitutional limits on national power would preserve "the blessings of union" and prevent the generation of "factions intent upon the gratification of their selfish ends."[30] In private communications and an address to a special session of Congress, Tyler elaborated on his constitutional concerns with the more ambitious aspects of the Whig program advanced by Clay. While happy to concur with Congress in a new financial plan, he necessarily reserved "to myself the ultimate power of rejecting any measure which may in my view of it, conflict with the Constitution . . . a power which I could not part with even if I would."[31] Former president John Quincy Adams wailed to his diary that Tyler, "who styles himself President of the United States . . . is a political sectarian, of the slave-driving, Virginian, Jeffersonian school."[32] Nonetheless, Clay, who had already bullied President Harrison into calling the special session and

---

[28] Henry Clay, quoted in Michael F. Holt, *The Rise and Fall of the American Whig Party* (New York: Oxford University Press, 1999), 99. In this 1839 letter to the Virginia Whigs, Clay was immediately concerned with forging an alliance that could control the Senate and secure his own nomination for the presidency.

[29] Quoted in Oliver Perry Chitwood, *John Tyler* (New York: D. Appleton-Century, 1939), 191.

[30] John Tyler, "Inaugural Address, April 6, 1841," in Richardson, *Messages and Papers*, 4:39.

[31] John Tyler, "Special Session Message, June 1, 1841," in Richardson, *Messages and Papers*, 4: 46.

[32] John Quincy Adams, *The Diary of John Quincy Adams*, ed. Allan Nevins (New York: Longmans, Green, 1929), 522 (16 April 1841), 520 (4 April 1841).

been rebuked by him for being "too impetuous," expected to be able to steamroll the new president, thirteen years Clay's junior and the youngest person to assume the presidency to that date.[33] Clay laid out his legislative program for one of Tyler's confidantes, Virginia representative Henry Wise, who complained, "These are his cardinals, and he is their pope."[34] When Clay insisted on bringing forward a bank bill in the special session, Tyler advised him that such an action would be premature and threaten the party. When Clay refused to consider a more modest proposal that seemed to meet the president's constitutional scruples and had already won Webster's endorsement, Tyler exploded, "Go you now then, Mr. Clay, to your end of the avenue, where stands the Capitol, and there perform your duty to the country as you shall think proper. So help me God, I shall do mine at this end of it as I shall think proper."[35]

Tyler advanced various aspects of the Whig program in Congress, but when Clay pushed through an unreconstructed version of the bank, the president balked. In his veto message, Tyler explained that the constitutionality of the bank "has been a question of dispute from the origin of the Government" and remained an "unsettled question" in the country at large. Given that his "own opinion has been uniformly proclaimed to be against the exercise of any such power by this Government" and having taken "an oath that I would 'preserve, protect, and defend the Constitution of the United States,'" it "would be to commit a crime" to sign the bank bill now.[36] Less than a month later he vetoed a lightly revised bank bill on the same grounds. While he admitted that the veto power "ought to be most cautiously exerted," the president's "duty is to guard the fundamental will of the people themselves from (in this case, I admit, unintentional) change or infraction by a majority in Congress," and he could not

[33] Harrison quoted in Merrill D. Peterson, *The Great Triumvirate* (New York: Oxford University Press, 1987), 301. Clay told a colleague, "Tyler dare not resist; I will drive him before me." Quoted in Chitwood, *John Tyler*, 210n31.

[34] Henry Wise, "To Beverly Tucker, May 29, 1841," in *The Letters and Times of the Tylers*, ed. Lyon G. Tyler, vol. 2 (Richmond, VA: Whittet & Shepperson, 1885), 34. Wise later complained that Clay was "madly jealous" of Tyler and wanted "to drive him to a veto if he can," and Tyler was in turn bound to veto Clay's "full-grown central monster." Wise, "To Beverly Tucker, June 5, 1841," in Tyler, *Letters and Times*, 2:38.

[35] Quoted in Chitwood, *John Tyler*, 215. See also Robert V. Remini, *Henry Clay* (New York: Norton, 1991), 578–99.

[36] John Tyler, "Veto Message, August 16, 1841," in Richardson, *Messages and Papers*, 4:64. Kentucky governor Robert Letcher complained to holdover attorney general John Crittenden, who soon resigned, "After I saw he had some four or five Virginia schoolmasters around him, I confess I lost all hope. Ah, that was too bad!—our chief cook, in whom we placed all confidence, to poison our favorite dish!" R. P. Letcher, "To J. J. Crittenden, September 3, 1841," in *The Life of John J. Crittenden*, ed. Mrs. Chapman Coleman, vol. 1 (Philadelphia: J. B. Lippincott, 1873), 161.

abandon it simply "because a majority in Congress have passed a bill" and held a contrary opinion.[37]

Like Jackson before him, Tyler was assailed by many Whigs for claiming an independent authority to interpret the Constitution. Tyler could afford to be more modest in his departmentalism, however. Jackson's actions had cleared a path for Tyler to act on his own constitutional sensibilities without disparaging the judicial authority to settle constitutional meaning. Secretary of State Daniel Webster contributed to an anonymous editorial in the prominent Whig paper, the *National Intelligencer*, urging conciliation. It might have been hoped that Tyler would distinguish "between the legislative and executive character, which would allow of his signing an act in one capacity which he would vote against in the other," but his veto was an honorable one and the party should move on.[38] Other Whig politicians and outlets were more bitter. Clay among others pointed out that when Tyler asserted that the constitutionality of the bank had been a disputed one, he ignored "that department, whose interpretations of the Constitution . . . are binding upon all, and which, therefore, may be considered as exercising a controlling power over both the other departments," the Supreme Court. Only "pride" and "vanity" could prevent a president from "yield[ing] his private opinion to the judgment of the nation."[39] Far more dangerous to the Constitution than the elected representatives of the people was a president "relying on [his] own preconceived opinions, [who has] resolved to administer the Constitution just as [he] understand[s] it, not caring for the solemn adjudication of our courts of justice."[40]

---

[37] Tyler, "Veto Message, September 9, 1841," in Richardson, *Messages and Papers*, 4:68, 69.

[38] "The Veto," *National Intelligencer*, 17 August 1841, 3. See also Daniel Webster, "President Tyler's Veto of the United States Bank Bill, August 16, 1841," in *The Writings and Speeches of Daniel Webster*, vol. 15 (Boston: Little, Brown, 1903), 135. Tyler later did distinguish between his legislative and presidential responsibilities, saying in a signing statement on a congressional apportionment bill, "When I was a member of either House of Congress I acted under the conviction that to doubt as to the constitutionality of a law was sufficient to induce me to give my vote against it; but I have not been able to bring myself to believe that doubtful opinion of the Chief Magistrate ought to outweigh the solemnly pronounced opinion of the representatives of the people and the States." Tyler, "Special Message, June 25, 1842," in Richardson, *Messages and Papers*, 4:159. His restraint was hardly appreciated. John Quincy Adams authored a report for a House select committee denouncing the statement as "a defacement of the public records." *President's Reasons for Signing a Bill for the Apportionment of Members of the House of Representatives*, 27th Cong., 2nd sess., July 16, 1842, H.R. Rept. 909, 2.

[39] *Congressional Globe*, 27th Cong., 1st sess. (19 August 1841), app. 364, 369, 365 (Sen. Henry Clay).

[40] *Congressional Globe*, 27th Cong., 1st sess. (10 September 1841), app. 392 (Rep. Samson Mason).

Tyler and the supporters of his veto carefully refrained from questioning the authority of the Court, however. He had already framed his strategy during the presidential campaign, citing to the Democratic editors of the *Richmond Enquirer* Harrison's own statement: "There is not in the Constitution any express grant of power for such a purpose [to incorporate a bank], and it could never be constitutional to exercise the power, save in the event the power granted to Congress could not be carried into effect without resorting to such an institution."[41] The Supreme Court had allowed a bank if it were "necessary and proper" to the implementation of legitimate federal objectives but had left the determination of whether a bank was in fact necessary up to the political branches. For the bank's opponents, Jackson's earlier destruction of the bank had already demonstrated that the powers of Congress could be carried into effect "without resorting to such an institution." While Tyler thought Jackson's own financial arrangements were inexpedient and needed to be changed, there was a range of alternatives available that did not encroach on the authority of the state governments like a national bank would.

Tyler's assertion of authority was directed at Congress, not the courts.[42] As Henry Wise, a close advisor to the president and a fellow Virginian Whig, noted, Tyler only claimed the authority to independently interpret the laws when acting in his legislative, not in his executive, capacity.[43] His departmentalism had limits. The Court had left room for the exercise of political judgment in determining the constitutional propriety of a national bank, and Clay's adversaries intended to use it. It would not bring "the Legislative directly into conflict with the Judiciary department" to refuse to *revive* a law that the Court once accepted as constitutional.[44] Regardless of the situation when Madison approved the Second Bank of

---

[41] Quoted in Chitwood, *John Tyler*, 190.

[42] Unsurprisingly, this only heightened the fury of the Whigs in Congress. Upon receiving Tyler's first bank veto, Clay took to the floor to advise the president that, given his constitutional concerns, he should have either allowed the bill to pass into law without his signature or resigned from office. *Congressional Globe*, 27th Cong., 1st sess. (August 19, 1841), app. 365. Perhaps understandably, given that the Court was no longer allied with Clay, he did not suggest to Tyler that he allow the bill to become law and let the new bank be tested in the courts. Clay preferred to focus on the judicial decision already in hand. When Tyler issued two more vetoes in the regular legislative session, a select committee chaired by John Quincy Adams reported that it preferred impeachment, would settle for a constitutional amendment to restrict the veto power, hoped for electoral reinforcement, and expected the judiciary to come to its aid against an executive who had assumed "the exercise of the whole Legislative power to himself." *Report on Veto of New Tariff of Duties*, 27th Cong., 2nd sess., August 16, 1842, H.R. Rept. 998, 35.

[43] Ibid., 415.

[44] *Congressional Globe*, 27th Cong., 1st sess. (2 August 1841), app. 293 (Rep. Romulus Saunders). See also ibid., app. 176 (Rep. Robert McClellan).

the United States in 1816, things were different by 1841. As Democratic Senate leader Thomas Hart Benton had earlier argued, through his actions Jackson had "demonstrated, by the fact itself, that a national bank is not 'necessary' to the fiscal operations of the Federal Government, and in that demonstration . . . knocked from under the decision of the Supreme Court the assumed fact on which it rested."[45] While that response would hardly have been decisive to John Marshall, Marshall was no longer chief justice. Chief Justice Taney and his recently appointed colleagues might well take a different view of the matter.[46] The reconstituted Court was a "lion in the path . . . a roaring lion," and the "temporary majority, doubtful in its character" in Congress was hardly in a position to claim that there was now settled support for a bank.[47]

Tyler was not the last antebellum president to raise constitutional objections to a bill, but he was the last to generate such controversy. Rather than challenging the constitutional beliefs of legislative majorities, the later vetoes by Democratic presidents served only to remind legislators of their shared commitments. The last Whig president, Millard Fillmore, threw his lot in with moderate Whigs and Democrats and signed on to the Compromise of 1850 put together by Stephen Douglas. It sought to throw crucial constitutional questions regarding slavery into the courts for resolution. In his first state of the union address, Fillmore admitted a willingness to use the veto on any bills that "should appear to me unconstitutional," but he promised that in "domestic policy the Constitution will be my guide, and in questions of doubt I shall look for its interpretation to the judicial decisions of that tribunal which was established to expound it." But in truth the most important work of his presidency was already done, and he exhorted Congress and the nation to embrace the "irrevocable" compromise as "a final settlement" of the slavery controversy.[48]

Fillmore's unwillingness to follow the "Conscience Whigs" into more fundamental abolitionist opposition subsequently cost him a presidential nomination in his own right. When pressed on the constitutionality of the Fugitive Slave Act, a component of the compromise, Fillmore placed his

---

[45] *Register of Debates*, 24th Cong., 2nd sess. (12 January 1837), 387 (Sen. Thomas Hart Benton).

[46] *Congressional Globe*, 27th Cong., 1st sess. (2 August 1841), app. 293 (Rep. Romulus Saunders); ibid., app. 301 (Rep. John Thomas Mason). Daniel Webster shared that opinion, which was one reason he urged the congressional Whigs to unite with the president rather than "beat the field of constitutional argument all over again." Quoted in Peterson, *The Great Triumverate*, 306. See also Mark A. Graber, "The Jacksonian Makings of the Taney Court," unpublished paper.

[47] *Congressional Globe*, 27th Cong., 1st sess. (6 August 1841), app. 414 (Rep. Henry Wise).

[48] Millard Fillmore, "First Annual Message, December 2, 1850," in Richardson, *Messages and Papers*, 5:79, 93.

reliance on Attorney General John Crittenden, who declared that the act was "sanctioned by the decisions of the Supreme Court."[49] To which abolitionist Lewis Tappan sighed, "[I]t is a common thing for a time-serving President to endeavor to shelter himself under the wing of his legal advisor, when he is unwilling to take the responsibility the Constitution devolves upon him," and Charles Sumner thundered that Fillmore had sunk into the "depths of infamy" and that what was needed was a leader of "inflexible will" and "back-bone."[50] Fillmore responded in turn that "the main opposition is aimed at the Constitution itself" and the "issue which they present is one which involves the supremacy and even the existence of the Constitution." Rather than reopen the debate, the president urged a "general acquiescence" to the commands of "our cherished inheritance from our Revolutionary fathers."[51]

A kind of domesticated departmentalist rhetoric was employed by the next elevated vice president, Andrew Johnson. Like Tyler, the former Democrat Johnson was the southern half of a cobbled together ticket designed to secure a majority for an oppositional party. In this case, however, the oppositional party had launched an effort at constitutional reconstruction, and Johnson was not an entirely willing partner. With the end of major combat operations in the South, Johnson saw the opportunity for a speedy reconciliation and the realization of his major objective of a restored union, which sounded to Republican lawmakers too much like the Democratic wartime motto of "the union as it was, and the Constitution as it is."[52] With the onset of peace and Reconstruction rupturing wartime partisan alliances, the newly installed protégé of Andrew Jackson found himself assuming an oppositional stance within the still consolidating Republican regime, and congressional leaders took up the dropped standard of constitutional transformation.

Faced with a Congress thoroughly dominated by his ideological antagonists producing a stream of legislation at odds with constitutional requirements as he understood them, Johnson soon turned to the veto. He quickly outstripped Jackson, Tyler, and his other predecessors in the num-

---

[49] "Constitutionality of the Fugitive Slave Bill, September 18, 1850," *Official Opinions of the Attorneys General of the United States*, vol. 5 (Washington, DC: Government Printing Office, 1852), 256. Crittenden advised those critical of the act to "keep their consciences to themselves." Quoted in Albert D. Kirwan, *John J. Crittenden* (Lexington: University of Kentucky Press, 1962), 269.

[50] Lewis Tappan, *The Fugitive Slave Bill*, 3rd ed. (New York: William Harnard, 1850), 10n*; Charles Sumner, "Our Immediate Antislavery Duties, November 6, 1850," in *Works*, 3:130, 146.

[51] Millard Fillmore, "Second Annual Message, December 2, 1851," in Richardson, *Messages and Papers*, 5:138.

[52] "The Union as it Was, and the Constitution as it is," *New York Times*, 18 October 1864, 4; Joel H. Silbey, *A Respectable Minority* (New York: Norton, 1977), 69.

ber of vetoes issued, but he also had the dubious distinction of being the first to have a veto of an important piece of legislation overridden. Veto overrides became a routine feature of the Johnson presidency, and he accumulated more than any other president before or since. In exercising his veto power, Johnson was emphatic on his responsibility to act on his own understanding of the Constitution. When Congress first met after Appomattox, Johnson presented them with newly reconstituted Southern governments, a policy "attended with some risk" but "in the choice of difficulties, it is the smallest risk" and called for the restoration of fully functioning civilian government and courts throughout the union.[53] Congress refused to seat the Southern representatives and, after Johnson exercised his first veto of a Reconstruction measure in part because the states most affected were "shut out . . . from the representation to which [they are] entitled by the Constitution," the legislature passed a concurrent resolution stating that they would not be seated "until *Congress* shall have declared such State entitled to such representation."[54]

Like Tyler, Johnson's constitutional objections were aimed at Congress and did not seek or need to question the interpretive authority of the courts. As Johnson explained to a group of supporters, "I say, then, when you comply with the Constitution, when you yield to the law, when you acknowledge allegiance to the Government—I say let the door of the Union be opened, and the relation be restored to those who had erred and strayed from the fold of our fathers." Instead, Johnson charged, congressional Republicans were attempting "now to concentrate all power in the hands of a few at the federal head, and thereby bring about a consolidation of the Republic, which is equally objectionable to its dissolution." By contrast, "I stand to-day prepared to resist encroachments on the Constitution, and thereby preserve the Government." With the end of the war, Johnson declared, the Constitution "is again unfolded, and the people are invited to read and understand it, and to maintain its provisions" against transient factions.[55] Congress understandably reacted with alarm. Maine Republican William Fessenden observed that the president's objection "goes to the foundation" and "strike[s] at the very existence of this body as a power in the government," and he called on Congress "to assert its

<hr />

[53] Andrew Johnson, "Annual Message, December 4, 1865," in *The Political History of the United States of America during the Period of Reconstruction*, ed. Edward McPherson (Washington, DC: Solomons & Chapman, 1875), 64, 65.

[54] Andrew Johnson, "Veto of the Freedmen's Bureau Bill, February 19, 1866," in McPherson, *Political History*, 71; *Journal of the House of Representatives*, 39th Cong., 1st sess. (20 February 1866), 300 (emphasis added).

[55] Andrew Johnson, "Speech of the 22nd February, 1866," in McPherson, *Political History*, 59, 60, 62, 63.

own rights and its own position with reference to all these questions."[56] While congressional dissenters pointed to judicial opinions suggesting that the Southern states were immediately entitled to their constitutional representation in Congress once peace had been restored, the majority emphasized that it was for Congress alone "to fix the political relations of the States to the Union."[57] His first veto of Reconstruction legislation was narrowly sustained, but it was the last time Johnson was able to muster enough votes to sustain his negative on important legislation. After his veto of the Civil Rights Bill a month later, one Ohio Republican concluded that Johnson could no longer be part of the effort to "consolidate the Union party and secure its future power."[58] As Fessenden grimly explained to his son, "It is all important now that we should have two-thirds in each branch," and with the expulsion of the Democratic senator from New Jersey and the firming up of the "weak and unreliable" in Republican ranks, they did.[59]

Fresh from victory in the midterm elections of 1866, the congressional Republicans imposed a new plan of Reconstruction on the administration and the South. On March 2, 1867, Congress dismantled the state governments in the South and divided the region into military districts, required that all military orders from the president go through General Ulysses Grant, who was himself protected from presidential removal or transfer, and prohibited the president from removing civil officers without the consent of the Senate.[60] The Reconstruction Act and the Tenure of Office Act were passed over a presidential veto. Johnson issued a signing statement containing "my protest" against the provision of the Army Appropriations Act that "virtually deprives the President of his constitutional functions as Commander-in-Chief," but did not attempt to veto "these necessary appropriations."[61] When the president and state and federal civil

[56] *Congressional Globe*, 39th Cong., 1st sess. (23 February 1866), 986, 987 (Sen. William Fessenden).

[57] "Majority and Minority Reports of the Joint Committee on Reconstruction, June 18, 1866," in McPherson, *Political History*, 85. See also, Andrew Johnson, "Veto Message, July 19, 1867," in Richardson, *Messages and Papers*, 6:541.

[58] Warner Bateman, quoted in Eric L. McKitrick, *Andrew Johnson and Reconstruction* (Chicago: University of Chicago Press, 1960), 303. Indiana governor Oliver Morton warned Johnson that a veto of the Civil Rights Bill "would be the rock upon which the President and the Republican party would separate," and that "all roads out of the Republican party led into the Democratic party." Quoted in ibid., 309.

[59] Quoted in ibid., 323, 323n105.

[60] Government of the Rebel States, *U.S. Statutes at Large* 14 (1868): 428; Army Appropriation Act, *U.S. Statutes at Large* 14 (1868): 485, 486–87; Tenure of Civil Officers Act, *U.S. Statutes at Large* 14 (1868): 430.

[61] Andrew Johnson, "Message Accompanying the Approval of the Army Appropriation Bill, March 2, 1867," in McPherson, *Political History*, 178.

government officials interfered with military commanders in the South, Congress gave the latter further power to disregard and replace civil officials, leading Johnson to moan that it "is a great public wrong to take from the President powers conferred on him alone by the Constitution."[62] In the wake of those overrides, Johnson informed Congress in his next state of the union address that he had "deliberated much" of late on the "very serious and important question" of "[h]ow far the duty of the President to 'to preserve, protect, and defend the Constitution' requires him to go in opposing an unconstitutional act of Congress." He feared "violent collision" and even "civil war," but circumstances were becoming visible in which "plainly unconstitutional" acts might compel "Executive resistance." Nonetheless, he remained hopeful that measures "which are peaceable remain open to him or to his constituents," notably a "judicial remedy."[63]

These laws led to presidential action that finally galvanized a majority of the House to impeach Johnson, which in turn led to the strongest and most explicit departmentalist claims made on behalf of the Johnson presidency.[64] The president, rather ineffectually, dismissed Secretary of War Edwin Stanton against the wishes of the Senate and in arguable violation of the Tenure of Office Act, an action that the statute defined as a "high misdemeanor."[65] Johnson was promptly impeached. In his initial answer to the articles of impeachment, Johnson pointed out that he had been clear in his veto message that the power to remove executive officials was "lodged [in him] by the Constitution . . . and that, consequently, it could be lawfully exercised by him, and Congress could not deprive him thereof." Though the veto override was "an expression of the opinion of Congress" to the contrary, the Tenure of Office Act was necessarily "wholly inoperative and void by reason of its conflict with the Constitu-

[62] Andrew Johnson, "Veto Message, July 19, 1867," in Richardson, *Messages and Papers*, 6:544.

[63] Andrew Johnson, "Third Annual Message, December 3, 1867," in Richardson, *Messages and Papers*, 8:3766.

[64] Radicals in the House had begun to push for an impeachment as soon as the results of the midterm elections were in. Early investigations were focused on whether Johnson had been a conspirator in the Lincoln assassination, a particularly cruel twist given that Johnson had likely himself been a target for assassination. Elizabeth D. Leonard, *Lincoln's Avengers* (New York: Norton, 2004), 46.

[65] Tenure of Civil Officers Act, *U.S. Statutes at Large* 14 (1868): 430, 432. Johnson first tried, "under the authority given by the Constitution," to replace Stanton with Grant, but when the Senate disapproved, Grant got cold feet and surrendered the office back to Stanton, rather than "awaiting a decision of the question by judicial proceeding." "Correspondence Between Gen. Grant and President Johnson," in McPherson, *Political History*, 283, 284. Johnson eventually convinced retired General Lorenzo Thomas to take on the job, but he too gave way to Stanton.

tion." Far from denigrating judicial authority to interpret the Constitution in asserting this robust executive authority, however, Johnson tried to appeal to judicial supremacy. On a matter of such "gravity and importance" and "upon which the legislative and executive departments of the government had disagreed," the president had merely sought to have the issue "submitted to that judicial department of the government intrusted by the Constitution" with the power to say what the law means.[66] The president had the authority to independently interpret the Constitution in the course of carrying out his responsibilities and could not be bound by Congress, but the Supreme Court, he proposed, stood above them both.[67]

This constrained departmentalist argument became a prominent part of the impeachment trial.[68] Former Supreme Court justice Benjamin Curtis opened Johnson's defense, and contended that it was the "high and patriotic duty of a citizen to raise a question whether a law is within the Constitution of the country." Curtis assured the Senate that the president did not mean to "occupy any extreme ground"; he "is not to erect himself into a judicial court and decide that the law is unconstitutional." Refusal to enforce an unconstitutional law would often "prevent any judicial decision from being made," and his duty was to "cause a judicial decision."[69] Whether the constitutional violation was clear or contestable, "it is impossible to draw any line of duty for the President." After due deliberation he must act on what "he believes" the Constitution requires, sometimes resisting the law in order to receive an authoritative interpretation of constitutional requirements from the Supreme Court.[70] Thomas Nelson, soon to be a judge on the Tennessee Supreme Court, explained that the "political training and education" of Johnson led him to follow the example of "Mr. Jefferson and General Jackson [who] undertook to construe the Constitution of the United States for themselves, and claimed that as executive officers they had the right to do so."[71] There were "questions peculiarly belonging to the executive department which the President of the United States of necessity must have the right of determining for himself," when he must "exercise something like judicial discretion . . . upon his own authority and upon his own construction of the Constitution."[72]

[66] *Trial of Andrew Johnson*, vol. 1 (Washington, DC: Government Printing Office, 1868), 39, 40.

[67] Johnson could have readily calculated that the Court would be supportive of his resistance to the congressional intrusion on traditional presidential prerogatives.

[68] See also Whittington, *Constitutional Construction*, 132–40.

[69] *Trial of Andrew Johnson*, 387.

[70] Ibid., 1:388.

[71] Ibid., 2:163, 164. Lincoln's example was not neglected. Ibid., 2:296 (William Evarts).

[72] Ibid., 2:165, 167.

"[E]ach and every department," William Groesbeck reminded the Senate, must observe "with the utmost fidelity the provisions of the written Constitution," and the "first paramount duty" of the president was that he adhere to its requirements as best he could understand them.[73]

These arguments were primarily marshaled to limit the authority of Congress, which the president's lawyers asserted was the most dangerous branch.[74] In doing so, they reinforced rather than tore down judicial supremacy. It remained true that the "Supreme Court . . . by the very terms of the Constitution itself [is] the highest and final interpreter of the constitutionality of congressional enactments." Even in doubtful cases, it is "right and proper" for the president to adhere to "a long established interpretation of the Constitution" and seek "to test the accuracy of the new [congressional] interpretation in the forum which is the highest and final interpreter of such questions."[75] Chief Justice Salmon Chase privately endorsed the president's position and the "clear duty of the President to disregard the law, so far at least as may be necessary to bring the question of its constitutionality before the Judicial Tribunals," as did a leading constitutional treatise that was in press at the time of the impeachment.[76]

As Johnson and his defenders developed a constrained version of departmentalism to justify his actions in resisting Congress, congressional leaders showed themselves to be, in one sense at least, the true heirs of Jefferson, Jackson, and Lincoln, articulating a departmentalism consistent with their own reconstructive posture. With Lincoln's death, constitutional leadership had passed to Congress. The House managers of the article of impeachment strongly denied that the president had any authority to question the constitutionality of an act of Congress. The executive has "no constitutional power to inquire for himself whether the law was constitutional or not"; he must enforce it until it is "repealed for its unconstitutionality, or for any other reason."[77] The president claimed he

[73] Ibid., 2:198, 199. See also ibid., 2:292–93, 272–73 (William Evarts) ("the President . . . [is] bound to the special fidelity of watching that all the departments of this government obey the Constitution, as well as that he obeys it himself").

[74] Ibid., 2:134.

[75] Ibid., 2:200. See also 2:382 (Henry Stanbery).

[76] Salmon Chase, "To Gerrit Smith, April 19, 1868," quoted in J. W. Schuckers, *The Life and Public Services of Salmon Portland Chase* (New York: D. Appleton, 1874), 577; John Norton Pomeroy, *An Introduction to the Constitutional Law of the United States* (New York: Hurd & Houghton, 1870), 444–45. Though my interest is in the public argument developed by Johnson about judicial and presidential authority to interpret the Constitution, it is possible to question how much effort the administration actually made to develop a test case for the Tenure of Office Act. See Christopher N. May, *Presidential Defiance of "Unconstitutional" Laws* (Westport, CT: Greenwood Press, 1998), 60–64.

[77] Ibid., 2:72, 71 (George Boutwell). Boutwell did accept the right of the Supreme Court to annul a statute as unconstitutional. Ibid., 72.

wanted a test case for the statute, but he "has already seen it tested and decided by the votes, twice given, of two-thirds of the senators and the House of Representatives." If he still doubted the constitutionality of a law "twice tested" by congressional vote, then he should have resigned.[78]

The managers admitted a judicial authority to interpret the Constitution and annul an unconstitutional law, but the practical effect of the admission was limited.[79] Their departmentalist claims on behalf of Congress and to the derogation of both the judiciary and the presidency recognized few bounds, but such strong congressional departmentalism did not live beyond the reconstructive moment. Representative Ben Butler laughed that the president might as well assume the "stupidity, ignorance, and imbecility, or worse" of the members of Congress as imagine that Congress would have passed an unconstitutional law. The record of judicial review of acts of Congress to date, Butler asserted, indicated that "possible doubts" had been thrown on acts of Congress "hardly one to a generation," and even then only when the act directly affected the judicial power and not when the constitutional issue had been "much discussed on its passage."[80] The judiciary was not to attempt to settle constitutional controversies; it was to correct inadvertent constitutional errors. In arguing to keep evidence of the cabinet's belief regarding the constitutionality of the Tenure of Office Act out of evidence at the impeachment trial, House manager James Wilson thought such beliefs irrelevant, for the president's sole duty was to enforce the laws "regardless of the opinions of cabinet officers, *or decisions of the judicial department*" for so long as "they remain on the statute-book."[81] Not only would it be "no relief" for the president "if the court itself had pronounced the [statute] to be unconstitutional," but the mere fact that the president attempted to draw "into controversy, in the courts and elsewhere, the validity of laws enacted by the constituted authority of the country" was itself impeachable.[82] It "is not to be presumed, even for the purpose of argument," that Congress would violate the Constitution.[83] Congress was, of course, limited by the Constitution, but if it were to violate its own constitutional responsibilities "the question is, before what tribunal is the Congress to answer?

---

[78] Ibid., 2:223, 299 (Thaddeus Stevens).

[79] Ibid., 1:688 (James Wilson), 2:72 (George Boutwell), 2:405 (John Bingham).

[80] Ibid., 1:108, 110. Butler cited *Hayburn's Case, Gordon v. United States, Ex Parte Garland*, but suggested that even those were "nearly unintelligible." He dismissed other cases "wherein the validity of acts of Congress have been discussed before the Supreme Court" as obiter dicta and "open to other criticisms." Ibid., 1:108–9.

[81] Ibid., 1:684, 668 (emphasis added).

[82] Ibid., 2:74.

[83] Ibid., 2:91 (George Boutwell).

Only before the tribunal of the people."[84] The judiciary is mainly "of an advisory character." Congress alone is "the mouthpiece of the people," and thus is "uncontrolled by any other department" and indeed had "authority . . . over the executive and the judiciary" and "is the superior power in the three departments of government."[85] It is "not a supposable contingency" that Congress would pass a clearly unconstitutional law, and in the case of a "doubtful law" the "legal rule is that the presumption is in every case in favor of the law," a presumption so strong that "none has ever been reversed."[86] For all "practical affairs," the Constitution is what Congress says it is.[87]

Presidential Assertions in the Twentieth Century

After Johnson, constitutional arguments took a less prominent role in presidential veto messages. Presidents, affiliated and preemptive alike, ceased to take the responsibility on themselves to guard the Constitution from legislative violations. While constitutional objections were the primary justification for exercising the veto power in well over half the vetoes issued by the first seventeen presidents, less than 10 percent of the vetoes of public bills issued by subsequent presidents relied on constitutional arguments.[88] In successfully urging the override of President Taft's lame-duck veto of a prohibitionist measure, Republican representative Nathan Kendall hoped that presidents would soon lose the "venerable pretext" of constitutionally based vetoes, for "there is a suitable tribunal organized and maintained to determine [its constitutionality]—a tribunal before whose arbitrament every patriotic citizen of the Republic submits with absolute unreserved. If [the bill] offends against the organic law of the land, let the Supreme Court so declare."[89] In his analysis of presidential vetoes, Bruce Peabody has shown that even when mentioning constitutional concerns, twentieth-century presidents often did not say enough to provide substantive guidance, or encouragement, to any congressional

[84] Ibid., 2:415 (John Bingham).

[85] Ibid., 2:28 (John Logan).

[86] Ibid., 2:256 (Thomas Williams).

[87] Ibid., 2:91 (George Boutwell).

[88] Bruce Peabody, "Recovering the Political Constitution: Nonjudicial Interpretation, Judicial Supremacy, and the Separation of Powers," Ph.D. diss., University of Texas, 2000, 119, 137.

[89] *Congressional Record*, 62nd Cong., 3rd sess. (1 March 1913), 4442. But Representative Augustus Stanley responded to those who "advised to close our eyes to its glaring defects, to shirk our high obligation, and let the Supreme Court pass upon this measure; that this is no concern of ours," that such "is the code of a coward and the philosophy of a fool." Ibid.

deliberation on the constitutional issues at stake, and what they did say tended to point to the superior authority of judiciary.[90]

Instead of vetoing potentially unconstitutional laws, twentieth-century presidents instead adopted the device of the signing statement, by which they could express constitutional reservations while nonetheless allowing the bill to become law. Such statements are rarely a precursor to any presidential action to secure constitutional commitments against the new law. They are generally offered for later judicial consumption, in the hopes that the courts will either use the presidential statement as part of the legislative history of the statute that might guide its interpretation or take its signal to review the legislation and authoritatively settle any constitutional issues raised.[91] Subsequent acts of presidential noncompliance with statutes deemed unconstitutional have primarily involved separation-of-powers questions with little political salience.[92] Thus, Grover Cleveland followed Chester Arthur in submitting a nominee for Senate confirmation for the office of chief examiner of the Civil Service Commission, in violation of the statutory scheme that called for the commission to appoint its own examiner, and Woodrow Wilson removed a postmaster in Portland, Oregon, in violation of a successor to the Tenure of Office Act, sparking the lawsuit that led the Supreme Court to declare that Andrew Johnson had been right in his constitutional claim regarding the removal power.[93]

The president does not so much stand on his own authority as a constitutional interpreter as borrow the authority of the judiciary and seek to draw the Court into his dispute with Congress. As the Office of Legal Counsel concluded under President Bill Clinton, the Supreme Court in the twentieth century seemed to accept a limited power of presidential nonenforcement of apparently unconstitutional statutory provisions. The critical considerations for the president "exercising his independent judgment" was whether the Court would agree with the president's judgment and whether noncompliance helped or hindered the effort "to afford the Supreme Court an opportunity to review the constitutional judgment of the legislative branch."[94] This "court-centered approach," as one critic

---

[90] Peabody, "Recovering the Political Constitution," 136–40.

[91] May, *Presidential Defiance*, 72–76.

[92] These episodes through the Carter administration are compiled in ibid., 101–18.

[93] On the Civil Service Commission, see Act of January 16, 1883, ch. 27, § 3, 22 Stat. 403, 404; "Civil-Service Bill," in *Opinions of the Attorneys General*, 17:506; "Civil Service Commission—Chief Examiner," in *Opinions of the Attorneys General*, 18:409. On the postmaster removal, see Act of July 12, 1876, ch. 179, § 6, 19 Stat. 78, 80–81; Myers v. United States, 272 U.S. 52, 166–68 (1926). See also May, *Presidential Defiance*, 121–22.

[94] "Presidential Authority to Decline to Execute Unconstitutional Statutes, November 2, 1994," *Opinions of the Office of Legal Counsel of the United States Department of Justice*, vol. 18 (Washington, DC: Government Printing Office, 1999), 199. For elaboration, see

dubbed it, to the exercise of presidential constitutional judgment is consistent with a distinctly domesticated version of departmentalism, one that is targeted at Congress alone while reinforcing judicial supremacy.[95]

Rather different were the ambitious constitutional assertions of the Nixon administration. As we saw with Andrew Johnson, presidential efforts to bring the Constitution into play in substantive political and policy disputes soon gave way to presidential concern with maintaining the powers of the office itself against legislative encroachment. Richard Nixon continued this latter tendency. His administration showed a distinct willingness to make aggressive constitutional claims, but primarily on behalf of presidential power rather than in opposition to central features of the broader constitutional regime. Such presidential constitutional interpretation is consistent with the politics of opposition, in which preemptive presidents find themselves both searching for instruments by which they can affect policy and besieged by hostile political forces. Where the departmentalism of the politics of reconstruction is an offensive weapon by which the president attempts to enhance his own authority to remake the constitutional regime, the domesticated departmentalism of the politics of opposition becomes a defensive shield by which the president seeks, with an appeal to legality, to ward off the political blows of opponents.

Soon after the conclusion of the Nixon presidency, James MacGregor Burns offered a "tentative judgment" in his book on leadership: "Nixon was the utter opportunist, shifting ideological stances, repudiating (making 'inoperative') previous positions. . . . Finally, cornered and trapped, he seemed to make a last desperate effort to retrieve what scraps of influence he could from the inner recesses of the executive." Contrasting Nixon to Franklin Roosevelt, Burn noted that the former "resorted to bargaining rather than moral leadership."[96] He was what Burns would call a "transactional" leader rather than a "transforming" one; Skowronek would note the difference between Nixon's constrained strategic circumstance and Roosevelt's more expansive one, an opportunity structure that allowed only the latter to convert the politics of opposition into a politics of reconstruction. Of course, the Nixon administration felt those constrained circumstances acutely. The sense, as one presidential aide

---

Dawn E. Johnsen, "Presidential Non-Enforcement of Constitutional Objectionable Statutes," *Law and Contemporary Problems* 63 (2000): 7.

[95] David Barron, "Constitutionalism in the Shadow of Doctrine: The President's Non-Enforcement Power," *Law and Contemporary Problems* 63 (2000): 63.

[96] James MacGregor Burns, *Leadership* (New York: Harper & Row, 1978), 395–96. See also Richard P. Nathan, *The Administrative Presidency* (New York: John Wiley & Sons, 1983), 26 ("Nixon's domestic program cannot be summarized as conservative, centrist, or progressive. Its tone and emphasis changed as political conditions changed").

often put it, was of "the White House surrounded."[97] Frustrated by its inability to mark legislative accomplishments that were distinctively its own, the administration paid gradually "[m]ore attention . . . to opportunities to achieve policy aims through administrative action as opposed to legislative change, . . . taking advantage of the wide discretion available to federal officials under many existing laws."[98] Like Andrew Johnson before him, with little power to lead, Nixon was left dependent on the formal powers of his office. It would not be surprising that he would reach too far in attempting to maximize those powers and then suffer a devastating reaction as a consequence.

The Nixon administration was prone to making bold constitutional claims on behalf of presidential power, but it did not challenge the ultimate judicial authority to interpret the Constitution. Even as he campaigned for the presidency in 1968, Nixon announced: "Let me be very clear about this: The next President must take an activist view of his office. He must articulate the nation's values, define its goals and marshal its will." The "passive Presidency," Nixon noted, perhaps recalling his own days in the Eisenhower administration, was gone, part of "simpler past."[99] Nixon intended to fully exploit the tools of the modern, twentieth-century presidency. In doing so, he preferred to operate along the path laid down by earlier presidents but where the Court had not yet tread.

Both presidential war powers and presidential authority to impound appropriated funds were implicit in Article II of the Constitution, according to the administration. In the midst of the Watergate crisis, Congress overrode Nixon's veto of the War Powers Resolution of 1973. The administration denounced the resolution as "clearly unconstitutional," but was vague about the source and scope of presidential war powers. A State Department lawyer had earlier testified in a Senate hearing that they rest "on his general authority under Article II of the Constitution. I think it would be difficult for anyone to be more precise than that. The Constitution is not such a precise document."[100] But presidential defenders pointed to a long history of "usage and practice" that gave concrete meaning to the presidential war power and rendered the War Powers Resolu-

---

[97] Anonymous White House aide, quoted in Richard P. Nathan, *The Plot That Failed* (New York: John Wiley & Sons, 1975), 82. Chief of Staff H. R. Haldeman quickly concluded, "I don't think Congress is supposed to work with the White House." Quoted in Stanley I. Kutler, *The Wars of Watergate* (New York: Norton, 1990), 128.

[98] Ibid., 7.

[99] "Excerpts from Text of Speech by Richard Nixon on Conception of the Presidency," *New York Times*, 20 September 1968, 33.

[100] Senate Committee on Foreign Relations, *War Powers Legislation, 1973: Hearings before the Committee on Foreign Relations on S. 440*, 93rd Cong., 1st sess. (1973), 100 (Charles Brower).

tion a "serious attack on the Constitution."[101] Similarly, when questioned at a press conference on the constitutional basis for the increasingly aggressive presidential impoundments of Nixon's second term, the president replied simply that "the constitutional right of the President of the United States to impound funds . . . that right is absolutely clear" and gave examples of such actions by previous presidents.[102] In support of that claim, administration officials pointed to the many instances of past impoundments and the inherent authority of the president as chief executive.[103] Judicial intervention to authoritatively settle these matters was hardly to be expected in what were widely regarded to be political questions. Both were effectively resolved through legislative action, and the president made no special claims as to the presidential authority to interpret the Constitution in the course of these debates.

The courts did rebuff the Nixon administration's reliance on inherent presidential powers to defend its warrantless electronic surveillance. Though the 1934 Communications Act outlawed wiretaps and the courts excluded evidence collected by wiretaps from trial, electronic surveillance had been authorized by presidents and used by federal agents for decades prior to the Nixon administration.[104] The Omnibus Crime Control Act of 1968 regulated the practice to some degree by allowing their use with a judicial warrant in the investigation of domestic crimes, but explicitly refrained from regulating so-called "national security wiretaps."[105] The

---

[101] *Congressional Record*, 91st Cong., 2nd sess. (1970), 19686–93 (Sen. Barry Goldwater). See also Louis Fisher, *Presidential War Power* (Lawrence: University Press of Kansas, 1995), 114–33; Whittington, *Constitutional Construction*, 173–86.

[102] Richard Nixon, "The President's News Conference of January 31, 1973," in *Public Papers of the Presidents of the United States: Richard Nixon, 1969–1974*, (Washington, DC: Government Printing Office, 1971–75), *1973*, 62.

[103] See, e.g., *Federal Register* 38 (6 February 1973): 3474; Senate Ad Hoc Subcommittee on Impoundment of Funds of the Senate Committee on Government Operations and the Subcommittee on Separation of Powers of the Senate Committee of the Judiciary, *Impoundment of Appropriated Funds by the President: Hearings on S. 373*, 93rd Cong., 1st sess. (1973), 369–72. See also Whittington, *Constitutional Construction*, 162–73; Edward S. Corwin, *The President*, 5th ed. (New York: New York University Press, 1984), 149–51; Louis Fisher, *Presidential Spending Power* (Princeton: Princeton University Press, 1975); James P. Pfiffner, *The President, the Budget, and Congress* (Boulder, CO: Westview Press, 1979); Arthur S. Miller, "Presidential Power to Impound Appropriated Funds: An Exercise in Constitutional Decision-Making," *North Carolina Law Review* 43 (1965): 502.

[104] See *Warrantless Wiretapping and Electronic Surveillance*, 94th Cong., 1st sess., February 1975, S. Print 75-S522–6; Barton J. Bernstein, "The Road to Watergate and Beyond: The Growth and Abuse of Executive Authority Since 1940," *Law and Contemporary Problems* 40 (1976): 58.

[105] 82 Stat. 214, 18 U.S.C. 2511(3) (1970). "Congress took what amounted to a position of neutral noninterference on the question of the constitutionality of warrantless national security wiretaps authorized by the President." Gerard J. Kenny, "Note: National Security

Nixon administration claimed broad authority to conduct searches and electronic surveillance without prior judicial approval as part of the presidential obligation to protect national security, and had surreptitiously done so in a wide variety of circumstances. Administration officials contended most narrowly that the president had independent authority to say what was required by the Fourth Amendment's prohibition on "*unreasonable* searches" and most broadly that the president must act on his own understanding of what was necessary to fulfill his constitutional responsibility "to protect the security of the nation."[106] Even so, the administration tested those arguments in court, requesting that judges put their approval on this interpretation of the constitutional division of powers and defer to executive judgment on particular searches.[107] The administration cooperated with judicial proceedings and, apparently, complied with judicial conclusions as to the proper constitutional and statutory boundaries of executive authority and discretion.[108]

The administration followed a similar pattern in the case of executive privilege. Under investigation by Congress and its own special prosecutor for the events surrounding the Watergate affair, Nixon attempted to protect tapes, documents, and witnesses from scrutiny by placing them under the umbrella of executive privilege. The Constitution gave to the president, Assistant Attorney General William Rehnquist explained to Congress, the right to withhold any information that in "his judgment . . . would be harmful to the national interest."[109] As Eisenhower's attorney general William Rogers had earlier emphasized, "the President and heads

---

Wiretap: Presidential Prerogative or Judicial Responsibility," *Southern California Law Review* 45 (1972): 888, 889.

[106] United States v. Smith, 321 F.Supp. 424, 429 (C.D. Calf. 1971).

[107] See, e.g., United States v. United States District Court, 407 U.S. 297 (1972) (requiring warrants in domestic security cases, including bombing of Central Intelligence Agency office); Laird v. Tatum, 408 U.S. 1 (1972) (declining judicial involvement in passive monitoring of public demonstrations by government); United States v. Brown, 484 F.2d 418 (5th Cir. 1973) (upholding surveillance of foreign embassy); United States v. Butenko, 494 F.2d 593 (3rd Cir. 1974) (upholding surveillance of Soviet national at United Nations); Zweibon v. Mitchell, 516 F.2d 594 (D.C. Cir. 1975) (requiring warrants in security cases not involving foreign powers); United States v. Ehrlichman, 376 F.Supp. 29 (D.D.C. 1974) (rejecting national security defense for break-in of office of psychiatrist of Pentagon Papers leaker). For discussion, see Philip A. Lacovara, "Presidential Power to Gather Intelligence: The Tension Between Article II and Amendment IV," *Law and Contemporary Problems* 40 (1976): 106; Louis Fisher, *Constitutional Conflicts between Congress and the President*, 4th ed. (Lawrence: University Press of Kansas, 1997), 271–74.

[108] See, e.g., Fred P. Graham, "High Court Curbs U.S. Wiretapping Aimed at Radicals," *New York Times*, 20 June 1972, 1.

[109] Senate Committee on the Judiciary, *Hearings on Executive Privilege before Senate Subcommittee on Separation of Powers on S. 1125*, 92nd Cong., 1st sess., August 4, 1971, 422.

of departments must and do have the last word" subject only to the "force of public opinion."[110] Consistent with its recent predecessors, the Nixon White House asserted a presidential authority to identify the existence of an executive privilege, to define its scope, and to determine whether any particular piece of information fell within its ambit.

As the issue increasingly became one of whether the White House would obey a judicial subpoena to turn over tapes of Oval Office conversations, the administration's position on the relative authority of the president, the Court, and Congress was not always consistent. Early in 1973, as a Senate investigation committee chaired by Sam Ervin pressed the administration, Nixon directed his aides to research the precedents on executive privilege. Confident in those results but worried that he was losing the political battle for public opinion, the president announced to a press conference, "[I]f the Senate feels that they want a court test, we would welcome it. Perhaps this is the time to have the highest Court of this land make a definitive decision in regard to this matter. . . . And we think that the Supreme Court will uphold, as it always usually has, the great constitutional principle of separation of powers rather than uphold the Senate."[111] A month later, Attorney General Richard Kleindienst told a Senate committee that if Congress did not like the presidential exercise of executive privilege, then it had constitutional weapons of its own by which it could attempt to compel presidential compliance: "[Y]ou have a remedy, all kinds of remedies, cut off appropriations, impeach the President."[112] As in the past, the possibility of Congress employing such remedies still seemed remote.

As the administration's political support, always limited, collapsed completely, it knew it could not question the supremacy of the judiciary. By the end of the summer, both the Ervin committee and the special prosecutor (through Judge John Sirica) subpoenaed White House tapes. The White House put off the Senate, but in the face of reporters pressing such

---

[110] William P. Rogers, "The Power of the President to Withhold Information from the Congress," Senate Committee on the Judiciary, *Freedom of Information and Secrecy in Government, Part 1: Hearings before the Senate Subcommittee on Constitutional Rights*, 85th Cong., 2nd sess., 6 March 1958, 146, 57. See also William P. Rogers, "Constitutional Law: The Papers of the Executive Branch," *American Bar Association Journal* 44 (October 1958): 941.

[111] Richard Nixon, "The President's News Conference of March 15, 1973," in *Public Papers, 1973*, 211.

[112] Senate Committee on Governmental Affairs, *Executive Privilege, Secrecy in Government, Freedom of Information: Hearings before the Subcommittee on Intergovernmental Relations*, 93rd Cong., 1st sess., 10 April 1973, 51. Administration lawyers likewise told the courts that impeachment was the appropriate remedy to presidential abuse of executive privilege, but that the courts should not exercise authority in this area. Warren Weaver, "Tape Case Argued in Federal Court," *New York Times*, 23 August 1973, 29.

questions as "Where is the check on authoritarianism by the executive if the President is to be the sole judge of what the executive branch makes available and suppresses?" it announced that it "would abide by a definitive decision of the highest court" and appealed the district court's subpoena.[113] While Nixon might cite what he called "the Jefferson rule" of exercising presidential judgment as to how far to comply with judicial orders for information from the executive and worry about the precedent a negative decision in the Supreme Court might set, Nixon recognized the political reality that he was in no position to subordinate judicial authority to presidential authority.[114] He had little choice but to seek the Supreme Court's support for his constitutional claims and to help him fend off his adversaries. In happier times, Nixon himself had praised the justices as "the ultimate custodians and guardians of that priceless asset," respect for law.[115] Even the relatively friendly editorial page of the *Wall Street Journal* admonished that executive privilege could not "be left to the total discretion of the President" or "resolved by a unilateral assertion of the congressional power." Only the courts, drawing on "a body of law," were "the appropriate agency to decide."[116]

As the president realized, he was grasping at straws. Though the courts would not assist even a congressional impeachment investigation to penetrate the veil of executive privilege, public opinion did, and Nixon soon made "a major exception to the principle of confidentiality" despite the fact that it had "been recognized by the courts, whenever tested, as inherent in the Presidency."[117] The Supreme Court did, however, regard judicial proceedings as more important than presidential privileges. While the

[113] Richard Nixon, "The President's News Conference of August 22, 1973," in *Public Papers, 1973*, 722; Deputy White House Press Secretary Gerald L. Warren, quoted in R. W. Apple Jr., "Nixon Contests Subpoenas, Keeps Tapes; Hearing Set Aug. 7 on Historic Challenge," *New York Times*, 27 July 1973, 1.

[114] Richard Nixon, "The President's News Conference of November 17, 1973," in *Public Papers, 1973*, 958; Richard Nixon, *RN* (New York: Grosset & Dunlap, 1978), 1019–20, 1052. Nixon's attorney, James St. Clair, refused to say what the president would do if the Court ruled against him, consistent with his argument in court that the judiciary had no proper jurisdiction over the president in this case. Philip Shabecoff, "St. Clair Silent on Obeying the Court," *New York Times*, 23 July 1974, 1. Special Prosecutor Leon Jaworski said he was "appalled" at this "parrying" tactic, since the "President has a sworn duty to obey the law" and presumably the law was what the Supreme Court said it was. "White House Stand Dismays Jaworski," *New York Times*, July 24, 1974, 23.

[115] Richard Nixon, "Remarks Announcing the Nomination of Judge Warren Earl Burger to be Chief Justice of the United States," in *Public Papers, 1969*, 388.

[116] "Hard Cases and Bad Law," *Wall Street Journal*, 8 July 1974, 10.

[117] Richard Nixon, "Address to the Nation Announcing Answer to the House Judiciary Committee Subpoena for Additional Presidential Tape Recordings, April 29, 1974," in *Public Papers, 1974*, 390. On congressional subpoena powers, see Senate Select Committee v. Nixon, 498 F.2d 725 (C.A.D.C. 1974).

president might be the sole judge of his constitutional powers vis-à-vis Congress, the justices insisted that the Court was the "ultimate interpreter" of his powers vis-à-vis the judicial branch.[118] The special prosecutor could have his subpoena. "[A]fter checking with some of our strongest supporters in Washington," Nixon later reported, "we concluded that full compliance was the only option."[119] The president quickly announced that he "respects and accepts the Court's decision."[120] Days later, Nixon resigned from office.

The political obstacles facing oppositional presidents tempt them toward emulating their reconstructive cousins and asserting the presidential authority to say what the Constitution means. Their precarious position, however, makes that unrealistic. Instead, they have found themselves attempting to borrow from the authority of the courts in order to hold off their political adversaries. They have not hesitated to give their understanding of the Constitution, but have known that their understanding is subordinate to the Court's. Rather than challenge judicial authority, these presidents have often bolstered judicial authority and then sought to align themselves with the courts against Congress. While the Court may not be a reliable ally to these presidents, the "political reality" left them little choice but to look for assistance where they could.

MANAGING THE JUDICIARY

As the preceding discussion already makes evident, some preemptive presidents are more oppositional than others. Oppositional politicians manage to reach the presidency by a variety of routes, and frequently the disadvantaged political party must sacrifice oppositional ideology for the chance at electoral victory. Political outsiders, carefully balanced tickets, and ideological moderates are the rule for preemptive presidencies. More full-throated oppositional figures—candidates who reflect the reconstructive potential of the disadvantaged party—frequently either lead their party to inglorious defeat or find themselves sitting on the sidelines as less stalwart candidates carry the party banner. Thus, Generals Har-

---

[118] United States v. Nixon, 418 U.S. 683, 704 (1974). For analyses of United States v. Nixon, see "Symposium: United States v. Nixon," *UCLA Law Review* 22 (1974): 1. For a critical analysis of presidential claims of executive privilege, see Raoul Berger, *Executive Privilege* (Cambridge: Harvard University Press, 1974). For an excellent narrative account of the confrontation, see Kutler, *The Wars of Watergate*.

[119] Nixon, *RN*, 1052.

[120] Richard Nixon, "Statement Announcing Intention to Comply with Supreme Court Decision Requiring Production of Presidential Tape Recordings, July 24, 1974," in *Public Papers, 1974*, 606.

rison, Taylor, and Eisenhower were ushered to the head of desperate parties, so that military glory might overshadow party ideology. A place on the ballot was held open for party-switchers Tyler and Johnson, who might encourage voters to do the same. Safe moderates such as Cleveland, Wilson, Nixon, and Clinton, appealing to potential crossover voters, were embraced as "electable."[121] Oppositional firebrands such as Henry Clay, William Jennings Bryan, Robert Taft, and Barry Goldwater are shut out, at least until the regime is in collapse, when a Franklin Roosevelt or a Ronald Reagan can come to the fore. Whereas it is easy to imagine a Henry Clay running afoul of the Taney Court, a William Jennings Bryan at odds with the Fuller Court, or a Barry Goldwater grating against the Warren Court, and perhaps launching reconstructive efforts of their own, those actually elevated into the politics of preemption had less to fear from the Court and more to gain.

Oppositional presidents are less likely than affiliated presidents to view the Court as generally friendly, but they may not view the judiciary as universally hostile either. In a generally unfavorable environment, these presidents must exploit opportunities to advance their agenda, and the judiciary may provide a vehicle for doing so. In contrast to the openly partisan and hostile legislature, the judiciary may be an outlet for presidential ambitions to alter policy. Moreover, the president has relatively close contact with the judiciary. The president plays the leading, though not the exclusive, role in selecting judicial personnel. The president has nearly a free hand in determining the official position of the federal government on issues that come before the bench. Through control over the Justice Department, the president can exercise significant influence over what cases are moved through the appellate process and what arguments are presented before the Court. In other words, the federal government is a powerful and often successful litigant, and the president has almost exclusive control over that dimension of the government.

Oppositional presidents find themselves in three kinds of position relative to the Court. The first we have already seen. Presidents may turn to the courts to help them defend the constitutional prerogatives of the executive branch. While oppositional presidents are not the only ones who may feel the need to resist congressional encroachment onto their constitutional turf, they may face the most severe pressures and have the

---

[121] As the Democratic Party made the shift from populism to progressivism, the *New York World* crowed, "[T]he Democratic slate is wiped clean. The party is back to first principles again, under leadership that is fit to lead." Quoted in Arthur Link, *Woodrow Wilson and the Progressive Era, 1910–1917* (New York: Harper, 1954), 8. The *New York Times* likewise concluded that "mere politicians have been convinced by repeated defeat that Byranism is not a profitable cult." "Democratic Leadership," *New York Times*, 9 March 1911, 10.

fewest alternative resources to draw upon. When the precedents accumulated under affiliated presidents no longer hold the same appeal to partisan legislators, presidents must hope that the courts are more sympathetic to their legalistic arguments on behalf of institutional power. Institutional clashes are often driven by substantive disagreements over policy, and the uncertain status of the preemptive president relative to both his copartisans and the dominant party may make serious institutional clashes particularly likely. As Skowronek observed, over the course of American history it is preemptive presidents who have faced serious impeachment threats—Tyler, Johnson, Nixon, and Clinton—an unenviable track record both in its uniformity and as a proportion (half) of the total number of administrations that have found themselves operating in that strategic environment.[122] Such presidents may well turn defensively to the courts to fend off legal and political attacks on the administration and to defend the uses that they make of executive powers. Even within the impeachment trial itself, President Johnson tried to tie the hands of the senators as much as possible by looking to Chief Justice Salmon Chase, as the presiding officer, to impose a judicial, rather than political, tone on the proceedings. Such a use of the courts may be more grudging than enthusiastic, but where presidential authority cannot stand on its own, the president must seek to bind others to judicial settlements on the best terms that he can. As Nixon well knew, his best hope was that there would be "some air in the Court's ruling."[123] It was a slim hope, but with little or no support left in Congress it was all the hope he had left. For the oppositional president, better a "court test" than dependence on the "unilateral assertion of congressional power."

The other two positions are more welcome, as the president looks upon the Court as a substantive interpreter and enforcer of the Constitution.[124] Putatively oppositional president may in fact share many of the constitutional commitments of the Court. On key constitutional issues central to the regime, the preemptive president may not be particularly "oppositional" at all. He may therefore share many of the same incentives as an affiliated president to extol judicial supremacy. The other situation is more mixed, and presidents will be more opportunistic. Preemptive presidents may well find areas of relative agreement with the Court, even while

---

[122] Skowronek, *The Politics Presidents Make*, 44–45.

[123] Nixon, *RN*, 1052.

[124] Of course, it should again be emphasized that constitutional interpretation is not the only form of policymaking that presidents might pursue through the courts, and the judiciary is not the only instrument of policymaking to which presidents might have preferential access. The claim is not that constitutional law is the only vehicle of presidential policymaking, but that the ability of oppositional presidents to turn constitutional law in their favor gives them reason to support the judicial authority to interpret the Constitution.

they disagree with the Court in others. Unable to challenge the Court in areas of disagreement, such presidents may settle into a pattern of cooperating with the judiciary in areas of agreement. In the relevant time horizon of the administration, there is more to be gained by reinforcing the authority of the Court than by attempting to tear it down.

Few putatively oppositional presidents have been more comfortable with the central constitutional commitments of the established regime than was Grover Cleveland. New York, the financial and business center of the nation, was crucial to the Democrats' postbellum presidential prospects. New York's Samuel Tilden nearly took the White House for the Democrats in the contested election of 1876. In 1884, New York governor Grover Cleveland became the first Democratic president since secession. Comfortable with Wall Street and free of any personal history with wartime Southern sympathizers or postwar political machines, Cleveland had developed a reputation as a reformer and a friend of business. His successful campaign of 1884 did not emphasize great divisions between the parties, but instead focused on the need for "honest administration" after what he characterized as the long, profligate, and corrupt Republican reign.[125]

Cleveland's own constitutional sensibilities were fully attuned to the principles that were increasingly being emphasized by the Supreme Court. Cleveland promised in his first inaugural "to be guided by a just and unstrained construction of the Constitution" and in his second to defend "all its restraints when attacked by impatience or restlessness."[126] The Jeffersonian and Jacksonian resonances of Cleveland's expressions of faith were perhaps at odds with the more expansive programs of Republican politicians, but they were in keeping with the emerging jurisprudence of the Court. Indeed, these inherited constitutional notions were being carried forward and reconceptualized for a new postbellum era in no small part by current and former Democrats such as Justice Stephen Field and Michigan judge Thomas M. Cooley.[127] But this was an updated constitutionalism that not only reflected the influence of antislavery think-

---

[125] Concerns with "economy" and the prevention of "corruption" were themselves longstanding themes of the nineteenth-century Democratic Party. Gerring, *Party Ideologies*, 166–84.

[126] Grover Cleveland, "Inaugural Address, March 4, 1885," in Richardson, *Messages and Papers*, 8:300; Cleveland, "Inaugural Address, March 4, 1893," in Richardson, *Messages and Papers*, 9:393.

[127] See Gillman, *The Constitution Besieged*; Alan Jones, "Thomas M. Cooley and 'Laissez-Faire Constitutionalism': A Reconsideration," *Journal of American History* 53 (1967): 751; Charles W. McCurdy, "Justice Field and the Jurisprudence of Government-Business Relations: Some Parameters of Laissez Faire Constitutionalism, 1863–1897," *Journal of American History* 61 (1975): 970. See also Graber, "Jacksonian Origins," 17.

ing but also the nationalization and industrialization of the economy. While Cleveland aggressively vetoed appropriations that he did not think could be justified as benefiting the general welfare, he recognized a broader federal role in society than would have been accepted by his antebellum predecessors.

As the president-elect waited to take office for the first time, the Cleveland-allied *New York Times* recommended Stephen Field as the ideal justice, one who would not allow the "General Government to construe every doubtful power in its own favor." Field had been appointed by Abraham Lincoln and was, in 1885, the last Democrat appointed to the Supreme Court. The *Times* was particularly influenced by the legal tender cases, but Field had also often expressed his eagerness to use the Fourteenth Amendment to reign in the regulatory ambitions of the states. A few years later the *Times* expressed the hope that, with the old divisive questions settled and a Democrat in the White House, the "Supreme Court may be raised above all contentions of party."[128] In fact, it assured its readership, there was nothing in the principles of the Cleveland Democrats that was "not entirely consistent with the doctrines laid down by the Supreme Court in a long series of decisions while it has been made up wholly of Judges appointed by Republican Presidents," the dubious approval of legal tender being the notable exception.[129] As the Court prepared for rearguments on the constitutionality of the federal income tax, which had passed into law without President Cleveland's signature, the *Times* emphasized that the case should not be understood to be "magnifying the function of the Supreme Court." The Court was merely being asked to resume "a function that has been to some extent abandoned, and with unfortunate, with really deplorable, results."[130]

As the Court felt its way toward one of its great periods of constitutional activism, Cleveland did not question the judiciary's authority to do so. Instead, after his first term of office, he presided over an elaborate celebration of the centennial of the Supreme Court in New York City. The Court was well deserving of praise, he declaimed, as its creation "more than any other" feature of the constitutional founding "gave safety and promise of perpetuity to the American plan of government." No matter how well written it was, there were bound to be "diverse constructions" of the Constitution, and the nation could hardly have survived "without an arbiter to determine finally and conclusively the rights and duties embraced by the language of the Constitution." Having learned the "cost of

---

[128] "The Supreme Court," *New York Times*, 5 January 1885, 4; "The Chief-Justice," *New York Times*, 24 March 1888, 4.

[129] "The New Chief-Justice," *New York Times*, 1 May 1888, 4.

[130] "Psychology of the Supreme Court," *New York Times*, 2 May 1895, 4.

the struggle to wrest liberty from the grasp of power," the Founders had created a tribunal to which "all questions arising under their newly-formed Constitution, affecting the freedom and the protection and safety of the citizens" were to be referred for authoritative resolution. The former president went so far as to compare the Court to God himself, for just as God brought forth light upon an earth that was "without form and void," so "a light in the temple of justice and law, gathered from the Divine fountain of light, illuminated the work of the fathers of the Republic."[131]

Cleveland had little cause to curse the light that the Court was shining on the Constitution. As a staunch ally of the New York banking community, he could hardly be displeased by the bulk of the Court's work in his first term, striking down state schemes to avoid paying creditors and blocking state interference with the creation of a national marketplace.[132] The Cleveland-friendly press, for example, judged the constitutional issue in the important *Wabash* case, in which the Court struck down the state regulation of interstate railroad shipments during Cleveland's first term, to be "fundamental to the existence of the Union and to the existence of trade" and asserted that the "pretensions of the State legislatures and railroad commissions . . . cannot be broken down too soon or too thoroughly," though national regulation might be appropriate.[133]

Near the end of his second term, the Court dramatically struck at the powers of Congress, but Cleveland took no offense. Shaken by their first electoral loss to Cleveland, the Republicans had passed the Sherman Antitrust Act in 1890 in a bid to let the steam out of an antimonopoly movement that was putting heat on the Republican Party's own favored eco-

---

[131] Grover Cleveland, "On Taking the Chair at the Celebration of the Organization of the Supreme Court, February 4, 1890," in *The Writings and Speeches of Grover Cleveland*, ed. George F. Parker (New York: Cassell, 1892), 125–27.

[132] Augustus Garland, the new attorney general and the first southern cabinet member since secession, did unsuccessfully intervene in favor of state sovereign immunity against creditors in the *Virginia Coupons Cases*, throwing some narrow legal support to a Republican plan for dealing with the state debt that the new Democratic majority in Virginia had accepted, while declining to speak to its morality. The *Times* called on the Virginia Democrats to "meet the situation calmly and firmly . . . [and] bow to the decision of the highest tribunal in the Union," which would enable them to work out a reasonable repayment plan with the state's creditors. "Virginia and Her Debt," *New York Times*, 24 April 1885, 4. The *Nation* saw in the decision the congenial "breaking down of the partisan line in the consideration of broad issues," but also admitted that the case was a difficult one. While "the broad requirements of justice" were on the side of the bondholders, the Court's constitutional argument to rescue them "seems to be forced" and had to be recognized as "a virtual change of the Constitution itself." "The Week," *Nation*, 7 May 1885, 371; "The Week," *Nation*, 23 April 1885, 331. See also Poindexter v. Greenhow, 114 U.S. 270 (1885).

[133] "The Week," *Nation*, 28 October 1886, 339. See also *New York Times*, 27 October 1886, 4; Wabash, St. Louis and Pacific Railway Co. v. Illinois, 118 U.S. 557 (1886).

nomic policies, notably protectionist tariffs, but there was little agreement in Congress about how far the new federal law could constitutionally reach. The Harrison administration initiated few prosecutions under the statute, and met with little success in winning indictment or conviction when it did.[134] The attorney general during Cleveland's second administration, Richard Olney, was a long-standing critic of the Sherman Antitrust Act, and he was less than enthusiastic in pursuing cases under it.[135] Many thought his defense of the act before the Supreme Court in the inherited *E.C. Knight* case was less than robust. He later confided to his secretary, "You will have observed that the government has been defeated in the Supreme Court on the trust question. I always supposed it would be and have taken the responsibility of not prosecuting under a law that I believed to be no good."[136]

When the attorney general's expectations were fulfilled in an opinion by the Cleveland-appointed chief justice sharply limiting the federal government's constitutional power to reach manufacturing, the president raised no complaint. Instead, in his next annual message to Congress, the president explained that it was "not because of any lack of disposition or attempt to enforce" antitrust measures on the part of the administration that the monopoly problem remained unaddressed. It was simply that "the laws themselves as interpreted by the courts do not reach the difficulty." Following the "decision of our highest court on this precise question" of the scope of federal authority over the trusts, the president urged Congress to limit itself to the proper and narrow sphere of "transportation or intercourse between States" and leave the rest to the states.[137] From the perspective of many of the Republicans who had contributed to passing the Sherman Act, the actions of the affiliated Court in limiting its reach was part of a useful collaboration. From the perspective of the Democratic Cleveland administration, the Court's interpretation of the constitutional constraints on congressional power was equally ideologically welcome.

In the same term, the Court struck down the newly passed federal income tax, which was even more a reflection of the autonomous judgment of the Court but was no more politically unwelcome to the Cleveland

---

[134] William Letwin, *Law and Economic Policy in America* (New York: Random House, 1965), 92–116; Albert H. Walker, *History of the Sherman Law of the United States of America* (New York: Equity Press, 1910), 63–86; Hans Thorelli, *The Federal Antitrust Policy* (Stockholm: P. A. Norstedt, 1954), 371–80.

[135] See, e.g., *Annual Report of the Attorney General* (Washington, DC: Government Printing Office, 1893), xxvi–xxvii.

[136] Quoted in Thorelli, *The Federal Antitrust Policy*, 388.

[137] Grover Cleveland, "Fourth Annual Message, December 7, 1896," in Richardson, *Messages and Papers*, 9:745. See also Keith E. Whittington, "Congress before the *Lochner* Court," *Boston University Law Review* 85 (2005): 821, 841–45.

administration. Though Olney mounted a stout defense of the income tax before the justices, the administration never embraced the measure.[138] In pressing a reduction in protectionist tariffs, the president's highest priority for his second term despite a growing budget deficit, Cleveland had told Congress that he would accept "a small tax on incomes derived from certain corporate investments" as part of the overall fiscal adjustment, but he opposed the broad income tax that the populist wing of the party in Congress appended to the tariff bill.[139] Those pressing most strongly for freer trade nonetheless warned that inclusion of an income tax to satisfy the South and West and close the budget gap would destroy the Democratic Party.[140] Prominent Democratic journalist and party operative Manton Marble noted that the income tax was the favorite of German political economists and complained that a "race unpracticed in liberty is teaching American Democrats taxation and Democracy."[141] Nonetheless, given the unyielding opposition of the Republicans, Democratic leaders in Congress concluded that they would not have the votes to pass even modest tariff reform unless they agreed to the demands of their populist colleagues to package the tariff bill with a tax on corporate profits, inheritances, and personal income above $4,000. The president wrote to the chairman of the House Ways and Means Committee that it was essential that the legislative session not end without the passage of some kind of tariff law. Tariff reform "is so interwoven with Democratic pledges and Democratic success that our abandonment of the cause of the principles upon which it rests means party perfidy and party dishonor" and quite likely electoral defeat. While the president knew that "adjustment and compromise" would be required to get a bill through Congress, he drew the line at those items "which embod[y] Democratic principle so directly that [they] cannot be compromised," but it was "party duty" to "defer to the judgment of a majority of our Democratic brethren" on the inclusion of the income taxes, "which do not violate a fixed and recog-

---

[138] In his argument, the attorney general warned the justices of the criticism to come, that the plaintiffs were asking the Court to "overlook and overstep the bounds which separate the judicial from the legislative powers." His co-counsel was more explicit: "Upon such subjects ["political economy"] every freeman believes that he has the right to form his own opinion, and to give effect to his opinion by his vote. . . . When the opposing forces of sixty millions of people have become arrayed in hostile political ranks upon a question which all men feel is not a question of law, but of legislation, the only path of safety is to accept the voice of the majority as final." Pollock v. Farmers' Loan and Trust Company, 157 U.S. 429, 513, 531–32 (1895).

[139] Cleveland, "First Annual Message, December 4, 1893," in Richardson, *Messages and Papers*, 9:460.

[140] Festus P. Summers, *William L. Wilson and Tariff Reform* (New Brunswick, NJ: Rutgers University Press, 1953), 168–69.

[141] Quoted in ibid., 173.

nized Democratic doctrine."[142] Opposition to protectionist tariffs had been a fundamental Democratic commitment since the age of Jackson. The party had not yet given deliberate consideration to the issue of the income tax. Facing a revolt in his legislative coalition in the midst of continuing depression and with no other hope of reducing the tariff, Cleveland allowed his own tariff reform to pass into law without his signature.

Others within the party were less willing to swallow the income tax. Nebraska Representative William Jennings Bryan, the emerging leader of the populist wing of the Democratic Party, was a primary sponsor of the amendments. Although the tax was small, it introduced a greatly feared principle of progressive taxation of income (rather than the traditional basis of federal government revenue, consumption taxes and the sale of national resources), and it was expected that the entire burden of the tax would be borne by the residents of only four eastern states (New York, New Jersey, Pennsylvania, and Massachusetts).[143] Two of these states (New York and New Jersey) happened also to be important swing states in Gilded Age presidential elections, and New York in particular was essential to Democratic Electoral College calculations. It was the centrality of New York that led to reformist New York governor Grover Cleveland's own Democratic presidential nomination in 1884, 1888, and 1892 and the integration of the Mugwumps (a breakaway group of Republican professionals and businessmen centered in New York) into the Cleveland coalition.[144] Democratic New York senator David Hill warned his populist colleagues, "I have hoped that with the Supreme Court as now constituted this income tax will be declared unconstitutional. . . . [T]he times are changing; the courts are changing; and I believe that this tax will be declared unconstitutional. At least I hope so."[145] When Republicans in Congress expressed astonishment that the Democrats were now supporting an income tax, "an unnatural position for the Democratic party . . . a new departure," northeastern Democrats were quick to deny that the tax was a party measure. "Democratic state papers," from which "the creed of the party" was derived, included " a declaration in favor of a tariff for revenue only, a declaration that the imposition of custom-house duties

---

[142] Grover Cleveland, "To William L. Wilson, July 2, 1894," in *Letters of Grover Cleveland, 1850–1908*, ed. Allan Nevins (New York: Houghton Mifflin, 1933), 355, 357.

[143] Arnold M. Paul, *Conservative Crisis and the Rule of Law* (Gloucester, MA: Peter Smith, 1976), 161–62.

[144] On the centrality of New York to national Democratic politics and policymaking in the Gilded Age, see Scott C. James, *Presidents, Parties, and the State* (New York: Cambridge University Press, 2000), 42–56.

[145] *Congressional Record*, 53rd Cong., 2nd sess. (21 June 1894), 6637 (Sen. David Hill). See also *Congressional Record*, 53rd Cong., 2nd sess. (30 January 1894), 1644 (Rep. Franklin Bartlett).

for purposes of protection is unconstitutional, and a promise to have a tariff for revenue only." The income tax, by contrast, was something to be found "in the platform of the People's party, or the Populist party . . . the Socialist Labor party," and adherents to those foreign ideologies had "crept into the citadel" of the Democratic Party and "propose by their mad folly to deliver it to the enemy."[146] When the Court struck out the income tax, the populists exploded at the audacity of the "Cleveland Court," while both the Cleveland Democrats and the Republicans rallied around the independence and authority of the federal judiciary.[147]

The president took great pleasure in the Court's other significant decision of his last full year in office, *In Re Debs*, which Cleveland took as fully vindicating his dramatic intervention in the Pullman strike the year before.[148] In 1894, the newly organized American Railway Union, under the leadership of Eugene Debs, launched a sympathy boycott against any train that included Pullman cars, quickly expanding a small strike at a railcar manufacturer into a general railway strike in Chicago, a central hub of national rail traffic. While the administration had held back from involving the federal government in some previous labor disputes, Attorney General Richard Olney was quick to act against the Pullman strike. Once the post office informed the Justice Department that the strike was delaying the transportation and delivery of the mails, Olney instructed local U.S. attorneys across the country to initiate court proceedings against anyone obstructing the mail. As factories and communities nationwide began to feel the pinch from the lost rail links to the national market, the attorney general expanded his directive.[149] Though he had been skeptical of the application of the Sherman Act to such cases, he authorized U.S. attorneys to join the railroad lawyers in making use of it.[150] Responding to one such request from the U.S. attorney in San Francisco, Olney noted, "Act upon your view of the law, which is certainly

---

[146] *Congressional Record*, 53rd Cong., 2nd sess. (30 January 1894), 1643, 1642 (Rep. Franklin Bartlett).

[147] "Clevelandism Again," *New York Times*, 21 November 1896, 4.

[148] In Re Debs, 158 U.S. 564 (1895).

[149] Olney also worried about the "spread over the entire country" of the labor unrest and hoped that if "the rights of the United States were vigorously asserted in Chicago," the contagion would be contained and stamped out. He later observed that "as was anticipated, the termination of the strike in Chicago terminated it everywhere else, and, with one exception, the use of troops in connection with the strike was no longer required." Quoted in Henry James, *Richard Olney and his Public Service* (Boston: Houghton Mifflin, 1923), 47, 206–07.

[150] *Annual Report of the Attorney General*, 1893, xxvi–xxviii. On his earlier doubts, see Thomas K. Fisher, "Antitrust During National Emergencies I," *Michigan Law Review* 40 (1942): 969, 977.

sustained by adjudication so far as they have gone."[151] He instructed his special counsel in Chicago to win an injunction, "whether under inter-state-commerce law, act of July 2, 1890 [the Sherman Act], or on general grounds."[152] While Olney believed the "President might have used the United States troops to prevent interference with the mails and with inter-state commerce on his own initiative—without waiting for action by the courts and without justifying the proceeding as taken to enforce judicial decree . . . it is doubtful—at least it seemed doubtful to me at the time—whether the President could be induced to move except in support of the judicial tribunals."[153] When the injunctions were violated, Cleveland authorized the use of federal troops to free the trains and disperse the strikers. When Democratic governor, and labor sympathizer, John Altgeld objected to the introduction of federal troops without a request from state government officials as doing "violence to the Constitution," the president responded crisply that the federal responsibility in this situation was clear.[154]

Once the strike was broken, there was still the question of what to do with Debs and other strike leaders. While Olney was primarily focused on "securing earliest end of business paralysis," his special counsel on the scene in Chicago had his eye on "final results instead of temporary advantage," which meant making this "the last railway strike . . . in this country for many years" by punishing "with a firm hand" the union leaders in the courts.[155] In December, Debs and others were held in contempt and jailed for violating the injunction, and they appealed both their sentences and the validity of the underlying injunction to the Supreme Court. In the spring of 1895, the Court upheld the actions of the lower court and the authority of the federal government to reach into railroad strikes. The Supreme Court declined to pursue the question of whether the Sherman Antitrust Act might apply to this situation, as had been argued by both the government and the lower court. The Supreme Court instead focused on the "broader ground," including the fundamental responsibility of the federal courts to assist in keeping the "highways of interstate

[151] Richard Olney, "Telegram to Charles A. Garter, June 29, 1894," in *Appendix to the Annual Report of the Attorney General* (Washington, DC: Government Printing Office, 1896), 18.

[152] Olney, "Telegram to Edwin Walker, July 1, 1894," in *Appendix*, 61.

[153] Richard Olney, "Extracts from a Memorandum Dictated by Olney in 1901," in James, *Olney and Public Service*, 203.

[154] John P. Altgeld, "To Grover Cleveland, July 5, 1894," in *Letters of Grover Cleveland*, 360.

[155] Richard Olney, quoted in Gerald G. Eggert, *Richard Olney* (University Park: Pennsylvania State University Press, 1974), 147; Edwin Walker, "To Richard Olney, July 9, 1894," in *Appendix*, 77; Walker, "To Richard Olney, July 14, 1894," in *Appendix*, 85; Walker, "To Richard Olney, July 2, 1894," in *Appendix*, 64.

commerce free from obstruction."[156] Unlike *E.C. Knight* and the Income Tax Cases, *Debs* upheld the constitutional authority of the federal government to act, but, as in those cases, the Court acted in a way that reinforced the administration's own political and ideological commitments.

The conservative Cleveland administration was in general sympathy with the constitutional understandings pronounced by first the Waite and then the Fuller Court in the closing decades of the nineteenth century. The Clinton administration at the end of the twentieth century had a somewhat less agreeable relationship with the conservative Rehnquist Court. Even so, the conflicts between the administration and the Court were fairly mild, and the Court's constitutional jurisprudence often offered opportunities to the administration as well as the occasional frustration.

Five out of six of the previous presidential elections had been won by the Republican Party when Arkansas governor Bill Clinton emerged from a weak field of candidates to capture the Democratic presidential nomination in 1992. Clinton had just served as a chairman of the Democratic Leadership Council, which had been working within the party to pull it to the right since Walter Mondale's embarrassing showing in the 1984 presidential election.[157] Once he had sewn up the party nomination, Clinton took pains to distance himself from its liberal wing and position himself as a "new," post-Reagan Democrat with such symbolic actions as denouncing black rapper and activist Sister Souljah at a Rainbow Coalition conference and interrupting the campaign to return to Little Rock to visibly weigh and deny the last-minute clemency appeal of a death-row inmate. Although 1992 was originally expected to be a mere "tryout" for the 1996 campaign, a sudden economic downturn and strong independent presidential run by businessman H. Ross Perot gave Clinton the White House with the lowest share of the popular vote since Woodrow Wilson's victory in 1912.[158]

In his acceptance speech to the 1992 Democratic convention, Clinton promised a "new covenant" that was "not conservative or liberal. In many ways, it's not even Republican or Democrat. It's different. It's new . . . [but] rooted in the vision and values of the American people."[159] The Democratic Leadership Council soon labeled this the "third way" between "traditional liberalism and conservatism," while sometime Clinton political advisor Dick Morris called it "triangulation." After some early

---

[156] In Re Debs, 158 U.S. 564, 600, 586 (1895).

[157] Kenneth S. Baer, *Reinventing Democrats* (Lawrence: University Press of Kansas, 2000).

[158] A. L. May, "'92 Race Seen as Tryout for '96," *Atlanta Journal-Constitution*, 14 July 1991, D1.

[159] "Transcript of Speech by Clinton Accepting Democratic Nomination," *New York Times*, 17 July 1992, 14.

leftward digressions on homosexual rights and national health care, the administration soon settled into a program aimed at winning plaudits on Main Street and in the bond markets, building a domestic policy record on such traditionally Republican issues as deficit reduction, crime fighting, and welfare reform.

For such an administration, the conservative Rehnquist Court could not be regarded as a reliable ally, but it could be usefully managed on some issues. Especially once the Republicans took control of both chambers of Congress after the 1994 midterm elections during Clinton's first term, the administration was unlikely to do better in Congress than in the judiciary. For those within the Clinton Justice Department who wanted the administration to pursue a more straightforwardly liberal agenda through the courts, the politics of opposition was marked primarily by frustration. Thus, to Deval Patrick, former NAACP attorney and head of the Civil Rights Division in the Department of Justice, the White House was not sufficiently "goal oriented." Instead, as the deputy to Clinton's first and most liberal solicitor general concluded, "The Administration worked more day-to-day, reacting to cases and issues. The general attitude was not to look too liberal. . . . The Administration generally seemed to want to keep things the same as they had been in the Reagan-Bush administrations."[160] Linda Greenhouse, the Supreme Court correspondent for the *New York Times*, observed the difference during Clinton's first term: "The [Clinton] Administration's self-protective crouch contrasts sharply with the Reagan and Bush Administrations' approaches to hot-button cases on the Court's calendar. . . . [The latter could] turn a case into a useful vehicle for staking out political ground. By contrast, the [Clinton] Administration's concern now seems to be to avoid getting run over."[161] On such issues as affirmative action and criminal justice, where both the Court and Congress were to the administration's right, it often simply sought to keep its options open while minimizing political controversy. On other issues, such as the admission of women to the Virginia Military Institute or legal restrictions on abortion, the administration could be more aggressive in seeking support from the Court that it could not get from Congress.

Like Cleveland a century before, President Bill Clinton even benefited from the Supreme Court's saving him from a disagreeable statutory amendment that he had to swallow in order to get a significant legislative

---

[160] Assistant Attorney General for Civil Rights Deval Patrick, quoted in Richard L. Pacelle Jr., *Between Law and Politics* (College Station: Texas A&M University Press, 2003), 183; Principal Deputy Solicitor General Paul Bender, quoted in ibid.

[161] Linda Greenhouse, "For Clinton, the Supreme Court's Docket is a Mine Field of Politically Sensitive Cases," *New York Times*, 18 November 1994, B9.

package through Congress. In February 1996, the president finally signed the Telecommunications Act, the most important telecommunications reform since the New Deal and an administration priority from the beginning of Clinton's term of office. He marked the occasion by traveling to the Library of Congress on Capitol Hill to sign a law that he promised would unleash the "free flow of information." He praised its potential "to build our economy. . . , to bring educational technology into every classroom, and to help families exercise control over how media influences their children."[162] The last was in recognition of the legislation's requirement of the "V-chip," the administration's favored technological fix to sex and violence on television. The president did not mention another high-profile element of the law, the Communications Decency Act, which the Justice Department would soon be defending in court.

The Communications Decency Act (CDA) was a last-minute amendment on the floor of the Senate to the telecommunications reform bill. Democratic senator James Exon of Nebraska had originally introduced the measure in February 1995 to extend "the standards of decency which have protected telephone users to new telecommunication devices."[163] The stand-alone bill had languished, with the president observing that he favored "some action" to protect children from pornography on the Internet, as long as it was within the "very strict" standards set by the Supreme Court under the First Amendment.[164] As the Senate neared final deliberations on the telecommunications bill that summer, Exon and Republican senator Daniel Coats offered a revised version of the CDA as an amendment. With lurid photos downloaded off the Internet available on his desk for his colleagues to view, Exon quickly won a lopsided vote to include the CDA in the reform bill.

The CDA placed the Clinton administration in a difficult bind, ratcheting up the tension between Clinton's New Democratic interest in protecting family values and the liberal commitment to expansive civil liberties. The Court offered a way to relieve that tension. The Department of Justice and the Clinton administration had repeatedly voiced their opposition to the measure, judging it both unworkable and unconstitutional, but as Senator Orrin Hatch complained of the Senate vote, "It's kind of a game, to see who can be the most against pornography and obscenity. . . . It's a political exercise." The administration was unable to prevent

---

[162] Clinton, "Remarks on Signing the Telecommunications Act of 1996, February 8, 1996," in *Public Papers, 1996*, 186; Clinton, "Statement on Passage of Telecommunications Reform Act of 1995, February 1, 1996," in *Public Papers, 1996*, 127.

[163] *Congressional Record*, 104th Cong., 1st sess. (1 February 1995), 3203 (Sen. James Exon).

[164] Clinton, "Remarks and a Question-and-Answer Session with the American Society of Newspaper Editors, April 7, 1995," in *Public Papers, 1995*, 485.

addition of the CDA to the bill.[165] The House of Representatives had already passed the reform bill with the administration's preferred indecency provision calling for the Justice Department to study the issue, and Speaker Newt Gingrich had denounced the Exon proposal as unconstitutional. After Senate passage, however, the Clinton administration relented, concluding, according to a senior administration official, "No way are you going to get yourself in a position where the president isn't willing to go as far as a Democratic senator in restricting child pornography on the Internet" in an election year.[166] It was initially hoped that the Senate's amendment would be excised in the privacy of the conference committee, but in a surprise victory for social conservatives the conference narrowly voted to adopt the Senate's language.[167] At the same time, however, the conference did entrust enforcement to the Department of Justice (rather than the Federal Communications Commission) and provide for expedited judicial review of its indecency provisions. The president announced that he would not allow the inclusion of the CDA to hold up telecommunications reform, and with political attention now focused on it the Justice Department pledged to defend the measure "so long as we can assert a reasonable defense consistent with Supreme Court rulings in this area."[168]

The courts agreed with what the Justice Department told Congress rather than with what it said in its legal briefs. After a special three-judge panel struck down the CDA as unconstitutional in the summer of 1996, Clinton affirmed, "I remain convinced, as I was when I signed the bill, that our Constitution allows us to help parents by enforcing this act," but said that the Justice Department would be responsible for a decision as to whether to appeal and trumpeted the administration's support for filtering software to block "objectionable materials."[169] The administration quickly concluded that it would be politically costly not to appeal—the administration could not be seen as killing the act. The Supreme Court struck down the provision in *Reno v. American Civil Liberties Union*, severing it from the Telecommunications Act.[170] The White House issued

[165] Senator Orrin Hatch, quoted in Edmund L. Andrews, "Senate Supports Severe Penalties on Computer Smut," *New York Times*, 15 June 1995, D6.

[166] Quoted in Jacob Weisberg, "Strange Webfellows," *Slate*, 14 December 1996 (http://slate.msn.com/id/2257).

[167] Howard Bryant and David Plotnikoff, "How the Decency Fight Was Won," *San Jose Mercury News*, 3 March 1996, 1D.

[168] Assistant Attorney General Andrew Fois, quoted in John Schwartz, "Language on 'Indecency' Sparks Telecommunications Bill Protest," *Washington Post*, 5 February 1996, A8.

[169] Clinton, "Statement on the Court Decision on the Communications Decency Act, June 12 1996," in *Public Papers, 1996*, 906.

[170] Reno v. American Civil Liberties Union, 521 U.S. 844 (1997). Clinton had previously claimed credit for the CDA, even as he admitted that it was unlikely to survive constitutional

a statement reemphasizing its commitment to protecting children from inappropriate material and announcing plans for a conference to study filtering technology similar to the V-chip.[171] Exon lamented the Court's decision from his retirement in Nebraska, while his local paper hailed his "good try."[172]

APPOINTMENT POLITICS

Judicial appointment politics both shape and reflect the complicated relationship between an oppositional president and the Supreme Court. Vacancies on the Supreme Court create opportunities for oppositional presidents to influence the development of constitutional law, and the possibility of judicial appointments can encourage even oppositional presidents to buy into judicial supremacy. At the same time, oppositional presidents are often constrained in their options in choosing justices and have been unable and unwilling to take the Court in radically new directions. The existence of preemptive presidents and their judicial appointments has not derailed the close relationship between the Court and the affiliated leader. But as with affiliated leaders, judicial appointments create opportunities for oppositional presidents to add new elements and points of emphasis to the interpretation of the predominant constitutional order.

Until the late nineteenth century, the appointment politics surrounding Supreme Court vacancies was brutal for oppositional presidents. Oppositional presidents and their parties were so weak that they proved incapable of leaving any significant mark on the membership of the Supreme Court. After Andrew Jackson and Martin Van Buren had remade the Court with eight Democratic appointments (helped in part by the two-seat expansion of the Supreme Court by the Democratic Congress, a parting gift to the lame-duck Andrew Jackson), the first Whig in the White House, William Henry Harrison, died before getting the opportunity to fill a seat on the Court. Joseph Story, who thought that under the Jacksonians the "vital principles of the Constitution are uprooted and disregarded," had planned to retire from the bench once the White House was in friendly hands, but Harrison's quick death and the rapid break between

---

challenge. Clinton, "Remarks at a Town Hall Meeting on Education at Clarksburg, West Virginia," May 22, 1997," in *Public Papers, 1997,* 647.

[171] Clinton, "Statement on the Supreme Court Decision on the Communications Decency Act, June 26, 1997," in *Public Papers, 1997,* 829.

[172] Fred Knapp, "Exon Laments Porn Ruling Internet Decision," *Lincoln Journal Star,* 27 June 1997, A1; "Exon's Decency Act a Good Try, But Sleaze is Difficult to Fight," *Omaha World Herald,* 29 June 1997, 12b.

his successor and the Whigs in Congress kept Story on the bench.[173] Soon after the Twenty-eighth Congress was gaveled into session in December 1843, Justice Smith Thompson, an appointee of James Monroe, died. With the presidential election less than a year away and the prospect that the nomination could be made by a President Henry Clay, the Whig majority in the Senate was resolved to block any Tyler nominee.[174] Four months later, the death of Justice Henry Baldwin created a second vacancy on the bench, but the additional opening only strengthened the resolve of the Senate Whigs. The leading Whig paper declared, "Better . . . the Bench should be vacant for a year than filled for half a century by corrupt or feeble men, or partisans committed in advance to particular views of duty," which to committed Whigs defined any individual willing to accept a nomination from the hated Tyler. In the "emergency created by the occurrence of another vacancy on the bench of the Supreme Court," the Senate was expected to stand firm.[175] Throughout 1844, the president and the Senate dueled, with the Senate voting to reject or postpone four times the three names that Tyler put forward.[176] Tyler's choices were all eminent, but personally controversial and ranged from intolerable to less than ideal to the Whig majority. Tyler took advantage of James Polk's surprising defeat of Henry Clay in the presidential contest to offer New York's widely admired chief justice, Samuel Nelson, to the Senate. Perhaps preferring a Democratic justice chosen by Tyler to one chosen by Polk, the Senate relented and finally allowed the seat that had stood vacant for fourteen months to be filled. Even so, it took no action on Tyler's final nominee, leaving Tyler with five defeated nominations for the Supreme Court—equaling the total of all the defeated nominations of the prior nine administrations and setting a record of presidential futility that still stands.[177]

[173] Quoted in R. Kent Newmyer, *Supreme Court Justice Joseph Story* (Chapel Hill: University of North Carolina Press, 1985), 307. On Story's retirement plans, see William W. Story, ed., *Life and Letters of Joseph Story*, vol. 2 (Boston: Charles C. Little and James Brown, 1851), 523.

[174] The Whigs had earlier blamed Tyler for Taney being on the Court, for Tyler had resigned his seat in the Senate when he could no longer support the Jackson administration. Virginia returned a loyal Jacksonian to Washington, giving the president the majority he needed to confirm Taney. Warren, *Supreme Court*, 2:288n1.

[175] "The U.S. Judiciary," *National Intelligencer*, 27 April 1844, 2.

[176] Tyler did little better with his Cabinet nominations. Senator Thomas Benton later recalled the end of the session in March 1843 as a time when "[n]ominations and rejections flew backwards and forwards as in a game of shuttlecock—the same nomination, in several instances, being three times rejected . . . within the same hour." Thomas H. Benton, *Thirty Years' View*, vol. 2 (New York: D. Appleton, 1865), 629.

[177] Over two years after Henry Baldwin's death, James Polk filled his seat with Robert Grier.

The next Whig in the White House did little better. Like Harrison before him, Zachary Taylor did not live to see a Supreme Court vacancy. Taylor's vice president, however, was only marginally more successful in placing justices on the Court than Harrison's had been. When the Democratic justice Levi Woodbury died in 1851, a year after Millard Fillmore had assumed the presidency, the moderate Fillmore had little difficulty winning Senate confirmation of his choice of the moderate Benjamin Curtis, who went on to author an important dissent in *Dred Scott*. He had less luck when Justice John McKinley died during the summer of 1852. By then the presidential election was in sight and the Democratic-controlled Senate was in a less accommodating mood, especially with a seat representing a southern district at stake. Even senatorial courtesy was not enough to win confirmation for Fillmore's nomination of North Carolina senator George Badger, a conservative but a Whig. The seat remained open until after the inauguration of Democrat Franklin Pierce, who promptly nominated John Campbell, a leading Alabama litigator whose name had been unanimously urged on the president by the sitting members of the Court.[178] Though the Whigs had opportunities to influence the Jacksonian Court, they were sharply constrained in their ability to exploit those opportunities and make any mark on the Court at all. The Jacksonian dominance of the antebellum Court was total.

Appointment politics for the Democrats during the long Republican era between the Civil War and the New Deal was more mixed, but it began in a familiar fashion for an oppositional president. Andrew Johnson might have repeated Tyler's experience, but Congress saved him the trouble of an extended fight. Justice John Catron, one of two of Andrew Jackson's justices still serving on the Court, finally succumbed at the end of May 1865. The last Jackson justice, James Wayne, died just over two years later. Congress would not allow Johnson to claim either seat, however. Johnson had only assumed the presidency a month before Catron's death, and the details of southern reconstruction took priority over finding a replacement. By the time Johnson nominated Ohio lawyer Henry Stanbery for the vacant seat in April 1866, whom the president regarded as a "sound man . . . right on fundamental constitutional questions" and "with us thoroughly, earnestly," he had broken from Congress over Reconstruction and it was too late.[179] It was rumored in Washington that Stanbery had written Johnson's veto message against the Civil Rights Bill, which Congress had just managed to override in March. Stanbery's apparent hostility to the Republicans' growing interest in black civil

---

[178] Henry J. Abraham, *Justices, Presidents, and Senators* (Lanham, MD: Rowman & Littlefield, 1999), 84.
[179] Quoted in Welles, *Diary*, 487.

rights was more than enough to disqualify him in the party's eyes, but the public record did not give senators much ground for raising objections.[180] Fortunately the House had already approved a bill to simply eliminate the vacancy by reducing the number of justices by one (having just increased the size of the Court to ten justices in 1863), and the senators recognized their solution. The Senate saw the House's bid and raised it, proposing to cut the size of the Court by two members (eliminating the next seat that might come open, presumably giving the five Lincoln-appointed justices not only a clear majority but a cushion on an eight-person Court), and the House soon agreed.[181] Seeing the writing on the wall, Johnson offered Stanbery the position of attorney general, a position the Senate was willing to let him hold, before the amended bill was even taken up in the House. The Republican Congress discovered the need to restore one seat immediately after Ulysses S. Grant occupied the White House in 1869.

Since the late nineteenth century, oppositional presidents have had more success in placing justices on the Court. The opportunity to influence the Court through appointments can give oppositional presidents a further stake in accepting judicial supremacy. Judicial vacancies also invite oppositional presidents to express their attitude toward the Court, whether their agenda is a conservative one that accepts the main elements of the existing constitutional regime or a reformist one that seeks to complicate, but not repudiate, the predominant constitutional order.

Given Grover Cleveland's comfort with the primary constitutional dimensions of the Republican political order of the Gilded Age, it is unsurprising that his judicial picks were well within the mainstream of the constitutional jurisprudence of the era. Ironically, Cleveland had more difficulty securing confirmation of his proposed justices during his second term when the Democrats held the majority of seats in the Senate than during his first when the Republicans held sway. Even so, politics complicated matters. The first vacancy to confront Cleveland in 1887 was for a southern seat (justices were still expected to represent a geographic circuit), and Cleveland quickly named former Mississippi senator Lucius Q. C. Lamar. The previous occupant of the seat, Justice William B. Woods, had been a native of Ohio and risen to the rank of major general in the Union army before deciding to remain in occupied Alabama at the conclusion of the Civil War. Now that was the postbellum Republican idea of someone

---

[180] John H. Cox and LaWanda Cox, "Andrew Johnson and His Ghost Writers: An Analysis of the Freedmen's Bureau and Civil Rights Veto Messages," *Mississippi Valley Historical Review* 48 (1961): 460, 477–79.

[181] On the motivation behind the Court reduction, compare Kutler, *Judicial Power*, 48–63 (primarily to solidify a northern majority on the Court) and Friedman, "Transformation in Senate Response," 22–24 (primarily to deny Johnson any influence over the Court).

to head the Deep South judicial circuit! By contrast, Lamar had been a secessionist and member of the Confederate government and army, though he had reestablished himself as an advocate of national reconciliation after Reconstruction.[182] His nomination came just months after the Republicans had gleefully embarrassed the Cleveland administration over its plan of returning those captured Confederate battle flags still being held in the War Department.[183] With the "rebel battle flag issue" still close to mind, a narrowly divided Senate found itself once again debating the Civil War. Cleveland was able to swing just enough votes to win Lamar's confirmation with minimal support from the northern states.[184] His choice of Melville Fuller to become chief justice shortly thereafter was similarly subjected to a long Senate debate, this time focusing on the charge that the nominee had been an Illinois "Copperhead" during the war, but Fuller was confirmed by a comfortable margin.[185] Both Lamar and Fuller easily joined with their conservative colleagues on the Court to emphasize the limitations on government power.

The judicial appointment politics of Cleveland's second term were, if anything, more eventful, but for reasons that were even less substantive. The late nineteenth century was a period of extraordinary conflict between presidents and senators over control of appointments. Individual senators, especially those from the powerful New York machines that depended on patronage for their strength, claimed the right to dictate to the president appointments involving offices and people within their states, and presidents in turn resisted such strong claims of senatorial privilege in the appointments process, resulting in pitched battles over the

---

[182] On Woods, see Louis Filler, "William B. Woods," in *The Justices of the United States Supreme Court, 1789–1978*, ed. Leon Friedman and Fred L. Israel, vol. 2 (New York: Chelsea House, 1980). On Lamar, see Wirt Armistead Cate, *Lucius Q. Lamar* (Chapel Hill: University of North Carolina, 1935), 68–113, 153–63, 258–303.

[183] Harry Thurston Peck, *Twenty Years of the Republic, 1885–1905* (New York: Dodd, Mead, 1917), 144–47.

[184] Lamar's nomination initially received warm and bipartisan support from the senators, but as the confirmation process lingered, the Republican faithful made known their hostility to any former Confederate, and his senatorial supporters wavered. Lamar himself thought the Republicans were trying to wave the bloody shirt one more time as they positioned themselves for the 1888 campaign. Edward Mayes, ed., *Lucius Q. C. Lamar* (Nashville, TN: Methodist Episcopal Church, 1896), 524–25. After his confirmation, the Republican *Cincinnati Commercial Gazette* concluded that it should at least teach the people "who do care for our nationality, and who do not trust the Confederate Democratic party, that the Supreme Court is in danger as well as the Senate of the United States . . . and that the only salvation for them is to elect the next Republican candidate for President of the United States." Quoted in Mayes, 536. See also Willie D. Halsell, "The Appointment of L.Q.C. Lamar to the Supreme Court," *Mississippi Valley Historical Review* 28 (1941): 399; Friedman, "Transformation in Senate Response," 1, 37–39.

[185] See, e.g., "Their Action Cowardly," *New York Times*, 3 July 1888, 1.

selection of such things as custom house officials. While executive offices were the primary spoils in these political wars, the Supreme Court, with its tradition of seats tied to the geographically drawn circuit jurisdictions, had not yet fully escaped the conflict.[186] When Justice Samuel Blatchford of New York passed away in 1893, President Cleveland naturally looked to his own home state for a suitable replacement. Unfortunately, New York's senior senator, David B. Hill, who had once succeeded the reformist Cleveland as governor of the state and had challenged him for the 1892 Democratic presidential nomination, had his own ideas about what constituted a politically suitable New Yorker. The rivalry between Cleveland the independent reformer and Hill the machine regular was personal and local, however, not ideological. Even with a Democratic majority (or perhaps, *especially* with a Democratic majority), Hill was able to rally a majority of his colleagues to his view that the president could not be allowed to appoint a justice who was personally offensive to the home state senator. As a result, two respected but antimachine New York attorneys went down in defeat in rapid succession.[187] Finally, the president in frustration broke from the geographical constraints and turned again to a southern senator, in this case Senate majority leader Edward Douglass White of Louisiana. Although the Democracy in the South was increasingly subject to populist pressure, and the sugar-farming senator was an in-party foe of Cleveland's free trade initiatives, White was a staunch conservative and a good match for Cleveland's first-term picks.[188] When Justice Howell Jackson, who hailed from Tennessee, died the following year, Cleveland moved to rectify the apparent geographic imbalance created by the White appointment. This time the president chose to make peace with the senator from New York and sought his approval for the nomination of Rufus Peckham. Though Peckham's brother, Wheeler, had been the subject of the second Supreme Court nomination killed by Hill the year before, Rufus was personally uninvolved in the intraparty squabbles and corruption investigations that had doomed Wheeler, and Hill

[186] Hill's dubious crusade brought to mind the similar recent, and recently repudiated, efforts of New York senator Roscoe Conkling. The public reaction to the spectacle of the Senate bowing to Hill on Cleveland's nominations was harsh, and individual senators thereafter effectively lost the prerogative to block Supreme Court appointments. See Friedman, "Transformation in Senate Response," 52–54. On the earlier patronage battles of the 1870s and 1880s, see Wilfred E. Binkley, *President and Congress* (New York: Vintage, 1962), 187–204.

[187] See Carl A. Pierce, "A Vacancy on the Supreme Court: The Politics of a Judicial Appointment, 1893–94," *Tennessee Law Review* 39 (1972): 555.

[188] See Robert B. Highsaw, *Edward Douglass White* (Baton Rouge: Louisiana State University, 1981); Marie C. Klinkhamer, *Edward Douglass White, Chief Justice of the United States* (Washington, DC: Catholic University of America Press, 1943).

assented to the selection of the conservative New York state judge.[189] Less than a decade later Peckham would author the defining opinion of the turn-of-the-century Court, *Lochner v. New York*.[190]

Woodrow Wilson was the first oppositional president who was willing and able to use the appointments process to steer the Court in a different direction and work through the judiciary to question and reform the predominant constitutional order. His oppositional role was to publicize constitutional alternatives, not rework the landscape. With a Democrat-controlled Senate, Wilson had a fair amount of flexibility in filling the three vacancies that arose on the Court during his first term of office, and the former professor of jurisprudence hoped to entrench a Progressive voice on the bench. His first choice did not accomplish that goal. James McReynolds had been a trust-buster in the prior Republican administrations, but had broken with the Taft administration for not punishing monopolies hard enough. McReynolds was rewarded with an appointment as attorney general. He was not personally known to Wilson, but his attitude on the antitrust question gave him a progressive reputation and his legal skills were held in high regard. In part wanting to avoid ethical or political entanglements, the president kept himself at arm's length from his attorney general and the Justice Department, leading McReynolds to complain that he never had any substantive policy discussions with the president. Nonetheless, McReynolds irritated his colleagues in the Cabinet, and Wilson apparently hoped he would do more legal good, and less political harm, in the more isolated environs of the Supreme Court, and the Senate readily agreed. One former Cabinet member praised his "monumental work" on trusts and his fierce independence, but hindsight showed "that the tides of liberalism have never reached him," and he became the "most reactionary justice on the bench."[191] Wilson himself was said to have regretted the nomination.[192]

Wilson's other two choices were more reliable. Louis Brandeis was a leading legal advocate for Progressive causes and had become a trusted advisor to President Wilson. Stymied in his initial desire to appoint Brandeis to be his attorney general, Wilson was willing to enter a bruising

[189] Grover Cleveland, "To David B. Hill, November 18, 1895," in *Letters of Grover Cleveland*, 415.

[190] Lochner v. New York, 198 U.S. 45 (1905).

[191] Josephus Daniels, *The Wilson Era* (Chapel Hill: University of North Carolina Press, 1946), 540. See also David Lawrence, *The True Story of Woodrow Wilson* (New York: George H. Doran, 1924), 77; Link, *Wilson and Progressive Era 17*, 28; Arthur Walworth, *Woodrow Wilson*, 3rd ed. (New York: Norton, 1978), 271, 328.

[192] Ray S. Baker, *Woodrow Wilson: Life and Letters*, vol. 6 (Garden City, NY: Doubleday, Page, 1937), 113.

political battle to get him on the Court.[193] Nominated in January 1916, Brandeis's confirmation was a bitterly contested, highly partisan affair. With solid Democratic support and less than a handful of Progressive Republican defections, his eventual confirmation seemed assured, but it came only after months of rancorous debate in the Senate and the press.[194] Having dragged the confirmation out until the beginning of the summer, the Republicans had at least given themselves a campaign issue for the fall. Their concern for what Wilson would do to the Court with a second term was weirdly reinforced by the presence of Charles Evan Hughes at the top of the Republican ticket, whose resignation from the Court days after the Senate's confirmation of Brandeis created a third and, as it turned out, last vacancy for Wilson to fill. Wilson quickly nominated district court judge John Clarke. After some investigation, the president was satisfied that the judge "could be depended upon for a liberal and enlightened interpretation of the law" (though, as with earlier appointments, Wilson seemed more concerned about antitrust matters than constitutional ones), and the fact that he was a prominent figure in the swing state of Ohio did not hurt.[195] The exhausted Senate immediately confirmed Clarke. Brandeis's distinguished tenure on the Court amply realized Wilson's aspirations for him, as the justice became the leading spokesman for a liberal constitutionalism, though often through dissenting opinions. Clarke, however, soon grew tired of the Court and turned over his seat for Wilson's Republican successor, Warren Harding, to fill (which he did, with archconservative George Sutherland).

In all, Wilson managed only modestly to affect the balance of the Court, which remained staunchly conservative through Franklin Roosevelt's first term. By elevating Brandeis to the Court, however, Wilson helped legitimate and promote a liberal constitutional vision that challenged the presumptions and conclusions of the dominant constitutional order. Even when allying with relatively progressive members of the Court, Brandeis was in no position to carry the majority and obstruct the legislative agenda of conservative lawmakers. With a seat on the Court, however, Brandeis was in a position to advocate for constitutional change. In this, he was extremely successful. He thought it not enough to urge the majority to get out of the way of progressive legislation, as did his colleague Holmes. For Brandeis, his opinions were a vehicle to instruct public and

---

[193] Wilson was apparently persuaded that Brandeis "just doesn't fit in that particular place because he is known all over the country as a crusader and it would shock the sensibilities of the public to appoint him to that particular position." Quoted in Lawrence, *True Story*, 75. See also, Link, *Wilson and Progressive Era*, 28.

[194] Melvin I. Urofsky, "Wilson, Brandeis, and the Supreme Court Nomination," *Journal of Supreme Court History* 28 (2003): 145.

[195] Quoted in Abraham, *Justices, Presidents, and Senators*, 138.

political opinion, and to agitate not just for a value-neutral judicial restraint but for a freer and more just polity that could be realized through positive government action. As Harold Laski concluded, "[T]he importance of Mr. Justice Brandeis' accession to the Court [is] that where Holmes was a liberal by negation he was a liberal by positive affirmation. He brought to the court not only a willingness to doubt its traditional outlook but an alternative philosophy which might reasonably supersede it."[196] Though many particulars of Brandeis's constitutional vision were not adopted by the New Dealers, other aspects of his thought became touchstones of constitutional opposition in the 1920s and were incorporated into liberal constitutional sensibilities in the 1930s.

After the New Deal, Republicans likewise introduced discordant elements into the Court's constitutional jurisprudence. With greater success in winning the White House during the Cold War, however, the post–New Deal Republicans also had more opportunities to place justices on the Court than had any previous oppositional party. At the same time, these preemptive Republican presidents were constrained by a Senate controlled by the Democratic Party, albeit one with a sizable conservative southern wing. As a consequence, they did more to define and shape the constitutional jurisprudence of the era than previous oppositional parties were able to do, with the possible exception of the Cleveland Democrats.

Despite a Senate that was either effectively evenly divided or held by the Democrats, Eisenhower successfully placed five justices on the Court. Moderation was the watchword of the Eisenhower presidency, and it guided his judicial picks as well. When his brother criticized the president during his early days in office as being "little different[t]" from the Truman administration and exhorted him to "operate this country on a constitutional basis . . . assuming for the Federal Government only those limited powers that the Constitution intended that it should have," Ike admonished,

> You keep harping on the Constitution; I should like to point out that the meaning of the Constitution is what the Supreme Court says it is. Consequently no powers are exercised by the Federal government except where such exercise is approved by the Supreme Court (lawyers) of the land. . . . But until some future Supreme Court decision denies the right and responsibility of the Federal government to do certain things, you cannot possibly remove them from the political activities of the Federal government. . . . [I]t is quite clear that the Federal government cannot avoid or escape responsibilities which the mass of the people firmly *believe* should be undertaken by it. The political processes of our

[196] Harold J. Laski, "Mr. Justice Brandeis," *Harper's Monthly* 168 (January 1934): 212. See also Samuel Konefsky, *The Legacy of Holmes and Brandeis* (New York: Macmillan, 1956).

country are such that if a *rule of reason* is not applied in this effort, we will lose everything—even to a possible and drastic change in the Constitution. This is what I mean by my constant insistence upon "moderation" in government. Should any political party attempt to abolish social security, unemployment insurance, and eliminate labor laws and farm programs, you would not hear of that party again in our political history. There is a tiny splinter group, of course, that believes you can do these things. Among them are H. L. Hunt (you possibly know his background), a few other Texas oil millionaires, and an occasional politician or business man from other areas. Their number is negligible and they are stupid.[197]

He largely entrusted the task of identifying judicial candidates to his moderate liberal attorney general, Herbert Brownell, though with a general expressed preference for judicial experience and strong legal qualifications. The president wanted "highly qualified" "middle of the road" candidates, such as Earl Warren, but no "left-wingers."[198] Given Eisenhower's own bias toward professionalism and the political need to advance impeccable nominees who could not be viewed as political or presidential cronies, as Harry Truman's nominees to the Court often were, the president wanted merely to confirm, not challenge, the post–New Deal jurisprudence. The position of chief justice, however, was somewhat different, and Eisenhower wanted an administrator and consensus-builder in the role. The president had also effectively promised a Supreme Court appointment to former California governor Earl Warren, whose popularity crossed party lines and who had played a key role in throwing the Republican Party presidential nomination to Eisenhower rather than the more conservative Robert Taft.[199] Though his confirmation was briefly delayed by reluctant southern Democrats, Warren soon received unanimous approval. In the aftermath of *Brown*, southern Democratic wariness and hostility was even stronger to Eisenhower's next nominee, John Marshall Harlan II, but he too easily won confirmation.[200] When a third vacancy appeared weeks before the 1956 election, any nomination would necessarily be a campaign event as much as an act of governance, and the president wanted a nominee with cross-party appeal who could shore up his own electoral support. He found what he wanted in William Brennan,

---

[197] Dwight Eisenhower, "To Edgar Newton Eisenhower, November 8, 1954," in *Papers*, 1386.

[198] Dwight Eisenhower, quoted in Yalof, *Pursuit of Justices*, 42.

[199] Given his political bind, Eisenhower struggled to rationalize the selection of Warren despite his lack of judicial experience. See Yalof, *Pursuit of Justices*, 44–51.

[200] Eisenhower bypassed political calculations (which called for a Catholic nominee) to choose Harlan and held the announcement of his nomination until after the midterm elections. Ibid., 54.

a moderately liberal Democrat, a New Jersey Catholic, and a state supreme court judge with enthusiastic support from the legal establishment.
Eisenhower eagerly gave Brennan a recess appointment, as had been his
practice while president, with Senate confirmation to come after the election, which it did with only Joseph McCarthy (of whom Brennan had
been a vocal critic) voting no.[201] In his second term, Eisenhower was able
to name two more to the Court: Charles Whittaker and Potter Stewart.
Whittaker was confirmed for the Court easily, but proved to be ill-suited
for it and gave up the seat after only a few years. Stewart was strongly
opposed by southern Democrats as a proponent of *Brown* and desegregation, but eventually won confirmation.

Despite having replaced a majority of the justices from the New Deal
Court he inherited, Eisenhower managed, if anything, to push it in a somewhat more liberal direction, a trajectory that was consistent with the inclination of his Justice Department. Warren and Brennan became the core
of the activist liberal Court of the 1960s (once the deferential Felix Frankfurter was replaced with the self-consciously activist Arthur Goldberg)—
a Court that made the centrist Harlan and Stewart look more conservative
than they were initially thought to be. Although Potter Stewart may have
been closer to Eisenhower's own ideal point as a justice, and Ike famously
complained that placing Warren and Brennan on the bench were his biggest mistakes as president, the Warren Court was his Court also.[202] *None*
of Eisenhower's appointments to the Court was more conservative than
the justice he replaced.[203] The judicial choices of John Kennedy and Lyn-

---

[201] Abraham, *Justices, Presidents, and Senators*, 200. Eisenhower at one point indicated
a preference for an "anti–New Deal" Democrat but did not press the point. Yalof, *Pursuit
of Justices*, 229n98. See also Stephen J. Wermiel, "The Nomination of Justice Brennan:
Eisenhower's Mistake? A Look at the Historical Record," *Constitutional Commentary* 11
(1994): 515; Michael A. Kahn, "Shattering the Myth about President Eisenhower's Supreme
Court Appointments," *Presidential Studies Quarterly* 22 (1992): 47.

[202] For different versions of the complaint, see Wermiel, "Nomination of Justice Brennan," 535–36. Eisenhower and Brownell were particularly disappointed in the Court's decisions limiting anti-Communist investigations, which Warren and later Brennan joined.
Yalof, 65, *Pursuit of Justices*, 229nn108–9. The appointments of Warren and Brennan were
also the most politically driven nominations, whereas the selection of Harlan and Stewart
arose through the procedures and criteria that Eisenhower generally preferred.

[203] The subsequent voting records of the justices demonstrate the liberalizing effect of
each of Eisenhower's appointments. Bernard Grofman and Timothy J. Brazill, "Identifying
the Median Justice on the Supreme Court through Multidimensional Scaling: Analysis of
'Natural Courts' 1953–1991," *Public Choice* 112 (2002): 55; Lawrence Baum, "Membership Change and Collective Voting Change in the United States Supreme Court," *Journal
of Politics* 54 (1992): 3. Moreover, it is notable that a content analysis of newspaper editorials about the justices at the time of their nominations indicates that informed contemporary
observers not only recognized that Brennan and Warren were quite liberal appointments
but also saw *all* of Eisenhower's Supreme Court appointments as fairly liberal, ideologically

don Johnson were crucial in transforming the Warren Court of the 1950s into the Warren Court of the 1960s—from a Court centered around Truman's Tom Clark to a Court centered around Eisenhower's Bill Brennan—but the Republican alternative offered by Eisenhower was self-consciously friendly to the existing constitutional order.[204] Although it was also a Republican alternative constrained by the need to reach across party lines, it is telling that Eisenhower's preferred alliance on judicial nominees was with the liberal northern wing of the Democratic Party rather than the conservative southern wing. Eisenhower's influence on the Court reflected a liberal bipartisan coalition, not the conservative coalition.

A decade later Richard Nixon made the opposite alliance, famously looking to the white South for his crossover voters and his potential Supreme Court justices. As the Republican presidential nominee in 1968, Nixon ran as much against his old California rival, Earl Warren, as against his immediate Democratic opponent. With urban riots and street crime at the front of the public's consciousness, Nixon made "law and order" a central campaign theme and blamed federal judges for contributing to the "shocking crime and disorder in American life today" by "weakening the peace forces as against the criminal forces." If elected, Nixon promised to appoint only "strict constructionists," judges who would refrain from imposing their "social and political viewpoints on the American people." His judicial nominees would have "experience or great knowledge in the field of criminal justice" and a "deep and abiding concern for these forgotten rights" of crime victims.[205]

Anticipating a Republican victory in November, Chief Justice Earl Warren informed President Johnson in June 1968 of his intention to retire, "effective at your pleasure," hoping that a like-minded successor could be appointed before the curtain closed on the Great Society. The president and the chief justice agreed that recently appointed associate justice Abe Fortas would be the perfect replacement. Brilliant lawyer, committed liberal, and longtime political advisor to President Johnson, a Chief Justice Fortas could be counted on to preserve and extend Warren's jurisprudential legacy. Once Johnson had lined up sufficient support in the Senate for

---

on par with Truman, Kennedy and Johnson's appointments. Jeffrey A. Segal, Lee Epstein, Charles M. Cameron, and Harold J. Spaeth, "Ideological Values and the Votes of U.S. Supreme Court Justices Revisited," *Journal of Politics* 57 (1995): 812.

[204] On the pivot points for the Warren Court, see Andrew D. Martin, Kevin M. Quinn, and Lee Epstein, "The Median Justice on the United States Supreme Court," *North Carolina Law Review* 83 (2005): 1275; Powe, *Warren Court*, 651; Andrew D. Martin and Kevin M. Quinn, "Dynamic Ideal Point Estimation via Markov Chain Monte Carlo for the U.S. Supreme Court, 1953–1999," *Political Analysis* 10 (2002): 134.

[205] Quoted in E. W. Kenworthy, "Nixon, in Texas, Sharpens His Attacks," *New York Times*, 3 November 1968, 79.

easy confirmation of Fortas, he went public with Warren's resignation letter and his own acceptance of that resignation "effective at such time as a successor is qualified."[206] The strategic nature of Warren's retirement was all too transparent, however, and once coupled with Johnson's choice of longtime protégé Homer Thornberry to fill the vacancy created by Fortas's shift to the center seat, the initial optimism for an easy confirmation faded. California governor Ronald Reagan took Warren to task for trying to choose his own successor, and candidate Richard Nixon called for "leaving the selection of the new justice to the next President."[207] Support evaporated when the sitting justice's testimony at his confirmation hearing became an opportunity for senators to express all their accumulated dissatisfactions with the Warren Court, culminating with Strom Thurmond denouncing the Court's criminal justice decisions as "calculated to bring the courts and the law and the administration of justice in disrepute."[208] When further disclosures revealed more of the justice's financial improprieties and continuing entanglements with the White House, the nomination was clearly dead, and Fortas eventually asked the president to pull the plug. Twisting the knife, Thurmond suggested that "Mr. Fortas now go a step further and resign from the Court for the sake of good government."[209] When further press investigations into Fortas's finances revealed his generous and ongoing "consulting" agreement with a well-connected financier under investigation for securities fraud, Warren performed one of his last acts as chief justice in helping to convince Fortas to accept Thurmond's earlier suggestion.

Approaching his then-inevitable victory over the hapless vice president, Nixon explained to voters that he would take the Court in a new direction. Nixon avowed, "The Supreme Court is not infallible. It is sometimes wrong. Many of the decisions break down 5 to 4, and I think that often in recent years, the five-man majority has been wrong and the four-man minority has been right." As president, Nixon intended to bolster that minority. Meanwhile, he was not afraid to criticize the Court. By contrast, Hubert Humphrey's time in the administration's "obedience school" had taught him only to maintain "respectful silence on these far-reaching matters"; whenever Nixon sought to discuss the Supreme Court, the vice president "acts like we're in church."[210] On the campaign trail, Nixon did not speak in hushed tones about the Court (or about the vice president).

---

[206] "Warren-Johnson Letters," *New York Times*, 27 June 1968, 30.

[207] Quoted in Powe, *Warren Court*, 468–69.

[208] Senator Strom Thurmond, quoted in Powe, *Warren Court*, 471–72.

[209] Quoted in Bruce Allen Murphy, *Fortas* (New York: W. Morrow, 1988), 525.

[210] Quoted in R. W. Apple, "Nixon Intensifies Blows at Humphrey on Ohio Train Tour," *New York Times*, 23 October 1968, 28.

Perhaps the immediate appearance of two vacancies on the Court obviated the need for Nixon to assume a more reconstructive posture in the White House. The president might express his own disagreement with past decisions and he might try to affect the course of future decisions through his appointments to the Court, but the judicial authority to say what the Constitution means could go unchallenged. Nixon did not need to claim an authority of his own to trump the Court's majority; he could simply seek to influence the composition of that majority. Nixon's disagreement with the Court was also relatively narrow, not touching on the basic purposes, powers, and structures of American government. There was no broader constitutional regime to be built from the starting point of presidential criticism of the Court for being insufficiently tough on crime. Nixon hoped to jawbone the Court, not supplant it as the authoritative interpreter of the Constitution.

Filling the position of chief justice proved to be deceptively easy. Nixon had drawn some of the material for his campaign criticisms of the Court from a widely publicized 1967 speech by Warren Burger, the chief judge on the U.S. Court of Appeals for the D.C. Circuit. An Eisenhower appointee and a leading conservative on the federal bench, Burger had been an outspoken critic of the Court's recent criminal justice decisions. Even so, Nixon strongly considered following former president Eisenhower's advice of nominating either former attorney general Herbert Brownell or Associate Justice Potter Stewart, possibilities that both White House aides and aspirant Warren Burger thought hardly consistent with Nixon's campaign promises.[211] Both Brownell and Stewart asked to be taken out of the running, however, and the job fell to Burger, who breezed through the Senate.

Burger's confirmation still left the Fortas vacancy to fill, and here things went awry. After having almost stiffed his southern supporters with his choice for chief justice, Nixon was determined to reward them with his next selection. He gave Attorney General John Mitchell strict marching orders; the president wanted a young Republican from the South with an established record as a law-and-order judge. For eight years the Democrats had expanded the federal bench and filled it with loyal Democrats, and while Republican presidential candidates were now able to attract voters in the South the region's judges were still solidly Democratic. Nixon's ideal candidate for this vacancy did not exist in the political world of 1969. Some compromises would have to be made. The Virginian lawyer Lewis Powell was a Democrat, a bit too old, and had never served

---

[211] Burger angrily wrote Brownell about the Potter candidacy that "someone ought to do a close check on *all* the bad 5–4 holdings. . . . It just *can't* be that they could be serious." Quoted in Yalof, *Pursuit of Justices*, 102.

as a judge, but he was a prominent member of the legal establishment (descendant of one of Virginia's first families, former president of the American Bar Association, respected chairman of the Richmond school board who had managed its peaceful desegregation) and had recently criticized the Court's criminal justice decisions. Powell, however, told the administration that he did not want the job.[212] That left Clement Haynsworth Jr., a nominal Democrat who had been appointed to the Fourth Circuit by Eisenhower and was being pressed forward by southern Democratic senators. The White House proved overconfident about the prospects for confirmation and was slow to respond when labor unions and the NAACP leapt on the nomination with complaints of ethical improprieties by Judge Haynsworth. So soon after the Fortas affair, even a whiff of scandal was enough to scare away jittery senators, and the nomination was narrowly defeated on the floor. The bright side for the president was that he won kudos from the South for sticking with the embattled nominee. The administration resolved to go back to the not-very-deep well, and it came back with G. Harrold Carswell, a longtime prosecutor and trial judge recently confirmed to the Fifth Circuit. After a cursory background check primarily concerned with ensuring that the judge's finances were above reproach, his name was rushed to the Senate. Despite his recent promotion, Carswell's career had been undistinguished, and the administration was again caught by surprise when it was revealed that he had dallied with segregationists in Georgia and Florida in the 1940s and 1950s. He was also narrowly defeated in an increasingly exhausted and disgruntled Senate.

Tired of the distraction and needing a sure thing, the White House turned away from Dixie and looked north. Enjoying the warm support of his own childhood friend Warren Burger as well as close friends of the attorney general, Minnesota's Harry Blackmun had the great virtue of being confirmable. Apparently conservative on criminal justice and moderate on civil rights, and with a safe background of a Harvard education and a Minneapolis legal practice, Blackmun was Nixon's olive branch to the Senate, which gave him its swift and unanimous approval. A little over a year later, the terminally ill Hugo Black and John Marshall Harlan resigned from the Court. With a revamped selection process, the administration hoped to avoid further confirmation troubles, but the new more extended process was also prone to leaks, and weeks passed as possible candidates were batted around—and beaten up—in the press. With the presidential election a year away, the White House wanted to score political points with the dual nomination, but suitable candidates again proved hard to find. Increasingly desperate, Nixon personally persuaded Lewis

---

[212] Yalof, *Pursuit of Justices*, 106.

Powell to accept the nomination to finally get a southerner on the Court, and at the last minute Justice Department insider William Rehnquist got the nod as a genuine and smart strict constructionist.[213]

William O. Douglas, the last of Franklin Roosevelt's justices, had been the only justice to urge Fortas to stay on the Court and weather the controversy, and he took his own advice when disclosures of his own lesser financial improprieties led House minority leader Gerald Ford to call for his impeachment in 1970. After serving for longer than any other justice in the Supreme Court's history, declining health finally forced Douglas off the bench in 1975. The task of naming a successor fell to the same Gerald Ford, who was then serving out Richard Nixon's unexpired second term. In the shadow of Watergate and never having won a national election, Ford had pledged to "be the President of all the people," one who had "not subscribed to any partisan platform," had told Congress that his "motto toward Congress is communication, conciliation, compromise and cooperation," and had admitted that he was no longer "my own man. . . . I am your man, for it was your carefully weighed confirmation that changed my occupation."[214] The Democratic landslide in the 1974 midterm election further weakened the president's hand. His primary goal in selecting a nominee for the Supreme Court was to reinforce the belief in the integrity of the courts and to win an easy confirmation. To accomplish that mission, he handed over the task to his apolitical attorney general, Edward H. Levi, the former dean of the University of Chicago Law School. Levi was so apolitical that he neglected to seek outside input before submitting a list of names to the American Bar Association for its review, necessitating the submission of a supplemental list that included two women as well as additional possibilities suggested by Democratic senators. Even so, the president agreed to Levi's first choice, John Paul Stevens, a "careful" jurist from Chicago with no apparent ideological slant that would either complicate confirmation or suggest that Ford was being political in his choice of nominee.[215]

Within a single term of office Nixon had been able to place four new justices on the Court, with Ford filling yet another vacancy. The necessity

---

[213] Ibid., 124.

[214] Gerald Ford, "Remarks on Taking the Oath of Office, August 9, 1974," in *Public Papers of the Presidents of the United States: Gerald R. Ford, 1974* (Washington, DC: Government Printing Office, 1975), 1; Ford, "Address to a Joint Session of Congress, August 12, 1974," in *Public Papers, 1974*, 7.

[215] Edward Levi, quoted in Yalof, *Pursuit of Justices*, 128. Substantively, Ford was particularly concerned that environmentalists would not object to Stevens, given that the president was trying to neutralize that issue before the 1976 elections. Yalof, 256n184. See also David M. O'Brien, "The Politics of Professionalism: President Gerald R. Ford's Appointment of Justice John Paul Stevens," *Presidential Studies Quarterly* 21 (1991): 103.

of winning support from a Democratic Senate and the happenstance of the pattern of vacancies, however, prevented Nixon from turning the Court in a dramatically different direction. The replacement of Warren and Fortas with Burger and Blackmun ended the solid liberal majority that had remade constitutional law in the 1960s, but Blackmun moved steadily to the left over the course of his tenure on the Court, and the replacement of Warren-Court dissenters Black and Harlan with Powell and Rehnquist did not create a solid conservative bloc. Instead, Byron White, Stewart, and Blackmun became the erratic swing votes. "Law and order" was the one policy criterion on which the president insisted, and at least in that area Nixon's appointments paid off. Although the Burger Court declined to overturn the most prominent criminal justice decisions of the Warren Court, it did rein in the most liberal legal decisions of the 1960s so as to realize Nixon's goal of "strengthening the peace forces." Elsewhere the Court tended to follow the lead of the Warren Court, though generally with greater moderation and less certainty. Rather than orchestrating a reversal, the Burger Court looked for ways by which conservatives could live with what the Warren Court had wrought. It was, in Mark Tushnet's apt characterization, a Court of "country-club Republicanism," concerned about street crime but otherwise in tune with liberal opinion favoring, for example, sexual liberty and modest affirmative action.[216] The so-called Nixon Court was a fractured Court.[217] Amidst a welter of conflicting opinions, the justices were comfortable with the exercise of judicial power, but they could no longer agree on how that power should be used. The Republicans within the New Deal order had finally made their ability to make judicial appointments felt, but their contribution to the constitutional regime was primarily jurisprudential confusion. The justices could no longer articulate the clear foundations of the liberal order that had first been laid down by Franklin Roosevelt, but they could elaborate nothing else.

Within this framework, Bill Clinton also played the role of oppositional president operating within a political environment decisively shaped by Ronald Reagan. After George H. W. Bush's appointment of Clarence Thomas, a working five-justice conservative majority across a number of issues had emerged on the Court. With an opportunity to name the successors to two swing justices from the Burger Court, Byron White and Harry Blackmun, Clinton had the ability to help shape the scope of Republican

---

[216] Tushnet, "Burger Court."

[217] With greater focus on at least some substantive issues, Nixon's appointments to the Court were a more cohesive group than were Eisenhower's. Stefanie A. Lindquist, David A. Yalof, and John A. Clark, "The Impact of Presidential Appointments to the U.S. Supreme Court: Cohesive and Divisive Voting within Presidential Blocs," *Political Research Quarterly* 53 (2000): 804–5.

constitutional jurisprudence by hedging in the tentative majority (or majorities, depending on the movement of the individual justices in the center
of the Rehnquist Court) that the Reagan and Bush appointed justices
formed. White, the last of the New Frontier justices and apparently still
the Democratic loyalist, retired from the bench soon after Clinton's inauguration. Enjoying the benefit of a solid Democratic majority in the Senate, Clinton initially hoped to hit a "home run" by appointing a pragmatic
politician who could be counted on to defend abortion rights to the
Court.[218] In a drawn-out, very public process, however, the president discovered that his preferred politicians did not want to give up political life
for life on the bench, and they risked a messy confirmation battle in the
Senate as well. Already encountering legislative and political difficulty in
getting his administration up and running, and under increasing pressure
to settle on a nominee, Clinton offered up Ruth Bader Ginsburg, who
could simultaneously claim a moderate record as a judge on the Court of
Appeals and the mantle of the "Thurgood Marshall of gender equality
law" for her work with the American Civil Liberties Union in the 1970s.[219]
She was not the "home run" Clinton was initially looking for, but her
nomination was an easy base hit in the Senate, where a quiet confirmation
was assured. When Harry Blackmun retired a few months later, Clinton
again sought a high-profile politician for the Court. This time rebuffed
by Senate majority leader George Mitchell, who thought the confirmation
process would jeopardize the Democrats' ambitious legislative agenda,
Clinton again vacillated over the decision. Not needing to invite further
trouble in a Senate already enmeshed in debates over the president's
health care plan and growing scandals surrounding his past behavior,
Clinton finally took the advice of senators and aides to make the politically safe choice of Stephen Breyer.[220] Clinton had far fewer appointments

[218] Quoted in Thomas L. Friedman, "The 11th Hour Scramble," *New York Times*, 15
June 1993, A1. Mark Graber has noted that abortion was nearly the only area in which
Clinton did not "sound . . . Republican." Mark A. Graber, "The Clintonification of American Law: Abortion, Welfare, and Liberal Constitutional Theory," *Ohio State Law Journal*
58 (1997): 731.

[219] The Thurgood Marshall comparison was by Erwin Griswold and touted to the White
House in a letter-writing campaign organized by Ginsburg's husband; quoted in Yalof, *Pursuit of Justices*, 200. See also, Richard B. Davis, *Electing Justice* (New York: Oxford University Press, 2005), 136–37, 140–41.

[220] As one White House official noted of the nomination of Breyer, "He was the one with
the fewest problems." Quoted in Neal A. Lewis, "As Political Terrain Shifts, Breyer Lands
on His Feet," *New York Times*, 15 May 1994, 30. See also Mark Silverstein and William
Haltom, "You Can't Always Get What You Want: Reflections on the Ginsburg and Breyer
Nominations," *Journal of Law and Politics* 12 (1996): 459. But see Ken I. Kersch, "The
Synthetic Progressivism of Stephen Breyer," in *Rehnquist Justice*, ed. Earl M. Maltz (Lawrence: University Press of Kansas, 2003).

to change the personnel on the high Court than did Richard Nixon, but the vacancies did come in recent swing seats that potentially mattered. Unlike Nixon, Clinton was not determined to push the Court in a new direction. The opportunity costs of making a controversial nomination in a context in which the administration's political resources were already seriously taxed were high, and there were relatively few gains to be made by undertaking a confirmation battle and challenging the constitutional status quo. Clinton was not willing to fight for his version of a Brandeis who would be a progressive visionary on the Court. Perhaps he did not even want a Brandeis—his "home run" politicians were not liberal ideological icons like Brandeis but low-key pragmatists like Bruce Babbitt. In terms of constitutional philosophy, this was a muted opposition.

Conclusion

The elevation of a member of the partisan opposition to the presidency does not necessarily indicate the beginning of a period of constitutional reconstruction. Oppositional presidents may lack either the ambition or the authority to launch a reconstructive project. Instead, they must operate within the established constitutional regime, while perhaps seeking ways to reform it. For presidents such as Grover Cleveland, partisan opposition to the dominant party of the era did not imply serious disagreement with the constitutional commitments being articulated by government leaders and the Supreme Court. Political disputes over patronage and policy did not extend into the constitutional sphere. For other presidents such as Richard Nixon, the constitutional interpretations offered by the Court are more disagreeable. Even so, such oppositional presidents do not position themselves as leaders free to envision a new constitutional future.

The diversity of preemptive presidents should remind us that these categories describing different presidential leadership situations are ideal types, clarifying extremes on a continuum, with most historical presidents occupying space further down the continuum, where conditions are less distinct and more fluid. Although the leaders of the normal out-party in a given historical era may have important differences with the interests, constituencies, and policy preferences of the normally dominant political party, they may well accept the constitutional baselines that were established by and are most associated with the other party. From the perspective of the constitutional commitments that the Court seeks to articulate and uphold, these presidents may not be particularly "oppositional" at all. Part of the power of the constitutional regime is the extent to which its basic contours are accepted by the national leaders of both parties. The controversies that remain are generally manageable within the politics of the era. They do not threaten to rupture normal politics and the expected relationships among the institutions of government.

A review of the strategic situation in which the presidents considered in this chapter have found themselves is also a reminder of how difficult the politics of reconstruction is to launch and sustain. The position of the president is rarely secure. For preemptive presidents, who often find themselves at odds with Congress and standing on a fragile electoral base, picking fights with the judiciary would be self-defeating. The independence and supremacy of the judiciary is as much a strategic asset for these presidents as it is for affiliated leaders.

Indeed, these presidents create opportunities for the Court to display and enhance its own independent, leadership role within American constitutional development. Whether they are actively turning new problems over to the courts or simply expressing their willingness to live with whatever decisions that the Court might make, these presidents invite the Court to actively put its stamp on the Constitution. The potential friction between the constitutional commitments of the justices and the immediate legislative calculations of the opposition party is productive for the further expansion and deepening of the constitutional regime as it is interpreted by the Court. It is the Democratic administration of Grover Cleveland that sets the table for the Republican Court of free labor and property to make some of its boldest pronouncements on behalf of a laissez-faire Constitution. At the same time, the judicial appointments of preemptive presidents add new voices to the Court. These appointments help distinguish the Court from its closest allies in the political arena, even if they do not always do so in the most obvious ways. The interventions of Bill Clinton and Woodrow Wilson are the most expected, slowing down or dampening the consolidation of conservative majorities on the Court and creating opportunities for progressive coalitions to form on at least some issues. Less expected, but perhaps more consequential, are the additions that Cleveland and Eisenhower made to the Court. The late-Jacksonian, small-government inclinations of Cleveland's appointments complemented and enriched what would soon become known as the *Lochner* Court. The appointments of a midcentury Republican administration solidified the post–New Deal Court's willingness to take on the southern Democracy and its segregationist stain. Rather than challenging the leadership of the Court within the constitutional order, these presidents have, in their own ways, contributed to its supremacy and activism.

FIVE

The Growth of Judicial Authority

IN DECEMBER 2000, the U.S. Supreme Court determined the presidency. The Founders could have hardly imagined such an event. When representative government was young, electoral rules were relatively few, and elections were local affairs involving a small electorate and handwritten ballots or a voice vote, there was little room for the type of election dispute that emerged in Florida in 2000. To the extent that election results were contested or not clear, legislatures were widely regarded as the appropriate institution to resolve such disputes. This understanding found its way into the constitutional text. The jealously guarded right of the British Parliament to judge the election returns of its members was carried over into the United States.[1] The Constitution specified that the House and Senate were each to serve as the "Judge of the Elections, Returns and Qualifications of its own Members."[2] Likewise, the ballots of the presidential electors were to be authoritatively counted, and presumably if necessary contested, in Congress. If no candidate could win a majority of the electors, then the duty of selecting a president fell to the members of the House of Representatives.[3] To the Founding generation, no one could be more trusted to judge election returns and resolve election disputes than the collected representatives of the people.

One of the striking features of the 2000 presidential contest was the willingness to have the matter resolved in the courts rather than the state and national legislatures.[4] Of course, Democratic candidate Al Gore and

---

[1] Thomas Pitt Taswell-Langmead, *English Constitutional History*, 10th ed. (London: Sweet and Maxwell, 1946), 372–74. The rise of political parties had already put pressure on that system of judging election returns, however, by the time of American independence. Ibid., 649.

[2] U.S. Const., Art. I, § 5.

[3] U.S. Const., Art. II, § 1.

[4] This was much more clearly true on the Democratic side than the Republican, with the latter publicly contemplating "the constitutional remedy" of carrying the dispute into the Florida legislature and the U.S. Congress, if necessary. James Baker, quoted in Roberto Suro, "Nation Awaits Court's Decision; Both Bush and Gore Camps Warn of Taint on Presidency, but Foresee Reconciliation," *Washington Post*, 11 December 2000, A1. Even when Gore aides considered continuing the fight after the U.S. Supreme Court's ruling, the focus was on the judiciary. David Von Drehle and James Grimaldi, "Careful Decision to End It; After His 36-Day Fight, Gore Studies Verdict, Polls Advisors, Meets Defeat with Calm Resolve," *Washington Post*, 14 December 2000, A1.

his allies initiated the judicial contest in Florida, but in the course of keeping Democratic lawmakers on board with continuing legal appeals the Gore camp signaled that they would not carry the fight beyond the judiciary and into the legislatures. The courts would provide "finality."[5] Even when the U.S. Supreme Court intervened in the dispute to Gore's apparent detriment, his camp still accepted judicial resolution, with Gore's chief lawyer telling the press before the justices' decision that "[t]heir voice is final."[6] For many, the mere existence of the Supreme Court case of *Bush v. Gore*, not to mention the ready acceptance of it, marked the apogee of judicial authority and showed the great distance that the Court had traveled since its founding.[7]

One must be careful of reading too much into *Bush v. Gore*. Although the case certainly says something about the status of the judiciary in modern American politics, it says little about the authority of the Court to interpret the Constitution.[8] Ironically, the Supreme Court was exercising a far more of a court-like role in December 2000 than the modern Court usually does—that is, *Bush v. Gore* was primarily a matter of conflict resolution for two identifiable parties rather than of judicial lawmaking through constitutional interpretation.[9] As might be expected in a case of such magnitude, the identity of the litigants and the details of the facts of the dispute demanded the justices' attention and swamped most other considerations. The plurality opinion itself strove to minimize the legal impact of the decision and the broader significance of the constitutional understandings laid down by the Court. The case of a disputed presidential election is almost *sui generis*, and the Court's intervention in that dispute largely provided "a restricted railroad ticket, good for this day and train only."[10] Nonetheless, the willingness of an array of national political officials to carry a presidential election into the courts and to abide by the Court's decision at the end of the twentieth century stands in sharp contrast to the expectations and behavior of political actors ear-

[5] Statement of U.S. Representatives Cal Dooley and Jim Moran, quoted in Ken Foskett, "Reaction: Democrats Support Appeals Process; Gore Camp Agrees Court's Judgment is the End of the Line," *Atlanta Journal-Constitution*, 5 December 2000, 12A.

[6] David Boies, quoted in Howard Gillman, *The Votes that Counted* (Chicago: University of Chicago Press, 2001), 129.

[7] See, e.g., Laurence H. Tribe, "eroG v. hsuB and its Disguises: Freeing *Bush v. Gore* from its Hall of Mirrors," *Harvard Law Review* 115 (2001): 170; Richard E. Barkow, "More Supreme Than Court? The Fall of Political Question Doctrine and the Rise of Judicial Supremacy," *Columbia Law Review* 102 (2002): 237.

[8] On the immediate constitutional and institutional background to *Bush v. Gore*, see Richard L. Hasen, *The Supreme Court and Election Law* (New York: New York University Press, 2003).

[9] On this "basic social logic of courts," see Shapiro, *Courts*, 1.

[10] Smith v. Allwright, 321 U.S. 649, 669 (1944) (Roberts, J., dissenting).

lier in the nation's history and is indicative of the robust authority that the modern Court enjoys. The awkward tie of Thomas Jefferson and Aaron Burr in the presidential election of 1800 was resolved in Congress. The scheming of the lame-duck Federalist majority to derail the national will brought threats of extraconstitutional solutions, not litigation.[11] The corrupted election of 1876 was resolved by an ad hoc electoral commission created by Congress and largely composed of congressmen. Supreme Court justices served on the commission in a distinctly extrajudicial capacity, though their participation in that personal way was welcomed as lending equitableness to the proceedings.[12] In 2000, the prospect of the involvement of legislators and politicians in resolving the election dispute brought forth hand-wringing over a possible "constitutional crisis." Only judges, it was widely thought, could be trusted to impose a settlement.[13]

To this point, we have focused on the somewhat cyclical set of incentives that lead presidents sometimes to oppose but usually to support judicial authority to interpret the Constitution. In placing these recurring patterns in the foreground of our analysis, development across time has been placed in the background. This chapter will look more closely at that background. Focusing on this background will allow us to see how the strategic contexts examined in the previous chapters have altered over time. The previous chapters have called our attention to important factors that affect judicial authority, and we should be alert to the possibility that the relative prevalence of those factors that tend to bolster judicial authority may also have changed over time.

Indeed, institutional and coalitional pressures that push political actors to turn to the Court for constitutional leadership have become more pervasive over the course of American history. Political leaders have found increasing reason to support the Court, and decreasing capacity to resist the Court, over time. Unsurprisingly, this favorable environment has encouraged the Court to make ever more grandiose claims for its own authority to stand as the "ultimate interpreter" of the Constitution while recognizing ever fewer reasons to defer to the constitutional understandings of others.

This chapter overviews some aspects of this growth of judicial interpretive authority. It begins with an early, and unsuccessful, effort to construct judicial supremacy by the first affiliated leaders, the Federalists. It then turns to the rather different and more successful efforts of the late nine-

---

[11] See Bruce Ackerman, *The Failure of the Founding Fathers* (Cambridge: Harvard University Press, 2005).

[12] See Charles Fairman, *Five Justices and the Electoral Commission of 1877*, vol. 7 of *History of the Supreme Court of the United States* (New York: Macmillan, 1988).

[13] See Keith E. Whittington, "Yet Another Constitutional Crisis?" *William and Mary Law Review* 43 (2002): 2093.

teenth and early twentieth centuries to elevate the courts to a privileged place in the constitutional order, before concluding with the place of the judiciary in the fragmented politics of the late twentieth century.

JUDICIAL SUPREMACY AND THE "BANEFUL INFLUENCE OF FACTION"

One of the earliest assertions of judicial supremacy in the United States came within a decade of ratification of the Constitution. Despite the historical novelty of the power of judicial review, it did not take long for the notion of judicial supremacy to emerge. The power of the judiciary to strike down, or at least to refuse to apply, laws that the judges regarded as unconstitutional was anticipated by at least some at the time of the founding. Nonetheless, the theory and practice of such a power were still in rudimentary form, and judges were most concerned with arguing that the courts were not inferior to other constitutional interpreters.

The possibility of the courts acting as constitutional interpreters and laying aside laws that they deemed unconstitutional was recognized gradually over the course of the 1780s and 1790s, first in the states and then in the federal government. In his well-known 1791 "Lectures on Law," James Wilson, a leading draftsman and proponent of the U.S. Constitution, argued that "whoever would be obliged to obey a constitutional law, is justified in refusing to obey an unconstitutional act of the legislature— and . . . when a question, even of this delicate nature, occurs, every one who is called to act, has a right to judge."[14] The duty of constitutional interpretation was a general one, but one that was at least shared by judges. As Wilson noted elsewhere in his lectures, "If that constitution be infringed by one [branch of government], it is no reason that the infringement should be abetted, though it is a strong reason that it should be discountenanced and declared void by the other."[15] More particularly, James Iredell, among the most original and influential of the early advocates of judicial review, noted in 1786 that under the American theory of limited government, "an act of Assembly, inconsistent with the constitution, is *void*, and cannot be obeyed. . . . The judges, therefore, must take care at their peril, that every act of Assembly they presume to enforce is warranted by the constitution, since if it is not, they act without lawful authority."[16] "It is not," Iredell assured Richard Spaight, then participat-

---

[14] James Wilson, *The Works of James Wilson*, ed. Robert Green McCloskey, 2 vols. (Cambridge: Harvard University Press, 1967), 1:186.

[15] Ibid., 1:330.

[16] James Iredell, *Life and Correspondence of James Iredell*, ed. Griffith J. McRee, vol. 2 (New York: D. Appleton, 1858), 148.

ing in the federal constitutional convention, "that the judges are appointed arbiters, and to determine as it were upon any application, whether the Assembly have or have not violated the Constitution; but when an act is necessarily brought in judgment before them, they must, unavoidably, determine one way or another" if they are to do their own duty as constitutional agents of the people.[17] Wilson concurred, noting that this "regulation is far from throwing any disparagement upon the legislative authority. . . . It does not confer upon the judicial department a power superiour, in its general nature, to that of the legislature; but it confers upon it, in particular instances, and for particular purposes, the power of declaring and enforcing the superiour power of the constitution."[18]

Even so, state assemblies sometimes reacted with alarm to early suggestions of a power of judges to set aside their legislative handiwork. In New York, a state court merely hinting at a power of judicial review was enough to provoke the state legislature to adopt a resolution in 1784 denouncing the judicial opinion as "subversive of all laws and good order, and lead[ing] directly to anarchy and confusion," and to declarations in the press that the judicial power was merely "to declare laws, not to alter them. Whenever [the courts] depart from this design of their institution, they confound legislative and judicial powers."[19] Two years later, after Rhode Island judges claimed a power of judicial review, the state legislature forced them, under threat of impeachment, to "totally disavow any the least power or authority, or appearance therefore to convene or controul" state statutes.[20]

The courts had been more successful in laying claim to the power of judicial review in Virginia. Judge George Wyth declared in an early case in 1782 that he would "feel the duty; and, fearlessly, perform it" if asked to enforce an unconstitutional law, though his senior colleague, Edmund Pendleton, was less certain as to the appropriate answer to this "tremendous question."[21] A few years later, Judge William Nelson rejected the view that the "judiciary, by declaring an act of the legislature to be no law, assumes legislative authority, or claims a superiority over the legislature." The judges were not "the champions of the people, or of the Constitution,"

[17] Ibid., 2:173. Spaight had earlier written to Iredell denouncing the "despotic" and "insufferable" power of judicial review as it was recently exercised by the North Carolina Supreme Court. Ibid., 2:169.

[18] Wilson, *Works*, 1:330.

[19] Quoted in Larry Kramer, "We the Court," *Harvard Law Review* 115 (2001): 56, 57.

[20] Ibid., 58. On the early state cases, see Haines, *American Doctrine*, 73–121; Snowiss, *Judicial Review*, 13–89; Philip Hamburger, "Law and Judicial Duty," *George Washington Law Review* 72 (2003): 1701; Kramer, *The People Themselves*, 35–114; William Michael Treanor, "Judicial Review before *Marbury*," *Stanford Law Review* 58 (2005): 455.

[21] Commonwealth v. Caton, 4 Call. 5, 8, 17 (Va. 1782).

they merely had an obligation to find the applicable law in the cases before them.[22] Judge James Tyler declared, "I cannot consent" to being made "an agent . . . for the purpose of violating the constitution . . . as a public servant, filling an office in one of the great departments of government, I should be a traitor to my country to do it."[23] The power of the courts to refuse to abet constitutional violations, according to Justice William Paterson in a federal circuit court eight years before the *Marbury* decision, was grounded in the basic principle "that the judiciary in this country is not a subordinate, but co-ordinate, branch of government."[24] By 1803, John Marshall was following a well-trod path in arguing that the Constitution was a rule to be followed by the courts as well as by the legislature.[25]

The first Congress that convened under the new U.S. Constitution was faced with numerous basic decisions about the proper organization of the new federal government, and in making those decisions they often encountered the ambiguities of the constitutional text and were compelled to make at least an initial resolution of those constitutional uncertainties. Several of these decisions were immediately controversial and provoked substantial constitutional debate within Congress and elsewhere.[26] In the midst of those debates, legislators recognized the possibility of judicial review of their actions. In defending the constitutionality of a measure to create a national bank, Representative Elias Boudinot addressed one "last objection," that the judiciary might regard the bill as unconstitutional and would "not lend their aid to carry it into execution." This objection did not cause Boudinot any concern, however, for he welcomed such a "remedy" in preventing "a wrong measure from effecting his constituents" if "from inattention, want of precision, or any other defect, he should do wrong."[27]

More remarkably, and idiosyncratically, William Loughton Smith denied that Congress could play any interpretative role in determining whether the president had a unilateral right to remove executive officials. Smith objected to the claim that it would be proper to give a "legislative construction" on the removal power, for doing so "would be an infringement on the powers of the Judiciary." Rather than inviting the "mischief"

---

[22] Kamper v. Hawkins, 1 Va. Cases 21, 30 (1793).

[23] Ibid., 61.

[24] VanHorne's Lessee v. Dorrance, 2 U.S. 303, 309 (1795).

[25] Marbury v. Madison, 5 U.S. (1 Cranch) 137, 180 (1803). See also Jack N. Rakove, "The Origins of Judicial Review: A Plea for New Contexts," *Stanford Law Review* 49 (1997): 1031; Graber, "Establishing Judicial Review: *Marbury*," 609; Klarman, "How Great," 1111.

[26] For an overview, see Currie, *The Constitution in Congress*, 7–116; Mark Graber and Michael Perhac, eds., *Marbury v. Madison* (Washington, DC: CQ Press, 2002), 263–75.

[27] *Annals of Congress*, 1st Cong., 3rd sess. (1791), 1978, 1979.

of "Legislatures undertaking to decide constitutional questions," Congress should refrain from exercising "the powers of judges in expounding the constitution."[28] Elbridge Gerry perhaps clarified the issue by noting that the matter of removal was something for the Senate and the president to resolve between themselves, as the two bodies that shared the appointment power. To the extent that they could not reach an accommodation, "the judges are the constitutional umpires on such constitutional questions" and the "House of Representatives have nothing to do with it."[29] For those favoring a legislative settlement in favor of a unilateral executive removal power, it was "proper for the Legislature to speak their sense upon those points on which the Constitution is silent."[30]

Rather than filling in a constitutional gap, Representative James Madison preferred to think of Congress as expounding the implicit meaning of the original constitutional scheme in locating the removal power in the president. He expected that this decision "will become the permanent exposition of the Constitution" on this point, and he was particularly emphatic in rejecting Smith's claim that the "Legislature has no right to expound the Constitution."[31] He demanded to know "upon what principle it can be contended, that any one department draws from the constitution greater powers than another, in marking out the limits of the powers of the several departments?" None of "these independent departments has more right than another to declare their sentiments" on such constitutional points. Such matters must be "adjusted by the departments themselves," and failing that by the larger "will of the community, to be collected in some mode to be provided by the constitution, or one dictated by the necessity of the case."[32] As Madison had earlier explained to Thomas Jefferson, "as the Courts are generally the last in making their decision, it results to them . . . to stamp it with its final character. This makes the Judiciary Dept paramount in fact to the Legislature, which was never intended, and can never be proper."[33] Simply from speaking last in the ordinary course of things, the judiciary was likely to have inordinate influence over constitutional meaning. Far better for Congress to set a firm

---

[28] *Annals of Congress*, 1st Cong., 1st sess. (1789), 489. Smith believed executive officials could only be removed by impeachment.

[29] *Annals of Congress*, 1st Cong., 1st sess. (1789), 491, 492. Gerry, who had opposed passage of the Constitution on these same grounds, later in the debate argued that the Constitution was often obscure, but "if Congress are to explain and declare what it shall be, they certainly will have it in their power to make it what they please." Ibid., 523.

[30] Ibid., 505 (John Laurance).

[31] Ibid., 514, 520.

[32] Ibid., 520.

[33] James Madison, *The Papers of James Madison*, ed. Robert Rutland, vol. 11 (Charlottesville: University Press of Virginia, 1979), 293.

precedent on general principles, before particular disputes became intertwined with factional politics. Courts could take their guidance from that prior congressional deliberation.

More significant than William Smith's curious suggestion of judicial supremacy in those early congressional debates, however, was the debate following passage of the Alien and Sedition Acts of 1798. The congressional passage of the acts reflected the tense political climate of the late 1790s. The ratification of the Constitution had not put an end to basic political divisions within the new republic, as many had hoped that it would. Despite the general support for the presidency of George Washington, it quickly became apparent that both Congress and the cabinet were divided over fundamental principles of government, as well as over personality, ambition, and interest. One faction, which retained the name of Federalists, came to dominate Congress and the administration and favored a larger and more active national government that would encourage the development of a commercial republic allied with Britain. Another faction, which traveled under various names including Democratic-Republican, came under the informal leadership of Thomas Jefferson and James Madison and was skeptical of the Federalist nation-building project and more sympathetic to the new republican government in France. Despite the Founders' antipathy to political parties, two opposing legislative coalitions and electoral organizations were rapidly forming by the time John Adams succeeded Washington in 1797.[34]

Foreign affairs provided the trigger for the administration to take a more strong-armed approach to domestic political opposition. In an attempt to weaken Britain, the French navy increasingly attacked American shipping. When an American mission arrived in France to negotiate a settlement, the French foreign minister, in what became known as the "XYZ Affair," demanded a bribe and an American loan to France before formal discussions would be allowed to begin. The popular and political outcry in the United States was immediate upon arrival of the news, and the government stepped up preparations for war. The pro-French Republicans were placed on the defensive, especially since they continued their general resistance to a military buildup. Against this background, the Federalist senator Theodore Sedgwick wrote, "[The XYZ affair] will afford a glorious opportunity to destroy faction."[35] President Adams believed that the "tongues and pens of slander" were "instruments with which our

---

[34] See also Richard Hofstadter, *The Idea of a Party System* (Berkeley and Los Angeles: University of California Press, 1969), 40–121; James Roger Sharp, *American Politics in the Early Republic* (New Haven: Yale University Press, 1993); Joanne B. Freeman, *Affairs of Honor* (New Haven: Yale University Press, 2001).

[35] Quoted in Smith, *Freedom's Fetters*, 21.

enemies expect to subdue our country," and that "disorganizers" had been "too long permitted to prevail," but he trusted that the towns that were "free of them will ever prove their federalism in elections."[36] With heightened international tensions, the preexisting distrust of factions in the fledgling republic grew into open hostility against Republican organizations and newspapers that had sprung up around the country.[37] As Federalist newspapers declared, "Whatever American *opposes* the Administration is an Anarchist, a Jacobin, and a Traitor. . . . It is *Patriotism* to write in favor of our Government—it is Sedition to write against it."[38]

The Sedition Act was intended to give greater legal heft to such common Federalist sentiments, making it a crime to publish "false, scandalous, and malicious writing or writings, against the government of the United States," to bring in "into contempt or disrepute," or to "excite" against it "the hatred of the good people of the United States."[39] Representative John Allen explained the need for the law by reading on the floor of the House from the *Philadelphia Aurora*, a leading Jeffersonian outlet.[40] Particularly disturbing to Allen was the publication of a speech by one of his congressional colleagues, Edward Livingston, who had declared, "[W]henever our laws manifestly infringe the Constitution under which they were made, the people ought not to hesitate which they should obey. If we exceed our powers we become tyrants, and our acts have no effect. . . . [O]ne of the first effects of measures such as this, if they be not acquiesced in, will be disaffection among the States, and opposition among the

[36] Quoted in Michael Kent Curtis, *Free Speech, "The People's Darling Privilege"* (Durham: Duke University Press, 2000), 61–62.

[37] "Democratic-Republican societies" first emerged during the Washington administration, but most dissolved by 1796. They were in many ways precursors to the more formal Republican Party organization that developed during the Adams administration, however. See Eugene P. Link, *Democratic-Republican Societies, 1790–1800* (New York: Columbia University Press, 1942); Noble E. Cunningham Jr., *The Jeffersonian Republicans* (Chapel Hill: University of North Carolina Press, 1957). A typical proclamation of the societies emphasized their duty "to *detect* and *publish* to the world every violation of our Constitutions, or instance of Mal-Administration." Philip S. Foner, ed., *The Democratic-Republican Societies, 1790–1800* (Westport, CT: Greenwood Press, 1976), 320.

[38] Quoted in Curtis, *Free Speech*, 62.

[39] 1 Stat. 596, July 14, 1798. The Alien Acts, passed at the same time, enhanced presidential authority to detain and deport aliens and extended the period of residency required for naturalization to citizenship.

[40] President Adams likewise thought that if the U.S. Attorney "does not think this paper libellous, he is not fit for his office; and if he does not prosecute it, he will not do his duty." Indeed, the president suggested to his secretary of state that the editor of the *Aurora* "merits the execution of the alien law. I am very willing to try its strength upon him." John Adams, "To T. Pickering, August 1, 1799," in *The Works of John Adams*, ed. Charles Francis Adams, 10 vols. (Boston: Little, Brown, 1854), 9:5.

people to your Government."[41] Allen concluded his reading by noting, "This, sir, was a foul calumny on the good people of the United States, or the gentleman has a more intimate acquaintance with treason and traitors than I had been ever in the habit of ascribing to him. . . . This is an awful, horrible example of 'the liberty of opinion and freedom of the press.' "[42] Representative Albert Gallatin mused, "If an individual thinking, such as [I myself] did, that the present bill was unconstitutional, and that it had been intended, not for the public good, but solely for party purposes, should avow and publish his opinions . . . would a jury, composed of the friends of that Administration, hesitate much in declaring the opinion ungrounded, or, in other words, false and scandalous, and its publication malicious" and thereby convict him of sedition?[43]

The (indirect) exchange between Allen and Livingston is instructive as to more than just the Federalists' constricted understanding of acceptable political discourse in a republican government.[44] It also exposed a sharp division over the proper locus of authority in constitutional interpretation and the remedy of constitutional violations. Allen is astonished that Livingston would turn to the people to act "whenever they think we exceed our Constitutional powers; but, I ask the gentleman, who shall determine that point? I thought the Constitution had assigned the cognizance of that question to the Courts." "The people," Allen assured his colleagues, "I venerate; they are truly sovereign; but a section, a part of the citizens, a town, a city, or a mob, I know them not."[45] Such sentiments marked the decline of what Larry Kramer has called a "popular constitutionalism" that was regnant at the time of the American Revolution and that endorsed a wide range of public action in defense of constitutional understandings, ranging from voting, petitioning, and pamphleteering, to jury nullification and "mobbing," and which formed part of the background of judges refusing to aid the enforcement of unconstitutional laws.[46] The

[41] *Annals of Congress*, 5th Cong., 2nd sess. (1798), 2095, 2098.

[42] Ibid., 2096.

[43] Ibid., 2162.

[44] On the Federalists' understanding of speech in a democracy, see James P. Martin, "When Repression is Democratic and Constitutional: The Federalist Theory of Representation and the Sedition Act of 1798," *University of Chicago Law Review* 66 (1999): 117.

[45] *Annals of Congress*, 5th Cong., 2nd sess. (1798), 2096.

[46] Kramer, *The People Themselves*, 18–34. As Pauline Maier notes, "When someone suggested during the Stamp Act riots that the militia be raised [Sheriff Stephen] Greenleaf was told it had already risen. This situation meant that mobs could naturally assume the manner of a lawful institution." Pauline Maier, "Popular Uprisings and Civil Authority in Eighteenth Century America," *William and Mary Quarterly*, 3rd series, 27 (1970): 19. See also Christian G. Fritz, "Legitimating Government: The Struggle Over People's Sovereignty, 1776–1900," unpublished manuscript.

traditions of political activity that gave rise to the Boston Tea Party did not immediately disappear with the attainment of national independence.

The Federalists had already had difficulties with the unruliness of early American democracy. By the end of his presidency, George Washington had grown bitter at the criticism he received in the press, and he denounced "certain self-created societies," the Democratic-Republican clubs, that "have disseminated, from an ignorance or perversion of facts, suspicions, jealousies, and accusations of the whole Government," which ultimately led to "insurrection" such as the tax protests in western Pennsylvania.[47] Congressional preparation for war in 1798 provoked new unrest in the region. When a mob freed eighteen tax resisters from federal custody in 1799, President Adams authorized military force to pacify the region and locate the instigators. Upon arrest, John Fries and others were transported to Philadelphia and tried for treason, among other offenses, in federal court. Although federal law required that capital cases be tried in the county of the crime, the judges regarded Philadelphia to be the better venue for the trial and jury selection since the home county of Fries and his colleagues was too sympathetic to the defendants' cause, "public justice," they argued, "ought to be as well guarded as the prisoner's convenience."[48] The defense counsel argued strenuously that the actions of the defendants did not meet the constitutional definition of treason, but the judges instructed the jury to follow a broad definition of treason that assured conviction. Secretary of State Timothy Pickering reported the good news, "anxiously expected by the real friends to the order and tranquility of the country," to the president: "The examples appear singularly important in Pennsylvania, where treason and rebellion have so repeatedly reared their heads. And painful as is the idea of taking the life of a man, I feel a calm and solid satisfaction that an opportunity is now presented, in executing the just sentence of the law, to crush that spirit."[49] When evident jury bias resulted in a second trial for Fries, Supreme Court justice Samuel Chase opened the proceedings with a legal opinion precluding the defense from arguing the definition of treason, explaining later that it was the duty of the court to prevent the defense from an "improper

---

[47] George Washington, *The Writings of George Washington*, ed. John C. Fitzpatrick, vol. 34 (Washington, DC: Government Printing Office, 1940), 29, 35. See also Elkins and McKitrick, *The Age of Federalism*, 451–88; Thomas P. Slaughter, *The Whiskey Rebellion* (New York: Oxford University Press, 1986); Saul Cornell, *The Other Founders* (Chapel Hill: University of North Carolina Press, 1999), 195–218. On Washington and the press, see Marshall Smesler, "George Washington and the Alien and Sedition Acts," *American Historical Review* 59 (1954): 322.

[48] Francis Wharton, *State Trials of the United States During the Administrations of Washington and Adams* (Philadelphia: Carey and Hart, 1849), 488.

[49] Timothy Pickering, "To John Adams, May 10, 1799," *Works of Adams*, 8:644.

attempt, to mislead the jury."[50] Having been denied their only legal strategy, the defense counsel withdrew from the case in protest, but Justice Chase assured Fries that the "court will be your counsel, and will do you as much justice as those who were your counsel."[51] Fries was quickly convicted again and sentenced to hang.[52]

The Federalist judiciary's controversial handling of the Fries case reflected emerging disagreements over the role of judges and juries in applying the law. One aspect of revolutionary-era popular constitutionalism was jury nullification. If unconstitutional laws are "*a mere nullity,*" then juries as well as judges could refuse to apply them, especially if juries are understood to be a particular instantiation of the popular sovereign.[53] The integration of juries, adding "a mixture of popular power," according to a younger John Adams, into the legal machinery, was another check on the power of government, requiring popular support for the laws to be made effective.[54] In his law lectures, James Wilson exhorted, "[T]he jury must do their duty, and their whole duty; they must decide the law as well as the fact," even when the judge and the jury disagreed "with regard to a point of law," noting that "[n]o punishment can be inflicted without the intervention" of a jury.[55] In a famous case from colonial New York the jurors responded to the defense attorney's call that they "see

[50] *Trial of Samuel Chase, An Associate Justice of the Supreme Court of the United States,* vol. 2 (Washington, D.C.: Smith and Lloyd, 1805), 166.

[51] Case of Fries, 9 F. Cas. 924, 942 (C.C. Pa. 1800). Wharton quotes Chase somewhat differently. Wharton, *State Trials,* 629. The ideas of the justice as to an adequate defense proved peculiar. In his jury charge, he pointed out that Fries had previously been convicted of treason on the same set of facts and law. Wharton, 635. But Judge Richard Peters, sitting on the trial with Chase, later wrote that the justice conducted himself well in the remainder of the trial. Stephen B. Presser, *The Original Misunderstanding* (Durham, NC: Carolina Academic Press, 1991), 112.

[52] Against the advice of his cabinet, Adams later pardoned those convicted of participating in "Fries's Rebellion." The Fries trial, and Justice Chase's behavior, fed Republican polemics and later figured in Chase's impeachment. See also Whittington, *Constitutional Construction,* 20–71.

[53] Boston *Gazette,* quoted in Kramer, "We the Court," 29.

[54] Adams, *Works of Adams,* 3:481. In the years leading up to the Revolution, Adams had believed that juries were the "Voice of the People," and "the common people should have as compleat a Controul, as decisive a Negative, in every Judgement of a Court of Judicature," especially since the "great Principles of the Constitution, are intimately known" to every juror. Quoted in Shannon C. Stimson, *The American Revolution in the Law* (Princeton: Princeton University Press, 1990), 71, 79. See also Kramer, "We the Court," 28–33; John Phillip Reid, *In a Defiant State* (University Park: Pennsylvania State University Press, 1977), 27–64; William E. Nelson, *Americanization of the Common Law* (Athens: University of Georgia Press, 1994), 3–35; Jeffrey Abramson, *We, the Jury* (Cambridge: Harvard University Press, 2000), 22–88; J. R. Pole, "Reflections on American Law and the American Revolution," *William and Mary Quarterly,* 3rd series, 50 (1993): 123.

[55] Wilson, *Works,* 2:540; 1:74.

with their own eyes" and refused to convict John Peter Zenger for the seditious libel of criticizing the royal governor, and colonial Massachusetts jurors lent their support to John Hancock's circumvention of British customs laws by refusing to convict him of any crime.[56]

By the early nineteenth century the power of juries was in decline, but in the 1790s they still created obstacles to the Federalists.[57] Reducing the role of the jury in the articulation and defense of constitutional principles was consistent with their larger rhetorical effort to construct constitutional interpretation as outside of the realm of legitimate popular and political action. The passage of the Sedition Act was motivated in part by the "nearly epidemic degree of [unpunished] seditious libel that infected American newspapers" and the unreliability of common-law prosecutions and the more locally responsive state courts.[58] Federalist supporters of the Sedition Act continued to praise juries as a "barrier to liberty," but exercised great care in selecting their jurors and then hemmed them in with more active judicial management of the courtroom so that they might not develop "erroneous impressions" from constitutional arguments from the defense.[59] In refusing to allow defense attorneys to argue the unconstitutionality of the act to the jury in a sedition trial in Virginia, Justice Chase explained that "no jury would wish to have a right to determine such great, important, difficult questions." The "judicial power of the United States [i.e., federal judges] is the only proper and competent authority whether any statute made by congress (or any of the state legislatures) is contrary to, or in violation of, the federal constitution."[60] The Sedition Act proved to be an effective legal weapon for the Federalists, but such judicial excesses were also a substantial political liability.[61]

---

[56] James Alexander, *A Brief Narrative of the Case and Trial of John Peter Zenger*, ed. Stanley Katz (Cambridge: Harvard University Press, 1963), 93. On John Hancock, see Reid, *In a Defiant State*, 32, 51–52.

[57] On the decline of juries, see Nelson, *Americanization of Common Law*, 165–74; Mark DeWolfe Howe, "The Changing Role of the Jury in the Nineteenth Century," *Yale Law Journal* 74 (1964): 170.

[58] Quote from Leonard W. Levy, *Emergence of a Free Press* (New York: Oxford University Press, 1985), x, as modified by Curtis, *Free Speech*, 46.

[59] *Annals of Congress*, 6th Cong., 2nd sess. (1801), 925 (Samuel Dana); *Trial of Chase*, 1:33. Federal juries were selected by federal marshals, who were appointed by the president. Unlike locally elected sheriffs, Jeffersonians regarded the federal marshal as a "creature of the Executive" and "but the breath of the nostrils of the prosecutor." *Annals of Congress*, 5th Cong., 2nd sess. (1798), 2164 (Albert Gallatin); *Annals of Congress*, 11th Cong., 1st sess. (1809), 77 (John Randolph). Justice Chase was accused of further tampering with jury selection, by explicitly instructing the marshal to strike "any of those creatures called democrats" from the jury for a sedition trial. *Trial of Chase*, 1:194.

[60] United States v. Callender, 25 F. Cas. 239, 257, 256 (C.C. D. Va., 1800).

[61] John Fries, for example, had been a Federalist, but the brutal tactics of the administration turned him and the entire German community into die-hard Republicans. Elkins and

There were clear obstacles to continuing the protest of the act after its passage. A member of the U.S. House of Representatives, Matthew Lyons, was the first to be convicted under the Sedition Act, for two public speeches and a letter to the editor of a Vermont newspaper critical of the Adams administration.[62] In Massachusetts, several individuals were convicted of sedition after erecting a "liberty pole," whose inscription began, "No Stamp Act, No Sedition, No Alien Bills."[63] Several Jeffersonian newspapers were shut down, and others were hampered by federal prosecutions. A maverick Federalist member of the New York state legislature, Jedidiah Peck, was arrested for circulating a petition demanding repeal of the act.[64]

With the terms of the Sedition Act being aggressively implemented through the Federalist judiciary, the Jeffersonian opposition turned to the states as a platform from which to continue the criticism of the legislation. Resolutions passed by the Virginia and Kentucky state legislatures in the final months of 1798 were among the most important protests to the Alien and Sedition Acts. The Virginia resolution was secretly drafted by James Madison, as the Kentucky resolution was by Thomas Jefferson.[65] Madison subsequently joined the Virginia state legislature and drafted an extensive report on the resolutions that was published in early 1800.[66] The resolutions denounced the acts as unconstitutional and became canonical texts of the emerging Jeffersonian Republican Party.

For present purposes, the resolutions are most notable for their assertion of state authority to interpret the Constitution. Both resolutions develop a strict constructionist approach to constitutional meaning based on a state compact theory of the origins of the Constitution, contending that the Constitution and the federal government resulted "from the com-

---

McKitrick, *The Age of Federalism*, 699–700. On the implementation of the Sedition Act, see Smith, *Freedom's Fetters*, 176–417; Curtis, *Free Speech*, 80–104.

[62] Wharton, *State Trials*, 333–36.

[63] Curtis, *Free Speech*, 88; Smith, *Freedom's Fetters*, 260–70.

[64] Elkins and McKitrick, *The Age of Freedom*, 705–6; Smith, *Freedom's Fetters*, 390–98. Peck was transported to New York City for trial, but the journey became a public relations disaster for the Federalist authorities, "nothing less than the public exhibition of a suffering martyr for the freedom of speech and the press, and the right of petitioning." Jabez D. Hammond, *The History of Political Parties in the State of New York*, 4th ed., vol. 1 (Cooperstown, NY: H. & E. Phinney, 1846), 132. As a result, the prosecutor decided that "more Good will flow from suspending the Prosecution [and keeping Peck under threat of it], than from Pursuit of it" in an immediate trial. Quoted in Smith, 397. Peck was released and overwhelmingly reelected to the legislature.

[65] Madison, *Writings*, 6:326–31; Jefferson, *Writings*, ed. Ford, 7:289–309. On the drafting of the resolutions, see Adrienne Koch and Harry Ammon, "The Virginia and Kentucky Resolutions: An Episode in Jefferson's and Madison's Defense of Civil Liberties," *William and Mary Quarterly*, 3rd series, 5 (1948): 145.

[66] Madison, *Writings*, 6:341–407.

pact to which the States are parties" and that the powers of the federal government are strictly limited to "the grants enumerated in that compact."[67] The Sedition Act "exercises a power nowhere delegated to the Federal Government . . . subvert[s] the general principles of free government . . . [and is] expressly and positively forbidden by one of the amendments."[68] Madison's Virginia resolution finds a general responsibility of the states to "interpose for arresting the progress of the evil" that threatened their citizens, realized in this case by publicly "declaring . . . that the acts aforesaid are unconstitutional" and calling on the other states to join Virginia in taking "the necessary and proper measures" to maintain reserved "authorities, rights, and liberties."[69] Jefferson's Kentucky resolution is more explicit in grounding the legislature's action in the claim that unconstitutional acts are "unauthoritative, void, and of no force," and that the federal government "was not made the exclusive or final judge of the extent of the powers delegated to itself." As authors of the Constitution, the states had a preeminent "right to judge for itself" whether the Constitution had been violated and how such violations should be remedied.[70] Jefferson, unlike Madison, went on to suggest that the state "nullification of the act is the rightful remedy," in which "each [state might] take measures of its own" to prevent the unconstitutional acts from being "exercised within their respective territories."[71]

State legislative protests against the actions of the federal government were not entirely unprecedented, but the constitutional theory put forward by the resolutions of 1798 was distinctive.[72] Unsurprisingly, the Federalists, who still controlled the remainder of the state legislatures, did not respond positively to Virginia's and Kentucky's call to protest. No

---

[67] Ibid., 6:326.

[68] Ibid., 6:328.

[69] Ibid., 6:326, 331.

[70] Jefferson, *Writings*, ed. Ford, 7:291, 292.

[71] Ibid., 7:301, 306.

[72] In 1790, for example, the Virginia legislature adopted a memorial to Congress attempting "to call the attention of Congress to an act of their last session" regarding the federal assumption of state debts, "which the General Assembly conceive neither policy, justice nor the constitution warrants." As "guardians" of their constituents the Virginia legislators were obliged to "sound the alarm," but they concluded simply by expressing the "hope" that Congress would reconsider its actions. Herman Ames, ed., *State Documents on Federal Relations* (Philadelphia: University of Pennsylvania, 1900), 5, 6, 7. In 1799, the Virginia legislature issued a similar address to the people explaining their obligation "to warn you of encroachments" on the people's constitutional liberties. Madison, *Writings*, 6:332. In other cases, state governments expressed defiance of federal judicial decisions that went against their interests or issued public instructions to their U.S. senators to work against particular federal policies. See, e.g., Ames, 7–15; Slaughter, *The Whiskey Rebellion*, 97–98; Koch and Ammon, "Virginia and Kentucky Resolutions," 152–53. Cf. Kramer, "We the Court," 96 (finding, based on such prior protests, that the 1798 resolutions were not so "radical" and built on practices that were "well established").

state adopted resolutions approving of the resolutions, and nine states in New England and the mid-Atlantic issued critical replies.[73] The replies ranged from the brief pronouncements of Delaware and Connecticut simply stating that the Virginia and Kentucky resolutions displayed a "dangerous tendency" to more elaborate rebuttals of particular arguments put forward by the resolutions.[74]

In responding to the Jeffersonian critics, the Federalist state legislatures could have mounted a variety of defenses, but they overwhelmingly and somewhat surprisingly resorted to the assertion of judicial supremacy. The legislatures could have easily argued the case on substantive grounds, rehearsing the points made by the Federalists in Congress. Massachusetts, for example, included in its reply, "lest their silence should be construed as disapprobation," a substantive defense of the Sedition Act as "expedient and necessary." Rhode Island, in deference to the federal judiciary, merely noted its "private opinions" that the federal laws were "within the powers delegated to Congress, and promotive of the welfare of the United States."[75] The legislatures could have asserted congressional supremacy in construing the terms of the U.S. Constitution and denied the authority of a state legislature to challenge the federal legislature on matters of national concern. Especially in this early period before the firm establishment of even the power of judicial review, pointing to congressional passage of the acts as conclusive to resolving such constitutional disputes would seem to have been a natural move.[76]

The most common Federalist response by far was to raise up the federal judiciary as the proper authority for resolving constitutional controversies. The argument for judicial supremacy was indeed so common in the debates that one historian labeled it as "Federalist doctrine," and of course there was no doubt as to what the Federalist judiciary thought of the Sedition Act.[77] Rhode Island, for example, stated its opinion that Constitution granted "the Federal Courts, exclusively, and the Supreme Court of the United States, ultimately, the authority of deciding on the

---

[73] Those states were all firmly in Federalist control. New Jersey did not reply, regarding that to be a "waste of time and the public money," but did take a formal vote to dismiss the resolutions. The remaining states, all in the South, where Republicans had greater strength in the legislatures, appear to have made no formal response. Frank M. Anderson, "Contemporary Opinion of the Virginia and Kentucky Resolutions," *American Historical Review* 5 (1899): 47, 225.

[74] Ames, *State Documents*, 16.

[75] Ibid., 19, 17.

[76] See, for example, Pennsylvania's argument that republican government is necessarily founded on "confidence" in government, not in "jealousy" as Kentucky asserted, and that elected national representatives (given "their virtues and their talents") oversee "the province of the whole" and the "combined will." Minorities had an obligation of "acquiescence" to the "voice of the greater number." Ibid., 21, 22.

[77] Anderson, "Contemporary Opinion," 54.

constitutionality of any act or law of the Congress."[78] Massachusetts likewise concluded that the power to interpret the Constitution was "exclusively vested by the people in the judicial courts of the United States,"
leaving to the states only the "power of proposing" constitutional amendments, not of acting as "judges." Such statements were at the heart of the
responding resolutions passed by Pennsylvania, New York, New Hampshire, and Vermont, and were featured in a Maryland legislative report.[79]
In Massachusetts, Republican editors were jailed for sedition for endorsing "the monstrous positions" of the Virginia and Kentucky resolutions
and for criticizing Massachusetts legislators for avoiding their own responsibilities by embracing judicial supremacy.[80] Many Federalists
seemed to regard it as self-evident that the Constitution had "in plain
terms" removed questions of its own interpretation from the states and
vested them in the federal courts.[81] Second-guessing of the constitutionality of federal laws by the state legislatures invited "civil discord" and
disunion and undermined confidence in the federal government, while
leaving constitutional controversies unsettled or susceptible to the opinions of "less competent tribunals" than the courts.[82] The Federalist legislatures echoed arguments developed just a few years earlier by Columbia
law professor James Kent, who posited that constitutional interpretation
was "a JUDICIAL act, and requires the exercise of the same LEGAL DISCRE-
TION, as the interpretation and construction of a Law." Courts alone
would be "exempt . . . from the baneful influence of Faction," and thus
the "most proper power . . . [to] maintain the Authority of the Constitution."[83] Rather than rely on their own authority to reaffirm the constitu-

[78] Ames, *State Documents*, 17.

[79] Ibid., 18. See also pp. 20 (Pennsylvania on the Supreme Court's "high authority of
ultimately and conclusively deciding upon the constitutionality of all legislative acts"); 23
(New York on the "judicial power" to decide constitutional cases); 25 (New Hampshire
resolving that the "duty of such [constitutional] decision is properly and exclusively confided to the judicial department"); 26 (Vermont resolving that "this power ["to decide on
the constitutionality of laws" is] exclusively vested in the judiciary courts of the Union");
Anderson, "Contemporary Opinion," 47 (Maryland legislative committee, arguing that
the constitutional evaluation of federal laws was "exclusively vested in the Courts of the
United States").

[80] Frank Maloy Anderson, "Contemporary Opinion of the Virginia and Kentucky Resolutions II," *American Historical Review* 5 (1899): 228.

[81] Ames, *State Documents*, 17.

[82] Ibid., 17. In his 1800 report for the Virginia legislature, Madison responded to such
criticisms of the resolutions by noting that some constitutional controversies may "never
draw within the control of the judicial department" and, especially relevant in that controversy, that the courts "also may exercise or sanction dangerous powers beyond the grant of
the Constitution." Madison, *Writings*, 6:351.

[83] James Kent, "An Introductory Lecture to a Course of Law Lectures," in *American
Political Writings during the Founding Era*, ed. Charles S. Hyneman and Donald S. Lutz,
vol. 2 (Indianapolis: Liberty Fund, 1983), 942. Such sentiments had become common in

tionality of the Sedition Act, Federalist politicians responded to challenge by urging deference to the authority of the federal courts.

As we have already seen in chapter 2, this strategy was unsuccessful. Not only did the Federalists lose the White House, both chambers of Congress, and several state legislatures in the elections of 1800, but the Jeffersonians also trumpeted their departmentalist understanding of the relative institutional authority to interpret the Constitution. Every component of the Federalist justification for judicial supremacy fell into disrepute. Whereas the Federalists were nationalists and questioned the authority of the states to interpret the Constitution, the Jeffersonians were localists who celebrated the autonomy of the states as constitutional actors. Whereas the Federalists were skeptical of democracy and held up the judiciary as a necessary counterpoise to popular authority in the new republic, the Jeffersonians embraced democracy and questioned whether any institution of government should be independent of the people. Whereas the Federalists held up the federal judiciary as an important instrument of the national will, the Jeffersonians mistrusted it as corrupted by faction and subversive of constitutional principles. As the fragile Federalist regime sought refuge outside of politics and laid its hopes on the judiciary, the Jeffersonians carried the constitutional contest to the people and won the authority to dismantle the nascent Federalist state.

The injury to judicial authority in 1800 was serious but not fatal. The victorious Jeffersonians undid what they could of the Federalist entrenchment in the judiciary, withholding undelivered commissions from unlucky magistrates such as William Marbury, repealing the Judiciary Act of 1801 and in so doing eliminating the offices of many of the "midnight judges" installed by the lame-duck Adams, and impeaching two Federalist judges who strayed too far into partisan politics. In the midst of these efforts, a few Jeffersonians suggested that the judiciary had no authority to look into the Constitution, but this was the minority view even within the Republican Party. Mainstream Jeffersonians had no problem with judges who would apply constitutional limits on federal power. John Marshall's 1803 defense of the power of judicial review drew little negative comment (even as his toothless assertion of the judicial authority to second-guess how the executive conducted his duties was met with cries of outrage in the Jeffersonian press).[84] As we saw in chapter 3, such orthodox successors of Jefferson as Madison and James

---

Federalist legal thinking. See, e.g., Whittington, *Constitutional Construction*, 40–65. See also, Kramer, "We the Court," 94–95 (noting Kent's countermajoritarian justification for judicial review). Kent did go on to argue, however, that judges could be held accountable for their constitutional opinions by threat of impeachment; an argument Federalists did not maintain after Republicans gained control of Congress. Kent, 2:943–44.

[84] See Ellis, *The Jeffersonian Crisis*; Whittington, *Constitutional Construction*, 20–71; Warren, *Supreme Court*, 1st ed., 1:244–55.

Monroe lent their support to judicial authority in order to help control conflicts among the states, and Chief Justice Marshall raised the specter of interstate violence to help justify the Court's role as a constitutional arbiter in *McCulloch*.[85]

At the same time, the courts played a limited role in the Jeffersonian regime. In this early period, notions of judicial supremacy were too closely associated with the withering Federalist Party, and departmentalism was too central to Jeffersonian lore for the Republicans to push judicial authority too far. Even if Marshall is, as Mark Graber has persuasively argued, better understood as a friend of the nationalist Republicans of the 1810s and 1820s than a fossilized Federalist, the Marshall Court had relatively little to offer the politicians of the period.[86] Recalling the rationales for making active use of a friendly judiciary discussed in chapter 3, the Jeffersonians did come to worry about the problems of regime enforcement and hoped that the Court would help alleviate sectional and interstate tensions, but the local threats to Jeffersonian constitutional principles were far fewer than those facing later administrations, and consequently the Court was a less important tool of routine constitutional management. Other rationales for supporting judicial authority that would come to the fore later in American history were of little significance in the early nineteenth century. The Jeffersonians were relatively united on constitutional essentials and enjoyed unparalleled preeminence over electoral and legislative opponents. Jeffersonian politicians could realize their modest policy agenda on their own and did not need judges to help shoulder the burden or overcome legislative obstacles. They did not need the added legitimacy of favorable judicial opinions or the security of entrenched judicial allies. In this era, the judiciary had a recognized authority to interpret the Constitution but little claim to enhanced authority relative to the other branches of government. The judges did not have to "close their eyes on the Constitution," but no one would have believed that they were its "ultimate interpreter" either.[87]

Avoiding the "Distracting Question"

Like the Jeffersonians, the early Jacksonians had little need for a robust judicial authority. In keeping with his reconstructive stance, of course, Jackson himself was willing to assert his own warrants as a constitutional interpreter and drown out Marshall's voice. Within Jackson's own coali-

---

[85] See also Whittington, "The Road Not Taken," 365, 369–73.
[86] Graber, "Federalist or Friends," 229.
[87] Marbury v. Madison, 5 U.S. 137, 178 (1803); Baker v. Carr, 369 U.S. 186, 211 (1962).

tion, John Calhoun and the South Carolina nullifiers paused hardly at all to consider the judiciary's possible claim to hear their constitutional objections to the protectionist tariff.[88] It was self-evident to them that the late Marshall Court was not the proper venue for discussing, let alone resolving, the extent of congressional power over trade. Nullification did, however, reinforce the belief of the elderly Madison, among others, in the need for a peaceful arbiter for such disputes.[89] In later years, however, like the Jeffersonians before them, the Jacksonians were generally secure both in their political power and in their constitutional beliefs. They were fully capable of enforcing their constitutional orthodoxy at the national level through presidential vetoes and congressional majorities.[90] While preserving a limited federal government on their own, Jacksonian political leaders had little need to bolster or rely upon judicial authority to articulate their strict constructionist vision.

The political environment became more supportive of judicial authority over time, however. Most notably, the slavery issue added a dimension to party politics that, at least temporarily, redounded to the benefit of the judiciary. As long as the prominent constitutional disputes tended to reinforce the existing political structure, elected officials were willing to deliberate on constitutional meaning. Although the Democratic Party contained the strongest proslavery element and the Whig Party had periodically served as a vehicle for antislavery agitation, both parties tried to finesse the slavery issue, especially in relation to the territories. As sentiment at both extremes on the issue grew more intense, however, strategies of avoidance and compromise became less politically viable. In order to preserve their existing organizations, leaders of both parties sought to shift final resolution of the slavery issue into some other forum where national political leaders would not have to take a position.

The favored compromise was to shift the decision to the territorial legislatures and to the federal judiciary in the hope of compartmentalizing the dispute, moving it away from national electoral politics and removing the fuel from the political fires of both the northern abolitionists and the southern fire-eaters. The 1848 compromise plan introduced in the Senate on the eve of the presidential elections by a close ally of Henry Clay,

[88] See John C. Calhoun, "To Frederick W. Symmes, July 26, 1831 [Fort Hill Address]," in *Papers*, 421–24; Whittington, *Constitutional Construction*, 72–112.

[89] See James Madison, "To N. P. Trist, February 15, 1830," in *Writings*, 9:355; McCoy, *Last of the Fathers*, 119–70; Ellis, *The Union at Risk*.

[90] For examples of Jacksonian vetoes based on a narrow understanding of federal powers, see Richardson, *Messages and Papers*, 4:64 (John Tyler on banks), 4:68 (same), 4:462 (James Polk on internal improvements), 5:247 (Franklin Pierce on insane asylums), 5:256 (Pierce on internal improvements), 5:386 (same), 5:543 (James Buchanan on agricultural colleges), 5:601 (Buchanan on internal improvements), 5:608 (Buchanan on land grants).

Delaware Whig John Clayton, for organizing the California and New Mexico territories was silent on the issue of slavery, leaving its future to depend "on the Constitution, as the same should be expounded by the [territorial] judges, with a right to appeal to the Supreme Court of the United States." Clayton recommended his measure as allowing Congress to "avoid the decision on this distracting question, leaving it to be settled by the silent operation of the Constitution itself."[91] In "referring it to the Supreme Court, it adopted the very best course, because the people, being law-abiding, would submit to the decision of that court, which occupied the place of highest confidence."[92] Recounting the difficulty of reaching any agreement in the special committee on the territories, Clayton pointed out to his colleagues that "this bill resolves the whole question between the North and South into a constitutional and a judicial question. It only asks of men of all sections to stand by the Constitution, and suffer that to settle the difference by its own tranquil operation. If the Constitution settles the question either way, let those who rail at the decision vent their indignation against their ancestors who adopted it," who were fortuitously beyond the reach of the ballot box.[93]

The proposal initially met a great deal of skepticism from those firmly ensconced in either proslavery or antislavery constituencies. It is easy to imagine in hindsight that southerners would be eager to put the question before the Taney Court, anticipating a result such as *Dred Scott*. In fact, many southerners had no greater confidence on this score than had many northerners. George Badger of North Carolina, for example, complained that he "had respect for the Supreme Court, but he was not willing to leave the decision of the question to a court, so large a portion of which were opposed to slavery." Indeed, raising the real issue, "he would willingly see his candidate for the Presidency defeated, rather than that this question should not be settled."[94] Reverdy Johnson of Maryland opined that "this was not the best moment for the consideration of the subject because we are on the eve of a Presidential election," and that he "would have preferred its postponement until the Presidential election has been terminated," but once the issue was raised, it was critical that it be settled correctly through "concessions on both sides."[95] Alexander Stephens, future vice president of the Confederacy, threatened disunion in the face of this "compromise" under which "the Supreme Court of the United States, to whom the matter was to be referred in the last

---

[91] *Congressional Globe*, 30th Cong., 1st sess., 19 July 1848, 950. This section owes its inspiration to Graber, "The Non-Majoritarian Difficulty," 35.

[92] *Congressional Globe*, 30th Cong., 1st sess, 31 August 1848, 1031.

[93] *Congressional Globe*, 30th Cong., 1st sess., 19 July 1848, 950.

[94] *Congressional Globe*, 30th Cong., 1st sess., 26 July 1848, 1001.

[95] *Congressional Globe*, 30th Cong., 1st sess., 10 June 1848, 917.

resort, could not be expected, under the principles of numerous decisions already made, to decide otherwise than that slavery cannot be protected" in the territories.[96]

The Ohio Whig Thomas Corwin, who would later become a Republican, was equally firm on the other side. He had no wish to ask the Court to "instruct the Senate of the United States as to constitutional duty in the matter."[97] But given the course of the debate in the Senate, he asked, "Can I have confidence in the Supreme Court of the United States, when my confidence fails in Senators around me here? Do I expect that members of that body will be more careful than the Senators from Georgia and South Carolina to form their opinions without any regard to selfish considerations?" Although, Corwin attested, "I admire the Supreme Court of the United States as a tribunal" and "rejoice in the good consequences to this Republic from the exercise of its functions," he chided his Democratic colleagues who seemed to "have had some new light upon the subject within the last few years" and "have been smitten with new love for the power and wisdom of the Supreme Court." "Jackson Democrats" once cried, "We are judges for ourselves" and treated John Marshall's *McCulloch* decision with "infinite scorn." Corwin readily agreed that once the justices had spoken, "their decision, whether right or wrong, controls our action," but the Court had not yet spoken and he was amazed that Democrats would now claim that "there is only one tribunal competent to put the matter for rest forever. We are to thank God, that though all should fail, there is an infallible depository of truth, and it lives once a year for three months, in a little chamber below us."[98] Corwin thought the precedents were on his side if the issue were to go to court, but declared, "Let us not evade the question altogether."[99]

Although Clayton's bill was defeated in the antislavery-leaning House, his proposal became the basis of the last great territorial compromise of the antebellum era.[100] The Compromise of 1850 adopted the policy of "popular sovereignty," or congressional nonintervention, in leaving the adoption of territorial slave codes to the eventual territorial governments. Senator Henry Clay defended the compromise by arguing that the "bill leaves in full force the paramount authority of the Constitution. . . . Now what ought to be done more satisfactory to both sides of the question . . .

---

[96] *Congressional Globe*, 30th Cong., 1st sess., 7 August 1848, app. 1107.

[97] *Congressional Globe*, 30th Cong., 1st sess., 24 July 1848, app. 1158.

[98] *Congressional Globe*, 30th Cong., 1st sess., 24 July 1848, app. 1161. Corwin later explained, "I could see no reason why the opinions of the Senators should not be as free from party bias as the opinions of the judges of the Supreme Court." Ibid., app. 1171.

[99] *Congressional Globe*, 30th Cong., 1st sess., 24 July 1848, app. 1162.

[100] See also Fehrenbacher, *The Dred Scott Case*, 11–235; Graber, "The Non-Majoritarian Difficulty," 46–50; Mendelson, "Dred Scott's Case—Reconsidered," 16.

[than] to leave the question of slavery or no slavery to be decided by the only competent authority that can definitely settle it forever, the authority of the Supreme Court of the United States?"[101] A few northerners in particular proposed "clarifying amendments" that would legislatively determine the issue, arguing with Senator Roger Baldwin of Connecticut that "the people demand a law, a rule for their conduct clear and intelligible. They do not ask us to give them a Delphic response."[102] But Senator Albert Brown of Mississippi gave the eventual southern view, noting that though he too preferred "directness in legislation" when it could be achieved, "if Congress will refrain from intimating an opinion, I am willing that the Supreme Court shall decide it."[103] Samuel Phelps of Vermont, one of the architects of both the 1848 and 1850 proposals, asked for nothing more, hoping only that "all parties" would be willing "to submit the question to the tribunal created by the Constitution for the purpose of deciding it."[104]

As Corwin wryly noted of the original plan, Congress had enacted a lawsuit, not a law.[105] But it was a lawsuit that, at least initially, had a great deal of support from across the political spectrum, from Abraham Lincoln to Jefferson Davis.[106] The Democrats in particular hoped to ride that horse

[101] *Congressional Globe*, 31st Cong., 1st sess., 7 June 1850, 1155.

[102] *Congressional Globe*, 31st Cong., 1st sess., 6 June 1850, 1146.

[103] *Congressional Globe*, 33rd Cong., 1st sess., 24 February 1853, app. 232.

[104] *Congressional Globe*, 31st Cong., 1st sess., 23 January 1850, app. 95.

[105] *Congressional Globe*, 30th Cong., 1st sess., 24 July 1848, app. 1161 ("this bill seems to me a rich and rare legislative curiosity. It does not enact 'a law,' which I had supposed was the usual function of legislation. No, sir; it only enacts 'a lawsuit' ").

[106] Abraham Lincoln, "Speech at Galena, Illinois, July 23, 1856," in *The Collected Works of Abraham Lincoln*, ed. Roy Basler, 9 vols. (Newark, NJ: Rutgers University Press, 1953), 2:355 ("I grant you that an unconstitutional act is not a law; but I do not ask, and will not take your construction of the Constitution. The Supreme Court of the United States is the tribunal to decide such questions, and we will submit to its decisions; and if you do also, there will be an end of the matter. Will you? If not, who are the disunionists, you or we?"); *Congressional Globe*, 31st Cong., 1st sess., 14 February 1850, app. 154 (Jefferson Davis). There is some dispute as to whether the Galena speech was accurately reported. See "Autobiography Written for John L. Scripps," in Lincoln, *Collected Works*, 4:67; Don E. Fehrenbacher, "Lincoln and Judicial Supremacy: A Note on the Galena Speech of July 23, 1856," *Civil War History* 16 (1970): 197. His support for the judiciary would have been consistent with his stance as a young Whig politician. See, e.g., "Speech on the Sub-Treasury, December 26, 1839," in ibid., 1:171 ("the Supreme Court—that tribunal which the Constitution has itself established to decide Constitutional questions—has solemnly decided that such a bank is constitutional. . . . [T]hese authorities ought to settle the question—ought to be conclusive"); "Speech in the Illinois Legislature Concerning the State Bank, January 11, 1837" in ibid., 1:62–63 (that the "Supreme Court have, in an official capacity, decided in favor of the constitutionality of the bank, would, in my mind, seem a sufficient answer to this. . . . I ask, then, if the extra-judicial decision . . . is to be taken as paramount to a decision officially made by that tribunal, by which and which alone, the constitutionality of the Bank can ever

at least through the 1856 elections, on the eve of which Senator Judah Benjamin declared to great acclaim that "in order to provide the means by which the Constitution could govern, by which that single undecided question could be determined, we of the South, conscious that we were right, the North asserting the same confidence in its own doctrines, agreed that every question touching human slavery, or human freedom, should be appealable to the Supreme Court of the United States for its decision." Let all sides, "being a law-abiding and law-observing people," allow this question to be "finally settled by a tribunal from which none of us will attempt an appeal."[107]

Although the *Dred Scott* case did not arise through the provisions of these acts, it offered the Court a vehicle for providing the constitutional answer that Congress had preferred to dodge. Several members of the Taney Court were anxious to settle the issue, and in the process, end the growing abolitionist threat to the established party system.[108] Moreover, the 1856 presidential election of Democrat James Buchanan was taken by some, including the president and the president-elect, as a mandate for the proslavery position.[109] Throwing the combined prestige of the Supreme Court and the presidency behind the constitutional protection of slavery in the territories promised to undercut support for the Republican insurgency and stabilize national politics.

In both public and private, the justices embraced the view that it was the judicial duty to resolve the issue. The chief justice himself emphasized that the Constitution was a legal document, marking out the powers of the various branches and governments, and the "path of duty" of the Court was to enforce the higher law. Taney readily blended the rules by which "any tribunal" must interpret the Constitution with the specifically "judicial character of this Court," which was "not created by the Constitution" to reflect popular opinion or the ideals of justice.[110] Likewise, Justice James Wayne emphasized that in deciding the case the justices had "only discharged our duty as a distinct and efficient department of the Government, as the framers of the Constitution meant the judiciary to

---

be settled?"). Lincoln's relationship to judicial supremacy and majoritarianism is explored in Graber, *Dred Scott and Constitutional Evil.*

[107] *Congressional Globe*, 34th Cong., 1st sess., 2 May 1856, 1093.

[108] Fehrenbacher, *The Dred Scott Case*, 308–14; Auchampaugh, "James Buchanan," 231. It should be noted, however, that dissenting Justice John McLean is often, though controversially, thought to have initiated the broader discussion of slavery in the territories in the *Dred Scott* case, reflecting his own antislavery sentiments and desire for a Republican presidential nomination.

[109] Graber, "The Non-Majoritarian Difficulty," 282–87; Mendelson, "Dred Scott's Case—Reconsidered," 24; Friedman, "Countermajoritarian Difficulty, Part One," 333, 415–16.

[110] Dred Scott v. Sandford, 60 U.S. 393, 426 (1857).

be." In Wayne's view, the case involved "constitutional principles of the highest importance," such "that the peace and harmony of the country required the settlement of them by judicial decision."[111] As the opinions were being written, Justice John Catron urged President Buchanan to use almost identical language in his inaugural address, reinforcing the message that the issue "*must* ultimately be decided by the Supreme Court."[112] Buchanan was only too happy to oblige.

Of course, things went terribly badly for the Court from there. Taney's holding on the territorial question—that neither Congress nor the territorial governments could exclude slave holders from bringing their slaves into any territory—undermined both the "popular sovereignty" stance of the northern Democrats and Whigs and the core goal of the Republican Party—to secure the territories for free, white labor. In the near term, the inconsistencies between *Dred Scott* and popular sovereignty were still abstractions, and Stephen Douglas and his allies could afford to paper over them. The Republicans were the most severely pinched by the decision and had the most to gain by further politicizing the issue, and they reacted accordingly. Republican newspapers denounced Taney's opinion as a "stump speech embodied into a judicial opinion," with "no more authority than the conversations of the judges held in the street." The Court was said to have "abdicated its just function and descended into the political arena."[113] Many Republicans, including Lincoln, found evidence in the Court's opinion that it was part of a larger "slave-power conspiracy," and "the justices of the Supreme Court and the leading members of the new administration are parties to it."[114] Taney had sought to add the Court's imprimatur as the final interpreter of the Constitution and to close off further debate on the slavery question. He was spectacularly unsuccessful in that attempt, despite the efforts of Democrats to continue to prop up the Court's authority. When Buchanan finally shattered his fragile coalition by accepting the disputed proslavery Lecompton constitution for Kansas, and then followed it up by embracing the strongest reading of *Dred Scott* and "congratulat[ing]" the American people "upon the final settlement by the Supreme Court of the United States of the question of slavery in the Territories" which "irrevocably fixed" the issue and put an end to the "dangerous excitement," the Court was implicated in its consequences.[115]

[111] Dred Scott v. Sandford, 60 U.S. 393, 454 (1857).

[112] Quoted in Auchampaugh, "James Buchanan," 236.

[113] *New York Daily Tribune*, quoted in Friedman, "Countermajoritarian Difficulty, Part One," 427n382, 427n383.

[114] *New York Evening Post*, quoted in Friedman, "Countermajoritarian Difficulty, Part One," 428n384. For Lincoln, see " 'A House Divided': Speech at Springfield, Illinois, June 16, 1858," in *Collected Works*, 2:465.

[115] James Buchanan, "Third Annual Message, December 19, 1859," in *Works*, 10:341–42.

Though the Court undoubtedly suffered a momentary blow to its authority as it was caught up in Lincoln's reconstructive politics, for present purposes the dynamics of the 1850s of political deference to the courts are more noteworthy. Up until this period the majority party of the time, whether the Federalists, the Jeffersonians, or the early Jacksonians, was relatively united on the key constitutional issues of concern to them, on matters ranging from the bank to internal improvements to protective tariffs. As a consequence, they were willing and able to act on those constitutional principles when making policy and had little need for the Court to back them up. Slavery, by contrast, was a classic wedge issue that left both the Democrats and the Whigs internally riven. While legislators from the heart of either the North or the South were capable of taking a firm stand on the issue, and indeed preferred to do so in order to satisfy constituent demands, legislators from border states and party leaders who had to bridge the national divide could not afford to be so clear. To hold their coalitions together, established party leaders such as Pennsylvania's James Buchanan needed to be able to distance themselves and their party from responsibility for any direct action on slavery. For northern Democrats such as Stephen Douglas, cross-pressured by party allegiances and home-state voters, doctrines of popular sovereignty and judicial supremacy were necessary shields against accountability. Such intraparty divisions introduced a new element into American constitutional politics that provided additional rationales for strengthening judicial authority. While the slavery issue itself disappeared with the Civil War, this new problem of coalition management did not.

Preserving the "Dignity and Influence of the Courts"

American political parties have never been able to recapture the kind of cohesion and security enjoyed by the Jacksonian Democrats before the slavery issue took center stage. Even Lincoln's Republican Party was torn on issues relating to the war, Reconstruction, and economic policy, not least because the party was struggling to cobble together a coalition of former Whigs and prowar northern Democrats to secure majority status. One result of this struggle was the appointment of former Democrats to the Supreme Court, as well as the selection of a former Democrat for the vice presidency in 1864, with foreseeable results for judicial review of federal policies.[116] Once the southern Democrats returned to Congress, party lines were much more sharply drawn. National legislators in the late nineteenth century displayed substantial party discipline, and the divi-

---

[116] See Graber, "Jacksonian Origins," 17.

sions between the two parties were stark.[117] Even as the parties achieved greater internal cohesion, however, they lost electoral security. The parties could claim only narrow majorities in the House of Representatives, and frequently lost them. The presidency was similarly closely contested and turned on a few swing votes. Divided government was common, but with Republicans always keeping a firm grip on the Senate and with only conservative candidates able to capture the White House.[118] Populist insurgencies were a frequent threat in Congress and in party conventions and were of growing significance in the states.

In such an environment, regime enforcement took on new significance. To the relatively conservative forces who largely had the upper hand in presidential contests, Republicans and Cleveland Democrats alike, the policy consequences of a sudden swing in the mass electorate were potentially severe and frightening. While the national government remained largely anchored to East Coast economic sensibilities, state governments in the South and West often reflected the more radical sentiments of their local constituents. The judiciary had a vital role to play in managing the conflicts between capital and labor, agriculture and industry. Thus, when able to control the House, the Republicans sought to expand the federal judiciary to hear such cases and then fill those seats with reliable members of the bar. Freed from electoral constraints and party pressures, the courts could be relied upon to sustain the nationalist free-market commitments of the postbellum constitutional order.[119]

Empowered by national elected officials and dismayed by the radical proposals for economic and social reform that were winning support in legislatures, the federal judiciary seized the opportunity to make expansive claims for its own authority to interpret and apply the Constitution in the late nineteenth and early twentieth centuries. Buffeted by electoral and coalitional pressures and similarly concerned to enforce the strictures of the laissez-faire regime, conservative politicians were quick to endorse such judicial assertions. At the same time, reformers were willing to offer radical challenges to judicial authority. The willingness of conservatives to meet these challenges during this crucial period placed the courts on a firmer foundation than had previously been the case.

It was in these decades that the power of judicial review took on its modern form. By the first decade of the twentieth century, the Court was

[117] Keith T. Poole and Howard Rosenthal, *Congress* (New York: Oxford University Press, 1997), 58–85.

[118] Charles H. Stewart III, "Lessons from the Post–Civil War Era," in *The Politics of Divided Government*, ed. Gary W. Cox and Samuel Kernell (Boulder, CO: Westview Press, 1991); Sundquist, *Dynamics*, 106–69.

[119] See Gillman, "Parties Can Use Courts," 521; Fiss, *Troubled Beginnings*; Bensel, *Political Economy*.

voiding nearly one congressional statute and over three state statutes per year on constitutional grounds. The last time the Supreme Court completed a term without striking down at least one state law was in 1893. The political importance of the decisions of the Supreme Court had increased along with their frequency. In 1890, the Court imposed new constitutional restrictions on the authority of the states to regulate railroad rates, the leading edge of progressive economic regulations in the late nineteenth century. Although the Court allowed that states, in this case Minnesota, could establish commissions with the power to set railroad rates, the states could not, consistent with the due process guarantees of the Fourteenth Amendment, shield the decisions of such commissions from judicial scrutiny. The Minnesota statute allowed railroads only to charge "reasonable" rates, and the "question of reasonableness of a rate of charge for transportation by a railroad company, involving as it does the element of the reasonableness both as regards the company and as regards the public, is eminently a question for judicial investigation, requiring due process of law for its determination."[120] Justice Joseph Bradley complained in dissent, "[B]y the decision now made we declare, in effect, that the judiciary, and not the legislature, is the final arbiter in the regulation of fares and freights of railroads and the charges of other public accommodations"—an "assumption of authority on the part of the judiciary," Bradley thought, "[that] it has no right to make."[121] The Court soon made clear that the "reasonableness" requirement had a constitutional, as well as a statutory, base, and later struck down a rate schedule as "so unreasonably low as to deprive the carrier of its property without such compensation as the constitution secures, and therefore without due process of law."[122]

In 1895, as discussed in chapter 3, the Supreme Court issued three important decisions with constitutional implications. The Court upheld the broad power of the federal courts to issue injunctions to prevent labor unrest from disrupting interstate commerce and the jailing of socialist leader Eugene V. Debs for violating such an injunction during a railway worker strike.[123] A few months earlier, however, the Court had allowed, over the government's languid objections, a merger to proceed that would give a single company control of 98 percent of the national market in refined sugar, ruling that federal regulatory power did not extend over manufacturing and sharply limiting the scope of the 1890 Sherman Anti-

---

[120] Chicago, Milwaukee and St. Paul Railway Company v. Minnesota, 134 U.S. 418, 457 (1890).

[121] Chicago, Milwaukee and St. Paul Railway Company v. Minnesota, 134 U.S. 418, 462–63 (1890).

[122] Smyth v. Ames, 169 U.S. 466, 526 (1898).

[123] In re Debs, 158 U.S. 564 (1895).

trust Act.[124] Responding to an appellant lawyer's charge that the 1894 income tax was "communistic in its purposes and tendencies," the Court also narrowly struck down most of the law as beyond the taxing power granted to Congress, noting that the Constitution was designed "to prevent an attack upon accumulated property by mere force of numbers."[125]

The political response to these decisions was immediate and substantively striking. In his manifesto supporting his 1892 presidential run, Populist James Weaver expressed amazement that the judges would assume the responsibility of evaluating the reasonableness of railroad rates given that they were "speaking beyond the reach of the ballot box." He recalled that when "judges [who] are not subject to popular control" had allied themselves with the slave power, "there was no alternative but the sword."[126] In 1896, William Jennings Bryan and his populist allies wrested control of the Democratic Party from the incumbent conservatives and continued the attack. According to insurgent Democrats, such decisions demonstrated that "our constitutional government has been supplanted by a judicial oligarchy."[127] It instead should be recognized that the "Supreme Court cannot, by mere decision upon a constitutional question, rob the people of the powers of self-government nor prevent the American people from deciding for themselves . . . whether they will accept the decision of the Supreme Court as being final."[128] The popular North Carolina state judge Walter Clark called for federal judicial elections in a prominent law review, arguing that the "most dangerous, the most undemocratic and unrepublican feature of the constitution, and the one most subject to abuse, is the [current] mode of selecting the Federal judges."[129] Former Republican congressman James M. Ashley declared the Court a "menace to democratic government" and proposed reforms to limit the power of judicial review and allow Congress to override judicial invalidations.[130] Echoing earlier reconstructive leaders, Democrats complained that the "Supreme Court as at present constituted does not spring from the people,

[124] United States v. E.C. Knight Co., 156 U.S. 1 (1895).

[125] Pollock v. Farmer's Loan and Trust Co., 157 U.S. 429, 532, 583 (1895). See also Pollock v. Farmer's Loan and Trust Co., 157 U.S. 601 (1895).

[126] James B. Weaver, A Call to Action (Des Moines: Iowa Printing Company, 1892), 122, 80, 81.

[127] Sylvester Pennoyer, "The Income Tax Decision and the Power of the Supreme Court to Nullify Acts of Congress," American Law Review 29 (1895): 550, 558.

[128] Governor John Altgeld, quoted in "Current Topics," Albany Law Journal 54 (1896): 259.

[129] Walter Clark, "The Revision of the Constitution of the United States," American Law Review 32 (1898): 7.

[130] James M. Ashley, "Should the Supreme Court be Reorganized?" The Arena 14 (1895): 221.

and therefore does not properly represent the people."[131] The "work of nine lawyers" had left "the people of the United States . . . powerless."[132] Bryan's bid to begin the politics of reconstruction at the turn of the century, however, met with decisive defeat at the polls.

Although in his acceptance speech for the Democratic presidential nomination Bryan carefully insisted that the party made "no suggestion of an attempt to dispute the authority of the Supreme Court" and recognized "the binding force" of judicial decisions, the Republicans seized the opportunity to highlight their growing differences with the Democrats and to paint their opponents as extremists.[133] The Republicans made respect for the courts a central theme of the campaign of 1896. In his letter accepting the Republican presidential nomination, William McKinley swore to defeat "the sudden, dangerous and revolutionary assault upon law and order."[134] Observing the Democratic convention, former president Benjamin Harrison told his fellow Republicans in New York City, "I cannot exaggerate the gravity and the importance of this assault upon our constitutional form of government" and the threat to "the high-minded, independent Judiciary that will hold the line on questions between wealth and labor, between rich and poor." The prominent Republican politician and railroad executive Chauncey DePew accused Bryan of wanting to "abolish the Supreme Court and make it a creature of the party caucus," while McKinley's campaign manager declared the Democratic platform to be a "covert threat to pack the Supreme Court of the United States."[135] A breakaway convention of conservative Democrats adopted a platform condemning "all efforts to degrade that tribunal or impair the confidence and respect which it has deservedly held."[136]

After twenty years of close electoral competition between the two parties, the Republicans won a crushing victory in 1896. For the first time since General U. S. Grant's reelection in 1872, a presidential candidate won a solid popular majority. Equally important, urban voters through the North and upper Midwest swung decisively into the Republican camp, where they would stay until shaken loose by the Great Depres-

---

[131] District of Columbia *Evening Star,* quoted in Barry Friedman, "The History of the Countermajoritarian Difficulty, Part Three: The Lesson of *Lochner,*" *New York University Law Review* 76 (2001): 1383, 1439.

[132] "Note: Triumph of the Sugar Trust Over the People of the United States," *American Law Review* 29 (1895): 293, 306.

[133] William Jennings Bryan, "Acceptance Speech, August 12, 1896," in *History of American Presidential Elections, 1789–1968,* ed. Arthur Schlesinger Jr. and Fred L. Israel, vol. 2 (New York: Chelsea House, 1971), 1853.

[134] "Mr. McKinley Accepts," *New York Times,* 27 August 1896, 5.

[135] Quoted in Donald Grier Stephenson Jr., *Campaigns and the Court* (New York: Columbia University Press, 1999), 127, 126.

[136] "Platform of the National Democratic Party," *New York Times,* 4 September 1896, 1.

sion.[137] The Republican victory was widely interpreted in newspaper editorials as a "determination on the part of the people everywhere to maintain the dignity and supremacy of the courts."[138] The image of the Democrats as the party of "radicalism" was entrenched.[139] The Court had thrown its weight behind "the constitutional position of the most conservative wing of the Republican Party," and that coalition emerged from 1896 in firm control of its party and the elected branches of the federal government.[140]

Far from slowing down after the decisive victory of its electoral allies, the very public support of conservative Republicans helped bolster the authority of the Court to promote aggressively its own understanding of constitutional requirements. After 1896, the Court continued to monitor state governments, especially in Democratic and populist strongholds in the West and the South, for legislation that imposed excessive restrictions on business and constrained the development of a nationally integrated market, as well as an increasing number of less politically salient federal statutory provisions.[141] It was during this period that the Court developed some of its characteristic constitutional doctrines that guided its work during the early twentieth century. In 1897, the Court broke new constitutional ground in *Allgeyer v. Louisiana*, finding a "liberty of contract" in the due process clause of the Fourteenth Amendment. In that case, the Court blocked Louisiana's efforts to exclude out-of-state companies from selling maritime insurance for goods shipped from the port of New Orleans.[142] In the first decade of the twentieth century, the Court still upheld the vast majority of state laws challenged on due process grounds, but the number of cases in which the Court struck down such laws was rapidly rising, and the Court became increasingly mistrustful of governmental motives in passing such regulations.[143] Most importantly, the Court claimed for itself the right to determine what constituted "reasonable" economic legislation and when such legislation was instead "arbitrary" or "unjust." Most famously, in *Lochner v. New York* in 1905, the Court's

---

[137] Sundquist, *Dynamics*, 154–69; Walter Dean Burnham, *Critical Elections and the Mainsprings of American Politics* (New York: Norton, 1970); Paul J. Kleppner, *The Cross of Culture* (New York: Free Press, 1970).

[138] *Indianapolis News* quoted in Westin, "Supreme Court, Populist Movement," 38.

[139] Sundquist, *Dynamics*, 165.

[140] Gates, *Partisan Realignment*, 68.

[141] Ibid., 78–83. See also Whittington, "Congress Before the *Lochner* Court," 821.

[142] Allgeyer v. Louisiana, 165 U.S. 578 (1897).

[143] Charles Warren, "The Progressiveness of the United States Supreme Court," *Columbia Law Review* 13 (1913): 294; Melvin I. Urofsky, "Myth and Reality: The Supreme Court and Protective Legislation in the Progressive Era," *Yearbook of the Supreme Court Historical Society* (1983): 53; Michael J. Phillips, *The Lochner Court, Myth and Reality* (Westport, CT: Praeger, 2001), 31–89.

majority argued that if states were to be prevented from circumventing the Fourteenth Amendment on a mere "pretext," the justices must be prepared to examine whether the legislation at issue is "a fair, reasonable, and appropriate exercise of the police powers of the states, or is it an unreasonable, unnecessary, and arbitrary interference with the right of the individual to his personal liberty." If legislatures could impose limits on the freedom to contract in the case of such relatively normal occupations as bakers, the justices fretted, then "there would seem to be no length to which legislation of this nature might not go" and indeed everyone would be "at the mercy of legislative majorities." The majority of the justices found it "impossible for us to shut our eyes to the fact that many laws of this character, while passed under what is claimed to be the police power for the purpose of protecting the public health or welfare, are, in reality, passed from other motives."[144]

Though the Bryan insurgency had been beaten back at the national level in 1896, conservatives faced new challenges in the first decades of the twentieth century from progressive reformers within the Republican Party. Progressive factions challenged Republican Party leadership in both the House and the Senate, fracturing apparent legislative majorities. The factional splits affected presidential elections as well, most consequently in 1912, when former President Theodore Roosevelt joined the Progressive Party to challenge his own Republican successor William Howard Taft.

Judicial reform was one of the issues that former president Theodore Roosevelt used to propel himself back onto the public stage and to set up his independent run for the White House. By the end of his presidency, Roosevelt was already pondering the problem. Writing to one of the dissenting justices after the *Lochner* decision, Roosevelt expressed the conviction that if the "spirit" of that decision became pervasive in the judiciary, then "we should not only have a revolution, but it would be absolutely necessary to have a revolution."[145] The sitting president was still looking for "some satisfactory scheme" by which he could raise a protest "without impairment of that respect for the law which must go hand in hand with respect for the courts," but he ended his term of office worried that "there is altogether too much power in the bench."[146] A few years later, he believed action was needed. He became vocally critical of the courts after he left office in 1908, and when he returned to the public stage in the years leading up to his independent run for the White House,

---

[144] Lochner v. New York, 198 U.S. 45, 56, 59, 64 (1905). On "the rise and demise of *Lochner*," see Gillman, *The Constitution Besieged*.

[145] Theodore Roosevelt, "To William Rufus Day, January 11, 1908," in *The Letters of Theodore Roosevelt*, ed. Elting E. Morison and John M. Blum, vol. 6 (Cambridge: Harvard University Press, 1952), 904.

[146] Ibid., 904, 1393.

he gave voice to the more radical criticisms of the courts that were gaining increased prominence in scholarly and political circles. In the very 1911 speech in which he announced his new campaign for the presidency, Roosevelt declared that judicial rulings invalidating laws on constitutional grounds "should be subject to revision by the people themselves" through a "right to recall" individual judicial decisions. "I believe in pure democracy," Roosevelt argued. "If the courts have the final say-so on all legislative acts, and if no appeal can lie from them to the people, then they are the irresponsible masters of the people."[147] In a 1912 campaign address, Roosevelt called the "right of the people to rule" the "first essential in the Progressive programme," and that commitment was in clear tension with active judicial review.[148] His Progressive Party platform of 1912 demanded "such restrictions on the power of the courts as shall leave the people the ultimate authority to determine fundamental questions of social welfare and public policy."[149] Roosevelt's critique was joined by Socialist presidential candidate Eugene Debs, the former labor leader from the Pullman strike, who called for the "abolition" of the "usurped" power of judicial review.[150]

Roosevelt's assault on the courts galvanized conservatives. The *New York Times* called one of Roosevelt's early articles criticizing the Court as "the craziest article ever published by a man of high standing and responsibility," reflecting the former president's "towering ambition" and creep toward "autocracy."[151] Even Roosevelt's close political ally, Henry Cabot Lodge, broke from him over the judiciary issue, writing to the former president that, "I found myself confronted with the fact that I was opposed to your policies . . . with great force in regard to changes in our Constitution and principles of government. . . . I knew, of course, that you and I differed on some of these points but I had not realized that the differences were so wide."[152] President William Howard Taft had, in fact, served as a federal appellate court judge through much of the 1890s, and serving on the Supreme Court was his highest ambition. The impatient Roosevelt sneered at what he called the "lawyers' Administration," but Taft was a firm supporter of the courts.[153] In 1911, he vetoed statehood

[147] Theodore Roosevelt, *Progressive Principles* (New York: Progressive National Service, 1913), 73, 47, 75.

[148] Ibid., 120.

[149] Arthur M. Schlesinger Jr. and Fred L. Israel, eds., *History of American Presidential Elections*, vol. 3 (New York: Chelsea House, 1971), 2188.

[150] Ibid., 2202.

[151] Special to the *New York Times*, "The Short Way with the Courts," *New York Times*, 6 January 1912, 12.

[152] Henry Cabot Lodge, "To Theodore Roosevelt, February 28, 1912," in *Selections from the Correspondence*, 2:423–24.

[153] Roosevelt, *Letters*, 7:113.

for Arizona and New Mexico in part because they had adopted recall provisions that the president regarded as "destructive of the independence of the judiciary," "injurious to the cause of free government," and encouraging of "tyranny of the popular majority."[154] Roosevelt's speeches hit Taft "like a bolt out of the clear sky," and he denounced his predecessor's proposals as "absolutely impossible" and thought Roosevelt himself was becoming "not unlike Napoleon" in his impatience with the law.[155] Taft had grown tired of the presidency, but Roosevelt motivated him to seek renomination and reelection himself. In letters, Taft avowed, "I represent a safer and saner view of our government and our Constitution than does Theodore Roosevelt, and whether beaten or not I mean to labor in the vineyard for those principles." Taft was convinced that he "represent[ed] a cause that would make it cowardly for me to withdraw now. . . . the only hope against radicalism and demagogy."[156] More important than winning the election, Taft and his supporters determined, was "retain[ing] the regular Republican party as a nucleus for future conservative action."[157] On the campaign trail, Taft declared, "I believe in the popular Government, but I believe in popular Government ordered by Constitution and by law." The president denounced Roosevelt for planting the seeds of tyranny and expressed confidence that the American people would "never give up the Constitution."[158]

As the campaign wore on, Roosevelt de-emphasized the judicial issue and turned instead to other themes. The Democratic nominee, Woodrow Wilson, remained largely silent on the judiciary, though occasionally expressing opposition to judicial reform. Taft, having found a campaign issue that he cared about, continued to insist that the Constitution was "the supreme issue" of the election and that he and the orthodox Republican Party "stand for the Constitution as it is." The independence and authority of the courts was essential "to that form of government which has made the United States the greatest nation in the world, which has fostered liberty, promoted equality of opportunity, and achieved a prosperity beyond the most sanguine dreams of our forefathers." The Court was "the bulwark of liberty, the protection of the weak against the strong, and the safeguard of the rights of the minority," and Taft pledged to resist those who would "experiment" with it and thereby "attempt to under-

---

[154] William Howard Taft, *The Collected Works of William Howard Taft*, ed. David H. Burton, vol. 4 (Athens: Ohio University Press, 2002), 150.

[155] Quoted in Pringle, *Life of Taft*, 573; Archibald Butt, *Taft and Roosevelt*, vol. 1 (Garden City, NY: Doubleday, Doran, 1930), 346.

[156] Quoted in Pringle, *Life of Taft*, 764, 772.

[157] Quoted in Pringle, *Life of Taft*, 808.

[158] Special to the *New York Times*, "All Taft Wants is a Square Deal," *New York Times*, 20 March 1912, 4.

mine that great bill of rights which is indispensable to the preservation of our liberties."[159] His letters thanking and consoling well-wishers after the election made clear what the campaign was about for him—the defeat of Theodore Roosevelt—and on that score, it could be judged a success. He consoled his campaign treasurer with the thought, "I feel that had we not gone all in and worked as hard as we did, we might have allowed Roosevelt to be elected. . . . We accomplished his defeat, and you and I, with our ideas of constitutional government and of what is valuable in our country's constitution, must hold that to be worthy of any effort."[160] After leaving the White House, Taft accepted a position teaching constitutional law at Yale in order to continue the fight. Once the Republicans reclaimed the presidency in 1920, Taft was rewarded for his service with an appointment to the Supreme Court as chief justice.

Unlike 1896, the election of 1912 was not a clear victory for the courts. After all, Roosevelt had the best showing of any third-party candidate in the twentieth century and outpolled Taft by over 600,000 votes. Nonetheless, the Court was able successfully to exercise judicial review at an even greater rate over the next two decades. Antijudicial sentiment was unable to coalesce into a political majority. The Wilson administration did not support such measures, and conservatives retained control of the national Republican Party apparatus. Progressives inside and outside of Congress were divided among themselves over the appropriate response to the courts, as they were in other matters of politics and policy. Such hostility to the courts insured that conservatives would continue to regard the preservation of judicial authority as a priority—as the "only breakwater . . . against the tumultuous ocean of democracy," in the words of one American Bar Association president—while the fragmented nature of the antijudicial forces insured that their challenges were not politically serious.[161] As now Chief Justice Taft observed in 1923, "[T]he truth is that the so-called radicals are vastly more noisy than they are important."[162] Meanwhile, the substantive policy successes of the progressive forces in both Congress and the states gave the conservative courts plenty of opportunities to exercise their constitutional veto. Because the Court's conservative ideological allies could not dominate the policymaking process, the Court found itself faced with a steady stream of laws that it regarded as constitutionally dubious. Because the Court's ideological foes could not dominate

---

[159] William Howard Taft, "The Supreme Issue," *Saturday Evening Post*, 19 October 1912, 3, 81, 4.

[160] William Howard Taft, "To George R. Sheldon, November 10, 1912," Presidential Papers Microfilm, Series B: Presidential, vol. 45, reel 515.

[161] John F. Dillon, "Address of the President," in *Report of the Fifteenth Annual Meeting of the American Bar Association* (Chicago: American Bar Association, 1892), 211.

[162] Quoted in Ross, *A Muted Fury*, 217.

national, and especially presidential, politics, however, they could not bring the Court to heel. The weakness of the political majority both motivated and expanded judicial authority.

This political situation endured until the onset of the Great Depression. Woodrow Wilson's victory against a divided Republican Party proved a temporary interruption to general Republican dominance of national politics. The Supreme Court reached unprecedented levels of activism against the federal government in the 1920s while continuing through the mid-1930s to strike down increasing numbers of state laws. In the 1924 elections, Progressive candidate Robert M. La Follette offered the expected criticisms of the courts but downplayed the issue in favor of other campaign themes. A Republican senator from Wisconsin, La Follette had long been a leading spokesman of the progressive movement and a visible critic of the conservative judiciary. Just two years before, La Follette had proposed a congressional override of the Supreme Court's constitutional decisions in order to overcome a "judicial oligarchy" that had "wrested sovereignty from the people."[163] The Republican and Democratic candidates again took the opportunity to bolster judicial authority. The political reporter for the *New York World* concluded that the Republicans in particular "did not want to permit La Follette to escape from the Supreme Court issue if it could be forced on him."[164] Calvin Coolidge argued, "Majorities are notoriously irresponsible," and judicial review was essential to prevent political majorities from voting away even the "most precious rights."[165] Stumping for Coolidge, Charles Evans Hughes warned that La Follette's proposals would leave "everything you have, the security of your person and life . . . at the mercy of Congress." Hughes provided a lengthy list of constitutional commitments that would be in danger without judicial supremacy to interpret and enforce their terms, from federalism and separation of powers to rights to religion, speech, the vote, and security of home and property.[166] The Democratic presidential nominee was John W. Davis, a Wall Street attorney, past president of the American Bar Association, and no friend of court-curbing. His nomination found favor with Chief Justice Taft, who was confident that, if elected, Davis would hold to the "preservation of constitutional principles and the dignity and influence of the Court."[167] Coolidge won in a landslide, and many observers attributed Republican success in part to La Follette's perceived

---

[163] Quoted in ibid., 195.

[164] Quoted in ibid., 268.

[165] Calvin Coolidge, *Foundations of the Republic* (New York: Charles Scribner's Sons, 1926), 95.

[166] Quoted in "Hughes Answers Critics of Party," *New York Times*, 5 October 1924, E1.

[167] Quoted in Ross, *A Muted Fury*, 282–83.

opposition to the Supreme Court.[168] Taft celebrated the "famous victory" and its lesson that the United States "is really the most conservative country in the world."[169]

The ground shifted under the Court's feet in 1932, as Franklin Roosevelt trounced incumbent President Herbert Hoover at the polls as the nation remained mired in the Great Depression. A veteran of progressive politics, Roosevelt finally broke the loyalty of urban voters to the Republican Party while retaining the traditional Democratic base in the South and the West. Backed by huge majorities in Congress and committed to a constitutional vision at odds with the constitutional edifice carefully constructed by the Court and defended by conservatives over the prior several decades, Roosevelt launched into a politics of reconstruction that required displacing the authority of the Court to fix constitutional understandings.

We have already seen the reconstructive and departmentalist elements of Roosevelt's presidency in chapter 2. What is worth noting for present purposes is how moderate even Roosevelt's Court-packing plan was relative to the standard progressive and populist proposals of the prior several decades, which emphasized the abolition of judicial review, a "judicial recall," or a congressional override of judicial constitutional decisions. Perhaps having learned from the failures of past progressive campaigns, the 1932 and 1936 Democratic Party platforms, and indeed the campaigns themselves, were notably silent on the question of judicial reform. Indeed, some on the left complained that it "clearly does not meet the issue of the judicial power as an obstruction to democratic action. It does not go to the root of the judicial oligarchy, but by reorganizing it seeks rather to perpetuate it."[170] Instead, Roosevelt pursued the common theme of reconstructive politics that emphasized his own independent and immediate warrants for construing the Constitution and the inappropriateness of regarding past judicial pronouncements as controlling present political decisions, a claim to authority that is by its nature highly contextualized and transient. Further, Roosevelt's proposal to pack the Court with his supporters contained no provision requiring judicial restraint at all. In order for the judiciary "to do its part in making democracy successful," what was needed was a "reinvigorated, liberal-minded Judiciary" that understood the "present-day sense of the Constitution."[171] As Robert Jackson later explained, "What we demanded for our generation was the right consciously to influence the evolutionary process of constitutional

---

[168] Ross, *A Muted Fury*, 282–83.

[169] Quoted in Russell Fowler, "Calvin Coolidge and the Supreme Court," *Journal of Supreme Court History* 25 (2000): 271, 284.

[170] "Purging the Supreme Court," *Nation*, 13 February 1937, 173.

[171] Roosevelt, *Public Papers and Addresses*, 5:641, 6:133, 6:127.

law, as other generations have done," to loosen the "firm grip" of a "past that was dead and repudiated."[172] Prominent legal scholars allied to the administration argued the same point in the press. According to Columbia's Karl Llewellyn, the president "proposes nothing so drastic" as getting "rid of the priest or the oracle." He "proposes only putting enough new blood into our college of priests to overcome the inertia of the more frozen members." The plan would neither cost the Court its independence nor "shake the authority of the court."[173]

The administration hoped to harness the power of the Court, not destroy it. Even as it sought to temporarily displace judicial authority, it was setting the stage for its reconstruction. The Court-packing plan, as Roosevelt's judicial reorganization bill immediately became known, sparked a political firestorm. Republicans, who might be expected to be critical of the plan, remained largely silent in order to avoid turning the dispute into a partisan contest and allowed conservative Democrats to lead the opposition to the bill. The administration had decided against one traditional court-curbing proposal that would seek to limit or eliminate the power of judicial review in favor of the more innovative and indirect plan of adding justices. In many ways, this was an important acknowledgment of the heightened authority of the Court by the 1930s. The administration's proposal exploited the widespread concern that life-tenured judges could be out of touch and infirm, while appealing to the undoubted right of Congress to alter the size of the Supreme Court and create new judicial offices. That congressional power had fallen into disuse; the size of the Court had remained at nine since 1869. The political intent to "pack" the Court with more sympathetic justices was obvious. Surprisingly, Senator Burton Wheeler, a staunch progressive and former running mate of Robert La Follette's, came out in opposition to the plan. Wheeler produced a letter from Chief Justice Charles Evans Hughes denying that the proposed bill would improve judicial efficiency.[174] The Court further weakened support for the plan in the spring of 1937 by releasing its decision upholding the minimum wage in Washington state, then another upholding the National Labor Relations Act, and yet another upholding the Social Security Act.[175] The Court had clearly turned a corner, with Justice Owen Roberts switching sides to ease restrictions on government power. With the approval of the NLRA, unions lost interest in Court

[172] Jackson, *Struggle for Judicial Supremacy*, xiv.

[173] K. N. Llewellyn, "A United Front on the Court," *Nation*, 13 March 1937, 288, 289.

[174] Leuchtenburg, *The Supreme Court Reborn*, 140–41.

[175] West Coast Hotel v. Parrish, 300 U.S. 379 (1937); National Labor Relations Board v. Jones & Laughlin Steel Corp., 301 U.S. 1 (1937); Steward Machine Co. v. Davis, 301 U.S. 548 (1937).

packing. Public opinion turned decisively against the plan.[176] In May, one of the Four Horsemen, Justice Willis Van Devanter, resigned, giving FDR his first vacancy on the Court and the opportunity to solidify the narrow progressive majority. A bipartisan Senate Judiciary Committee report denounced the plan as "an invasion of judicial power such as has never been attempted in this country."[177] Undaunted, the president pressed forward with his plan and launched an aggressive lobbying campaign to shore up congressional support. The sudden death of the Senate majority leader, Joseph Robinson, in the midst of the summer debates on the bill was the final blow. Support for the plan evaporated.[178]

The fate of the Court-packing plan was a testament to the Court's strength, and its vulnerability. Even a popular president, fresh from a landslide electoral victory, backed by overwhelming partisan majorities in Congress, and faced with stern judicial resistance to his policy program in the midst of economic crisis, could not win passage of even a relatively tempered proposal to meddle with the Court. The public and political opposition to the Court-packing plan demonstrated the substantial authority the Court still possessed, even among those who disagreed with many of its substantive decisions. The authority of the Court to interpret the Constitution and guard it against political violations, an authority that conservative political leaders had been building in the public mind for several decades, bore its ultimate fruit.

Many were distrustful of a plan that seemed to consolidate further power in the presidency, and congressional New Dealers rhetorically asked how they would have been expected to respond to such a proposal if a Republican president had made it.[179] As the Court grew more accommodating over the spring of 1937, affected interests such as labor unions split off from the antijudicial coalition. Although those close to the president who could foresee future potential conflicts with the Court, such as Democratic Party chair Jim Farley, might ask, "Why compromise?" others who had already had their particular policies upheld, such as Senator James Byrnes, began to wonder, "Why run for a train after you have already caught it?"[180] The huge Democratic majorities won in the previous election also papered over basic divisions within the New Deal coalition that the Court-packing fight began to lay bare. A substantial group

---

[176] Caldeira, "Public Opinion," 1139.

[177] Senate Committee on the Judiciary, *Reorganization of the Federal Judiciary*, 75th Cong., 1st sess., 1937, S. Rept. 711, 10.

[178] Leuchtenburg, *The Supreme Court Reborn*, 142–54.

[179] William G. Leuchtenburg, *Franklin D. Roosevelt and the New Deal* (New York: Harper & Row, 1963), 234–35.

[180] Farley quoted in Leuchtenburg, *The Supreme Court Reborn*, 144; Byrnes quoted in Leuchtenburg, *Roosevelt and New Deal*, 237.

of conservative Democrats, especially from the South, concerned about the direction of the party and the government, were unwilling to concede more power to the president. In the future, FDR would attempt to purge or circumvent such conservatives, but the "Conservative Coalition" became an important and enduring constraint on liberalism.[181] Although powerful, the Democratic majority had limits, and the Court, after initially overreaching, had found them.

Even supporters of the New Deal could foresee positive benefits from the power of judicial review, and this shaped what many had in mind in seeking a more "liberal-minded judiciary." Referring to the Court-packing plan, the owner of the *Nation*, for example, wrote, "If I were a Negro I would be raging and tearing my hair over this proposal."[182] Others pointed to the value of the Court in protecting free speech and religion.[183] To great excitement, New York governor Herbert Lehman publicly declared his opposition to any "dangerous precedent that could be availed of by future less well intentioned administrations for the purpose of oppression or for the curtailment of the constitutional rights of our citizens."[184]

Early in the twentieth century, the political and legal Left still saw judges as the agents of capital and constitutional law as a tool for limiting the power of democratic majorities to challenge private power-holders. In the decade preceding the Court-packing plan, however, this view had begun to shift and the Left began to develop a stake in judicial review.[185] The precursor to the American Civil Liberties Union was founded by opponents of America's entry into World War I and was defending through lobbying and litigation those prosecuted for resisting the war effort.[186] They had initially lobbied Woodrow Wilson and members of his administration to respect the "Anglo-Saxon tradition of intellectual freedom," but the president had brushed them off, saying that "there could be no such thing . . . it was insanity."[187] By the 1920s the ACLU had moved away from its early reliance on popular constitutionalism and had thrown its lot in with the courts.[188] Roger Baldwin, the founder of the ACLU, later

---

[181] See Patterson, *Congressional Conservatism*; Milkis, *President and the Parties*.

[182] Oswald Garrison Villard, quoted in Leuchtenburg, *Roosevelt and the New Deal*, 235.

[183] Leuchtenburg, *The Supreme Court Reborn*, 139.

[184] "Gov. Lehman's Letter," *New York Times*, 20 July 1937, 1. In addition to printing the governor's letter on the front page, the *Times* published eight articles on the move that same day.

[185] On the general transformation of progressives from advocates of state power to advocates of civil liberties, see Kersch, *Constructing Civil Liberties*.

[186] Peggy Lamson, *Roger Baldwin* (Boston: Houghton Mifflin, 1976), 71–78.

[187] Quoted in Blanche Wiesen Cook, "Democracy in Wartime: Antimilitarism in England and the United States, 1914–1918," *American Studies* 13 (1972): 58, 57.

[188] See Emily Zackin, "Popular Constitutionalism's Hard When You're Not Very Popular: Why the ACLU Turned to the Courts," unpublished paper.

recalled that the Roosevelt administration "was stacked with our friends and supporters."[189] Baldwin and his allies on the Left were hardly beguiled by the courts, which all too often, Baldwin thought, "do not help much as protectors of rights, for judges write economics as well as law, and usually on the side of established property relations."[190] Nonetheless, the experience of World War I and what even a progressive president might do had made many of the Left preferring unreliable judicial protection of constitutional rights to no judicial protection at all.

As soon as Roosevelt's appointments joined the Supreme Court, one of the architects of Roosevelt's Court-packing plan, Princeton constitutional scholar Edward Corwin, began laying out a positive agenda for it. Corwin argued that judicial "self-abnegation" would be "less laudable in the long run" in such areas as the extension against the states of "certain rights which the Bill of Rights protects in more specific terms against Congress."[191] The "enlargement of judicial review" had "its best justification" when the "Court empowered itself to give voice to the conscience of the country in behalf of poor people against local prejudice and unfairness." He singled out "freedom of speech and press and the right to a fair trial."[192] The justices generally agreed, and quickly began to lay the foundations for the Warren Court's constitutional resurgence. Given that the New Deal coalition was itself "an extraordinary assemblage of such traditional outgroups" as organized labor, Catholics, Jews, and blacks, it is not surprising that the political representatives of that coalition found new value in free speech and similar civil liberties.[193]

While some progressives would subordinate individual rights in general to democratic majorities, adopting a judicial posture of overall deference to legislative decisions, others sought to distinguish between different forms of liberty and to dedicate the judiciary to enforcing the "preferred freedoms" that were "indispensable conditions of a free society" in contrast to those that "derived merely from shifting economic arrangements" that these progressives saw the *Lochner* Court as attempting to enshrine.[194] One approach to distinguishing preferred from less preferred freedoms was procedural, or what constitutional scholar John Hart Ely later called "representation-reinforcing."[195] The classic expression of that

[189] Quoted in Lamson, *Roger Baldwin,* 255–56.

[190] Quoted in Paul L. Murphy, *World War I and the Origin of Civil Liberties in the United States* (New York: Norton, 1979), 244.

[191] Edward S. Corwin, *Constitutional Revolution, Ltd.* (Claremont, CA: Claremont Colleges, 1941), 110, 111.

[192] Ibid., 111–12.

[193] Klarman, "Rethinking Revolutions," 1, 44.

[194] Alpheus Thomas Mason, "The Core of Free Government, 1938–1940: Mr. Justice Stone and 'Preferred Freedoms,'" *Yale Law Journal* 65 (1956): 597; Felix Frankfurter, *Mr. Justice Holmes and the Supreme Court* (Cambridge: Harvard University Press, 1938), 51.

[195] John Hart Ely, *Democracy and Distrust* (Cambridge: Harvard University Press, 1980).

view was hidden away in a crucial footnote in the 1938 *Carolene Products* case upholding the Filled Milk Act. Having announced the deferential "rational basis" test for upholding laws regulating "ordinary commercial transactions," the Court explained in a footnote the conditions under which there would be "more exacting judicial scrutiny." Those conditions include apparent violation of "specific" textual prohibitions in the Constitution, legal restrictions on the political process, and "prejudice against discrete and insular minorities" that might likewise leave some unprotected by the normal political process.[196] The Court's role was not to second-guess the judgment of legislatures, but to insure that the "remedial channels of the democratic process remain open and unobstructed."[197]

An alternative approach to identifying preferred freedoms was substantive, exercising judicial judgment to determine which freedoms were simply too sacred to be infringed. The progressive justice Benjamin Cardozo gave eloquent statement to this approach in 1937, the very year of the Court-packing plan and the judiciary's retreat from the earlier regime. When rejecting the claim to a privilege against double jeopardy in state criminal trials, Cardozo articulated a judicial mission to protect rights that are "of the very essence of a scheme of ordered liberty" and whose loss would "violate a 'principle of justice so rooted in the traditions and conscience of our people as to be ranked as fundamental.' "[198] To all the justices, the "guarantees of civil liberty are but guarantees of freedom of the human mind and spirit and of reasonable freedom and opportunity to express them," as was "protection against torture."[199] Such formulations did not solve all problems, or satisfy those who regard the rights of property as fundamental, but they indicated a continuing judicial role in securing the "constitutional protection of the liberty of small minorities to the popular will."[200] Just as national conservatives in the Republican Party in the first decades of the twentieth century had welcomed judicial monitoring of the states and Congress for progressive legislation that violated their constitutional understandings, so national liberals in the Democratic Party in the middle decades of the twentieth century welcomed judicial action against conservative states and Congress that violated liberal constitutional commitments. World War II only solidified this commitment, as the Court reasserted itself, with the vocal approval of liberals, as the authoritative guardians of liberty that distinguished American democracy from European dictatorships.[201]

---

[196] United States v. Carolene Products Co., 304 U.S. 144, 152n4 (1938).
[197] Minersville School District v. Gobitis, 310 U.S. 586, 599 (1940).
[198] Palko v. Connecticut, 302 U.S. 319, 325 (1937).
[199] Gobitis, 604; Palko, 326.
[200] Gobitis, 606.
[201] See Richard A. Primus, *The American Language of Rights* (New York: Cambridge University Press, 1999), 177–224.

"Trying to Take the Country Back . . . as Far as the Constitution"

The great parties of the nineteenth century were formed, in part, to vindicate constitutional principles, and they were surprisingly capable of acting on those principles. Despite their own fear of "factions," Jefferson and Madison took the drastic step of organizing an opposition political party in the 1790s in order to save the constitutional experiment from the perceived Hamiltonian perversion.[202] Although they found themselves needing to compromise strict principle in order to govern and were criticized for doing so by their more doctrinaire allies, Jefferson and Madison were able to win firm control of the elected branches of the national government and uproot much of what the Federalists had planted there. Somewhat differently, Martin van Buren, in alliance with Andrew Jackson, built the Democratic Party to be an instrument for binding public officials to limited-government principles.[203] The Whigs organized in turn to oppose Jackson's presidential "despotism," as the Republicans later did to redefine American freedom. After the contest of principles was decided at the ballot box, the victorious party expected to be able to govern.

During the nineteenth-century heyday of American political parties, a Whig editor could declare that parties were "but the embodiment of principle" and became a mere faction only if they no longer were "to be guided by principle."[204] Denouncing the "heretical sentiment of 'no-partyism and no-principles,' " Georgia Democrat Howell Cobb told his colleagues on the floor of the House that parties were nothing but "an association of men acting in concert with each other, to carry out great fundamental principles in the administration of Government" and were the essential means for holding officials accountable to those principles. To weaken the parties would be to "paralyze the arm of the people."[205] Massachusetts senator Charles Sumner agreed on that much, explaining to the Young Men's Republican Union of New York City that "through parties, principles are maintained above men."[206] In an era in which most members of Congress served only one term, their most important qualification for office was their strict "fidelity and stern adherence to the principles" of the party "at all times and under all circumstances," whatever the "personal merits or demerits of a candidate" might be.[207]

---

[202] Hofstadter, *Idea of Party System*.

[203] Gerald Leonard, *The Invention of Party Politics* (Chapel Hill: University of North Carolina Press, 2002).

[204] *New York Courier and Enquirer*, July 28, 1858, quoted in Joel H. Silbey, *The American Political Nation, 1838–1893* (Stanford, CA: Stanford University Press, 1991), 72.

[205] *Congressional Globe*, 30th Cong., 1st sess., 1 July 1848, app. 775.

[206] Quoted Hofstadter, *Idea of Party System*, 269.

[207] New Hampshire Democrat John H. George, quoted in Silbey, *American Political Nation*, 126.

Things became more complicated by the end of the nineteenth century. Once the Democratic South returned to national politics after Reconstruction, neither party was able to secure a solid majority in the House of Representatives, even as the Republicans held the edge in the electoral college and the Senate. The result was the nation's first era of recurrent divided government.[208] In the first half of the twentieth century, first the Republicans and then the Democrats were able to establish themselves as the majority party with unified government but at the cost of integrating disparate ideological elements into their electoral and legislative coalitions that persistently resisted the direction of presidential and party leadership. Meanwhile, serving in Congress had become a career in itself. Incumbent legislators were now far more likely to seek additional terms of office and significantly more likely to win them when they did. By the latter twentieth century, congressmen had become notably successful in separating their personal electoral fortunes from that of their political party. Individual congressmen had become independent agents, skilled at maximizing their appeal and minimizing their offense to their constituents. The second era of divided government emerged, but this time with a relatively stable House and a somewhat more variable Senate and presidency.[209]

---

[208] Divided government was not unknown before the Civil War, but there were important differences in frequency and structure between such episodes before and after the Civil War, and again in the twentieth century. Before the Civil War, the government was divided in nine of the thirty-six possible terms, though all were during the eighteen terms between the beginning of John Quincy Adams's presidency and the end of James Buchanan's. Only Adams and the Whigs confronted two chambers of Congress controlled by the other party, and only they had to deal with divided government throughout their presidencies. More often, divided government consisted of only one chamber lost to the other party at the midterm elections. Divided government was thus understood to be transitory, "to be corrected in the next election," and it was marked "by the widespread expectation of a return to unified normality." Joseph H. Silbey, "Divided Government in Historical Perspective," in *Divided Government*, ed. Peter F. Galderisi, Roberta Q. Herzberg, and Peter McNamara (Lanham, MD: Rowman & Littlefield, 1996), 21. Between the return of the South to the electorate and the 1896 realignment, at least one congressional chamber was divided from the president in eight of eleven terms.

[209] Nelson W. Polsby, "The Institutionalization in the U.S. House of Representatives," *American Political Science Review* 62 (1968): 144; Samuel Kernell, "Toward Understanding 19th Century Congressional Careers: Ambition, Competition, and Rotation," *American Journal of Political Science* 21 (1977): 669; James C. Garand and Donald A. Gross, "Change in the Vote Margins for Congressional Candidates: A Specification of Historical Trends," *American Political Science Review* 78 (1984): 17; John R. Alford and David W. Brady, "Personal and Partisan Advantage in U.S. Congressional Elections, 1846–1990," in *Congress Reconsidered*, 5th ed., ed. Lawrence C. Dodd and Bruce I. Oppenheimer (Washington, DC: CQ Press, 1993); David C. Huckabee, "Length of Congressional Service: First through 107th Congresses," Congressional Research Service Report for Congress (2002); Cox and Kernell, *Politics of Divided Government*.

As a consequence, the political power of presidential reconstructions has become more attenuated. The constitutional vision of reconstructive politics is no less real and significant, but the legislative support that it can marshal is less robust than once was the case. Coalition leaders find themselves more quickly and more often operating within the strategic environments described in chapter 3. Unsurprisingly, the bulk of the illustrations of the logic of the utility of judicial review by affiliated leaders in chapter 3 are drawn from the twentieth century. Turning to the judiciary as an alternative forum for advancing constitutional goals is frequently a necessity if political coalitions from their origins are fragmented or insecure or if coalition partners disagree not just about one (perhaps big) issue such as slavery but myriad issues. Courts become more useful to coalition leaders to the extent that they cannot reliably and safely take action on their constitutional priorities themselves, an increasingly common situation in the twentieth century. At the same time, the courts can afford to be more independent agents when the signals about constitutional priorities that they receive from political leaders are so weak and the threat posed by such a fragmented political majority is so limited.

This was perhaps most dramatically true with the "Reagan Revolution." As indicated in chapter 2, Ronald Reagan was the most recent president to engage in reconstructive politics and to make departmentalist claims. At the same time, his departmentalism was relatively muted, being voiced most famously not by the president himself but by his attorney general. Similarly, his reconstructive project seemed less ambitious than that of his predecessors, more fully realized in rhetoric than in practice. This reflects in part, no doubt, Reagan's inability to win control of the House of Representatives for the Republican Party. While capable of putting together cross-party coalitions to achieve some legislative goals and willing to exploit the resources of the executive branch to advance other policies, Reagan rather more quickly and more explicitly encountered the limits of his coalition's strength than did even, for example, Franklin Roosevelt, who was stifled by the conservative coalition before his own second term of office was complete.[210]

---

[210] Myriad divisions within his own party likewise limited Reagan's policy program and encouraged a quick turn to the courts. Even the Republican-controlled Senate gave little support to initiatives favored by social conservatives, such as Jesse Helms's jurisdiction-stripping proposal regarding school prayer, prompting the administration to point to the "courts themselves" as the best vehicle by which to "restore a more balanced view of the first amendment" while admitting that it would be an "uphill battle." Ronald Reagan, "Statement on Senate Action on the Proposed Constitutional Amendment on Prayer in Schools, March 20, 1984," in *Public Papers, 1984*, 382; Reagan, "Remarks at a Fundraising Luncheon for Senator Jeremiah Denton in Birmingham, Alabama, June 6, 1985," in *Public Papers, 1985*, 729. George H. W. Bush likewise limited himself to expressing "disap-

Central to Reagan's constitutional vision was a more limited national government. As emphasized in his first inaugural address, Reagan thought it was "time to check and reverse the growth of government," to reduce "the intervention and intrusion in our lives that result from unnecessary and excessive growth of government." That task was manifold, but included within it was the need to rebalance the relationship between the federal government and the states. "It is my intention to curb the size and influence of the Federal establishment and to demand recognition of the distinction between the powers granted to the Federal Government and those reserved to the States or the people. All of us need to be reminded that the Federal Government did not create the States; the States created the Federal Government."[211]

Reagan's interest in "the constitutional concept of federalism" was closely related to his interest in limited government, and as a consequence had constitutional implications and broader ideological significance.[212] Reagan was as interested in "restor[ing] the constitutional symmetry between the central Government and the States and . . . reestablish[ing] the freedom and variety of federalism" as he was in "end[ing] cumbersome costs and spiraling administration at the Federal level" and ensuring that "programs will be responsive to both the people they're meant to help and the people who pay for them."[213] The Nixon administration had likewise pushed a federalism initiative, but did not regard federalism as a priority and viewed it largely as a pragmatic administrative issue with no implications for the basic role of the national government in the post–New Deal order.[214] Reagan, by contrast, viewed his central efforts to reduce federal taxes and regulation as part and parcel of a "quiet federalist revolution,"

---

pointment" with Court rulings in this area. George H. W. Bush, "Statement on the Supreme Court Decision on the Lee v. Weisman Case," *Public Papers, 1992*, 1009. See also Bradley D. Hays, "Party with the Court: Regime Politics and the Supreme Court," Ph.D. diss., University of Maryland, 2005.

[211] Ronald Reagan, "Inaugural Address, January 20, 1981," *Public Papers, 1981*, 2.

[212] Reagan, "Remarks at the Annual Convention of the National Conference of State Legislatures in Atlanta, Georgia, July 30, 1981," *Public Papers, 1981*, 683.

[213] Ibid.; Reagan, "Address Before a Joint Session of the Congress Reporting on the State of the Union, January 26, 1982," *Public Papers, 1982*, 76.

[214] The "Reagan domestic speeches in 1980 were addressed as much against his two Republican predecessors as against Johnson, the Democratic Congresses, and Carter." David B. Walker, *The Rebirth of Federalism*, 2nd ed. (New York: Chatham House, 2000), 141. See also Joan Hoff, *Nixon Reconsidered* (New York: Basic Books, 1994), 65–73; Demetrios Caraley, "Changing Conceptions of Federalism," *Political Science Quarterly* 101 (1986): 289; Richard P. Nathan and John R. Lago, "Intergovernmental Relations in the Reagan Era," *Public Budgeting and Finance* 8 (1988): 15; J. Mitchell Pickerill and Cornell W. Clayton, "The Rehnquist Court and the Political Dynamics of Federalism," *Perspectives on Politics* 2 (2004): 233.

part of the process of "renew[ing] the meaning of the Constitution" and "trying to take the country back . . . as far as the Constitution."[215]

The administration's ability to act decisively and consistently on its articulated federalism principles was limited. In some areas, such as cutting spending on federal outlays to state and local governments, the administration was relatively successful. In other areas, its accomplishments were more meager. Reagan's most dramatic initiative, his 1981 proposal to clearly differentiate the functions of the state and federal governments and withdraw the federal government from state functions, foundered on the rocks of the economic recession, the midterm loss of Republican congressional seats, and opposition from state and local officials who were not enthusiastic about taking political ownership of a range of government responsibilities and their associated tax bills. In other instances, the administration and its congressional allies found themselves succumbing to the temptation to deviate from their federalist vision when other policy goals or simple political gains were at stake.[216] Thus, for example, Reagan advocated or agreed to statutes imposing significant new mandates on state and local governments, even in areas that were well within what he regarded as traditional state functions, as with the Age Discrimination in Employment Act Amendments (eliminating mandatory retirement for public employees), the Asbestos Hazard Emergency Response Act (requiring asbestos removal from schools), and the Highway Safety Amendments (requiring states to raise the minimum legal drinking age).[217]

In part with these political lessons in mind, the administration eventually set its sights on judiciary as a vehicle for making its conservative commitments on federalism credible and effective. Although Congress could be faulted for its "grasping extensions" of national power, one internal administration report argued, it was the Supreme Court, "through the power of constitutional interpretation, [that] has been the dominant force in the decline of federalism."[218] The only impediment the Court had left to centralization was "Congress' sense of self-restraint," which the administra-

---

[215] Reagan, "Remarks at the Annual Convention of the National Conference of State Legislatures, July 30, 1981" *Public Papers, 1981*, 682, 683; Reagan, "Interview with Reporters on Federalism, November 19, 1981," *Public Papers, 1981*, 1082.

[216] Timothy J. Conlan, "Federalism and Competing Values in the Reagan Administration," *Publius* 16 (1986): 37; Hugh Heclo, "Reaganism and the Search for a Public Philosophy," in *Perspectives on the Reagan Years*, ed. John L. Palmer (Washington, DC: Urban Institute Press, 1986).

[217] Timothy J. Conlan and David R. Beam, "Federal Mandates: The Record of Reform and Future Prospects," *Intergovernmental Perspective* 18 (Fall 1992): 7.

[218] Domestic Policy Council, Working Group on Federalism, *The Status of Federalism in America* (Washington, DC: Government Printing Office, 1986), 2 (executive summary). This report is discussed in Dawn Johnsen, "Ronald Reagan and the Rehnquist Court on

tion well knew was hardly adequate.[219] In its *Guidelines for Constitutional Litigation*, designed "to help ensure that principled and consistent positions are advocated by all Executive Branch litigators," the Justice Department identified Supreme Court doctrine regarded as "inconsistent" with the administration's constitutional understandings and directed government litigators to "educate lower courts . . . on the original meaning of the relevant constitutional or statutory provision" while reminding them that "as an ontological matter" the Constitution is not what the judges say it is. One implication of that last point was that litigators were instructed that federal statutes inconsistent with the administration's understandings were to be regarded as "unconstitutional and should not be defended" in court.[220] The administration had rhetorically, fiscally, and administratively challenged the modern Court's nationalist vision of federalism. For the "choices ahead in constitutional interpretation," as one Justice Department report was subtitled, a reconstructed Court could circumvent political pitfalls and discipline elected officials to ensure stern adherence to principles.[221] In the near term, the administration hoped to steer the judiciary in the proper direction through education and advocacy. In the longer term, judicial appointments were expected to play a crucial role.

Associate Justice William Rehnquist was the model jurist for the Reagan administration. Nominated to the Supreme Court almost by accident by Richard Nixon after the administration had run out of more politically captivating options, Rehnquist had emerged as the premier voice of conservative strict constructionism in the nation. In public speeches and carefully reasoned solo dissents from the bench, he denounced the liberal precedents of the Warren and Burger Courts and sketched out an alternative constitutionalism that inspired a younger generation of conservative lawyers who populated the Reagan administration. The Justice Department's *Guidelines for Constitutional Litigation* drew heavily on Rehnquist's opinions to identify the administration's views of the limits of congressional power.[222] To department attorneys tasked with evaluating possible candidates for future Supreme Court vacancies, Rehnquist was the only logical choice to fill the center seat if Chief Justice Warren Burger were to leave the bench.[223] To them, Rehnquist "was quite clearly the

Congressional Power: Presidential Influences on Constitutional Change," *Indiana Law Journal* 78 (2003): 363.

[219] Ibid., Domestic Policy Council, *Status of Federalism*, 17.

[220] *Guidelines on Constitutional Litigation*, quoted in Johnsen, "Ronald Reagan," 389n138, 390, 391n152.

[221] Department of Justice, Office of Legal Policy, *Report to the Attorney General: The Constitution in the Year 2000* (Washington, DC: Government Printing Office, 1988).

[222] Johnsen, "Ronald Reagan," 391.

[223] Yalof, *Pursuit of Justices*, 142–55.

justice who most represented the judicial views of the Reagan administration."[224] Elevating the "Lone Ranger" of the Burger Court to the position of chief justice of the United States made the strongest possible statement about the Reagan administration's understanding of the Constitution and the Supreme Court.[225]

The implications for federalism were an important, though certainly not the sole, factor guiding the administration in evaluating judicial candidates. Among the attributes of an "ideal candidate for the Court," the Reagan Justice Department had highlighted two complementary commitments: "deference to states in their spheres" and "recognition that the federal government is one of limited powers."[226] As the *Guidelines* observed in regard to its notes on federalism, "Rather than the usual problem of exercising authority it does not have, this guideline concerns the judiciary's failure to exercise appropriately its power to hold invalid unconstitutional congressional actions."[227] Rehnquist himself embodied these commitments, with an extensive record of urging the Court to adopt doctrines giving more autonomy to the states and authoring the only, if short-lived, post–New Deal decision limiting congressional authority on federalism grounds.[228]

Of course, the Rehnquist Court launched a new federalism offensive that emphasized both the limits on congressional authority under the Constitution and the extent of judicial authority over it. The renewed interest in federalism on the Court was clearly part of the Reagan legacy. With the exception of the first two, relatively modest, decisions in this offensive in the early 1990s, these federalism decisions relied on five justices.[229] Of the five justices in the federalism majorities—William Rehnquist, Sandra Day O'Connor, Antonin Scalia, Anthony Kennedy, and

---

[224] William Bradford Reynolds, Assistant Attorney General for Civil Rights, quoted in David G. Savage, *Turning Right* (New York: John Wiley & Sons, 1992), 9.

[225] On Rehnquist, see Keith E. Whittington, "William H. Rehnquist: Nixon's Strict Constructionist, Reagan's Chief Justice," in *Rehnquist Justice*, ed. Earl M. Maltz (Lawrence: University Press of Kansas, 2003).

[226] Quoted in Yalof, *Pursuit of Justices*, 259n55, 143, 144.

[227] Quoted in Johnsen, "Ronald Reagan," 396.

[228] That decision was National League of Cities v. Usery, 426 U.S. 833 (1976), subsequently overruled in Garcia v. San Antonio Metropolitan Transit Authority, 469 U.S. 528 (1985). On Rehnquist and federalism, see Sue Davis, *Justice Rehnquist and the Constitution* (Princeton: Princeton University Press, 1989), 135–88; H. Jefferson Powell, "The Compleat Jeffersonian: Justice Rehnquist and Federalism," *Yale Law Journal* 91 (1982): 1317.

[229] The early decisions were Gregory v. Ashcroft, 501 U.S. 452 (1991) (limiting application of the Age Discrimination in Employment Act with regard to state judges, decided seven to two) and New York v. United States, 505 U.S. 144 (1992) (limiting federal authority to commandeer state officials, decided nine to zero). David Souter, later a dissenter from the federalism decisions, was the only other justice to join these O'Connor majority opinions in their entirety.

Clarence Thomas—three were Reagan appointees, and Reagan elevated the chief justice to that position. The remaining justice, Clarence Thomas, was appointed by George H. W. Bush and clearly reflected Reagan-era legal conservatism. Fed a steady stream of appropriate cases by litigating state governments and conservative public interest groups and encouraged by a long decline in public trust in the federal government, these five justices carved out a number of new doctrines subjecting Congress to new constitutional limitations.[230] By contrast, the Burger Court offered Rehnquist little support in federalism cases. Chief Justice Warren Burger, for example, voted with Rehnquist 87 percent of the time during their time together on the Court, an agreement rate with Rehnquist matched only by O'Connor on the Burger Court. In federalism cases, however, the Nixon-appointed Burger was no more likely to agree with Rehnquist on these issues than was the arch-liberal William Brennan.[231] Whereas Nixon was primarily concerned with criminal justice issues in selecting justices, when he focused on jurisprudential issues at all, Reagan and Bush appointed not just conservative justices, but justices who were much more conservative on federalism than were their predecessors.[232]

It is in the context of federalism cases that the Rehnquist Court made its boldest assertions of judicial supremacy, and those cases composed a large portion of the historically unprecedented number of federal provisions struck down by the Rehnquist Court.[233] In recent years, the Court

[230] Paul Chen, "The Institutional Sources of State Success in Federalism Litigation before the Supreme Court," *Law and Policy* 25 (2003): 455; Cornell Clayton, "Law, Politics, and the New Federalism: State Attorney Generals as National Policymakers," *Review of Politics* 56 (1994): 525; Keith E. Whittington, "Taking What They Give Us: Explaining the Court's Federalism Offensive," *Duke Law Journal* 51 (2001): 477; Steven Teles, *Parallel Paths* (Princeton: Princeton University Press, forthcoming).

[231] On all federalism cases during the Burger Court, the Burger-Rehnquist agreement rate was 62 percent, while the Brennan-Rehnquist agreement rate was 60 percent. On all constitutional federalism cases involving national supremacy in which both justices voted, the Burger-Rehnquist agreement rate was a mere 50 percent, while the Brennan-Rehnquist agreement rate was 51 percent. Agreement scores calculated from Harold J. Spaeth, *United States Supreme Court Judicial Database* (http://www.as.uky.edu/polisci/ulmerproject/sctdata.htm).

[232] Every Reagan-Bush appointee to the Supreme Court replaced a justice with an agreement rate with Rehnquist on constitutional federalism issues involving national supremacy in the low fifties with a justice with an agreement rate with Rehnquist in the nineties, with the exception of David Souter, who was no more likely to agree with Rehnquist in these cases than was his predecessor, William Brennan. See Whittington, "Taking What They Give Us," 506.

[233] The Rehnquist Court's activism has spawned a vast literature. For a general discussion, see Thomas M. Keck, *The Most Activist Supreme Court in History* (Chicago: University of Chicago Press, 2004); "Symposium: Congressional Power in the Shadow of the Rehnquist Court: Strategies for the Future," *Indiana Law Journal* 78 (2003): 1; "Symposium: Conservative Judicial Activism," *University of Colorado Law Review* 73 (2002): 1139;

has limited the scope of the commerce clause, barred Congress from "commandeering" state actors, limited congressional authority under Section Five of the Fourteenth Amendment to impose restrictions on state governments, and carved out greater sovereign immunity for states from lawsuits in federal courts. When Congress tried to reestablish a strict scrutiny standard for state legislation infringing the exercise of religion that the Court itself had recently abandoned, Justice Kennedy cited *Marbury v. Madison* to emphasize that "shifting legislative majorities could *change the Constitution*" if Congress "could define its own powers" under Section Five of the Fourteenth Amendment and alter the constitutional doctrines that the Court had laid down.[234] When Congress attempted to regulate intrastate crimes affecting women, Chief Justice Rehnquist observed, "No doubt the political branches have a role in interpreting and applying the Constitution, but ever since *Marbury* this Court has remained the ultimate expositor of the constitutional text. As we emphasized in *United States v. Nixon*, . . . 'In the performance of assigned constitutional duties each branch of the Government must initially interpret the Constitution, and the interpretation of its powers by any branch is due great respect from the others' . . . Many decisions of this Court, however, have unequivocally reaffirmed the holding of *Marbury* . . . that 'it is emphatically the province and duty of the judicial department to say what the law is.' "[235] The "limitation of congressional authority is not solely a matter of legislative grace."[236] John Marshall's precept on the judiciary's authority "to say what the law is" was frequently invoked by the Rehnquist Court.[237]

The policy effects of these decisions have been more modest than their number and constitutional assertiveness might suggest. When closing off one avenue of congressional action in these cases, the Court left many others open for Congress to effectuate its policy goals.[238] The Court has taken pains to avoid impinging on congressional authority on issues that Congress cares deeply about, such as environmental regulation and maternity leave.[239] The statutory provisions that the Court has struck down, by

---

"Symposium: The Constitution in Exile," *Duke Law Journal* 51 (2001): 1; "Symposium: The Rehnquist Court," *Northwestern University Law Review* 99 (2005).

[234] Boerne v. Flores, 521 U.S. 507, 529 (1997) (emphasis added).

[235] United States v. Morrison, 529 U.S. 598, 616n7 (2000).

[236] Ibid., 616.

[237] It appeared in thirty-seven cases between 1986 and 2004. By contrast, it appeared in only thirty-five between 1930 and 1985.

[238] On the modesty of the Rehnquist Court's doctrinal developments, see Mark Tushnet, *The New Constitutional Order* (Princeton: Princeton University Press, 2003), 33–95.

[239] Solid Waste Agency v. United State Army Corps of Engineers, 531 U.S. 159 (2001) (avoiding question of constitutionality of federal environmental regulation); Nevada Department of Human Resources v. Hibbs, 538 U.S. 721 (2003) (upholding the waiver of state sovereign immunity for cases involving violations of Family and Medical Leave Act). See

contrast, do not represent the central legislative goals of any particular political coalition—not even those of the Democratic Party.

By taking action in these federalism cases, the Rehnquist Court tended to solve the kinds of political dilemmas that hampered the Reagan administration. In the first case reviving commerce clause limitations on national power, for example, the Court struck down the Gun-Free School Zones Act, which made the possession of firearms on school grounds a federal crime.[240] The statute was a classic piece of position-taking legislation, replicating common state laws. As a legal counsel to the Senate Judiciary Committee later explained its 1989 origins, "[W]hen we wrote it, it was just an idea that was partly mine, and partly someone who worked for Senator Kennedy. . . . And we were just thinking that we wanted to do something in the realm of gun control that we thought could win. And we were sort of kicking around a bunch of ideas, and we thought gee, there was a drug free school zone law. . . . So why don't we create gun free school zones?" As he observed, "It was very uncontroversial. No Senator wanted to stand up *for* guns in schools."[241] The bill required no floor debate and only one brief hearing, before being packaged without a recorded vote into Crime Control Act of 1990, which was passed by a Democratic Congress and signed by President Bush. When conservative Texas senator Phil Gramm threatened to hold up the bill, supporters simply threatened to put his opposition on record: "[W]e said, 'ok fine, go down to the floor and vote against it—we're going to force a vote.' "[242] Instead, the bill became an opportunity for legislators, such as co-sponsor Democratic senator Herbert Kohl, to voice their support for "keeping our teachers and children safe."[243] In signing the Crime Control Act, however, President Bush waved the red flag at the Court. In his signing statement, Bush praised the bill taking credit for offering "further protection for children," but complained that Congress had stripped from the law several of the get-tough provisions that the administration wanted. The president was "also disturbed" by some provisions of the law, "most egregiously, section 1702 inappropriately overrides legitimate State firearms laws with a new unnecessary Federal law" and policies that "should not be imposed on the States by Congress," though he was not about to veto

---

also Tennessee v. Lane, 541 U.S. 509 (2004) (upholding application of American with Disabilities Act to provide access to courthouses). For elaboration, see Whittington, "Taking What They Give Us."

[240] United States v. Lopez, 514 U.S. 549 (1995).

[241] Anonymous Senate Judiciary Committee legal counsel, quoted in J. Mitchell Pickerill, *Constitutional Deliberation in Congress* (Durham: Duke University Press, 2004), 99.

[242] Ibid., 99.

[243] Quoted in Pickerill, *Constitutional Deliberation in Congress*, 101.

the larger Crime Control Act that his administration had championed.[244] Although the target of the president's criticism would not be transparent to the casual reader, section 1702 was more popularly known as the Gun-Free School Zones Act.

The Court's action simply created another opportunity for politicians to advertise their embrace of children. When the Court struck the provision down in 1995, Kohl complained about "judicial activism that ignores children safety for the sake of legal nit-picking," which drew a rebuke from the *Washington Post* but undoubtedly further amplified Kohl's support for child safety to the voters of Wisconsin.[245] President Clinton was more nuanced, expressing "terrible disappointment" and determination to maintain "school safety" but admitted, "I want the action to be constitutional."[246] The *New York Times* observed that the president's statement "has more symbolic import than practical effect" given the existence of state laws and the previous year's Gun Free Schools Act that tied federal education aid to schools' adopting "zero tolerance" policies on guns, but it was part of a broader effort at "casting himself as a defender of children's health and safety."[247] Even so, presidential aides rushed to explain that the president was not challenging the Court but merely recognized the "importance of signaling a strong stand against violence and the prospect of kids killing kids with guns."[248] Meanwhile, Senate Judiciary Committee chairman Orrin Hatch led Republicans in applauding the decision. While emphasizing that "[n]o one wants guns in or around schools," he "hope[d] that this ruling marks the beginning of a much-needed reform of the Court's Commerce Clause jurisprudence."[249]

Rather than bearing the political cost of casting votes against popular positions for the sake of abstract constitutional principles, elected officials on both sides of the political aisle are willing to accept judicial supremacy.[250] In response to federalism objections to the proposed Religious Liberty Protection Act, Democratic representative Jerrold Nadler saw little problem: "[T]he fact is we are not extending anything. The courts will tell us exactly what our authority is and whatever it is, it is, and that is

[244] George H. W. Bush, "Statement on Signing the Crime Control Act of 1990, November 29, 1990," in *Public Papers, 1990*, 1715.

[245] Quoted in "Federalism and Guns in Schools," *Washington Post*, 28 April 1995, A26.

[246] William J. Clinton, "Presidential Radio Address on Guns and School Safety, April 29, 1995," *Public Papers, 1995*, 610, 611.

[247] Todd S. Purdum, "Clinton Seeks Way to Retain Gun Ban in School Zones," *New York Times*, 30 April 1995, 1.

[248] Presidential advisor George Stephanopoulos, quoted in ibid., 1.

[249] Orrin Hatch, "Hatch's Statement on Today's Supreme Court Decision," *Congressional Press Releases*, 27 April 1995.

[250] See also Neal Devins, "Should the Supreme Court Fear Congress?" *Minnesota Law Review* 90 (2006): 1337.

how far it will go." To the suggestion that Congress might refrain from relying on the Court in this way, Nadler responded, "[Y]ou do realize that Members of Congress are not uniformly angels?"[251] As a Republican Congress considered a ban on "partial-birth abortions," the *New York Times* denounced the bill's supporters for "[t]humbing their noses" at the Supreme Court and in doing so "attack[ing] . . . the rule of law."[252] White House Counsel Alberto Gonzales explained the second Bush administration's view of dealing with the novel legal questions raised by the war on terror. "While being 'respectful' of constitutional rights, the administration's job 'at the end of the day' is 'to protect the country,' he says. 'Ultimately, it is the job of the courts to tell us whether or not we've drawn the lines in the right places.' "[253] In the case of campaign finance reform, President George W. Bush reluctantly signed the Bipartisan Campaign Reform Act but used the occasion to invite the Supreme Court to strike down key provisions as unconstitutional. While claiming credit for provisions that would "strengthen our democracy," the president also noted "certain provisions [that] present serious constitutional concerns" and departed from his recommendations. Fortunately, these "flaws" did not require the president to actually veto the popular measure; "I expect that the courts will resolve these legitimate legal questions as appropriate under the law."[254]

We now live in a time in which political leaders simultaneously defer to the authority of the Court to say what the Constitution means and criticize the justices in the strongest terms for how they exercise that authority. The constitutional issues alive today are too various, the political coalitions that dominate politics too diverse, and the grip of the parties on political power too tenuous for the Court to satisfy all coalition partners. The Court has cut its own path on many constitutional issues, often frustrating and irritating political leaders but carefully refraining from getting in the way of central party commitments. Unlike any previous Court in American history, the modern Court is as likely to be criticized when it refrains from exercising its power to invalidate government actions as when it does. "Judicial activism" apparently now includes decisions such as those leaving in place the University of Michigan's race con-

---

[251] Representative Jerrold Nadler, in House Committee on the Judiciary, *Religious Liberty Protection Act of 1999: Hearings before the Subcommittee on the Constitution of the Committee on the Judiciary*, 106th Cong., 1st sess., 12 May 1999, 163.

[252] "Reproductive Rights in Peril," *New York Times*, 12 March 2003, A24.

[253] Jeanne Cummings, "Gonzales Rewrites Laws of War; White House Counsel's Methods Outrage Military Legal Experts," *Wall Street Journal*, 26 November 2002, A4.

[254] George W. Bush, "President Signs Campaign Finance Reform Act, March 27, 2002," in *Public Papers of the Presidents of the United States: George W. Bush, 2002* (Washington, DC: Government Printing Office, 2002), 518.

scious admissions policies and those refraining from interfering with the town of New London's redevelopment plans. The "activism" of a deferential Court reflects the range of political hopes that are now invested in the judicial authority to identify the requirements of the Constitution.

In the nineteenth century, the task of the Court within the constitutional regime was fairly straightforward. The issues that came before the Court were relatively few, and when the Court was asked to say what the Constitution meant and recognized in its authority to do so, the imperatives of the task were fairly clear. Political leaders were willing to recognize a judicial authority to speak for the Constitution, but the advantages of the Court exercising a truly independent voice were relatively few. In the twentieth century, precisely when the Court's efforts at constitutional interpretation became more frequent and its perceived need to rein in the increasingly active political branches of government grew, judicial supremacy acquired new dimensions. The Court routinely spoke out on issues of national political salience, and those who sought to lead unruly legislative and electoral coalitions were ill positioned to assume the responsibility for settling those constitutional controversies. Hemmed in by conflicting commitments and demands, presidents have ceded ground to the justices. They reserve the right to complain and cajole, but they do not claim the authority to say what the Constitution means.

SIX

The Dynamics of Constitutional Authority

IT IS COMMONLY THOUGHT that the judicial authority to say what the Constitution means is absolute, intrinsic to the constitutional design and evident from the origins of the republic. Even Ronald Dworkin, not usually prone to accepting the dead hand of the past, tells us to listen to our elders and accept judicial supremacy as fixed at the time of the founding.[1] The myth of *Marbury* remains powerful. At the turn of the twentieth century, populists and progressives denounced *Marbury* as a judicial coup, John Marshall's clever stratagem by which he imposed an oligarchy of judges on the new republic. Conservatives responded by celebrating *Marbury* for the same reasons, praising Marshall for establishing judicial supremacy and keeping the Jacobins at bay. In the latter twentieth century, the Warren Court and its more conservative successors could at least agree on the preeminence of *Marbury* and its supposed lecture on the "basic constitutional proposition" that the "federal judiciary is supreme in the exposition of the Constitution." If there is one thing that the justices claim to know, it is that the paramount judicial authority to interpret the Constitution has always been "respected by this Court and the Country as a permanent and indispensable feature of our constitutional system."[2]

This view of judicial authority is wrong. The relative authority of the competing institutions of the American political system to give meaning to the Constitution is often contested. Far from being a bedrock principle of American constitutionalism, the preeminence of the judiciary in defining constitutional terms and values is something that has emerged by fits and starts over the course of American history. It was something for which the judges and their supporters have had to struggle against those who would distribute the authority to interpret the Constitution more widely or locate it in a different, more popular and more accountable, branch of the government. To be sure, the judiciary has generally won that struggle, and stony-faced assertions on the expansive scope of the Court's authority, backed by presidential willingness to use military force to support those assertions, are among the tools that the Court has used to construct its role of constitutional leadership.

---

[1] Dworkin, *Freedom's Law*, 35.
[2] Cooper v. Aaron, 358 U.S. 1, 17 (1958).

Judicial authority can be successfully challenged, as when reconstructive presidents seek to wrest the Constitution away from the courts in order to stamp it with their own vision of the nation's heritage and future and to repudiate the supposed errors that the Supreme Court has either introduced or allowed to be introduced into the fundamental law. As the task of reconstructing the political commitments and policies of the government becomes more foundational, the president finds that he needs to transform predominant understandings of the Constitution itself. Such political leaders split what the Court would have us regard as the constitutional atom, separating judicial supremacy from constitutionalism as such. Such presidents have emphasized, as Attorney General Edwin Meese did for the Reagan administration, the distinction between the Constitution and constitutional law.[3] They claim the authority to reject the latter in order to save the former. One measure of the depth, and success, of their reconstructive political projects is just how far they were able to carry those claims. For Reagan, the claim of authority for the president to say what the Constitution means was never much more than rhetorical. For others, their reconstructive credentials proved stronger, and the Court temporarily found itself playing a secondary role in guiding the evolution of the Constitution and had some of its cherished constitutional principles rudely brushed aside.

Within the politics of reconstruction, the judicial authority to determine constitutional meaning is vulnerable. Reconstructive leaders are pressed by the ambitions of their political project to challenge the Court for the authority to articulate the fundamental commitments of the nation. Even when the courts are not a serious obstruction to the president's policies, judicial supremacy in constitutional interpretation is a standing threat to the president's aspirations and to his ability to construct the warrants to supports his actions in other arenas. In a political culture in which the Constitution is the touchstone of political authority and legitimacy, the authority to interpret that sacred text is too valuable to be left outside the presidential ambit. Such presidents necessarily must demonstrate the contingency of the political order that they have inherited. They must show that political fundamentals are open to choice. In doing so, they subvert the foundations of judicial supremacy. The president breaks down the façade of technical administration that surrounds the Court's work and helps bolster his claims of authority over others who might seek to read the Constitution on their own. Constructing the constitutional future and defining the terms of our fidelity to the past are pitched as political tasks, perhaps *the* political task, and as such, properly subject to political leadership. Rather than displaying an unrelenting hostility to the judiciary

[3] Meese, "Law of the Constitution," 981.

and an arrogant impatience with constitutional forms and constraints, reconstructive leaders assume a posture of deep engagement with our constitutional faith. Their conflict with the judiciary is contingent, not categorical. They seek to settle central constitutional disputes of their age on their own, and having planted their banner, they rally others to their side. In this situation, presidents are willing to assert that self-government requires that vital constitutional questions be answered by elected political leaders, not by the courts.

That situation has not long endured. The politics of reconstruction soon passes, and with it go the superior claims of the presidency in construing the Constitution. As presidential authority to interpret the Constitution wanes, judicial authority waxes. This authority is not simply seized by the Court, however. It is surrendered, often willingly and even eagerly, by political officials. Presidents with reconstructive ambitions want to fight constitutional battles and can often muster the support to make a credible showing, if not always to emerge victorious. Presidents in more normal political circumstances, presidents more concerned with managing the inherited political order than with remaking it, have neither those ambitions nor that level of support. Their political movements are heavily circumscribed and they find themselves crowded by claimants of all sorts. It is challenge enough to hold together their political coalition and to identify and advance elements of its agenda. In seeking to uphold constitutional and political orthodoxy, they are persistently vulnerable to the charge of heterodoxy. Forced to choose between principle and unity, they are more likely to choose unity. For such beleaguered politicians, the heightened judicial authority to say what the Constitution means is a respite from the responsibility and burdens of leadership. In such unfortunate but ordinary circumstances, the Court and the president can have a working and mutually beneficial relationship. For most national political leaders most of the time, for those outside the politics of reconstruction, judicial supremacy and the Court's efforts at constitutional interpretation are at worst an annoyance and at best a godsend.

For most of the nation's political life, the circumstances within which political leaders operate have encouraged them to lend their support to the independent judicial authority to interpret the Constitution. Most political leaders do not gain authority by seeking to repudiate what has come before, as reconstructive leaders do. Most instead gain authority by claiming to advance incrementally the commitments already made, by servicing the needs of their existing coalition, and by avoiding unnecessary conflict. For such leaders, constitutional disputes are more likely to be a distraction than an opportunity, discussions that will divide rather than unify. As long as constitutional commitments are widely held and easily upheld, the special authority of the courts to say what those commitments are is hardly necessary. Ironically, it is precisely when those commitments have greater political bite and become more contestable and disruptive that judicial authority becomes both prominent and politically valuable. As political coalitions fragment on constitutional issues, as direct action to settle constitutional disputes becomes more difficult and costly, as political divisions become deeper and the consequences of defeat or compromise become more intolerable, judicial supremacy in constitutional interpretation becomes more attractive to political leaders. While backbenchers with unified constituencies can posture on such issues to electoral advantage, those who must manage large and multivocal coalitions and worry about the national electorate face harder choices. Although the reconstructive leader benefits from opening constitutional meaning up to political choice, most political leaders gain by bemoaning how the lawyers who wear robes have tied their hands.

THE JUDICIARY AND THE PRESIDENCY

This perspective on the judicial authority to interpret the Constitution emphasizes the ways in which recognizing and bolstering that authority can benefit sitting presidents and party leaders. In doing so, it builds on and extends the approach that Robert Dahl, Mark Graber, and others have taken to understanding judicial power and the place of the judiciary in the broader political system. The concern here has specifically been with the contested authority to give meaning to the Constitution, but this perspective also has implications for the foundations of judicial power and independence more broadly and for the particular substantive content of constitutional law, as various scholars are recognizing. It is certainly not the case that every decision rendered by the Supreme Court and every aspect of its jurisprudence can be reduced to the political interests of the party in power, but in understanding how the Court has successfully claimed and exercised the power of constitutional interpretation and judicial review, it is fruitful to understand the ways in which that power can coexist with the demands of political leadership. Dahl identified the political puzzle (how would an institution with a power like judicial review survive over time?), even if his answer (it would not) was inadequate. From the perspective of the early twenty-first century, Dahl's puzzle may not seem obviously puzzling. But the formalist response (the institution just does, doesn't it? and besides, the power must be implicit in the constitutional text, somewhere) is not very helpful when the power comes under challenge, as it has at various times in American history and as it often has elsewhere. How the president has related himself over time to the judicial authority to interpret the Constitution highlights the political foundations of that authority. Those political foundations have often been strong and firm, supporting expansive claims of judicial supremacy. At times, however, those political foundations have been shaken, and judicial authority has appeared more vulnerable.

The account of judicial authority offered here has emphasized the significance of fissures within political coalitions and the fragmentation of the political system. Federalism, separation of powers, and the particular structure of the American party system have played key roles in encouraging presidents to lend their support to the courts. This account can coexist with some other dynamics. Whereas this book has focused on the actions and words of elite political actors, public opinion scholars have emphasized the potential value of diffuse support in the mass public for shoring up the judiciary.[4] Though one might question how robust such support is and how effectively it constrains politicians who might otherwise be inclined to subvert the courts, the account offered here suggests one way in which courts have won that diffuse support.[5] When activists and politicians on the left challenged judicial authority in the early twentieth century, conservative politicians rushed to swing public opinion to their side and to encourage average voters to lend their support to powerful and activist courts by rejecting candidates such as William Jennings Bryan, Theodore Roosevelt, and Robert La Follette. Even as conservative politicians railed against the particular decisions of individual judges in the late twentieth century, they took care to endorse the judiciary as an institution and its role in interpreting the Constitution. To the extent that the American public is supportive of the Court, the incentives faced by political leaders generally reinforce that inclination.

This account is also consistent with a focus on veto players and the ways in which a fragmented political system creates opportunities for judges to act independently without fear of reprisal.[6] It seems clear that the many veto points built into the American system help protect the judiciary from hostile legislative action, and this in turn may allow the Supreme Court to be more assertive in exercising its power of constitutional interpretation than would otherwise be the case. Simply noting the politi-

---

[4] See, e.g., James L. Gibson, Gregory A. Caldeira, and Vanessa A. Beard, "On the Legitimacy of High Courts," *American Political Science Review* 92 (1998): 343; Gregory A. Caldeira and James L. Gibson, "The Etiology of Public Support for the Supreme Court," *American Journal of Political Science* 36 (1992): 635.

[5] Although the available evidence is sketchy, the Hughes Court could not have rested easily on public opinion during its confrontation with Franklin Roosevelt. Caldeira, "Public Opinion," 1139. More generally, the theory and evidence of public opinion suggests that the Court would be vulnerable during the politics of reconstruction. See Whittington, "Legislative Sanctions," 446.

[6] See, e.g., George Tsebelis, *Veto Players* (Princeton: Princeton University Press, 2002).

cal space opened up by the multiple veto players in the American system, however, would overlook the positive attractions that judicial supremacy has for political leaders and the many ways in which presidents have gone out of their way to reinforce judicial authority. Whereas the veto players perspective would emphasize the possibility of judges seizing power from impotent politicians, the relationship between the president and the courts is better described as a wary partnership. The American political system is the impetus for judicial supremacy, and not just its enabler. The American historical experience shows politicians actively helping to construct judicial authority. They are not the victims of judicial supremacy.

The incentives facing presidents and the actions that they have taken in response to them also provide a richer portrait of how partisan competition works to the advantage of courts. An independent judiciary does not often thrive in a one-party state.[7] The desire of outgoing legislators to entrench their interests against incoming legislators is a common explanation for the growth of judicial power in polities characterized by multi-party competition. Partisan entrenchment has been part of the American experience as well. Significantly, however, partisan entrenchment is not the whole story. If it were, then Dahl's tale of a passive Court happily rubber-stamping the actions of its legislative co-partisans would have been adequate to describe the history of judicial review in the United States. Political competition drives political leaders to support the courts and use judicial supremacy to their advantage, but regime-enforcing uses to which the judicial authority to interpret the Constitution can be put far exceed the simple provision of policy insurance against electoral defeat.

The judicial authority to interpret the Constitution has been dynamic over the course of American constitutional history. The supremacy and leadership of the judiciary in setting the meaning of the Constitution was neither fixed at any particular moment in time nor strictly a function of the Court's own interpretation of its powers under the Constitution. Judicial authority has been politically constructed and reconstructed over time, with later political actors building on what has come before. Although the proper scope of judicial authority can be asserted and argued

---

[7] See Matthew C. Stephenson, " 'When the Devil Turns. . .': The Political Foundations of Independent Judicial Review," *Journal of Legal Studies* 32 (2003): 59; Ran Hirschl, *Towards Juristocracy* (Cambridge: Harvard University Press, 2004); Tom Ginsburg, *Judicial Review in New Democracies* (New York: Cambridge University Press, 2003); Gillman, "Parties Can Use Courts," 511; Donald J. Boudreaux and A. C. Pritchard, "Reassessing the Role of the Independent Judiciary in Enforcing Interest-Group Bargains," *Constitutional Political Economy* 5 (1994): 1; J. Mark Ramseyer, "The Puzzling (In)dependence of Courts: A Comparative Approach," *Journal of Legal Studies* 23 (1994): 721; Eli M. Salzberger, "A Positive Analysis of the Doctrine of Separation of Powers, or: Why Do We Have an Independent Judiciary?" *International Review of Law and Economics* 13 (1993): 349.

as a matter of fundamental principle, as the Supreme Court did in *Cooper v. Aaron*, the ultimate success of such claims is an example of what I have elsewhere called constitutional constructions.[8] The operation and character of the American constitutional system are defined and refined through such arguments and practices. What our constitutional practices ultimately look like has turned not only on the formal and abstracted persuasive powers of the arguments that can be made on their behalf, but also on the incentives facing political actors who have the power to effectuate them and the distribution of tools and powers available to those who might benefit from or be harmed by those practices. Judicial supremacy, like the powerful presidency, the centralized state, or myriad other features of the constitutional landscape, has been carved out by the accumulated political actions of judges, politicians, and citizens over the course of more than two centuries.

It has recently been suggested that the study of American political development is best understood as the examination of durable shifts in governing authority.[9] The political construction of constitutional meaning should be central to that enterprise. As that literature has emphasized, a great deal of politics is precisely over the location and relocation of governing authority, whether the authority at issue is relatively limited (such as whether an administrative agency will gain additional jurisdiction or powers) or relatively expansive (such as the relocation of sovereignty over the American colonies from Britain to the United States with the American Revolution). The constitutional text is centrally about the definition and allocation of governing authority, defining offices and the powers and subjects over which they have authority, the processes by which governing authority may be exercised, and the exceptions and limitations to that authority. The constitutional choices made with the drafting and ratification of the text only partially cover the field, however. A great deal has to be worked out in subsequent practice, most familiarly through judicial interpretation of the Constitution but routinely and importantly through political action that construes, implements, and extends the constitutional text. The struggle over interpretive authority constructs the Constitution both directly and indirectly, by specifying, for example, whether the judicial power includes the authority to say what the law is when it comes to the Constitution (e.g., "The federal judiciary is supreme in the exposition of the law of the Constitution") and by privileging some institutional actors in future disputes about the substantive meaning of various aspects of the Constitution ("It follows that the interpretation of the Fourteenth

---

[8] Whittington, *Constitutional Construction.*
[9] Karen Orren and Stephen Skowronek, *The Search for American Political Development* (New York: Cambridge University Press, 2004), 123.

Amendment enunciated by this Court in the *Brown* case is the supreme law of the land" and every "state legislator and executive and judicial officer is solemnly committed by oath ... 'to support *this* Constitution' ").[10] This authority is not fixed. It has shifted over time. The construction of this authority to interpret the Constitution does not stand outside of politics and "political time" but rather occurs within American political development and requires political explanation and study.

As developed here, the president is a crucial player in this process. To be sure, the president is not the only player. The Court itself is an important actor in asserting and establishing its own interpretive authority, and Congress and its members help create the strategic context within which both the president and the Court assert their respective claims for authority. Over the course of American history, however, the president has been, at times, the primary challenger to the interpretive authority of the Court and, at other times, one of the most prominent supporters of judicial supremacy. Understanding the status of the Court within the American constitutional system requires, in important respects, understanding presidential politics and the leadership challenges faced by presidents and presidential candidates.

Examining the relationship between the Court and the president should shed light on both. For those who wish to understand the political foundations of judicial authority, the pressures and constraints of the White House are crucial. At the same time, those who want to understand how presidents cope with the leadership challenges that they face would do well to attend to how the judiciary can be and has been a help or a hindrance to that effort. The Court has been a resource, a stimulus, and a constraint on the president.[11] Not all presidents have been equally engaged with the Court and constitutional interpretation, but the scope of judicial authority is a recurring theme in the history of the presidency.

[10] Cooper v. Aaron, 358 U.S. 1, 18 (1958) (emphasis added).

[11] Even in asserting an expansive reading of the president's constitutional powers, the administration of President George W. Bush has been careful not to deny the authority of the Supreme Court to have the ultimate power to say what the Constitution means. As such, the Court could be a restraint on presidential ambitions. Outside the context of the war on terror, for example, the Bush administration pointedly declined, with minimal analysis, Representative John Hostettler's invitation that it refuse to enforce a court order to remove a display of the Ten Commandments from an Indiana courthouse on the grounds that such orders were based on an incorrect understanding of the constitutional requirements. See letter of Assistant Attorney General William Moschella, 19 April 2005 (http://www.house .gov/hostettler/News/Hostettler-news-2005–06–17-ten-commandments-statement.htm). In building on the theories of presidential power that have been influential in conservative legal circles since at least the Reagan administration, however, and appointing justices who are likely to be supportive of such claims, Bush has the potential of converting this authority to say what the Constitution means from constraint into a resource, from a check on presidential power to a shield for presidential power against legislative and public criticism.

JUDICIAL SUPREMACY AND DEMOCRACY

Since the late nineteenth century, the exercise of judicial review has often been posed as having legitimacy problems in a democracy. A countermajoritarian Court is thought to obstruct the will of the people's elected representatives and frustrate the realization of electoral outcomes. The rise of activist Courts able and willing to aggressively exercise the power of judicial review and pronounce new and controversial constitutional interpretations—the assumption of constitutional leadership by the judiciary—raises not only empirical puzzles but normative concerns. For some, the concerns are severe enough to suggest that the Constitution should be taken away from the courts, perhaps to be replaced with some form of "popular constitutionalism" by which "the people themselves" would interpret and enforce the Constitution.[12] Others have come to the defense of judicial supremacy as essential to American constitutionalism.

Recognizing the political foundations of judicial supremacy should lead us to recognize that the place of judicial interpretation of the Constitution in a democracy is more complicated than is often assumed. The Court has not taken the Constitution away from the people. The Constitution has often been entrusted to the hands of the judges, if not by the people themselves, then at least by their elected representatives. Moreover, the Court's elaboration of constitutional meaning often proceeds within the context of a broader political and constitutional regime, the broad outlines of which have been established by political actors. During these periods of reconstructive politics, "vital questions" are settled in the political arena through the leadership of presidents such as Lincoln. During more normal politics, the Court has acted to interpret and extend those principles and commitments, independently but often in dialogue with other government officials.

For supporters of judicial supremacy, it is departmentalism and extrajudicial constitutional interpretation that is the threat. The reconstructive challenge to judicial authority plants the seeds for the future resurgence of the courts, however. Far from subverting the foundations of American constitutionalism, these episodes of reconstructive politics have served to strengthen and renew them. Constitutional values and priorities have been redefined and adjusted through this public and political engagement with the Constitution. As presidents have thrust themselves into the position of constitutional leadership and sought to articulate a constitutional vision that would capture the political imagination, they have not argued that the nation must set aside the Constitution in the name of pure democ-

---

[12] See, e.g., Tushnet, *Taking the Constitution Away*; Kramer, *The People Themselves*; Waldron, *Law and Disagreement*.

racy or fomented legal chaos. They have instead argued that they are more attractive and more faithful guardians of our inherited constitutional order than are their political opponents or the majority of the justices on the Supreme Court, and those claims have been weighed and at least partly vindicated in the political and electoral arena. When the principled decisions at stake in key issues of constitutional interpretation are subject to deep and well-considered political disagreement, these presidents have sought broader participation in the process of deliberating on the meaning of the Constitution and have asserted their own authority to help settle those disputes.

Once the politics of reconstruction is over, different political incentives make themselves felt that drive political leaders to become more deferential to courts and allow judges to become more assertive. Judicial supremacy is established by political invitation, not by judicial putsch. Judges become prominent and trusted interpreters of the Constitution, gaining authority over other possible interpreters who have more dubious claims and less desire to articulate and uphold the fundamental commitments of the regime. Those likely to disagree with the Court occupy the political margins. Those close to the center of power, who overlook American politics as a whole, are not likely to raise serious objections to the Court's work. They may or may not welcome or agree with each particular interpretation of the Constitution offered by the Court, but they have little interest in challenging the Court's authority to give those interpretations and often have a strong interest in bolstering that authority.

The fact that judicial supremacy rests on political foundations does not obviate the normative concerns with the Court aggressively exercising that authority. As Robert Cover reminded us, judicial constitutional interpretations have a "jurispathic" quality, suppressing alternative understandings of our foundational principles and traditions.[13] It is this quality of judicial interpretation that should be of central concern to debates over extrajudicial constitutional interpretation. Judicial supremacy might be trumpeted so loudly that the justices might well act more aggressively than they should. Even within the context of normal politics, when there are reasonable disagreements about particular issues, it seems appropriate to allow broad participation in the decision as to the content of our principles rather than remove that decision to an elite institution that will then seek to impose its ruling on, or against, the people at large. The judiciary's most useful role may be in framing constitutional disputes for extrajudicial resolution and in enforcing the principled decisions reached elsewhere rather than in autonomously and authoritatively defining constitutional

---

[13] Robert Cover, "Nomos and Narrative," in *Narrative, Violence, and the Law*, ed. Martha Minow et al. (Ann Arbor: University of Michigan Press, 1993), 138–44.

meaning. By using the power of judicial review to quash challenges to reasonable but contested constructions of the Constitution, even those favored and supported by political leaders, the Court may well give greater authority to those constitutional understandings than they are entitled and shrink the legitimate sphere of political debate and decision.[14] Shifting constitutional debates into the courts also alters the relative influence of different participants in the process to affect outcomes. The presidential wings of the political parties gain while others find their influence reduced. Cleveland Democrats may have been satisfied with the Gilded Age Court but Populist Democrats were not. Conservative Republicans could look favorably on the Court in the early twentieth century but progressive Republicans could not. Liberal northern Democrats were pleased with the post–New Deal Court but conservative southern Democrats were aghast.

The political dynamics that give rise to judicial supremacy may be more troubling from a democratic perspective than judicial supremacy per se. As we have seen, political leaders defer to the Court precisely because they do not wish to accept the responsibility of deciding these issues themselves. Presidents need not make the politically difficult veto, and legislators need not cast the politically difficult vote if the Court is available to take the action that the politicians fear to take themselves. Judicial supremacy facilitates distortions in representation and accountability. It lets politicians off the hook and encourages a political sensibility of avoiding constitutional responsibilities.

It is not obvious, however, that our democratic politics would be better absent the temptation of judicial supremacy. Devices designed to shelter politicians and political decisions from the electorate are commonplace, and it is not at all clear that such devices should be universally condemned. If politicians simultaneously recognize the value of free speech but prefer to turn its protection over to politically insulated judges, we should perhaps be grateful. Although this may allow and encourage legislators to denigrate free speech values in public, it may also result in a more protective legal regime than would be the case if legislators were forced to make the difficult decisions themselves. The dynamics of interpretive authority within the constitutional system in many ways echo the constitutional founding itself. Governing authority is shifted among institutions so as to secure outcomes that might otherwise be difficult to achieve or maintain. The shift in authority is itself a political choice and made within the context of democratic politics. The interpretive authority

[14] See also Keith E. Whittington, *Constitutional Interpretation* (Lawrence: University Press of Kansas, 1999).

that the Court exercises is a contingent one, and the constitutional commitments it seeks to realize can claim a certain democratic pedigree.

The founders created a complicated constitutional scheme. Multiple political officials vie with one another for primacy, and leadership among them can shift over time and across issues. The judiciary, the third branch of government, does not seem to start from an envious position in such a struggle. It does not have a direct connection to the font of political power in a republic, the people, and its instruments of coercion are largely borrowed. Although at its origins a position on the Supreme Court was a respectable enough office, one of the first chief justices found the prospect of being a state governor to be a more attractive political plum, and justices were relegated to the basement of the Capitol building when they were not scattered across the countryside hearing cases. It took some time before the Court could find its own voice through which it could claim to speak for the people, and even so it was by no means certain that elected representatives who were sent to the seat of government by asking for and winning the support of the people could be expected to respect such a claim. Within its sphere, the judiciary has enjoyed a remarkable success. Though chosen by presidents and confirmed by senators, the justices have been able gain authority over the president and the Congress. They have asserted the right to say what the Constitution means, and political leaders have generally chosen to respect that right. Judicial supremacy is not intrinsic to the constitutional scheme, but it has often emerged out of it.

Index

PRINCETON STUDIES IN AMERICAN POLITICS: HISTORICAL, INTERNATIONAL, AND COMPARATIVE PERSPECTIVES

Politics and Industrialization: Early Railroads in the United States and Prussia by Colleen A. Dunlavy

The Lincoln Persuasion: Remaking American Liberalism by J. David Greenstone

Labor Visions and State Power: The Origins of Business Unionism in the United States by Victoria C. Hattam